Militarization, Democracy, and Development

HONDURAS

Militarization, Democracy, and Development

the perils of praetorianism in latin america

KIRK S. BOWMAN

the pennsylvania state university press university park, pennsylvania

Library of Congress Cataloguing-in-Publication Data

Bowman, Kirk S.
Militarization, democracy, and development : the perils of praetorianism in Latin America / Kirk Bowman.
p. cm.
Includes bibliographical references (p.) and index.
ISBN 0-271-02229-9 (cloth)
1. Latin America—Defenses—Economic aspects.
2. Latin America—Armed Forces—Recruiting, enlistment, etc.
3. Latin America—Defenses—Political aspects.
4. Latin America—Defenses—Social aspects.
5. Civil-military relations—Latin America.
6. Latin America—Defenses—Economic aspects—Case studies.
7. Latin America—Defenses—Political aspects—Case studies.
8. Latin America—Defenses—Social aspects—Case studies.
I. Title.

HC130.D4 B68 2002
338.98'009'045—dc21 2002012190

Printed in the United States of America
Published by The Pennsylvania State University Press,
University Park, PA 16802-1003

The paper used in this publication is both acid-free and totally chlorine-free (TCF). It meets the minimum requirements of the American National Standard for Information Sciences—Permanence of Paper for Printed Library Materials, ANSI Z39.48–1992.

Contents

List of Figures and Tables

Figures

Tables

Preface

When Albert O. Hirschman was asked how he came to hold the unorthodox views he proposed in *The Strategy of Economic Development*, he would reply: "I went to Colombia early in 1952 without any prior knowledge of . . . development. This turned out to be a real advantage. . . . [I later] discovered I had acquired a point of view of my own that was considerably at odds with current doctrines" (1984, 88). While this experience is only partially true for Hirschman, it is precisely what happened to me. I had the good fortune of living in Central America many years before I entered graduate school and encountered theories and explanations of development and democracy. I will always carry with me many sights, sounds, tastes, and even smells of the region. Most of my memories bring a smile to my face. Some do not. For example, I witnessed firsthand the power of the Honduran military in the early 1980s. Although certainly not the most brutal military injustice of the period, I was strongly affected by the horrors of forced conscription. One day I observed the army parking buses outside a movie theater that was playing a Sylvester Stallone or Arnold Schwarzenegger action feature. When the movie ended, the unsuspecting public found quite a surprise as they exited the auditorium. Young men were violently separated from weeping girlfriends, wives, and children and forcefully herded onto the buses: "You are in the army now!" It did not matter if they had just started a new job or a new business. It made no difference if they had a sick parent or children to support and feed. They were enlisted. I remember thinking, how can this country ever develop?

In the 1980s, the Doctrine of National Security dominated Honduras. According to this doctrine, *la Patria* was threatened by internal enemies (unions, students, human rights activists, communists) and the armed forces needed and deserved considerable resources and freedom of action to defend the country's "values." National security trumped citizen-centric development. The Honduran armed forces were modern-day equivalents of the Roman Praetorian Guards, whose initial granted powers expanded until they became the polity's dominant political force.

Just a few miles away, Costa Rica provided a dramatic counterexample to Honduras. For Costa Ricans, government investment in health care, education, and democracy provided greater security than more weapons and soldiers. Fellow citizens were generally treated with respect by the authorities, and not viewed as potential enemies of the state. Costa Rican development and democracy were the envy of the isthmus.

I started graduate school a decade after leaving Central America. As I began studying issues of development, my interpretations and understanding of the literature and debates were filtered by personal impressions of the effects of militarization on development in Central America. My research on this topic started during my first semester as an M.A. student at the University of Arizona, under the guidance of the late Edward N. Muller. Ned was one of those remarkable academics who thought out loud about the major issues of development. He was intellectually curious and willing to use an eclectic mix of methods and theories to find answers for his limitless questions. His untimely passing was a great loss to our profession and to many of us personally; this book is in many ways a humble personal tribute to him.

As I began to assemble a list of those who contributed to this project, I realized that I had acquired a very large intellectual debt. Larry Birns taught me a great deal about passion and praxis. Tom Wright at UNLV rekindled my interest in Latin America and, through his example, inspired me to change professions and become an academic. Yong Deng, Bill Dixon, Jerry Green, Jeff Kash, Jacqui True, and Ed Williams helped me and this study during my time in Tucson.

Many people at the University of North Carolina influenced this book, including Ron Ahnen, Ken Bollen, Christina Ewig, Claudio Fuentes, Jonathan Hartlyn, Lisa Jacobs, Tom Oatley, Tim McKeown, François Nielsen, Tom Schaller, Lars Schoultz, Zeric Smith, John Stephens, Greg Weeks, Jonathan Weiler, and the wonderful librarians. Funding for dissertation fieldwork was provided by the Social Science Research Council, the Ford Foundation, the Fulbright program, and the Graduate College of the University of North Carolina. The Graduate College at UNC also provided useful dissertation write-up funding.

The Sam Nunn School of International Affairs at the Georgia Institute of Technology has been very supportive. Joy Daniell, Wanda Moore, Arma Spencer, and Latanya Buckner solved all my little problems with ease and good humor. The Georgia Tech librarians, particularly Mary Axford, were lifesavers. The Nunn School and the Center for International Business Education and Research (CIBER) contributed research and travel money. Linda Brady and William Long have been remarkably encouraging school chairs. Jesus Felipe, Peter Brecke, and Brian Woodall critiqued and improved parts of the study. Scott Baker, Sean Patrick Eudaily, and Sonali Tare were forced to read the manuscript as research assistants and all made contributions.

Central American scholars and professionals have been particularly generous. In Honduras, Marvin Barahona, Rafael del Cid, Matías Funes, Ramón Oquelí, Leticia Salomón, Leticia de Oyuela, Mercedes Oyuela, Melvin Vega, the staff of the Honduran Tourism Institute (in particular Claudia Chávez, Tatiana Cirque, Digna de Domínguez, and Cristóbal Silva), and the staffs of the National Archives and Military Archives answered lots of questions and provided lots of information. Mario Argueta read the chapters on Honduras and provided astute comments and corrections. The Pineda Greens and Espinals have been my families in Tegucigalpa for more than two decades. In Costa Rica, Kevin Casas, Víctor Hugo Céspedes, Adolfo Chacón, José Antonio Cordero, Catarina García, Gerardo Hernández, Emilia Mora, Mercedes Muñoz, Jorge Rovira Mas, Steven Palmer, Héctor Pérez, Juan Pablo Pérez, Manuel Rojas, and Mario Samper all assisted me far more than I will ever be able to help them. The staffs at the Arias Foundation, the National Library, the National Archives, the Central Bank Library, the Library of the Arch-Diocese of San José, and the Costa Rican Tourism Institute (particularly Alfredo Oporta and Ireth Rodríguez) could not have been more helpful. Víctor Hugo Acuña and Iván Molina both read large sections of the manuscript and provided clarifications and critiques. Graduate courses at the University of Costa Rica's *Centro de Investigaciones Históricas de América Central* (CIHAC) taught by Víctor Hugo Acuña, Fabrice Lehoucq, and Mario Samper were particularly useful. Teresa, Emilie, Susan, and Stephanie provided lots of laughs, great tamales, superb babysitting, and needed distractions. Caetano Cersósimo lent access to his personal library.

John Booth, Raquel Fernandez, Douglas Kincaid, Jennifer McCoy, John Peeler, Michael Perkins, Tom Scheetz, and Bruce Wilson made suggestions, supplied information, or gave a needed pat-on-the-back at crucial stages. David Pion-Berlin and Mitchell Seligson generously read recent drafts and offered support and constructive criticism. Charles Brockett went far beyond the call of duty, reading and carefully commenting on every chapter. James Mahoney provided important suggestions as well as many hours of stimulating discussion.

Two people must be singled out. When I first went to Costa Rica as a green graduate student, Fabrice Lehoucq was in San José as a Fulbright

Scholar. Fabrice took me under his wing, introducing me to local scholars and teaching me where and how to get information. We spent countless hours discussing Costa Rica, democracy, political science, and other topics over his spectacular cappuccinos. Our different perspectives have led to a rich and rewarding intellectual discussion that has gone on for many years.

Evelyne Huber has been a wonderful mentor, providing the perfect mix of friction and encouragement. Her support of my research was constant, as was her concern for the temporal well-being of my family. Evelyne always returned marked-up drafts quickly and channeled enough grants and research money my way to keep my son in diapers. Despite the best efforts of Evelyne and the others, this book still contains shortcomings and errors. They are my responsibility alone.

Portions of this book have been presented at various conferences. A much longer version of Chapter 3 was published in the *Journal of Peace Research*. Versions of small sections of Chapters 4 and 5 have appeared in the *Revista de Historia* and the *Journal of Latin American Studies*.

It has now been nine years since I quit my job, started graduate school, and began this project. My parents and family have supported me financially and emotionally. Elena and "El Tigre" have provided the laughs and love that made it an exciting and pleasant journey. They also made the biggest sacrifices and will receive almost none of the credit. May we, along with our newest sidekick Micah, have many more similar adventures together.

Abbreviations

AFL	American Federation of Labor
ANACH	National Association of Honduran Peasants
CENPRO	Costa Rican Ministry of Foreign Trade Export and Investment Promotion Center
CIA	Central Intelligence Agency
CINDE	Costa Rican Investment and Trade Development Board
CODEH	Committee for the Defense of Human Rights
COFADEH	Committee of Relatives of the Detained/Disappeared in Honduras
CONDECA	Central American Defense Council
COSUFFAA	Superior Council of the Armed Forces
DEA	Drug Enforcement Agency
ELG	Export Led Growth
ESF	Emergency Stabilization Funds
FAO	UN Food and Agriculture Organization
FMLN	Farabundo Marti National Liberation
FUSEP	Public Security Force
GAO	U.S. Government Accounting Office
ICT	Costa Rican Institute of Tourism
IHT	Honduran Institute of Tourism
IMF	International Monetary Fund
IPM	Military Pension Fund
ISI	Import Substitution Industrialization
LDCs	Less Developed Countries
MCRL	Free Costa Rica Movement
MDO	Democratic Opposition Movement
MLSP	Military Spending or percent of GDP used for defense
MPR	Military Participation Ratio or number of soldiers per 1,000 inhabitants
OAS	Organization of American States
PD	Democratic Party
PLN	National Liberation Party
PUSC	Social Christian Unity Party
SOA	School of the Americas
TACA	Central American Air Transport

UCLA	University of California, Los Angeles
UDC	Central American Democratic Union
UFCO	United Fruit Company
UNAH	National Autonomous University of Honduras
WDS	worse democracy score
ZOLTs	Free Zones for Tourism

Country Abbreviations

ARG	Argentina
BOL	Bolivia
BRA	Brazil
CHL	Chile
COL	Colombia
CRI	Costa Rica
DOM	Dominican Republic
ECU	Ecuador
ELS	El Salvador
GTM	Guatemala
HON	Honduras
MEX	Mexico
NIC	Nicaragua
PAN	Panama
PRY	Paraguay
PER	Peru
URY	Uruguay
VEN	Venezuela

introduction

PART

1 Militarization and Development

the research question and the research design

This book examines the relationship between militarization and development in Latin America. I assess the effect of military size and budgets on three separate indicators of development—democracy, economic growth, and equity. I review past research and identify and solve a policy-relevant and theoretically important intellectual puzzle: while the conventional wisdom and case study evidence conclude that large militaries are negatively associated with development, a large body of cross-national research finds that lots of soldiers are good for economic growth and equity in developing countries. Why?

I use a simple typology of militaries to generate an explanation for the different effect of militarization on development in Latin America than in other regions of the developing world. I posit that the conservative historical trajectory of Latin American militaries, the Cold War influence of the United States, and, above all, the considerable internal focus of the region's armed forces combined to produce a particularly malignant pattern of militarization in the region. I expand the explanation using concepts of state capacity and priorities or focus. I test three hypotheses using several types of data and both quantitative and comparative historical research methods. I start at the general level, using statistical techniques and longitudinal data to test the effect of militarization on democracy, economic growth, and equity in both a universal sample of developing countries and in Latin America.[1] This exercise demonstrates that the different military missions, history, and external threat-levels result in a very different militarization-development relationship in Latin America than in a universal sample. The results are stark and unambiguous:

1. I examine eighteen Latin American countries in Chapter 3 and seventy-six developing countries in Chapter 6.

militarization has a substantial and significant negative effect on democracy, economic growth, and equity in Latin America.

Finally, I present a comparative historical analysis of the effect of militarization on development in Costa Rica and Honduras in the 1948–98 period. The comparative historical chapters establish agency and sequence in the relationship and illuminate the causal mechanisms. They also clearly reveal the serious opportunity costs of militarization and show how large and powerful militaries can undermine state capacity and trump efforts for greater economic growth, equity, and democracy. These chapters also reveal many novel insights about the democratic consolidation process and economic transformations in Costa Rica and Honduras in the 1948–98 period.

The Puzzle

The proposition that large militaries undermine democracy, equity, and economic growth is widespread in Latin America. The most visible advocate of this position has been Nobel Peace Prize Laureate and former Costa Rican President Oscar Arias Sánchez. While not discarding the possibility that geography, history, and differences in class and power relations may explain part of the variance, Arias posits that a great part of Costa Rica's success in the post–WWII era stems directly from the dissolution of the military in 1948 and argues that other countries would also benefit greatly from demilitarization.[2] For more than a decade, Arias has championed the vision that demilitarization is not a dependent variable, but rather a causal variable that can have significant positive developmental effects for Caribbean Basin nations individually and for the region as a whole.[3]

2. Arias's most explicit statements on the relationship between militarization and development are found in various unpublished speeches such as "Desmilitarización y Democracia," delivered in Panama in February 1991, and his keynote address to the Segunda Conferencia Internacional de las Democrácias Nuevas o Restauradas, Managua, 4 July 1994. Arias's views on development, peace, disarmament, and demilitarization are in a collection of speeches (1990), which include his ideas on breaking loose from the accepted views from the past that enslave our future actions (such as the idea that countries need strong militaries to be secure). An overview of Arias's latest demilitarization and development plan is in *Washington Report on the Hemisphere* (31 May 1996).

3. Arias has in recent years expanded his geographical interests and now advocates demilitarization as a developmental policy in all regions of the developing world.

When President Arias (1982–86) began exhorting his neighbors about the potential benefits of demilitarizing, the Cold War was raging. Arias was vilified by U.S. policymakers[4] and the very idea of another country going *sans armée* anywhere in Latin America was viewed by scholars as nothing more than a pipe dream. Even modest military reductions appeared unrealistic.[5] In the past several years, the environment has radically changed. With the Cold War over and the neoliberal ideology of efficiency dominant, tremendous pressures are now being exerted on Caribbean Basin countries by U.S. embassies, Japanese aid officials, the International Monetary Fund, and local business elites to drastically downsize and in some cases eliminate armed forces.[6] Panama recently disbanded its military, as has Haiti.[7] Vigorous yet difficult efforts are under way in other Latin American countries to divert funds from the armed forces to debt reduction, education, and health services.

While Arias and others have used moral persuasion and case study evidence to argue that lower levels of militarization lead to development, more rigorous cross-sectional statistical analyses have not necessarily concurred.[8] Indeed, the bulk of the quantitative research featuring inferential statistics shows a significant positive relationship between Third World militarization and economic growth and between militarization and equity/social development.[9] The vastly disparate results found by quantita-

4. The scorn that the right wing of the Republican Party held for President Arias is captured in Whelan and Jaeckle (1988, 186), who call Arias a "leftist" and mock the Nobel Prize award (257). See also Honey (1994, chapter 14).

5. See Aguilera (1994). With the end of the Cold War, U.S. policy shifted radically. The shift is exemplified by U.S. embassy actions in Honduras: "The wars have left behind monsters. The American Ambassador to Honduras, Cresencio Arcos, has lately been trying to undo the military power he helped to build during a previous posting in the early 1980s" (*New York Times*, 30 May 1993). For the growing international consensus to reduce military power in Latin America, see also Ball (1992), FBIS-LAT (19 August 1994), Franko (1994), IMF (1992), Latinamerica Press (8 July 1993), and Washington Office on Latin America (1995).

6. However, Arias fears that the recent change in U.S. policy to permit sales of sophisticated weapons in Latin America will lead to an expansion of militarization in the region (personal interview, November 25, 1998). The aftermath of the 11 September 2001 terrorist attacks on the World Trade Center may also lead to greater international support of militarization.

7. Both after U.S. invasions, which may or may not have been necessary preconditions.

8. See, for example, Bullock and Firebaugh (1990), Dixon and Moon (1986), and Weede (1986). A full literature review is presented in Chapter 6.

9. This is especially true when the measure of militarization is the size of the military as measured by the number of soldiers per thousand inhabitants.

tive techniques and qualitative case studies represent a major intellectual puzzle.[10] And this is a puzzle with important policy implications. With the end of the Cold War, domestic civil society groups and international actors are actively encouraging a reduction in military spending in many countries of the region even while a host of quantitative scholars arrive at the "somewhat awkward conclusion" that large militaries have a positive influence on economic growth and social development in Less Developed Countries (LDCs).[11] The prime objective of this book is to solve this puzzle and firmly establish the relationship between militarization and development.

The Research Design: Leverage and Dependent Variables

The overarching argument—militarization has a negative effect on development in Latin America—is stated in very general, broad terms for two important reasons. First, this permits leverage maximization; we want to explain as much as possible with as little as possible (King, Keohane, and Verba 1994, 29). Second, research questions or propositions should permit clear tests of falsification. This very general argument allows more specific and observable implications of "development" that in turn generate testable hypotheses.

What is development? Mittelman defines development as the "increasing capacity to make rational use of natural and human resources for social ends" (1988, 22). While these types of definitions are useful in some contexts, they are also very difficult to operationalize. Huntington takes a different approach, defining five distinct goals of development: autonomy (from external forces), economic growth, democracy, equity, and stability. A great deal of research in the social sciences in recent decades has focused on one or more of these five goals. Early research under the modernization rubric deemed these goals complementary—all good things go to-

10. For example, works by Barry and Preusch (1988), Funes (1995), Meza (1988), Morris (1984), Oquelí (1982), Rosenberg (1995), Schulz and Schulz (1994), Salomón (1992), and others argue that militarization has in various ways negatively affected Honduran democracy. Recent works by Jonas (2000), Schirmer (1998), and Scheetz, Pape and Kulikowski (1997) show the negative effect of militarization on development in Guatemala.

11. See Bullock and Firebaugh (1990), Chan (1989), Kick and Sharda (1986), Kick et al. (1990), Weede (1986, 1992), and many others.

gether.[12] Later research focused on the conflictual nature of these goals. Classic studies by Huntington (1968: modernization breeds instability), Kuznets (1955: economic growth leads to inequality), and O'Donnell (1973: economic growth leads to authoritarianism) are exemplars of the volumes of research dealing with the conflictual nature of the goals of development.

These goals of development are useful to my research for three reasons. First, they are much more easily operationalized than "development." Second, they allow various empirical tests and opportunities for falsification. Third, having various components of development provides leverage; it is possible that we can explain a lot with only one causal variable. Having various dependent variables sacrifices parsimony and may make this project more complex than the typical study that focuses on one dependent variable. However, sacrificing parsimony for leverage is a profitable trade-off; in this study I leverage the militarization causal variable.

I selected three of Huntington's five goals as separate dependent variables.[13] There is little disagreement among mainstream scholars that democracy, equity, and economic growth are worthwhile goals.[14] Stability and autonomy are another matter. I do not consider stability to necessarily be a long-term goal of development.[15] Indeed, in my own research on the relationship between economic growth and equity, I conclude that a shake-up of the landed elite (instability) is strongly related with long-term economic growth and income equality. Many growth-and-equity success

12. Exemplars being Lerner (1958), Lipset (1981), Organski (1965), and Rostow (1960).

13. Human rights are not a separate dependent variable. The selection of dependent variables was guided by Huntington's goals of development. One of those dependent variables is democracy, and by all current definitions of democracy, human rights (or civil liberties) are an important component. Civil liberties and human rights are discussed in some length in the democracy chapters (3 and 5). In addition, the negative relationship between militarization and human rights in Latin America is obvious and well documented.

14. There are serious debates within the mainstream over what type of democracy or what type of growth a country should seek (United Nations Development Programme 1996; Gills, Racamora, and Wilson 1993). There are also radical voices that make serious charges that democracy is a form of Western imperialism.

15. Some may argue that stability is an intervening variable: high militarization leads to instability, which in turn leads to lower levels of democracy, equity, and economic growth. However, King, Keohane, and Verba explain that intervening variables may be omitted from causal analysis. Indeed, they argue quite forcefully that "we should not control for an explanatory variable that is in part a consequence of our key explanatory variable" (1994, 173–74).

stories—Japan, South Korea, and Taiwan—experienced tremendous upheaval and instability that was a necessary requirement for a distribution of resources that set the stage for their long-term success (Bowman 1997). Hirschman also points out that wars and instability are necessary conditions for peaceful resource redistribution (1963, 137). And Olson argues that shocks are needed to break up rent-seeking coalitions (1971, 1982). Collier and Collier weigh in very astutely on the inherent normative value of this variable: stability may be desirable under some circumstances, but under "other circumstances and from other normative perspectives, stability and the reduction of conflict may be seen as blocking needed change, whereas polarization may open new avenues for change" (1991, 10). Stability is not a goal of development under apartheid or when widespread exploitation occurs. Many Costa Ricans would argue that the 1948 Civil War was positive in the long term but that stability is inherently good now under a democratic regime. Democratic stability is a goal of development; authoritarian stability is not.

The relationship between militarization and autonomy is also not directly examined. "Autonomy" has been extraordinarily difficult to define and operationalize. I see little face validity in measures using United Nations voting behavior as an indicator of autonomy. In the globalized, interdependent world that emerged after World War II, one might also question the meaning and desirability of "autonomy from external forces." No country, not even the United States, is autonomous from global economic forces.

This book directly examines three specific relationships stated in the following hypotheses:

Hypothesis 1: militarization has a negative effect on democracy
Hypothesis 2: militarization has a negative effect on equity
Hypothesis 3: militarization has a negative effect on economic growth

While I propose that militarization undermines development, I never claim that the militarization variable explains everything about Latin American development or even that it is the most important factor. Indeed, the multivariate analyses in Chapters 3 and 6 show that many variables affect democracy and development. Rather, I submit, and the evidence confirms, that the relationship is measurable, substantial, significant, and negative.

Methodology and Triangulation

This research design uses both quantitative and qualitative methodologies, similar to Jeffery Paige's groundbreaking 1978 work.[16] Good qualitative and good quantitative research designs share the same goals and logic (King, Keohane, and Verba 1994). However, the techniques are sufficiently different that each style has general strengths and weaknesses (Ragin 1987). Quantitative research generally lends itself to meeting higher standards of replicability, while qualitative research designs are generally more historically grounded. Quantitative designs are generally better for establishing relationships and their magnitudes; qualitative research is better for illuminating causal mechanisms and establishing sequence and agency.[17] For my research question, both methods can and will be used. Specifically, quantitative components were designed with the goal of establishing significant relationships and approximating the amount of the variance in the dependent variables explained by the explanatory variable. Qualitative sections are used to recheck the conclusions of the quantitative sections, flesh out causal mechanisms, document sequence and agency, and explore data and variables not amenable to quantification. The use of different methodologies and distinct sources and types of data to test a relationship is often referred to as triangulation.

Triangulation results from training distinct methodologies and datasets on the same empirical problem and then analyzing both the discrepant and similar results that obtain (Tarrow 1995, 473–74). King, Keohane, and Verba define triangulation as using the best methodology to analyze "data collected at different places, sources, times, levels of analysis, or perspectives, data that might be quantitative, or might involve intensive interviews or thick historical description" and concur with Tarrow that triangulation is the ideal in the quest of causal inference in the social sciences (1995, 479). If a large body of scholarship already exists, triangulation can marry existing research from one methodological school with original scholarly work on the same question but with different methods and different data

16. This is the combination method described by Ragin (1987, chapter 5) and praised by King, Keohane, and Verba (1994, 5).

17. "Statistical and case study methods are complementary in establishing the different claims necessary for causal explanation" (Bennett and George 1998, 6). For a defense of the virtues of comparative historical research in causal analysis, see Goldstone (1997), Mahoney (1999), Mahoney and Rueschemeyer (2003), Rueschemeyer and Stephens (1997), and Skocpol and Somers (1980).

sources.[18] As quantitative research on Latin America is relatively underdeveloped and we have no existing studies on the topic in the time and space domain that interests me, I perform all of the analyses.

This research design, therefore, leads to both quantitative and comparative historical chapters. The two quantitative chapters are based primarily on eighteen Latin American cases, although Chapter 6 includes an examination of seventy-six LDCs. The comparative historical chapters focus on two countries, Costa Rica and Honduras.

In the quantitative sections, my strong preference for studies of change over relatively long periods of time appears. Development is not a short-term proposition and it may take many years for the impact of the causal variable to appear in the dependent variable. My research on the Kuznets inverted U-curve has awakened me to the problems of snapshot single-year cross-sectional studies for demonstrations of causation (Bowman 1997).[19] In this study, I focus on mid- to long-term trends of change in the dependent variables.

The Comparative Historical Case Selection

The logic of the comparative method has been described in a number of well-known works (Collier 1993; Lijphart 1975; King, Keohane, and Verba 1994). In a perfect research setting, one could easily gauge the effect of a causal variable on a dependent variable. One would start with two cases identical in every conceivable way. Then, the causal variable or treatment would be applied to one case and a placebo to the other. If the cases were identical in every aspect except the causal variable and an outcome or dependent variable differed greatly in the two cases, then we could

18. One of the best examples is Rueschemeyer, Stephens, and Stephens (1992), in which original comparative historical data analyses are triangulated with a large existing pool of quantitative research.

19. The Kuznets inverted U-curve is one example of a paradigm resulting from snapshot single-year cross-sectional studies (Bowman 1997). The plethora of cross-sectional studies do not, however, test sequence and agency, and while the cross-sectional regressions consistently support the inverted-U for large-N samples of LDCs, we cannot identify a single case that has followed the trajectory in income distribution and economic growth predicted by the inverted-U hypotheses, and attribute the changes in distribution to the economic forces described by Kuznets. Rueschemeyer and Stephens (1997) present cogent illustrations of the challenges that quantitative techniques face in establishing causation. Assessing change over periods of time solves many of these problems.

conclude that there is some relationship between the causal and the dependent variables. Unfortunately, it is difficult if not impossible to create such an experiment in macro-social comparative research. The comparative method attempts to approximate the ideal. The approach is relatively straightforward. Cases should have variance in both the dependent variable and the causal or explanatory variable and little or no variance in other potential control variables that have been identified as having a potential impact on the dependent variable.

The selection process for this study began with the choice of Costa Rica as one of the cases, for it had the lowest level of militarization in the region. I then selected the other case. Since the five Central American Republics are often referred to as a single divided nation (Woodward 1985) and are all small countries with relatively small populations, I focused on El Salvador, Guatemala, Honduras, and Nicaragua. Honduras was selected as the second case, as it matches much more closely the case of Costa Rica on important control variables. Bananas and coffee are the two leading exports and the countries have *very* similar resource endowments. Neither case had the extensive forced labor conditions of El Salvador and Guatemala, and to a lesser degree of Nicaragua. Both are Mestizo countries and lack large marginalized ethnic groups that so strongly shape political conditions in Guatemala;[20] although both Costa Rica and Honduras have had and continue to have small marginalized ethnic groups.[21] Both had until the middle of the twentieth century agricultural frontiers and an escape valve for those seeking land. Neither had a history of an enduring strong military institution as did Guatemala and El Salvador. Neither experienced a civil war during the era of the Cuban revolution, as did the other three countries. Both share long borders with Nicaragua and faced serious pressures from the United States during the Sandinista years. The Sandinista revolution and Contra wars make comparisons with Nicaragua problematic. Neither Costa Rica nor Honduras had a violently repressive oligarchy. And these countries had the two strongest union movements in Central America circa 1950.[22]

20. Due to the large indigenous population, the tradition of large landed estates, and the widespread practice of forced labor, Guatemala is the most dissimilar case in Central America.

21. Needler observes that coups are more frequent in Latin America where large Indian populations exist, such as in Guatemala (1974, 152–59).

22. In 1950, Honduras had the region's most advanced union movement (Pérez Brignoli 1988, 125).

As shown in Table 1.1, these two countries are remarkably similar on these important control variables—perhaps as similar as any pair of countries in the world—and yet are different in important ways besides militarization. These differences include the level of influence of transnational corporations in the economy, the development of the state, and most nota-

Table 1.1 Socioeconomic and demographic measures

	Costa Rica	*Honduras*
Land area (thousands of hectares)[1]		
Total	5,110	11,209
Arable	285	1,610
Population[2]		
1900	310,000	420,000
1950	800,000	1,430,000
Urbanization (percentage standardized),[3] 1960	18.5	11.1
HEC Index of Social Development,[4] 1940	69.3	82.9
Native American population percent,[5] 1978	0.6	3.2
Catholic percent,[6] 1985	89.3	95.1
Real per capita GDP		
1930	284.3	288.2
1945[7]	282.0	209.0
Coffee and bananas (percentage of all exports),[8] 1955	87.3	90.1
U.S. direct foreign investment (millions of dollars),[9] 1950	60.0	62.0
Top 20% share of national income, circa 1960 (percentage)[10]	60.0	67.8
Literacy, percent of population 15 + years,[11] 1950	79.4	35.2
International aid[12] (millions $U.S.)		
Cumulative total U.S., 1946–88	709.5	772.2
Cumulative total intl. orgs., 1949–92	2,212.3	2,305.7

1. SALA 31, 1:20.
2. SALA 31, 1:109.
3. SALA 31, 1:142.
4. SALA 31, 1:178. This is a summary index of twelve Health, Education, and Communication indicators where equality with the United States would equal zero. For example, in 1940 the average for Latin America was 73.9. In other words, in 1940 the total Health, Education, and Communication gap between Costa Rica and Honduras was 19.6 percent. The gap grew to 46.9 percent by 1980.
5. SALA 22, 97.
6. SALA 31, 1:338–39.
7. Bulmer-Thomas (1993, 345). In 1970 $U.S.
8. SALA 31, 2:645.
9. SALA 31, 2:952.
10. Data for Costa Rica from González-Vega and Céspedes (1993, 46); for Honduras from Muller (1988, 54).
11. SALA 1972, 140.
12. SALA 31, 2:882, 883, 897.

bly human capital as measured by literacy. The importance of literacy and human capital in Costa Rica cannot be overemphasized. Therefore, as with most two-case studies, the results are to a degree indeterminate. Yet, the real strength of comparative historical research, and the utility of combining it with inferential statistics, is in illuminating the causal mechanisms and showing agency and sequence in the relationships.[23]

Chapter Previews

Chapter 2: Militarization: The Causal Variable, the Literature, and the Theory

Chapter 2 first precisely defines and conceptualizes the causal variable—militarization—and then presents an overview of the literature on the Third World military and identifies the important gap in the literature that this study fills. The theoretical foundations of much of the research on the military flows out of the groundbreaking work of Andreski (1954 [1968]), Huntington (1957), and Janowitz (1964). Three other important and distinct subgroups in the militarization literature are also introduced. First, I review the 1960s modernization literature that exhibits optimism

23. This selection process may be seen as problematic in one regard. As King, Keohane, and Verba emphasize, it is an "egregious error" to select cases when variance in the causal and dependent variables are known to vary together in ways that support the posited hypothesis (1994, 142). While I did not select on the dependent variable, I knew a priori that levels of democracy and militarization were inversely related in these two cases. However, it is inconceivable that a scholar could learn enough about the cases to minimize variance in the control variables without having a pretty good idea about the fit of the cases with the proposed hypothesis.

The problem of selection bias is greatly reduced in this study because each posited relationship is also tested with inferential statistics, and there are a larger number of cases where the outcome is not known a priori. In addition, the utility of comparative historical research for establishing causal inference goes far beyond just the mimicking of statistical methods that King, Keohane, and Verba purport. Comparative historical research is able to present evidence that not only links the causal variable with the dependent variable, but is also able to illuminate the causal mechanism. Good comparative historical research shows how the independent variable caused change in the dependent variable; it establishes sequence and agency. As Stephens argues, "[C]omparative historical analysis is actually superior to cross-national quantitative analysis, its only competitor in the study of these macro social developments, because it allows one to uncover the causal processes and thus to eliminate rival explanations for the phenomenon under study" (1998, 23). And McKeown reasons that just as process tracing in a single case can lead to a determination "beyond a reasonable doubt" of guilt or innocence in a singe court case, well-executed research on even a single case can generate causal inference in social science research (1998).

for the modernizing effect of large Third World armies. Second, I explore the quantitative literature that statistically assesses the relationship between militarization and various goals of development. And third, I incorporate the qualitative civil military literature that is focused on Latin America. A careful examination of these literatures results in a simple typology of Third World militaries. Then, using the explicit theoretical rationale of Andreski, Huntington, Janowitz, and others, I propose that militarization should have a negative impact on development in Latin America even if it has a positive impact in other regions in the developing world.

Chapter 2 ends with a discussion of the impact of militarization on state capacity and state priorities in Latin America. I propose that a combination of large militaries, internal military foci, and the international Cold War emphasis on anticommunism rearranged state priorities and undermined state capacity for development. The United States and many Latin American elites might have been in support of democracy and equity in theory, but during the Cold War anticommunism too often trumped democracy and conservative order trumped equity. Democracy and citizen-centric development were not priorities and where state resources and attention were concentrated on internal order and security, state capacity to pursue the goals of development was undermined. Large militaries, particularly where enemies are fellow citizens, have serious opportunity costs.

Chapter 3: Taming the Tiger: A Quantitative Analysis of Militarization and Democracy in Latin America

The chapter argues that militarization in Latin America negatively affects three power relations that are important for democratization: class, transnational, and state. Two dimensions of democracy—average level of democracy over time and the lowest level of democracy during a multiyear period of time—are regressed against two indicators of militarization: military spending and the number of soldiers per thousand inhabitants. The results strongly support the hypothesis that militarization has a negative effect on democracy in Latin America. Finally, the chapter reveals that the negative impact of militarization on democracy began to diminish in the late 1970s, such that the negative effect is stronger in 1973–74 than in 1985–86.

Chapter 4: When Ballots Trump Bullets: Demilitarization and Democratic Consolidation in Costa Rica

Extant theories of Costa Rican democratic exceptionalism are presented and I argue that they are incomplete explanations of democratization. The ignored period 1948–58 must be studied to capture the causal mechanisms of democratic consolidation for this important case. In the 1948–58 period, the evidence is unambiguous that democracy was neither consolidated nor largely the result of elite pacts, Costa Rican culture, socioeconomic conditions, nor institutions. I illustrate how class power relations and transnational power dynamics threatened the Figueres regime both in 1948–49 and in 1953–58. The constitutional proscription of the military and the serious weakening of that institution restricted the options of the opposition who were united in their desire to destroy Figueres and who sought violent means to overthrow him. A preference for ballots over bullets only materializes after 1958 as the absence of a military as a deliberative actor affected the calculus of political elites.

Chapter 5: When Bullets Trump Ballots: Militarization and Democratic Collapse in Honduras

Honduras shared many similarities with Costa Rica during this period. In 1950, Honduras did not have a professional and institutionalized military. A moderate social democrat similar to Costa Rica's Figueres took power in 1957 and initiated an ambitious program of economic, political, and social reform. Like Figueres, President Villeda was opposed by the oligarchy, the banana companies, and the CIA. Villeda, like Figueres, was often smeared as a "communist." One major difference between Costa Rica 1948–58 and Honduras 1954–63 was the very different trajectories of the armed forces. I detail the emergence of the Honduran military. In 1963, this new political actor ousted Villeda in a violent military coup. The chapter concludes that it would be difficult to imagine Figueres surviving with a strong Cold War military and that it would be easy to imagine Villeda surviving another day without U.S.-supported militarization of the country.

Finally, I argue that militarization was not the automatic destiny for Honduras. The decision to professionalize an army or follow the Costa Rican demilitarized example was a major public debate in the 1954–57 period. The debate continued during the Villeda presidency, and by the electoral campaign of 1963 was again a major national issue that was forcefully decided by the *golpe de estado* just days before the scheduled election.

Chapter 6: Guns Versus Butter: A Quantitative Analysis of Militarization and Material Development

This chapter has two purposes. The first is to assess the relationships between militarization and equity and between militarization and economic growth in Latin America. The second is to illuminate the importance of the boundedness of social explanation and illustrate how militarization has a different effect on equity and economic growth in Latin America than in sub-Saharan Africa or in the Middle East and East Asia.

I first establish that food consumption is a useful indicator of equity. I assess the relationship between militarization and calorie consumption for eighteen Latin American countries for the 1964–89 period and find that militarization has a strong, highly significant, and negative effect on food consumption. The same methodology is then applied to the relationship between militarization and economic growth. The results strongly support the hypothesis that militarization has a negative effect on economic growth.

This chapter also compares the militarization/food consumption and militarization/economic growth relationships in eighteen Latin American cases with a universal sample of seventy-six LDCs. I reveal how contextual differences in the militarization variable by region can lead to biased findings.

Chapter 7: Escaping the Lost Decade: Militarization and Economic Growth in Costa Rica and Honduras

Successful social and economic development requires sustained state intervention and two types of resources: economic resources and organizational resources. The decision to emphasize internal security and build up the armed forces has opportunity costs as scarce financial and organizational resources are consumed. This comparative historical chapter analyzes the trade-offs between militarization and economic development in the 1980s and 1990s, with foci on foreign-aid utilization and the tourism industry.

I show how a greatly reduced military budget and a decision to pursue citizen-centric security rather than doctrines of national security in Costa

Rica resulted in the state capacity and resources to transform the economy after the crisis of the early 1980s. In the rest of the Central American isthmus, the quest for internal security led to increased militarization during the Cold War. Large portions of the budget that could have gone to economic restructuring and infrastructure were consumed by the armed forces. Militarization also led to increased uncertainty, shortened time horizons, and a series of crises that thwarted the planning, implementation, and follow-through of the long-term policies that are necessary for economic development.

The book makes major contributions to both basic research and policy. A large body of statistical research on militarization and development is challenged and reassessed. The democratization scholarship for Costa Rica and Honduras is furthered and enhanced. In the Costa Rican case, the reassessment is considerable. This study also makes a significant positive contribution to the ongoing social science debate between the proponents of nomothetic findings and area studies. I show that area-specific context is crucial for understanding development. Social science may progress further by seeking area-bounded explanation than universal truths. However, this study also shows that area-bounded explanations should both clearly identify those area-specific manifestations that create context and carefully assess the claim that regional context alters the causal relationship.

Finally, the policy ramifications are immense. If militarization has an unambiguous negative effect on democracy, equity, and growth in Latin America, then civil society, politicians, business, and other domestic actors should make every effort to demilitarize the countries of the region. These efforts should be encouraged and supported by the United States, international financial institutions, and other international actors. Clinton and Bush administration initiatives to increase military sales to the region should be replaced with incentives to reduce the flow of arms into the hemisphere. Scarce resources should be diverted from the Latin American military and used to enhance democracy, reduce poverty, improve human capital, and lower debts. The era of the praetorian should end.

2 Militarization

the causal variable, the literature, and the theory

This chapter defines and operationalizes militarization, reviews the militarization and civil-military relations literatures, and presents a theoretical framework for the argument that militarization has a negative effect on development in Latin America. I provide a simple typology of Third World militaries to help develop an explanation for why the effect of militarization on development is more malignant in Latin America than in other regions of the developing world.

What is militarization and demilitarization? Militarization's primary definition is the expansion or relative size of some integral part, scope, or mission of the armed forces and may be observed in the size of the budget, the number of soldiers, and the training, equipping, war-readiness, and institutionalization of the armed forces. As a secondary definition, politics can also become militarized when one observes an increase in military prerogatives and influence in political decision-making.[1] Finally, society can become militarized when the military's role expands in societal institutions such as education or the development of rural paramilitary forces. Demilitarization is a reduction in the size of the armed forces or in the prerogatives, political influence, and autonomy of the military.

Most quantitative researchers and some qualitative scholars have operationalized militarization as the percent of the national budget or national GDP spent on defense.[2]

1. Other institutions such as the police can also become militarized. Some analysts have noted a growth of paramilitarism in U.S. police departments in recent years, which is ominous, as "the mindset of the soldier is simply not appropriate for the civilian police officer. Police officers confront not an 'enemy' but individuals who are protected by the Bill of Rights" (Weber 1999, 1).

2. The operationalization of militarization is further detailed in Chapter 3. Quantitative studies that employ the militarization causal variable are cited in Chapters 3 and 6. One notable recent example of qualitative research using "militarization" is Williams and Walter (1997).

This single indicator not only directly measures the primary definition of militarization (size of the military) but also indirectly captures part of the secondary definition of the political influence and prerogatives of the military. As Nordlinger notes, "[C]hanges in the size of the defense budget are a telling indicator of the political power and prestige of the armed forces" (1977, 68–71). In his influential work on civil-military relations in Argentina, Pion-Berlin characterizes the defense budget as the sine qua non of military power and interests (1997, 40). In the quantitative analyses, I use both size of the military budget as a percent of GDP and the number of soldiers per thousand inhabitants as indicators of militarization, treating militarization as a continuous variable. The comparative historical chapters employ militarization as a dichotomous variable, with low levels of military institutionalization and prerogatives in the Costa Rican case and greatly expanding levels in the Honduran case.

The Development of the Militarization Literature

The number of articles and books on the military in the Third World is impressive, especially since these works only began to appear in any number in the 1960s. The intellectual foundation of much of the theoretically oriented scholarship flows from three important scholars from the 1950s—Stanislav Andreski, Samuel Huntington, and Morris Janowitz. This section will review these three authors and the other important general theoretical works of the 1960s. I show that a careful reading of this work provides theoretically informed expectation for a negative relationship between militarization and development in Latin America. From these classic works emerge two distinct bodies of scholarship that at best ignore each other (and at worst belittle each other): statistical research and qualitative research. These literatures are reviewed and I argue that progress would be enhanced if these very different research traditions were bridged.[3]

Andreski's 1954 *Military Organization and Society* is an impressive display of deductive logic and comparative sociology. In his 1964 "Annotated Bibliography," Johnson refers to this work as the "most exciting of the theoretical studies of the armed forces and militarism." Indeed, it features

3. The quantitative-qualitative divide is an old battle line in the social sciences. In many quarters, this rather insipid debate has disappeared, resulting in beneficial interchange between quantitative and qualitative scholars.

bold assumptions, deductive logic, some apocalyptic predictions, and creative jargon.[4] Andreski is interested in the relationship between "militancy" (or war-making) and social stratification. He observes that militancy sometimes heightens social stratification and sometimes flattens it. The major assertion is that the difference depends on the proportion of the population serving in the military. This proportion is referred to as the *military participation ratio* or the MPR (1968, 33). The higher the MPR, the greater the leveling effect. But a high MPR by itself does not reduce inequalities without the threat of war and annihilation. It is this threat that induces adjustments in stratification. If war does ensue, the more ferocious the war the more egalitarian the army (30). While Andreski acknowledges that large militaries may lead to improvements in education and technical skills in the soldiers (34–35), the real linkage between MPR and reduced stratification is warfare: "A war, particularly when the very survival of the state is at stake, produces an adaptation to the requirements of bellic efficiency, whose nature depends above all on the techniques of warfare. The need for efficiency may impose considerable leveling of social inequalities, as well as an increase in vertical mobility" (196).

It is easy to incorrectly extend Andreski's logic and conclude that in Third World countries, large militaries will be associated with lower stratification. By 1968, Andreski seized the opportunity of a second edition to unambiguously correct this misrepresentation of his argument. Large militaries can lead to either greater or lower levels of stratification, depending on the nature of the threat. If the threat to the country is from an external enemy and highly credible, then national cohesion and efficiency exist and MPR will reduce social stratification (South Korea and Taiwan would be examples). However, the effect is likely the opposite when large armies exist with no credible external threat of state annihilation. Andreski singles out Latin America as a region with too high an MPR for police functions and too low an MPR for waging interstate war (215). Latin American military structures increase stratification due to the large numbers of officers, who, through "parasitism," appropriate surplus wealth; Argentina is bemoaned for having as many generals as the United States (215). "The military function has become introverted in the Latin Ameri-

4. Andreski invents a host of strange terms; for example a widely conscriptive military is "neferic," while a feudal military is "ritterian," and a restricted professional military is "mortasic."

can republics; with few opportunities to fight for their countries" (211). "It is sad to find that the absence of concern for the common good might be the result of (Latin America's) relatively unwarlike existence" (198).[5]

Huntington's 1957 classic, *The Soldier and the State: The Theory and Politics of Civil-Military Relations*, deals with the question of civilian control over the armed forces. Huntington's thesis is simple; professionalization of the military and a firewall between soldiers and society will ensure civilian control of armed forces and military neutrality in politics. Professionalism is comprised of three parts—expertness, social responsibility, and loyalty to fellow practitioners. Like Andreski's work, it is often contorted to support positions not held by the author. The belief that professionalization will lead officers in Latin America to respect the democratic order and to refrain from meddling in politics is enticing.[6]

Finer (1988, 21) exposes the weakness of Huntington's argument, noting that many highly professional officer corps have intervened in politics, such as the German and the Japanese. For Latin America, Huntington's argument is stood on its head as it is in the two countries with the least professional armies—Costa Rica and Mexico—where the armed forces have been least interested in seizing power.

However, much of the criticism of Huntington—at least from a Latin American perspective—is misguided. He is clear that his theories are oriented to civil-military relations in "modern industrial societies" (1962, 256). As Stepan points out, "the professionalization thesis was rooted in the assumption that armies develop their professional skills for conventional warfare against foreign armies" and has no applicability for Latin America (1986, 136). Huntington himself later clarifies his position:

> Antigovernmental war encourages civil-military relations different from those stimulated by interstate conflict. . . . In terms of military relations to the government, both the deterrent force and the limited war force had clearly defined missions and had to be highly responsive to the political leaders of the government in the performance of these missions. In domestic war, on the other hand,

5. Even with this explicit and unambiguous clarification of his view, the 1954 (1968) work is still improperly cited by scholars to support the proposition that large armies will improve social inequalities in developing countries.

6. The widespread confidence in this strategy keeps funds flowing into the School of the Americas and joint training exercises throughout the hemisphere.

> the political and military roles of the principal actors are merged on both sides, and political and military means become indistinguishable. . . . the change in function from interstate to domestic conflict may have drastic effect upon the attitudes of military officers toward their government and upon the amenability to the traditional forms of objective civilian control. (1962, 22)

Despite this clarification, the absurd notion endures that a little training and professionalization can transform the Latin American military into the U.S. model. Stepan's landmark studies (1971, 1973, 1986) correct this misunderstanding: "the concept of military professionalism is still widely misunderstood, and it is useful to formulate explicitly the differences between *old professionalism of external warfare* and the *new professionalism of internal security* and national development" (Stepan 1986, 136, emphasis mine).

By the early 1960s, a host of new nations were emerging from colonialism at the same time that modernization was a dominant theme in social science. Scholars were in many cases overly optimistic about the transformative power of militaries as a modernizing force:[7] militaries and one-party governments were seen as the solution to the corrupt and defective governments found in poor countries. Janowitz's *The Military in the Political Development of New Nations* (1964) is concerned with two major questions: "First, what characteristics of the military establishment of a new nation facilitate its involvement in domestic politics? Second, what are the capacities of the military to supply effective political leadership for a new nation striving for rapid economic development and social modernization?" (1964, 1). Janowitz asserts, among other things, that military expenditures lead to economic development by providing technical and administrative skills and through military management of economic enterprises (75). In addition to economic growth, the military also provides political modernization and is an agent of social change. The "army is a

7. "God may not be on the side of poor and developing countries but the academics are: and it really did seem as though whatever newfangled experiment in despotism was adopted in these states, it was the appropriate answer to their backwardness and poverty. When the one-party system spread like a rash through the Third World, the one-party system was all the rage (even though most of such regimes were only two or three years old). As military coups exploded over the Third World, a host of apologists rushed forward likewise" (Finer 1988, 288). Finer believed that Third World militaries have the limited technical ability to administer only the most primitive community (1988, 12).

device for developing a sense of identity" and can reduce ethnic cleavages (80). The military also has the capacity to improve human capital by providing education (81) and building morale (83).

It is important to note that his study deals exclusively with the "new" nations emerging out of colonialism. Janowitz emphatically excludes Latin America from the study's scope: "But there are fundamental differences in the natural history of militarism in South America. The forms of military intervention represent more than a century of struggle and accommodation that has produced political institutions different from those found in the new nations. Thus there is a logic for excluding Latin American nations from this analysis" (1964, v–vi).[8]

Three other important works dealing with modernization and the military appeared in the 1960s. Along with that of Andreski and Janowitz, these works are often cited as theoretical support of the empirical quantitative research in the 1980s and 1990s that finds a positive relationship between militarization and development. Levy's mammoth *Modernization and the Structure of Societies* includes a chapter on the role and potential of the armed forces. He asserts that the armed forces are "the most efficient type of organization for combining maximum rates of modernization with maximum levels of stability and control" (1996, 603). Soldiers learn to do things better than do non-soldiers; for example, they will learn the best way to drive trucks. They then make up a pool of skilled laborers and administrators. Levy follows Janowitz in wanting to tear down Huntington's fire wall between the armed forces and general civilian concerns and bemoans the possibility that keeping the military out of the modernization process "may turn out to be one of the great mistakes of the twentieth century" (605).

Another often cited source for the proposition that militaries are modernizing agents is Inkeles's chapter "The Modernization of Man" (1966). Inkeles states that the army "may play an especially important role in introducing men to the modern world, both in the direct instruction they offer and indirectly in the model of routine, scheduling, technical skill, and efficacy" (148). However, Inkeles views this as an idealized institution that may not work in many countries where "armies may be run so as

8. In 1977, Janowitz issued a second and revised edition now titled *Military Institutions and Coercion in the Developing Nations*, with increased focus on paramilitary forces and a shift towards the view that the Latin American militaries were converging on the modernizing military model of the new nations.

scarcely to induce a man to exert himself, to practice initiative, or to respect the dignity of others" (149).

The classic argument for the modernizing nature of the Third World military is from Pye (1964). As in Janowitz's 1964 work, Pye's argument is directed only at new nations in Africa and Asia that were in transition from colonialism to state building. "It occurred to few students of the underdeveloped regions that the military might become the critical group in shaping the course of nation-building. Now that the military has become the key decision-making element in at least eight of the Afro-Asian countries, we are confronted with the awkward fact that there has been almost no scholarly research on the role of the military in the political development of new states" (Pye 1964, 69). Pye is optimistic that the army is a modern institution that will provide skills, discipline, and "modernization." Armies are rival institutions with external enemies and must therefore have an external focus and keep up with technology and education and not merely adjust to local dynamics. The army can be a veritable factory for molding modern men. "In all societies it is recognized that armies must make those who enter them into the image of the good soldier. The underdeveloped society adds a new dimension: the good soldier is also to some degree a modernized man. Thus it is that the armies in the newly emergent countries come to play key roles in the process by which traditional ways give way to more Westernized ideas and practices" (80).

In 1964, a vintage year for scholarship on militarization and development, a book dealing exclusively with the military in Latin America appeared—Johnson's *The Military and Society in Latin America.* While it is true—as is often cited—that Johnson has certain hopes for the modernizing role that the Latin American military can play, those expectations are in fact quite meager.

> In every republic there can be found quite responsible citizens who insist that the officers do have qualifications that are not available or are in short supply to the civilian sectors. However, the weight of the evidence is overwhelmingly on the side of those who insist that today civilians have equal or greater competence than the officers. Furthermore, there is nowhere in Spanish America a situation comparable to what is found in some of the new nations of Africa, the Middle East, and Southeast Asia, where officers can claim the right to direct government activities on the basis of both acquired skills and moral leadership. (1964, 132–33)

For Johnson, the Latin American military could assist in limited ways to promote modernization, especially at the rural level. The limited scope of the armed forces' role in development is illustrated by one of Johnson's few specific suggestions—using soldiers as medical guinea pigs (266).

These are the foundation studies on militarization and development. They are still cited regularly in empirical studies showing a positive relationship between militarization and development.[9] They are often misrepresented to support the view that larger militaries in the Third World will lead to greater social and economic development. Andreski rejects this characterization of his work unless credible external threats exist.[10] Huntington's 1957 work deals only with advanced industrial nations. Janowitz's 1964 classic study explicitly excludes Latin America, as does Pye's 1964 article. Johnson makes very little of the modernizing nature of the Latin American military. Inkeles is less than emphatic in his endorsement of the Third World military as a producer of modern men. The only work that unambiguously claims that militarization leads to modernization and development in the Third World without excluding Latin America is that of Levy. Even it must be considered in context, for in this two-volume work of some 821 pages, the chapter on the military is only 17 pages. Those empirical scholars who rely heavily and often exclusively on this body of research to theoretically support their empirical research are on less than sound footing as they often overstate the original arguments.

The Second Generation Military Research

The 1950s and 1960s not only brought about the first generation of research on the Third World military, but also produced the behavioral revolution and a quantitative-qualitative divide in the social sciences. The quantitative militarization and development research began with early works by Putnam (1967), Adelman and Morris (1967), Bury (1968), and Nordlinger (1970), and dealt largely with the correlates of the coup or with the impact of regime type on economic and social performance. The

9. See Chapter 6 for literature.

10. Weede is one quantitative scholar who is sensitive to the argument that the impact of militarization on development depends on whether the military is oriented towards credible external threats (1986, 1993).

impact of regime type on development has continued in studies by Remmer (1990) and others.[11]

A second area of inferential statistical research ignores regime type and instead looks directly at the relationship between the size of the military and various indicators of development, including democracy, social development, and economic growth. These literatures are reviewed in Chapters 3 and 6. With very few exceptions, these studies are flawed, as they ignore two important dimensions of militarization that are critical in the works of Andreski, Huntington, Janowitz, and others. The first deals with the very important differences between militarization for national self-defense against an external enemy and militarization for internal warfare. The second is the very different historical institutional trajectory between Latin American countries that gained independence in the early nineteenth century and those countries that gained independence in the second half of the twentieth century.

An entirely distinct body of literature also flowed out of the classic studies of Huntington and Janowitz—the qualitative research. This is a highly varied body of scholarship that deals mainly with the tensions and dynamics between civilians and the armed forces. The coup d'état has been the most popular subject, with much prognostication on the possibilities of future *golpes* or military withdrawal from politics. With the Third Wave of democracy consolidating, many insightful recent studies have attempted to measure and explain shifts in civilian control of the armed forces. In much of the qualitative research, the quantitative research is merely ignored, but occasionally the disdain for inferential statistics raises its head as in this line from Finer: "Statistically minded researchers have devoted much labour to trying to relate the size or cost of the armed forces to the incidence of military intervention. They might as well have scrutinized the entrails of dead fowl" (1988, 225).[12]

The first major comprehensive survey of the military in Latin America was Lieuwen's 1960 classic study that argued against U.S. support of the region's military institutions. In the following decades, hundreds of articles, books, and edited volumes on the militaries of individual countries or regions have appeared. The great problem with such work in general is

11. Jackman (1976) reviews some of this literature. He identifies various methodological flaws and concludes that regime type makes little difference in social and economic performance.

12. See also Janowitz (1977, 24).

that while it is highly accumulative it is not very cumulative. The works can be heaped en masse but there is very little integration or continuation in the research. Each new edited volume contains new typologies, ideal types, and classifications that usually ignore previous typologies, ideal types, and classifications.

Despite this general weakness in the literature, many excellent works have been published. Due to the sheer number it is impossible to review them all here, but I will introduce a couple that bear directly on this study.[13] One of the best general works is that of Rouquié (1984, translated into English in 1987). An important point that is particularly prescient for today is his warning not to think that military institutions have changed just because we are currently in a democratic cycle when civilians rule throughout most of Latin America. Rouquié notes that a scholar as eminent as Lieuwen (1961) announced that the military had been, by 1960, permanently extirpated from politics in Bolivia, Uruguay, and Chile (1984, 13).

In a painstaking review of dozens of defense journals in many Latin American countries, Nunn (1983, 1992, 1995) employs content analysis to analyze the political thought of the military and the changes in that thought over time. His work shows that the end of the Cold War and a decade of democratization have not altered the perceptions of the military, who still cling to a belief in the special role of the military as the saviors of the nation. As of early 1995, "Officers continue to see extremism and subversion as ever-present threats; civilians see this concern as a pretext for retaining outmoded Cold War policies that justify authoritarianism, and that once served to sidetrack the development of democratic institutions. . . . Everywhere sociopolitical change outpaces change within the military" (1995, 28).

13. Stepan's work has already been cited, and remains the most important body of research on Latin America (1971, 1986, and 1988). A critical review of recent scholarship is found in Pion-Berlin (1995), and a literature review on the military in Central America is found in Seckinger (1981). Some of the best-edited volumes are those of Goodman, Mendelson, and Rial (1990), Loveman and Davies (1997), Lowenthal (1976), Lowenthal and Fitch (1986), Rodríguez (1994), Schmitter (1973), and Varas (1989). The long list of important recent books includes Agüero's (1995) excellent study of the democratic transition in Spain and Hunter's (1997) well-received study of democratic institutions and civil-military relations in Brazil. Notable recent studies of Latin America as a region include Black (1986), Fitch (1998), Loveman (1999), and Remmer (1989). There has been an interesting debate on the degree to which military power has been reduced in many countries. For Argentina, see McSherry (1997), Norden (1996), and Pion-Berlin (1997).

Another body of work worth singling out is that of Loveman (1993, 1999), which explains the emergence of the military's concept of its mission and *la Patria*, and details the historical and institutional roots of constitutional provisions in Latin America that provide for legal regimes of exception and the suspension of political and civil rights. Loveman describes the constitutions of Latin America as contradictory documents that include both liberal ideals of Europe and North America and colonial Spanish concern with order and stability. In this region, with more than a century of constitutional tension, where both political liberty and constitutional dictatorship are legally enshrined, it is no surprise that the military's regard for electoral democracy would be equivocal.

Militarization and the Boundedness of Social Explanation

In inferential comparative social science research, there are two widely different views of the scope of our research and the range of application for our findings (see Kohli 1995). On the one hand, some scholars seek nomothetic or universal explanation. The context in which social phenomena occur is unimportant and the notion of area-specific dynamics is discounted. Social science aims to discover grand theory and universal truths: given X, we should expect Y to obtain in any setting. Both the classical Marxist and the rational choice (in particular the public choice variant) theoretical programs seek universal explanation (Kohli 1995).

MacIntyre embodies the other extreme—concepts and indicators do not travel well and the most we can expect is highly bounded explanation (1971). Some even argue that any comparison across countries is counterproductive. Most scholars assert that while we can learn much from comparative research, we must carefully consider to what degree our relationship(s) are bounded by space and time (see Bahry 1991). To complicate matters, most of the important outcomes that interest social scientists are complex and involve multiple causes.[14]

I posit that causal understanding can be maximized by focusing this study on Latin America rather than by seeking universal relationships.

14. Ragin describes this as multiple-conjunctural causation and quite explains how this can bedevil inattentive quantitative research (1987).

First of all, better data[15] (or at least more data) are available for Latin America than for other regions of the Third World. Including more regions of the world would result in limiting the variables or indicators in the analyses. Second, political development is a very complex concept that involves many potential causal variables, some of which are cultural and historical and therefore not only difficult to quantify, but are often obscure, abstract, and not easily conceptualized. Religion, trading partner, and colonizer dummy variables have been used for control in some studies of development: it is my contention that these cultural-historical variables can be better controlled for by focusing on a relatively homogeneous region with limited variance in cultural and historical factors. All of the countries of Latin America share common or at least relatively similar linguistic, religious, dependency, trading partner, and colonial patterns, all important factors for development according to some researchers. Other scholars suggest that culture interacts with other variables in determining political outcomes and that Latin America has a distinct political culture.[16] Whether one believes that culture is an interactive causal variable or a residual variable, most scholars of Latin America would probably agree with Susan Eckstein, who notes that despite the heterogeneity and diversity in the region, "Latin America's broader repertoire is rooted in its distinctive political history" (1989, 10–11).[17]

Third, if data were available for all regions of the world it would be possible to use dummy variables for regions to isolate various region-specific dynamics. Yet, one must have some historical knowledge of the area to hypothesize relationships and interpret the results of empirical tests. Adding dummy variables for regions and then interpreting the results without prior knowledge of the areas and theoretical reasoning for differences by region may be nothing more than data dredging. Laitin (1995, 456) argues that, "researchers in the area-studies tradition do not seek

15. For example, on a 1–4 scale (4 best), Summers and Heston rate the Penn World Table data for the eighteen Latin American countries used in this study as an average score of 1.91. The African countries achieve an average score of 1.25, and the developing countries of Asia have an average score of 1.42 (1991).

16. The latest salvo in this regard, and one with limited empirical support, is Inglehart and Carballo (1997).

17. For an excellent overview of the commonalities and contrasts in Latin America, see Skidmore and Smith (1997, Prologue). Rial also argues that in spite of the heterogeneity in the region, "Latin America exists and can (we might say *must*) be treated as a unit" (1990, 3).

generality of explanation, because they hold that the 'context' in which politics gets played out is highly determinative of the outcomes." Many of the esteemed works of our discipline such as Ames (1987), Bates (1981), Putnam (1993), Rueschemeyer, Stephens, and Stephens (1992), and others are successful in interpreting the empirical results of a group of cases that have something in common beyond what is quantifiable in a manageable fashion. Those who study social policy in advanced industrial countries would find it inefficient and beyond their interest to include cases from Africa or South Asia in their regressions. Yet, is there any reason to believe that French-speaking and French-colonized Mali would be somehow more comparable to Argentina than to France? This study rejects the notion that much can be gained by adding additional highly dissimilar cases and tries to exploit Latin America as a "fertile laboratory for studying comparative economic, social, and political change" (Wiarda and Kline 1996, 533).

By focusing this study on Latin America, I am limited to eighteen cases in some quantitative analyses (many more when stacking countries in pooled time series).[18] On the downside, it is very difficult to achieve high levels of statistical significance with only eighteen cases. As the following chapters demonstrate, and as in Putnam's influential study on democracy in a similar number of Italian regions (1993), by focusing on Latin America the relationships are much more substantial than in the large-N studies, and produce highly significant findings.

Most important, there is considerable theoretical rationale for positing that the effect of militarization on development is different in Latin America than in other regions. Without carefully assessing the historical and geopolitical trajectories of militaries as institutions, many large-N quantitative scholars have understandably made a serious mistake by treating all LDC militaries as the same variable. In the typical empirical study of the relationship between militarization and some component of development, all LDCs in the world are thrown into the sample and results are generated. As previously mentioned, generally the relationship that obtains is positive; higher militarization leads to greater development.[19] If

18. The eighteen countries used in this study are Argentina, Bolivia, Brazil, Chile, Colombia, Costa Rica, the Dominican Republic, Ecuador, El Salvador, Guatemala, Honduras, Mexico, Nicaragua, Panama, Paraguay, Peru, Uruguay, and Venezuela. Cuba and Haiti are not included due to lack of complete data.

19. Especially when number of soldiers per thousand inhabitants or military participation ratio (MPR) is the indicator.

one has a conviction that area-specific context is important, one would likely sit back and ask whether there are any systematic differences between different sets of militaries in the world that may bias the large-N studies. I have concluded that all LDC militaries are not the same variable and that the difference is to such a degree as to create a "cat-dog" variable. This variable does not carry well across regions.

Comparability of the Latin American Military

First, there is a long and enduring historical tradition of Latin American security forces exhibiting an almost spiritual calling to protect the citizens of the *Patria* from progressive values and to reinforce traditional conservative values (Loveman 1993, 1994, 1999; Loveman and Davies 1997; Nunn 1992, 1995). "Officers were taught and came to believe, that they possessed virtues, expertise, and patriotic values that mere civilians could never attain" (Loveman 1999, 70). Latin American militaries have a long tradition of internal focus and self-appointed and often constitutionally sanctioned authority to override civilian governments, human rights, and political rights if the *Patria* is perceived to be threatened—and despite recent democratic stability this is an enduring perception of military officers (Nunn 1995). Alba singles out as distinct to Latin America the "militarist tradition, which has turned armies into instruments of political maneuver and has encouraged military men . . . to believe that their proper role is one of politics and power" (1962, 178).[20]

Latin American militaries have a long institutional history as professional and largely autonomous organizations, a history that is not found in

20. Alba also notes that Latin American militarism is distinct from other regions, as militarism "refers only to a country's armed forces, or a part of them, taking action against a civilian-democratic regime. The intervention by the military against a dictatorship is not considered militarism in the Latin-American context" (1962, 165). A total of six distinctions between the Latin American military and those in other Third World countries are listed, including the distinction that "Militarism in some of the underdeveloped areas is of a unifying nationalist character, while that of Latin America can no longer be described by these terms" (179). Sarkesian asserts that "Categories and concepts such as corporate interests, middle class, military-political influence, the size of military establishments, the complete separation between political power and military impact on modernization, and the perceived autonomy between civil and military sectors—all are of doubtful applicability to African regimes" (1978, 8). Horowitz claims that "Latin American regimes, in contrast to their African and Asian counterparts, have many exceptional features" (1975, 308).

many LDCs, where a professional military is either a recent development or where the military is often nothing more than a militia for political leaders or clans.[21] In his classic work on Third World militaries, Janowitz correctly observes that "a meaningful distinction could be made between the new nations of Africa, the Middle East, and Asia on the one hand, and the nations of Latin America, on the other" due to the much longer institutional existence of the latter. In addition, Latin American militaries are ideologically different from those in other regions of the world, for in this region, "The military emerged with an institutional perspective that was conservative and accepted the status quo" (1977, 14).[22] In an impressive examination of primary documents, Nunn argues that "[T]hroughout Latin America the basic attributes of all [military] officers are the same" but are variable and different in the rest of the world and that there is a "telling divergence between Latin Americans and others" (1992, 79).

Second, Latin America has been strongly affected by actions and policies of the United States, as highlighted by the Monroe Doctrine and the number of interventions in the region. In particular, the long shadow of the United States was crucial in shaping the face of Latin American militaries in the post–WWII period (Etchison 1975). U.S. Cold War policy magnified the internal focus that was already strong in the region and really turned up the pressure for Latin American armies to fight internal enemies after the Cuban revolution in 1959.[23] "Secretary of Defense Robert McNamara announced in 1963 that the newly trained military leaders'

21. In the 1960s, when militarism in Latin America reached its apex, Coleman and Brice observed that "Armies have been the last of the authoritative structures of government to be created in all but a few of the forty-odd political entities of Sub-Saharan Africa. With few exceptions, national armies are either non-existent, or they are fragile structures" (1962, 359).

22. Janowitz also claims that Latin American militaries in the 1960s began to develop a vision of social and political change and social justice (1977, 15). I would argue that this "commitment" to social change and progress was largely hollow, as internal security was the prime concern.

23. "U.S. policymakers and military advisers were generally ignorant of the Latin American armed forces' professional and institutional evolution. Likewise, they misunderstood the historical internal security mission, variations in national threat perception and military doctrine, and local political nuances. With missionary zeal these advisers sought to remake the Latin American militaries and deploy them as surrogates for U.S. forces in the regional war against communism. Usually biting their tongues, Latin American officers accepted training, weapons, equipment, and other resources to wage their own wars against subversion despite arrogance, paternalism, and misconceptions of many U.S. personnel" (Loveman 1999, 169–70).

responsibility was not 'hemispheric defense', but 'internal security'" (LaFeber 1984, 151). U.S. policy after 1950 to strengthen the Latin American military dovetailed nicely with the traditional internal focus of the militaries. "After 1961, with U.S. support, Latin American armies went to war against internal subversion and international communism" (Loveman 1999, 166). This is discussed at length in the comparative historical chapters on Costa Rica and Honduras.

U.S. interest in stability in the hemisphere has had two other important effects for our study. First, the United States has resisted the large-scale demise of the landed elite in Latin America that it encouraged and oversaw in Japan and Korea (Bowman 1997). Second, the power and the interest of the United States were such that progressive revolutions from above were likely if not pre-ordained to be ephemeral.[24] Due in part to U.S. power and interests, long-term reactionary or conservative military regimes were likely during the Cold War, progressive military regimes were not. U.S. influence enhanced the existing conservative impact of the military in Latin America. "[W]ithout the armed forces, . . . every republic in Spanish America except Uruguay, Costa Rica, and Cuba would stand politically to the left of where it is now" (Johnson 1964, 144). In 1966, Needler reported a pronounced decline in the number of reformist coups in Latin America after U.S. training of the military, while the number of reactionary coups increased, an observation seconded by Wolpin (1975).[25]

The third and most important feature of the Latin American military that sets it apart from many other regions of the developing world during the Cold War period has been the absence of credible threats of war from neighbors.[26] Desch theorizes that countries with challenging internal

24. An exception is the seven-year Velasco regime (1968–75) in Peru, which "had the distinction of leading one of Latin America's most ambitious and sincere attempts to cope with underdevelopment and social injustice in the twentieth century" (Wright 1991, 134). For more on the Peruvian experiment, see Lowenthal (1975) and Stephens (1980).

25. Fitch contends that U.S. assistance was detrimental in Latin America not because of any ideological effect but because of "the general effect of assisting military professionalization and thus worsening the existing imbalance in the relative institutionalization of civilian and military organizations" (1986, 37). This is contrary to Huntington's well-known thesis that the greater the professionalization of the armed forces, the lower the threat of military intervention in the state (1959). Stepan (1971, 1986, 1988) details how professionalization in Brazil "coexisted with increasing politicization in the years leading up to 1964" (1986, 135).

26. The near-complete lack of wars between Latin American countries provides an alternative explanation to the "democratic peace proposal" so popular in the social science journals. In the period 1900–1980, the vast majority of electoral democracies were in two

threat environments and limited external threats will have weak civilian institutions, weak state capacity, and an inward-oriented military with a proclivity to seize political power. Desch categorizes Southern Cone cases as malignant examples of civil-military relations with high internal threat and low external threat environments from the 1950s through the 1980s (1999).[27] Surveying the region in 1965, Lieuwen catalogs threats to security in Latin America: Red China, Cuba, the Soviet Union, and internal subversion were listed and expounded, while threats to the security of any particular Latin American country by its neighbor were not mentioned a single time.[28]

Carlos Escudé (1993) presents a very provocative case for the claim that security issues in Latin America (with particular emphasis on Argentina) were driven by international (U.S.) ideology and norms of neorealist power politics, and not legitimate concerns of external threats. "Theories based on realist assumptions have often led to internal repression, to the breakdown of democracy and to human rights abuses, as a consequence of the realists' obsession with 'national' security. . . . Furthermore, balance-of-power arguments have always been used to justify the deviation of development funds for arms purchases, *despite the fact that Argentina has not faced credible threats for more than half a century*" (29–30, emphasis mine).[29]

---

groups of countries, the advanced industrial countries and Latin America. If Kautsky is correct that the advanced capitalist states act as an oligopoly and do not fight, and if Latin American countries do not have wars among themselves regardless of regime type, then the democratic peace proposal may be spurious (See Bowman and Eudaily 1999).

27. Desch (1999) classifies Southern Cone Latin American cases as internal threat dominant from 1950 to the 1980s. His contention that Argentina and Brazil had a shift to an emphasis on external enemies after 1982 is only partially convincing, particularly for the Brazilian case.

28. This is not to say that conflict and even border skirmishes are absent in Latin America. Some may argue that the dozen or so border conflicts in Latin America in the past half century are evidence of credible external threats and a genuine need for powerful armed forces. I would counter that many of the border conflicts, such as the recent conflict between Ecuador and Peru over a small strip of uninhabited jungle, should be seen as an outgrowth of internal political dynamics and not as a manifestation of genuine security threats.

29. While many military journals and officials may identify external threats as a prime mission of the Latin American military, other officials are more forthcoming in the lack of credible external threats to national existence beyond border skirmishes. Argentine Colonel Mario Horacio Orsolini claimed in his 1964 book, *The Crisis of the Army*, that internal counterinsurgency "filled the void produced by the almost complete disappearance of the possibility of war between our country and its neighbors" (quoted in Rosenberg 1991, 109).

Escudé continues by asserting that real security in Latin American countries that do not face credible external threats does not come from expanding military capabilities, but rather from a citizen-centric notion of development. During the Cold War, when U.S. policies greatly enhanced the existing emphasis on internal security threats, citizen-centric development was difficult to imagine. I argue that despite its challenges and problems, Costa Rica is the exemplar of citizen-centric security.

Kruijt and Torres-Rivas, the noted Central American scholar, also point out the absolute uniqueness of the Latin American military and its internal focus (1991). They state that in the entire twentieth century, there have been only two international wars of any significance in Latin America. The first was the Chaco War between Bolivia and Paraguay that began as a conflict between two transnational oil companies over possible oil reserves. The second was the Malvinas/Falkland War, which was caused by internal Argentine political dynamics. The utter failure of the Argentine military as a fighting force is, according to Kruijt and Torres-Rivas, the best example we have of the internal-political nature of the Latin American military (1991, 8–9). Ramsey (1997) counts a total of two wars between countries of Latin America from 1830 until 1935, and only one since 1935 (1997, ix–x). The lack of equipment and training for prolonged external wars is another telling indicator of the internal focus of the region's armed forces (Loveman 1999, 150–54).[30]

Erich Weede, one of the principal quantitative scholars of the effects of

30. There is clear empirical evidence to support the proposition that Latin American countries rarely fight each other but are often plagued with internal warfare. The 1996 Correlates of War Dataset yields the following evidence (Singer and Small 1993). Between 1816 and 1992 there were 11,158 total country-years in the world. 24.4% of those country-years are in Latin America and the Caribbean (22.3% in Latin America). In the entire world, there were only 75 interstate wars with 1,000 or more battlefield deaths. Of those 75, only nine (12%) were wars between Latin American countries. Of these nine wars, only three had greater than 2,000 deaths and four barely met the COW standards, with the minimum number of 1,000 deaths. Since 1932, there has been only one war fought between Latin American countries, the 1969 Soccer War between Honduras and El Salvador. In addition to a relative paucity of wars, especially since 1932, interstate Latin American wars are much less deadly than those in other parts of the world. The median number of battlefield deaths in the nine Latin American wars is 1,300 and the mean is 51,244. In contrast, the median for the other sixty-six wars in the COW dataset is 11,550 and the mean is 1,657,672. The suggestion that Latin American countries are more likely than other countries to experience civil war is also supported by the COW dataset. Singer and Small identify 151 civil wars. While Latin America accounts for 22.3% of all country-years, they experience 32% of all civil wars (48/151) (see also Bowman and Eudaily 1999).

militarization, singles out the Latin American military region, which "seems to have suffered from parasitic praetorians more specialized in bossing, exploiting, killing, and torturing civilians than in fighting other nations' armed forces" (1986, 299).

Finally, with the Cold War over, U.S. military officials are providing compelling testimony on the nature of the Latin American military. One anonymous retired Army colonel who managed military intelligence assistance for the U.S. Southern Command put it bluntly: "Latin American militaries had no role in the defense of their country [against foreign threats]. The only real role they had was internal defense" (*Washington Post*, March 6, 1997, A1, A8).

This is not to say that other Third World militaries do not have significant and in many cases primary concern with internal rather than external security.[31] What makes Latin American militaries unique according to Andreski, Janowitz, and others, is the combination of long history as a relatively autonomous hierarchical institution and a dominant internal focus.[32] A simple 2 x 2 matrix is useful.

In sum, the historically conservative social and political role of the pro-

Table 2.1 Classification of militaries, 1950–1990

Autonomy and Institutionalization	*Internal Enemies Dominant*	*External Enemies Dominant*
High	Latin America	Middle East South Korea Taiwan Asian Subcontinent
Low	Sub-Saharan Africa	

31. Ayoob (1991) points out that internal security is important throughout the Third World. However, there are a sizable number of Third World countries with serious external military foci in the period 1950–90, including many in the Middle East, the Asian subcontinent, and China, Korea, and Taiwan. Many of these countries that have large militaries also had booming economies due to petroleum exports and Cold War dynamics. The results of quantitative studies of militarization and development using a universal sample of LDCs are driven by this group of cases and the sub-Saharan African cases that had very small militaries and very little developmental success, a point that is clearly demonstrated in Chapter 6. The militaries of Israel, Mali, and Chile are different in important ways that are not captured by size measures.

32. The organization of professional military institutions in Latin America occurred largely between the late nineteenth century and the middle of the twentieth century, making their history "long" in a relative sense among Third World countries.

fessional Latin American military, the influence of the United States, and especially the complete lack of credible external threats of national annihilation combined to create in Latin America a military whose focus was internal and whose justification for existence and funding depended on the perception that the institution was needed to protect the *Patria* from internal threats to God, church, and family (Loveman 1999). Latin American militaries are qualitatively different from those found in Mali, Taiwan, or Israel, and quantitative measures that do not account for this will continue to reach conclusions that puzzle scholars with area expertise. Militaries built for fighting other militaries are generally much larger than militaries with internal targets, and militaries with serious external enemies during the Cold War received assistance from the superpowers that countries with perceived internal threats did not.[33]

The internal versus external focus of the armed forces is crucial for understanding the consequences of militarization (Desch 1999). In his second edition, Andreski includes a postscript clarifying that the positive benefits of MPR for reducing levels of stratification hinge on the military being "extroverted" or "oriented primarily towards fighting the foreigners" (1968, 210). The Latin American military was distinct enough that Andreski's expected effect of militarization or MPR on equity was reversed: "When viewed as props of the social order the Latin American armies are highly defective and unreliable instruments. . . . The armed forces behave as cancerous growths which, instead of performing any service to the social organism, only harm it" (1968, 214). Hence, in Latin America we should find a negative relationship between size of military (MPR) and development.

The theorized malignant effect of Latin American militarization leads us to the three hypotheses presented in Chapter 1 (militarization has a negative effect on democracy, on economic growth, and on equity). In addition, it leads to the testable hypothesis that the effect of militarization on development will be significantly different in Latin America than in other developing regions.

33. For this reason, which cannot be over-emphasized, the claims made by some that Latin American militaries are relatively small and therefore could not have had a negative effect on development (South Korea's or Israel's military are much larger and are developing quite well so don't look at the military) are misleading (Gurr, Jaggers, and Moore [1991] are guilty of such claims, as are all who use militarization as a variable in large-N quantitative research without considering area-specific content of the variables).

This book is therefore domain-bounded in both space and time. Latin America during the Cold War exhibits a type of militarization that very strongly and negatively affects the goals of development.[34] Of course, not all Latin American militaries are the same. It is the variance that allows us to test the impact of militarization on development in the region. The setting or context, however, is similar throughout Latin America and permits a most-similar design approach in both the quantitative and qualitative analyses.

The State and Additional Theoretical Considerations

The role of the state is central to this book. The work of Gerschenkron (1962) and Hirschman (1958) posits that successful growth in developing countries results from an active role of the state. Since the early 1960s, an impressive and eclectic array of comparative social science research, capped off by Evans, Rueschemeyer, and Skocpol (1985), has featured the state as an important actor for development.[35] Successful development is often associated with policy coherence, professional bureaucracies, expert change teams, insulation, state autonomy, and embeddedness. Evans (1994) argues that differences in state structure are strongly correlated with levels of performance, and proposes a continuum of states with the "klepto-patrimonial" Zairian state at one end and the "embedded autonomy" of the East Asian state at the other.[36]

34. Janowitz (1989, 9) strongly advocates that studies of the armed forces be bounded by region. "I believe that a regional perspective would help in clarifying the distinctive style and results of political intervention by differing military groups. I believe that such a research strategy would throw light on the patterns of civil-military relations through the world arena. Specifically, I believe that we would find considerable uniformity within regions and considerable diversity between regions."

35. There is a plethora of good works that "bring the state back in"; some examples include Anderson (1986), Evans (1979, 1994), Hamilton (1982), Krasner (1978), Migdal (1988), and Stepan (1978). There are also many critiques of state-centered research such as Gibbs (1994). An excellent discussion is found in the responses to Gibbs in *Contention* (1994, number 3).

36. This book falls within that "eclectic" and "messy" body of work that Evans and Stephens (1988) denominate "new comparative political economy." This body of work shares certain characteristics: (1) it is sensitive to international factors but rejects the idea that external factors determine internal dynamics; (2) the state is an important actor for development—potentially with both negative and positive consequences; (3) conflict and alliance among classes or fractions of classes shape historical processes; (4) long-term processes of change at the macro-level are often studied.

Huber (1995) assesses state strength with reference to Latin America, conceptualizing state strength broadly as the ability to achieve four goals: "(1) enforcement of the rule of law throughout the state's entire territory and population (legal order); (2) promotion of economic growth (accumulation); (3) elicitation of voluntary compliance from the population over which the state claims control (legitimation); and (4) shaping of the allocation of societal resources (distribution)" (167). This book will clearly show that Latin American militarization during the Cold War led to reduced state capacity to pursue each of these four goals. National security often gained center stage among the priorities that the state could pursue, at times to such a degree that the pursuit of those goals was attacked as a threat to national security. Special constitutional provisions and de facto impunity for the armed forces—who often exhibited the opinion that a higher authority exempted them from simple legalities and respect for human rights—compromised the "legal order." Long-term economic growth (accumulation) was limited, as the economic and organizational resources necessary to achieve long-term economic growth were (mis)allocated to the military. "Legitimation" was undermined as coups, in the name of fighting communism, ousted elected leaders and forestalled elections. And finally, "distribution" was too often and too easily smeared as a socialist or communist conspiracy, and the militaries of the region too often acted to support the material and political interests of the oligarchy.

The causal argument linking militarization, state capacity, and development can also be presented very succinctly with the use of the proposition presented in Chapter 1 and two additional stylized facts.[37]

> *Democracy, equity, and economic growth are desirable goals.*
>
> *Sustainable progress towards any of the goals of development is difficult to achieve and requires resources, commitment, and prioritization.*
>
> *Third World states are limited in their capacity to pursue multiple difficult goals or policies. Obsession with any single policy will hamper efforts to pursue other goals.*[38]

37. Stylized facts are widely employed in economics and are defined as either "truisms that are so obvious that they can be stated baldly" (Kasliwal 1995, 39), or broad generalizations, which are true in essence, though perhaps not in detail.

38. Even in the most powerful and developed countries, multitasking is difficult when the government is fixated on security issues. After the terrorist attacks of 11 September

A combination of domestic and transnational forces led to varying levels of fixation with doctrines of national security and anticommunism in Latin America.[39] Military size is an indicator of these varying levels and of a country's priorities: a country's commitment to national security can be roughly measured by the resources dedicated to the security forces. An ideological and resource commitment to internal security affected state priorities. Militarization in Latin America has basic opportunity costs and none of the benefits that accrue to countries facing national annihilation (Andreski 1954). There are trade-offs between expending organizational and economic resources on the military or using those resources for social development (equity), human capital, infrastructure, investment (economic growth), or democracy. The argument is not that a focus on internal security transforms the goals of development from desirable to undesirable. All countries want economic growth. Elites want the poor to get proper nutrition. The United States always wanted democracy in Latin America. The issue is one of priorities. In countries with high levels of militarization, guns trumped butter and bullets trumped ballots. Doctrines of national security trumped citizen-centric security.

2001, many important domestic policy initiatives have been sidetracked in the United States as the government focuses on security issues.

39. Even when the military took power with the explicit goal of economic development, this was generally secondary to the prime concern of deterring communism and national security.

bullets versus ballots

militarization and democracy

Taming the Tiger

a quantitative analysis of militarization and democracy in latin america

3

This chapter examines the impact of militarization on democracy in Latin America. I present a theoretical discussion of the relationship and hypothesize that militarization has a negative effect on two indicators of democracy: average democracy scores over time and democracy troughs. I employ inferential statistics to test the relationship and show that militarization has a substantial and significant negative effect on democracy in the region. The results are visually displayed in bivariate scatterplots, and regressions are presented in Table 3.3.[1]

During the past four decades, numerous studies have demonstrated the strong relationship between economic development and political democracy (Lipset 1959/1981; Cutright 1963; Cutright and Wiley 1969; Bollen 1983; Bollen and Jackman 1985; Brunk, Caldeira, and Lewis-Beck 1987; Burkhart and Lewis-Beck 1994). As the wealthiest countries are typically durable democracies and the poorest are typically not, the continued widespread acceptance of the economic development thesis of democracy is understandable. There is a third group of countries, the middle-income countries that have experienced tremendous volatility and variance in levels of formal democracy. These countries occupy that area of economic development referred to by Huntington as the "transition zone" (1984) and by Seligson as near the "economic threshold for democracy" (1987).

Most of the middle-income countries that have had significant experience with both the establishment and decline of democracy have been in Latin America. In the 1980s, Latin America simultaneously experienced severe economic deterioration and previously unmatched high levels of for-

1. For technical information and a much larger number of regression models for this chapter, see Bowman (1996).

mal democracy. By 1989, more than half of the countries of the region had, after the so-called "lost decade" of the 1980s, levels of per capita GDP roughly equivalent to levels from the 1960s. At the same time, electoral democracy was sweeping the region. This presents a major paradox for the economic development thesis; seemingly stable formal democracy appears alongside hunger, slums, and a deterioration of infrastructure.

This chapter addresses two fundamental questions. First, what accounts for wide differences in levels of democracy in Latin America during the Cold War era? Second, why do increases in levels of democracy accompany sharp decreases in levels of economic development in the 1980s? I argue that militarization helps to answer these questions, positing that the larger the military in Latin America the lower the levels of democracy over time and the greater the propensity for democratic breakdown. I do not claim that militarization is the only important factor in explaining levels of democracy. Rather, I posit that for Latin American countries in the transition zone during the Cold War era, the militarization variable is of utility in explaining differences in levels in formal democracy.

Theoretical Issues

Former Costa Rican President Oscar Arias Sánchez has been one of the leading advocates of the proposition that a strong military negatively impacts democracy in Latin America.[2] Scholars have noted the Costa Rican experience. O'Donnell and Schmitter single out Costa Rica as the only nonpacted democracy in all of Latin America, adding that "Costa Rican governments have not been politically and economically saddled with a military establishment" (1986, 76; see also Rueschemeyer, Stephens, and Stephens 1992, 236). Concurrent with the end of the Cold War, international actors and policymakers pointed to the autonomous Latin American military as an impediment to democracy (Nagle 1992). The U.S. government's *Voice of America* accused Honduras of being an army with a country rather than a country with an army (Schulz and Schulz 1994, 6). International lenders, including the IMF, the World Bank, and the Japanese gov-

2. The qualitative literature on the impact of militarization on democracy is immense. Some examples include Black (1986), Blasier (1985), Finer (1988), Fitch (1998), Lieuwin (1960, 1964), and Lowenthal (1991).

ernment have linked much-needed aid to military reductions (see IMF 1992; and FBIS, 8/19/94).

Social scientists only recently began to focus on the military as an important independent variable in large-sample comparative studies on democracy.[3] Dahl's landmark study on polyarchy barely mentions the armed forces, and a large and powerful military institution is not listed as one of the twenty conditions unfavorable to democracy (1971, 203). Economic development, education, sub-cultural pluralism, social stratification, dependency, historical heritage, composition of trade, and landholding patterns generally dominate as the independent variables in studies on democracy. Concurrent with the end of the Cold War and the acknowledgment by international policymakers that the military is often a major impediment to strong democratic institutions, the relationship between the military and democracy has surfaced in large-sample social science research. Hadenius (1992) addresses the issue in a subchapter and presents the results of a statistical analysis indicating a significant negative effect of military spending on democracy in LDCs. Huntington (1991, 239–56) argues that a large, expensive military is an impediment to democracy while a small, expensive military is not (cut and purge the military but give them high salaries, more prestige, and better high-tech toys). Rueschemeyer, Stephens, and Stephens directly indict the strong Third World military as "one of the major obstacles to successful democratization" (1992, 68, see also chapters 5 and 6). I build my theory of the effect of militarization on democracy in Latin America largely on the comparative historical scholarship of Rueschemeyer, Stephens, and Stephens.

In their influential work *Capitalist Development and Democracy*, the authors disagree with modernization theorists that there is a direct causal link between economic development and democracy. Rather, they argue that capitalist development indirectly affects regime type, as

> it is power relations that most importantly determine whether democracy can emerge, stabilize, and then maintain itself in the face of adverse conditions. There is first the balance of power among different *classes and class coalitions*. This is a factor of overwhelming importance. It is complemented by two other power configurations—the structure, strength and autonomy of the *state apparatus*

3. Notable exceptions include Nordlinger (1977).

> and its interrelations with civil society and the impact of *transnational power relations* on both the balance of class power and on state-society relations. (292)

In Latin America, the military has resided at the intersection of these three power constellations and therefore a robust negative impact of militarization on democracy is expected.

State Apparatus: In many Latin American countries, the military often controlled the police and all intelligence functions, concentrating the entire repressive apparatus of the state within one organization. "If the organizations of coercion and violence—the police and the military—are strong within the overall state apparatus, the situation is quite unfavorable for democracy" (Rueschemeyer, Stephens, and Stephens 1992, 67). More important, there is a trade-off between military power and democracy that was recognized even in Pye's (1964, 89) pro-military article that points out that a danger or possible opportunity cost exists in professionalizing or building up Third World militaries, as it may result in the "stifling" of representative politicians. In countries with very powerful militaries, such as Guatemala and Peru, consolidated democracy is difficult given the overwhelming position of the armed forces within the state. In Chapter 7, I show how the Honduran military became so powerful that politics became dependent on military tutelage.

Transnational Power Relations: Muller (1985) quite ingeniously assesses the link between the Third World military and international actors, and the often detrimental impact that this relationship has for democracy. Muller finds a strong negative relationship between levels of U.S. foreign aid and democratic collapse during the Cold War. He concludes that because "precedence was given to the goal of containing Communism above all else, even the maintenance of democratic institutions, most of those developing democracies linked to the United States by the condition of 'economilitary partnership' underwent a transformation from democratic to authoritarian rule. By contrast, democratic institutions survived in most developing democracies that were not economilitary partners of the United States" (1985, 466). Rueschemeyer, Stephens, and Stephens conclude that the international state system had a detrimental effect on democracy in Latin America, specifically during the Cold War, when military assistance "strengthened the military as an institution and thus its potential to act autonomously not only from the incumbent government but from civil society and political institutions in general" (221). Lieuwin (1960, 230) discusses this trade-off:

> Another particularly relevant question is whether U.S. military aid tends to provoke militarism inside individual countries by encouraging the armed forces to play politics. In a situation where the energies of the armed forces of Latin America are mainly devoted to the sphere of internal politics, military equipment and support from the United States may be converted into political power. The quantity of arms is probably less important than the psychological effect. Where the civilian and military elements are vying for power, United States military aid could unwittingly tip the balance in favor of the armed forces.

The United States extended the 1949 Mutual Security Program to Latin America in 1951 because it feared communism would spread to the region. Building powerful military institutions became a core component of the war against communism. The first pact was signed with Ecuador in January 1952. In 1954, mutual defense agreements were signed with Honduras and Nicaragua in preparation for the overthrow of Guatemalan president Jacobo Arbenz. In 1955, Guatemala under Castillo Armas became the twelfth Latin American country to sign (Lieuwin 1965, 91–92). Since Costa Rica had constitutionally proscribed the military in 1949, the effect of U.S. policy was limited. The same was not true for Bolivia, where the *Movimiento Nacionalista Revolucionario* (MNR) wanted to emasculate the Bolivian military after the 1952 revolution—soon after the change in U.S. policy (Eder 1968; Malloy 1970, 184). With U.S. encouragement and assistance, the Bolivian military rose from the ashes and "became so powerful that they were able to overthrow Paz in November 1964" (Blasier 1985, 145). What was permitted in Costa Rica in 1948 was unacceptable in Bolivia only a few years later.[4]

Class Power Relations: In Latin America, the military has been called on

4. U.S. policy towards Latin America has critics and supporters. One of the most favorable interpretations of U.S. intentions is Tony Smith (1994); a more damning picture is painted by LaFeber (1984), LeoGrande (1998), and Schmitz (1999). Pastor asserts that on balance, U.S. policy has helped Latin American democracy more than it has harmed it (1992, 200). Schoultz posits that U.S. policy has been sub-optimal because it is based on the historical U.S. perception that Latin Americans are inferior and less than trustworthy (1998).

to tilt the scales of class power struggles, usually to the advantage of the oligarchy and away from democratization.[5] Latin American military establishments "acted either autonomously or in alliance with economic elites to repress challenges from civil society to their collective corporate as well as their own and the economic elite's economic interests" (Rueschemeyer, Stephens, and Stephens 1992, 231).

While progressive military coups have occurred, they are rare and ephemeral. According to one of the foremost observers of militarization and democracy, the Latin American military has generally "served to maintain the economic and social status of the oligarchs" and has "opposed social change whenever the social change involved the reduction of the power and privileges of the oligarchy" (personal interview with Oscar Arias Sánchez, November 24, 1997, San José, Costa Rica). Even in countries such as Uruguay where military intervention is relatively uncommon, "the Uruguayan army has intervened in the political scene every time it was necessary for the dominant groups" (Minello 1981, 195).

It is important to emphasize that militaries do not typically seize power alone. "A military clique rarely launches a 'putschist' adventure without a sectional endorsement or without an alliance with civilian groups" (Rouquié 1986, 133). Dana Munro noted in 1918 that in Costa Rica, El Salvador, and Guatemala, military officers were usually tools of civilians and politicians (1918, 42–43).

As an institutionally strong and autonomous Latin American military negatively impacts all three power relations most important for democracy, I posit that high levels of militarization result in low levels of formal democracy in Latin America. Countries throughout the hemisphere faced internal challenges to the status quo and demands for greater resource distribution, justice, workers' rights, citizenship, etc. Those countries that responded with greater militarization chose bullets over ballots and undermined the opportunities for a democratic solution to societal demands. This is illustrated in detail in the comparative historical chapters on Costa Rica and Honduras.

This chapter employs both cross-sectional and pooled time-series techniques to assess the relationship between militarization and democracy. A multiple-year time frame (1972–86) is used for several reasons. First, I

5. The Latin American military has at times challenged the landed and ruling elite. The best-known example is the Peruvian military under Velasco.

could find relatively good data for this period. Second, democracy over time exhibits moderate levels of volatility in Latin America, and I wanted to use a time frame that could illuminate medium-term patterns and allow a dynamic analysis. Third, these years fall within what Wright calls "the era of the Cuban Revolution"(1991). This era provides both significant variability in the independent variable (militarization)—as the rise of Castro triggered a response of militarization in some of the countries in the hemisphere but not in others—and relative stability in international Cold War context.

I restrict the cases to Latin America for several important reasons that were presented in Chapter 2. We should add two more that deal directly with democracy. First, Latin America is the single region of the world that has had significant experience with both the establishment and the decline of democratization. If one wants to study why democracy fails or succeeds in the Third World, this is the place. Second, the proposition that militarization has a particular and perhaps unique negative effect on democracy in Latin America has notable advocates (Arias Sánchez 1987, 1991; Rueschemeyer, Stephens, and Stephens 1992, chapters 4 and 5).[6]

Defining and Operationalizing Key Terms

Any study of the relationship between militarization and democracy is challenged by the operationalization of the terms, especially if that study includes statistical analyses. Punctuated by Dahl's title choice of *Polyarchy*, the study of democracy in comparative social science often uses a restricted connotation encompassing responsible government, high levels of participation, and high levels of contestation (free and fair elections). Even measuring formal democracy has proved difficult. Some scholars treat formal democracy as a dichotomous or trichotomous variable (Huntington 1991; Rueschemeyer, Stephens, and Stephens 1992; O'Donnell and Schmitter, 1986), while others advocate interval measures (Bollen 1980,

6. I am not claiming that all Latin American militaries are the same. Indeed, the differences in institutional strength of the Latin American militaries provide the variance in the militarization indicators used in the statistical analysis. It is also true that Latin American countries have tensions with external actors and occasional military confrontation. However, these confrontations have been generally limited to border skirmishes. The real wars in Latin America have been—and in Colombia and Mexico, continue to be—between soldiers and fellow citizens.

1991; Hadenius 1992; Muller 1988). Studies presenting statistical analyses generally use interval measures of democracy.[7]

There are a host of interval-level democracy data sources available. In this chapter, I present only findings using Freedom House scores. Freedom House scores are not without problems, and to check the robustness of my findings, I substituted two other scales in the statistical models, the Fitzgibbon-Johnson Modified Index and the POLITY II. The results were nearly identical, with no significant differences regardless of the choice of democracy scale used as the dependent variable. A full explanation of the different scales, results for each measure, a host of regression models, and technical details are found in Bowman (1996).

Institutional military power is also difficult to operationalize and measure. Two indicators of size have been used: military spending and military participation ratios. Neither is perfect; but it is reasonable to accept these indicators as symptoms of institutional military strength in Latin America. Poverty is widespread throughout the region; the ability of the armed forces to secure large expenditures when people need food, towns lack sanitation, and countries can barely pay their debts indicates institutional strength. Likewise, with pay for foot soldiers low and living conditions poor, high military participation ratios are often accompanied by forced drafts or conscription. High military participation ratios are an indication of both sufficient leverage to secure large expenditures required to feed, train, and clothe soldiers, and the military's lobbying strength—often in the form of implicit threats—to continue troop induction, which is abhorred by the citizenry.

To test his hypothesis that "large armed forces—with the potential for intervention this confers—have an adverse effect on democracy," Hadenius uses military expenditures as a percentage of the budget as the indicator, and reports similar statistically significant negative effects when substituting military spending as a percentage of GDP (1992, 141–43, 199).[8] In his inquiries into the relationship between the military and eco-

7. The operationalization of democracy has produced one of the more heated recent battles in political science, in which Bollen and Jackman (1989) lead the charge for a graded measure, while Sartori (1987) and Przeworski and Limongi (1997) counter that there is no such thing as being half-pregnant or half-democratic and that the proper operationalization is dichotomous. Collier and Adcock (1999) carefully examine the issue and conclude that the choice of a graded or dichotomous scale should not be made ex ante, but rather should be determined by the goals and context of the research.

8. Aside from Bowman (1996), Hadenius's is the only published cross-national statistical analysis of the military spending and democracy relationship that I could locate.

nomic performance, Weede (1983, 1986) includes military spending (MLSP) as an indicator, but favors military participation ratios (MPR). The reliability of MLSP data has been questioned (Brzoska 1981; Payne 1989)[9] and there is evidence that Latin American governments engage in a shell game to place actual defense expenditures into social expenditure reports (see Scheetz 1992).[10] The number of soldiers per thousand inhabitants (MPR) data are much more transparent than MLSP data and the reliability of these data has not been challenged.

While both military participation ratios (MPR) and military expenditures (MLSP) have been used as indicators of the size of the military, it has been argued that they are not coterminous variables. In research using military participation ratios (MPR) and military spending (MLSP) as indicators of economic growth and basic human needs, military participation ratios are regularly portrayed as having a significant and positive effect on a developing nation (Bullock and Firebaugh 1990; Dixon and Moon 1986; Weede 1983, 1986). Even though MLSP exhibits at least a 0.65 correlation with MPR, MLSP does not consistently exhibit the same significant and positive effect on economic growth and human needs.[11] High military participation ratios, the argument goes, lead to discipline, technical prowess, and social mobility. In addition to its indication of a large military, MPR has a sociological dimension absent in MLSP. As far as I know, the relationship between MPR and democracy has never been statistically evaluated. One might be tempted to extend the just-cited arguments and propose that due to its technical training, cultivation of discipline, and promotion of development, the "social mobilization" of MPR would have a stronger positive effect or weaker negative effect on democracy than would MLSP.

9. Brzoska notes that "Examples of governments 'cheating' on the reporting of military expenditures . . . abound" and these suspect data are often the only source for agencies such as SIPRI, which publishes time series of military spending (1981, 261). Payne's chief arguments against MLSP data are twofold. His first claim is that communist countries use coercion as a resource in their militaries (1989, 20); this study does not include communist countries. His second charge is that GNP figures are often understated for less developed countries so the percentage of GNP going to the military will be artificially high (23).

10. After an exhaustive examination of actual expenditures, Scheetz concluded that SIPRI data, which are used in this study, come closest to the actual data (1992, 186). Determining actual military spending is complicated by "military capitalism," which is a growing phenomenon in Central America. For a description of the growth of military capitalism in Honduras, see Chapter 7.

11. The Pearson's correlation of military spending and military participation ratios 1972–84 for eighteen Latin American countries is 0.82.

One might also support the opposite hypothesis that MPR has a stronger negative effect than military spending on democracy for two reasons. First, since the Cuban revolution, the Latin American soldier has been drilled with "the notion that national security also required the political reeducation of the populace to root out all ideas of Marxism, class conflict, and in some cases even the concept of liberal democracy that permitted Marxism to flourish" (Wright 1991, 157). Soldiers were often trained to think that courts, legislatures, political parties, unions, and free expression were enemies of the fatherland (see Nunn 1992, 1995; Schirmer 1999). Second, Latin America has been characterized by many as exhibiting a bureaucratic-authoritarian political culture. Military training would typically reinforce preferences for authority over compromise, especially in times of perceived crisis. Pateman (1970) argues quite persuasively that participation in democratic practices at work socializes the individual to expect democracy in the polity. Rather liberally extending Pateman's argument, one may conclude that Latin American military participation socializes the acceptance of authoritarianism.

I once found this argument persuasive (see Bowman 1996), but have since concluded that while the argument may be theoretically alluring, it is empirically unmanageable to finely separate the effect of MPR from MLSP. The problem is not merely one of multicollinearity, but the combination of multicollinearity with considerable measurement error in MLSP data. I have concluded that the prudent course is to use the different indicators of militarization as regressors in separate regressions and trust only those findings that are consistent with both MLSP and MPR. In the analyses presented in this chapter, MLSP and MPR both had similar effects on democracy, and I report only the MPR models.[12] Given the better quality of the MPR data, we might expect the effect of military participation ratios to be more robust than the effect of military spending.

The Findings

Hadenius (1992) tests the effect of military spending on democracy for a single point in time. This design is of questionable utility for Latin America. Democracy scores exhibit some volatility, and democracy levels

12. The MLSP models are available in Bowman (1996).

tend to be slightly cyclical across the region (Huntington's "waves"). Hence, the relationship between military spending and democracy based on a single set of cross-sections may be significantly affected by the year chosen.

I propose an alternative design to test the relationship between military institutional power and democracy in Latin America loosely based on Dahl's principal justifications for advocating formal democracy (1971). Dahl proposes two general reasons why formal democracy is important. The first is normative; it is inherently desirable to have civil liberties, free speech, and leaders chosen by the citizenry. Responsible government selected by the governed is good. To test this dimension of democracy, I examine the relationship between militarization and level of democracy during a fourteen-year period, 1973–86. Two different designs are employed to test the relationship. First, I examine average levels of democracy over the time period with cross-sectional models of eighteen cases. I then use multiple (stacked) observations of the eighteen cases, stacking eighteen cases over the fourteen years for 252 observations.[13] Control variables include the per capita GDP in the year preceding the observation year (t-1), adult literacy with a one-year lag (t-1), economic growth, and income inequality. In addition, to control for countries such as Costa Rica and Paraguay, which maintained stable democracy scores over the time period, democracy scores in 1972 are held constant.[14] After considerable investigation and experimentation, ordinary least squares (OLS) was chosen as the most appropriate estimator.[15]

13. This pooled time series analysis design for Equations 3.1.1, 3.1.2, and 3.1.3 were stacked over time merely to increase the number of cross-sections and not to make a temporal causal argument. A temporal causal argument is presented in Figure 3.4.

14. The data for this research came from the following sources: Military Spending is from SIPRI and reported in various editions of the *Statistical Abstract of Latin America;* Military Participation Ratios, GNP growth, GNP per capita, and FITZ democracy scores are from the *Statistical Abstract of Latin America;* Literacy is from various editions of the *Statistical Yearbook for Latin America and the Caribbean;* GINI coefficients of income inequality are from Muller (1988, 54) for all cases except Ecuador, which was provided by François Nielsen. Nielsen provided two Gini coefficients for Ecuador for the time period. Following Muller's (1988) methodology, the two Ginis were averaged. No Gini coefficient was available for the Dominican Republic.

15. Time-series regressions are often plagued with autocorrelation, which results in unbiased and consistent OLS estimators, but which are inefficient and produce inflated variance of estimates of coefficients (Kmenta 1986; Gujarati 1988). Generalized least squares (GLS) produce estimates that are BLUE, or estimates that are unbiased and efficient for time-series regressions. Unfortunately, GLS is not a magic bullet when it comes to pooled time-series models. The GLS-ARMA estimator is appropriate only "when de-

Table 3.2 shows the regression tables. Military participation and military spending both have a negative, significant, and substantial effect on democracy, with both time series models and cross-sectional models of average scores. This negative relationship between militarization and democracy holds up with any combination of control variables and with any of three different democracy scales. Figure 3.1 visually presents the negative relationship between militarization and democracy. In spite of the strong negative bivariate relationship between military participation ratios and democracy scores ($r = -.66$), there is no relationship between 1972 Freedom House democracy scores and future military participation ratios ($r = -.07$). This gives limited evidence as to the direction of causation, which will be explored in greater detail in a later section.

Dahl's second reason that formal democracy is important is empirical: in those countries with high levels of democracy, extreme levels of human rights abuses such as those committed under Stalin and Hitler are rare. "The lower the barriers to public contestation and the greater the proportion of the population included in the political system, the more difficult it is for the government of a country to adopt and enforce policies that require the application of extreme sanctions against more than a small

---

sign is time dominant and when explanatory variables are dynamic. If either of these conditions is not present, autocorrelation may be more a nuisance than a threat, and other considerations would dominate the choice of estimator" (Stimson 1985, 927). In our cross-sectional dominant case, with eighteen countries (*N*) and fourteen times (*T*), two other alternative estimators were considered. Ordinary least squares with dummy variables for each country (LSDV) often result in uninterpretable coefficients unless *T* is much greater than *N*, what Maddala (1971) calls "specific ignorance" instead of "general ignorance." The GLSE error components model is most appropriate when time is dominant and has been shown by Mundlak (1978, 68–73) to be either a biased or inefficient estimator. There frankly is no superior estimator when timewise autocorrelation is present and there are more cross-sections than times ($N > T$) (Stimson 1985, 929). The time-series regressions in Appendix 3.1 suffer from positive first order autocorrelation of about .7. The greatest risk in using OLS with positive autocorrelation is in claiming significance when there is none. The levels of significance for the military participation ratio variable are so high in all regressions that this threat is minimal, especially since autocorrelation is less threatening in cross-section dominant designs (Stimson 1985, 926, 298). Nevertheless, I wanted to be certain of the significance of the militarization indicators. Cook and Campbell (1979) propose detrending the data before the regressions are run. The most appropriate detrending for the proposition that militarization negatively effects levels of democracy over time where democracy scores are bounded and fluctuate in both directions is a purely cross-sectional analysis of the mean average democracy scores 1973–86 regressed against the mean average independent variables 1972–85. One referee suggested that the most difficult test of the models is a cross-validation analysis. A full cross-validation analysis was conducted and fully supported the models and regressions.

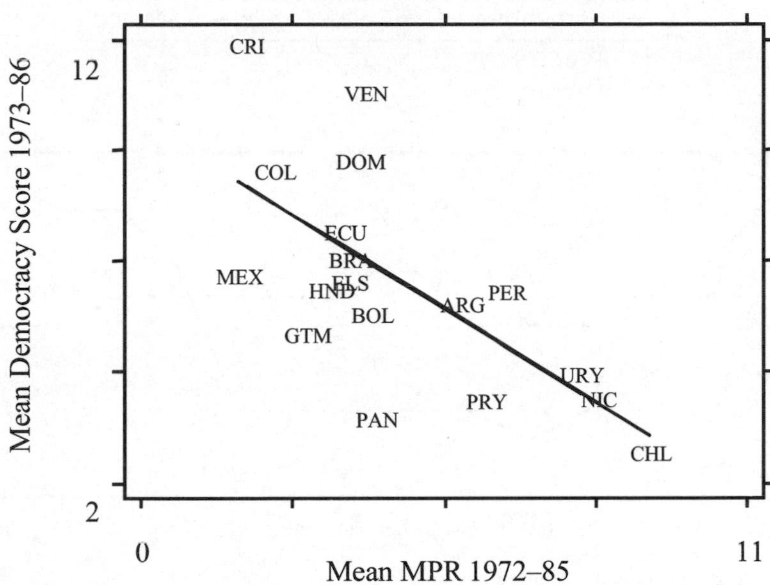

Fig. 3.1 The relationship between military participation ratios and average democracy scores, 1973–1986 (N = 18; r = −.658; p = .003)

percentage of the population; the less likely, too, that the government will attempt to do so" (1971, 26–27).

The gravity of this concept is appallingly clear in Latin America. The human tragedy of the disappeared under military authoritarians in Argentina, Chile, El Salvador, and other countries is incalculable. Levels of repression in Latin America have escalated during periods of extremely low levels of democracy. This crucial dimension of democracy cannot be properly assessed merely through average democracy scores; rather it is more important to see how low the level of democracy (and how high the potential for repression) can get at any point over a period of time. This concept is illustrated in Figure 3.2.

If Dahl is correct that widespread and massive human rights abuses are more likely to occur at very low levels of democracy—democracy troughs—then we would expect the chances of heinous abuses committed against a large number of the citizens to be most likely in that area of Figure 3.2 in which Argentina's democracy score falls to two. In the fol-

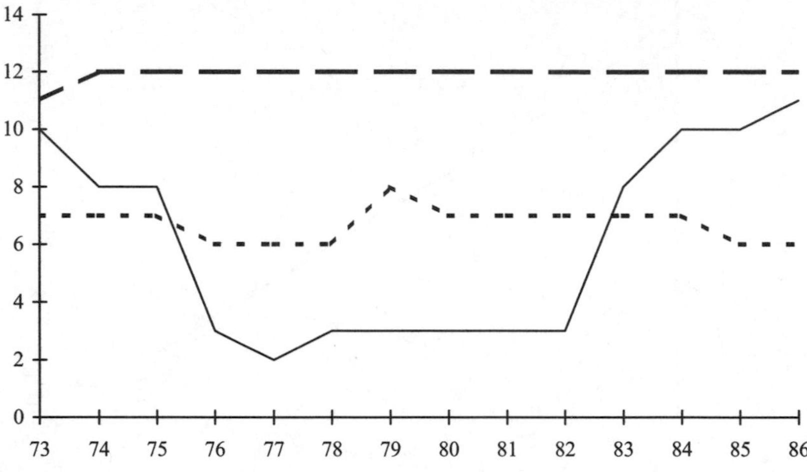

Fig. 3.2 Democracy troughs

lowing analysis, which uses the worst single score for a country over the 1973–86 period, the worst democracy score (WDS) for Costa Rica would be eleven, Mexico would be six, and the datum for Argentina would be two. In contrast, using the mean average democracy scores over the 1973–86 period treats Mexico and Argentina as roughly similar cases. Average scores were useful in verifying the effect of militarization on average democracy scores over time, but are of little use for analyzing the effect of militarization on democracy troughs.

The specific test of the relationship between militarization and democracy troughs regresses each nation's WDS for 1973–86 against the number of soldiers per one thousand inhabitants for 1972–85 (and military spending with results presented in Bowman 1996). Largely following Hadenius's lead, additional control independent variables include the previous democracy score (1972), adult literacy circa 1973, the log of GDP per capita for 1973, per capita GDP growth for 1973–86, and Gini coefficients of income inequality circa 1973. Research assessing the effect of these variables on democracy is ubiquitous and will not be reviewed here.

The results of the multiple regression analysis are presented in Table 3.3. The patterns are similar to the models of average democracy. In this model, using the WDS (from three separate scales) over a period of time, with any combination of control variables, militarization measured as either size of budget (MLSP) or number of soldiers per thousand inhabitants (MPR) has a substantial, highly significant, and consistently negative effect on democracy. Indeed, the MPR coefficient regularly outperforms the previous level of democracy as a predictor of democracy troughs.[16] Figure 3.3 presents the bivariate relationship between militarization and democracy troughs. Again, the visual bivariate relationship is compelling and negative; the bigger the military, the greater the probability of democracy troughs.

Direction of Causation

With the relationship between democracy and militarization established, the crucial question of direction of causation must be addressed: do high

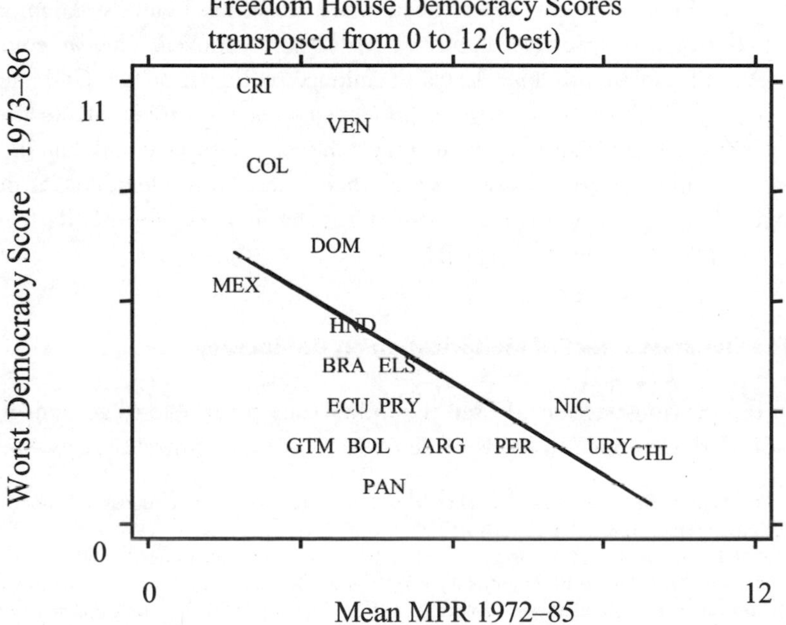

Fig. 3.3 The relationship between military participation ratios and lowest single-year democracy scores, 1973–1986 (N = 18; r = −.576; p = .012)

16. Again, when military spending is used as the indicator of militarization, it is also highly significant (see Bowman 1996).

levels of militarization cause low levels of democracy or do low levels of democracy cause higher levels of militarization? Published debates about the direction of causation in studies concerning democracy have been common at least since the publication of *Polyarchy* in 1971. A strong intuitive argument can be made for the alternative proposition that low levels of democracy cause high levels of militarization. Hadenius devotes a chapter to direction of causation and concludes that while there is strong evidence that military expenditures negatively impact democracy, an analysis of changes in military spending over time under various regime types reveals no effect of democracy on military spending (1992, 150).

The data support Hadenius's claim of no reversed causality from democracy to military spending, for there is no relationship at all between 1972 Freedom House democracy scores and future levels of military spending with a Pearson's correlation of .005. Likewise, there is no significant relationship between 1972 Freedom House scores and MPR levels 1972–85, with a Pearson's r of −.07. Table 3.1 reveals a quite remarkable degree of stability in military participation ratios throughout the examined period. While Argentina experienced very wide swings in levels of democracy during this period (see Figure 2), MPRs barely moved. The two countries with consistently high levels of military participation are Chile and Uruguay. While both countries experienced some increase in MPRs after their respective collapses in democracy, Chile and Uruguay both had high levels of military participation before their once-strong democracies declined.[17] Democracy was restored to Uruguay in 1985, and MPRs from 1986 to 1988 averaged a very high 9.8.[18]

The Dynamic Effect of Militarization on Democracy

In the previous sections, I used the militarization variable to account for part of the variance in levels of democracy in Latin America 1972–86. I

17. The military overthrow of Allende was in September 1973. Uruguay's democracy declined precipitously after 1973.

18. El Salvador and Nicaragua are the two cases that experienced sudden drastic changes in MPR levels; El Salvador after 1981 and Nicaragua after 1979. In these cases, the argument that a collapse in democracy led to increases in MPR is unsupported since neither case was very democratic when the MPRs were low. Rather, these drastic increases resulted from wars with strong international linkages and in the broader context are aberrations that may inflate the multivariate results. To check, all regressions were rerun excluding 1982–85 MPRs for El Salvador and 1980–85 MPRs for Nicaragua. These pruned regressions resulted in no significant changes and are not reported.

Table 3.1 Military participation ratios,[1] 1972–1985, for eighteen Latin American countries

	Arg.	*Bol.*	*Bra.*	*Chi.*	*Col.*	*Cri.*[2]	*Dom*	*Ecu.*	*E.S.*	*Gua.*	*Hnd.*	*Mex*	*Nic.*	*Pan.*	*Pry.*	*Per.*	*Ury.*	*Ven.*
1972	5.7	3.9	4.1	7.7	2.2	1.1	3.5	3.2	3.2	2.5	4.1	1.5	3.0	4.4	5.8	5.2	7.1	3.9
1973	6.5	4.0	4.1	7.6	2.2	1.1	3.4	3.1	3.1	2.3	4.0	1.5	2.9	4.4	5.6	5.1	7.1	4.2
1974	6.0	3.9	4.1	9.0	2.1	1.1	3.7	3.0	3.0	2.2	3.2	1.5	2.9	4.7	5.4	6.0	8.9	4.1
1975	6.3	4.3	4.2	10.8	2.1	1.0	3.6	2.9	2.9	2.1	3.8	1.6	2.2	4.7	5.4	6.1	8.9	4.3
1976	6.0	4.6	4.1	10.7	2.4	1.5	3.7	3.4	3.4	2.2	3.6	1.7	2.6	4.4	5.2	6.3	9.7	4.2
1977	5.9	4.0	4.0	10.6	2.4	1.4	3.6	4.1	4.1	2.2	3.5	1.6	2.6	4.4	5.0	7.7	9.7	4.0
1978	5.7	3.9	3.8	10.3	2.4	2.3	3.4	4.6	2.3	2.1	3.8	1.8	2.3	4.3	4.8	7.6	9.8	3.9
1979	5.6	3.8	3.7	10.2	2.3	2.6	3.3	4.4	3.0	3.0	3.8	1.8	2.2	4.2	4.6	7.4	9.7	3.8
1980	5.5	4.4	3.7	10.5	2.3	2.6	4.1	4.3	3.4	2.9	3.7	1.7	8.6*	4.1	4.4	8.7	9.7	3.7
1981	5.4	4.7	3.6	10.3	2.4	2.5	4.0	4.1	4.9	3.6	4.3	1.7	13.5*	4.5	4.3	8.8	9.7	3.6
1982	6.0	4.6	3.5	10.1	2.5	2.5	4.1	4.2	6.0*	3.9	4.2	1.8	13.8*	4.9	4.4	9.0	10.0	3.5
1983	5.9	4.7	3.5	10.8	2.5	2.8	3.7	4.4	6.7*	5.1	4.5	1.7	15.2*	4.8	4.3	8.9	10.3	3.4
1984	5.8	4.7	3.4	10.4	2.4	3.1	3.4	4.3	9.2*	5.0	4.6	1.7	21.6*	5.2	4.4	7.0	10.2	3.8
1985	4.3	4.6	3.5	10.3	2.3	3.0	3.3	4.6	9.6*	5.2	4.7	1.8	23.4*	5.5	3.5	6.5	10.2	4.1

*Excluded from regressions in nonreported tests. Excluding these data did not significantly alter results in any regression.

1. Military personnel per 1,000 inhabitants.

2. Costa Rica has no army and some measures of military participation give Costa Rica a score of zero. These data count civil and rural guards (police), which may greatly overstate Costa Rican militarization. I use the highest possible scores for Costa Rica, as I wanted to make it as difficult as possible for the statistical tests to support the posited hypotheses.

posited that three power configurations are most important for democracy—class power relations, state power relations, and transnational power configurations—and that a strong autonomous military contributes to a negative dynamic in each of the three. Given that levels of militarization did not significantly decline during this period, what accounts for the increase in formal democracy in the region in the 1980s? Surveying a world of poverty and polarization in 1984, Huntington concluded that without substantial economic development in the Third World, "the limits of democratic development in the world may well have been reached" (1984, 218). Poverty inhibits democracy. Yet in Latin America, both increasing poverty and democratization were the stories of the 1980s.

Rueschemeyer, Stephens, and Stephens posit that an increase in the relative power of the working class vis-à-vis the landed and ruling elite is favorable to democracy. In the 1980s, the opposite occurred in Latin America. Labor unions, the traditional organizational resource of the working class, declined in membership and prestige, and income distribution worsened in nearly every country (Psacharopoulos et al., 1994). A second power constellation important for Rueschemeyer, Stephens, and Stephens is the state, which has been under attack during the past decade. The third power relation that can strongly affect democracy is transnational. It is in this area, specifically the attitude of the United States towards the value of elected officials, that helps explain the recent increase in democracy in Latin America.

According to this hypothesis, beginning with Carter's emphasis on human rights and support for democratic political systems (Blasier 1987, 221; Pastor 1992; Schoultz 1981), there was a change in Washington's commitment to elected heads of state in the hemisphere. Perhaps as an ideological weapon against Nicaragua and Cuba, the Reagan administration's mantra was elections and capitalism. There emerged a "widespread validation of political democracy and free markets" (Lowenthal 1992, 64–65; see also Aguilera 1994), which began after Carter's election and reached its apex at the 1994 Summit of the Americas, where elected heads of state of every hemispheric nation except Cuba gloried in their "democracy" and dreamed of a free trade area from the Yukon to Patagonia.[19]

19. Unfortunately, not everyone at the summit was freely elected (see Hartlyn 1994). Whether or not levels of formal democracy have contributed to real representation and a distribution of power in many countries is debatable, but beyond the scope of this paper (see Gills, Racamora, and Wilson 1993).

My proposition is that the United States began strongly supporting formal democracy in conjunction with Carter's human rights policy, and that such support increased over time until it became a de facto demand (see Salomón 1991, 114–15). This is not to say that the United States expected substantial distributions of power and strong democracies, but multiparty elections were required for aid and trade (Schirmer 1991). Strong and influential militaries still persist in many countries, but they have been banished over time from the presidential palace. In Honduras in the fall of 1994, a group of leading professionals, educators, and political authorities issued a statement claiming that the "threat of a coup d'état is a latent condition in our country that is curbed only by international pressures" (FBIS, 8/17/94). Due to changing transnational power dynamics, I hypothesize that the negative effect of militarization on formal democracy declined during the 1973–86 period. This does not mean that there was a decline in militarization or MPR during this period. Indeed, as shown in Table 3.1, MPR increased during this time period, as did U.S. military aid to the region. This paradox of U.S. policy in the 1980s and early 1990s—support for militaries concurrently with insistence on elected presidents—resulted in considerable protest at the School of the Americas and in scholarship pointing out the hypocrisy of U.S. support for "low intensity" democracy (see, for example, Gills, Recamora, and Wilson 1993).

To test this proposition that the effect of MPR was attenuated, I regress three different democracy scales (Freedom House, Polity II, and Fitzgibbon-Johnson) against the log of per capita GDP, literacy, and military participation ratios using pooled time-series from 1973 to 1986. The models include dummy variables for six of the seven two-year time periods as well as interactive variables of the time periods with MPR. In order to compare the slope coefficients, all three democracy scales were standardized to a 1 (worst) to 20 (best) range.

Figure 3.4 presents the dynamic effect of MPR on democracy.[20] Holding the level of development constant (PCGDP and LITERACY), the negative impact of military participation is nearly identical for all three democracy scales. In the 1973–74 period, every additional soldier per thousand inhabitants results in a democracy decline of 1.357 points for the Freedom House scores and of 1.621 points for POLITY II (or approximately 8 percent on the 1–20 scale). In the 1985–86 period, for every

20. Regression table in Bowman (1996).

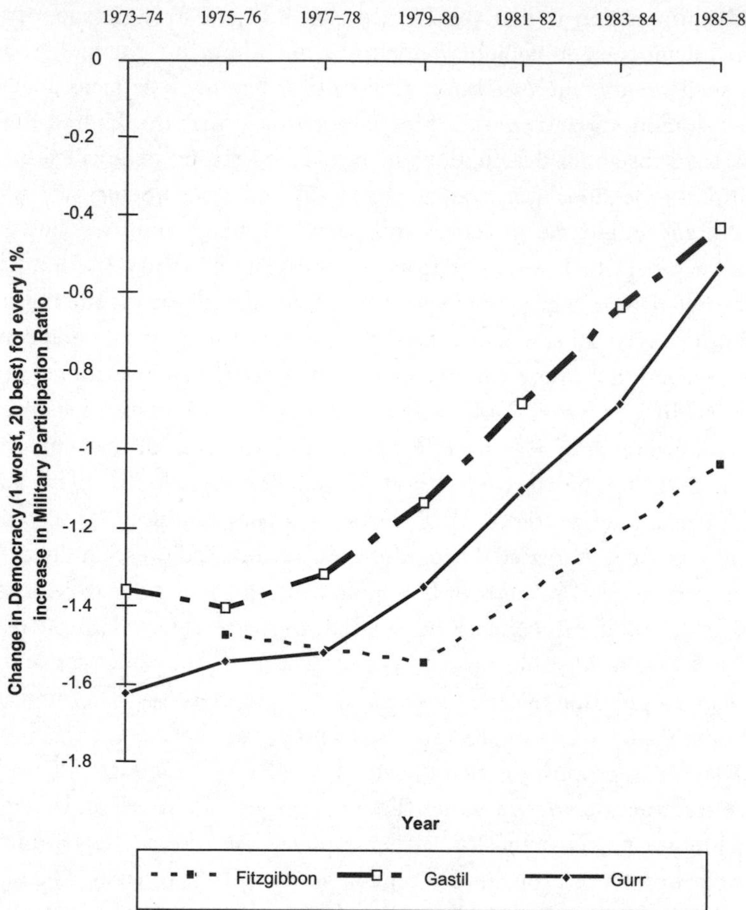

Fitzgibbon is Fitzgibbon-Johnson Modified Index, Gastil is Freedom House, Gurr is POLITY II. All democracy scores standardized (1 worst, 20 best). Literacy and Log GDP per capita in previous year held constant.

Fig. 3.4 The declining negative effect of military participation ratios on democracy over time

additional soldier per thousand inhabitants the democracy scores on average decline by .429 points for the Freedom House scores, .531 points for POLITY II, and 1.032 points for Fitzgibbon-Johnson (all 1–20 scales). The slopes follow the hypothesized pattern with all three scales: the negative impact of military participation on democracy decreases over time with the greatest decrease occurring after 1977–78. In the early 1970s, the negative impact was the greatest. Beginning in the late 1970s to early 1980s, the negative impact began to decline. This coincides very strongly with the theoretical expectations.[21]

Conclusion

This chapter tests three hypotheses. The first addresses the relationship between militarization and level of democracy over time. The effect of militarization (operationalized either as spending or military participation ratios) on democracy over time is robust and in the expected negative direction. The second hypothesis—that the size of military budgets or military participation ratios result in episodes of low levels of democracy within a set time period—is engendered by Dahl's empirical claim that widespread human rights abuses are more likely to occur in polities with very low levels of democracy. Cross-sectional multivariate models test and confirm the hypotheses with either militarization variable (MPR or MLSP). Finally, I hypothesize that due to shifts in transnational power dynamics, the negative effect of militarization on democracy declined beginning with the Carter administration. I used a pooled time-series analysis with dummy variables for two-year periods and interaction effects of MPR and two-year periods. As expected, there is a strong and significant difference in the effect of MPR across the time period. The negative effect of MPR on democracy was greatest in 1972–73 and lowest (while still negative and significant) in 1985–86.

Indeed, the number of soldiers per thousand inhabitants appears to have the single strongest impact on democracy in Latin America during this time period. Economic development and literacy generally have a very weak effect on democracy in the various models. This calls into serious question the enduring empirical claims of the modernization school that economic development directly leads to democracy. At least for nations in the wide middle range of development, these findings show that other forces are more important in determining the emergence and maintenance of formal democracy.

Given the tremendous negative effect of militarization on democracy

21. Even in the latest period, the negative effect of MPR is significant. Strong Latin American militaries still threaten democracy in countries as diverse as Guatemala, Honduras, and Chile with attempted coups, rumors or threats of coups, and human rights abuses.

in Latin America, it is not at all surprising that Costa Rica is the exception that proves the rule: no army and a strong democracy. Over the long term, if full democracies are to develop and endure in Latin America, Nobel Laureate Oscar Arias Sánchez may be correct in asserting that taming the tiger is not enough; demilitarization may be a necessary condition for strong and enduring democracies in the region.

Table 3.2 Democracy scores, 1973–1986, regressed against military participation ratios (pooled time-series 18 countries × 14 years in first three equations; cross-sections of averages, 1973–1986, in last three equations)

Dependent Variable	*Democracy Series*			*Democracy Average*		
Intercept	−1.41	5.87	7.14	6.07	4.94	−8.10
Literacy	−.050	.191**	.211**	.191	.167	.602*
	(0.64)	(2.42)	(2.52)	(0.68)	(0.70)	(2.11)
PCGDP	.117	−.029	−.005	.093	.061	−.014
	(1.50)	(0.39)	(0.06)	(0.35)	(0.26)	(0.06)
Democracy 1972	.335***	.308***			.365*	.467*
	(5.61)	(5.62)			(2.13)	(2.10)
MPR		−.423***	−.447***	−.728***	−.692***	−.791***
		(7.01)	(7.00)	(3.57)	(3.78)	(4.27)
GINI						.433
						(1.66)
GDP growth						−.377*
						(1.96)
R^2	.127	.272	.179	.497	.628	.760
Adj. R^2	.117	.260	.169	.390	.513	.616
F-ratio	12.05	23.05	18.00	4.62	5.48	5.28
	.000	.000	.000	.019	.008	.011
No. obs.	252	252	252	18	18	17

*** $p < .01$, ** $p < .05$, * $p < .10$

Two-tailed test; standardized coefficients in first cell rows; t-ratios in ( ).

Democracy — Freedom House democracy scores (0 lowest to 12).

Literacy — Adult literacy with one-year lag in first three equations; average literacy 1972–85 in last three equations.

PCGDP — Natural log of per capita GDP with one-year lag in first three equations; average log of per capita GDP 1972–85 in last three equations.

Democracy 1972 — Freedom House democracy score 1972 (0 lowest to 12)

MPR — Military participation ratio per thousand with one-year lag in first three equations; average 1972–85 in last three equations.

GINI — GINI coefficient of income inequality circa 1975.

GDP growth — Percent of total GDP growth per capita, 1973–86.

Note: Tables using POLITY II and the Fitzgibbon-Johnson Modified Index as the dependent variable are found in Bowman (1996). Results are virtually identical when using MLSP as the causal variable. For regressions and technical information, see Bowman (1996).

Table 3.3 Worst Freedom House democracy scores (WDS), 1973–1986, regressed against military participation ratios, 1972–1985

Dependent Variable		*WDS*	
Intercept	−1.58	−1.14	−19.82
Literacy	.013	.172	.588**
	(0.06)	(0.88)	(2.31)
PCGDP	.117	.091	−.028
	(0.51)	(0.48)	(0.15)
Democracy 1972	.591***	.533***	.785***
	(3.23)	(3.52)	(3.99)
MPR		−.601***	−.585***
		(3.88)	(3.71)
GINI			.555**
			(2.36)
GDP growth			−.223
			(1.24)
F-prob.	.013	.002	.003
R^2	.601	.714	.816
Adj R^2	.478	.626	.706
No. obs.	18	18	17

*** $p < .01$, ** $< .05$, * $< .10$
Dominican Republic excluded and N = 17 when GINI used.
Standardized coefficients in first cell rows; t-ratios in ( ); two-tailed test.

WDS	Worst Freedom House democracy score, 1973–86 (low worst to high best)
Literacy	Adult literacy, c. 1973
PCGDP	Log per-capita GDP, 1973
Democracy 1972	Freedom House democracy scores, 1972 (0 lowest to 12 highest)
MPR	Mean average military participation ratio per thousand, 1972–85
GINI	GINI coefficient of income inequality, 1965–75
GDP Growth	Percent of total GDP growth per capita, 1973–86

NOTE: Tables using MLSP as causal variable as well as POLITY II and the Fitzgibbon-Johnson Modified Index as the dependent variable are found in Bowman (1996). Findings are consistent regardless of choice of militarization variable or democracy scale.

4 When Ballots Trump Bullets

demilitarization and democratic consolidation in costa rica

The previous chapter shows that levels of militarization are strongly and negatively related with levels of democracy in Latin America. The following two chapters employ a comparative historical format to illuminate the causal mechanism and to establish agency and sequence in the relationship. I show that the lack of an autonomous and deliberative military played a crucial role in the consolidation of democracy in Costa Rica 1948–58 and that the emergence of a powerful and autonomous military played an equally important role in the collapse of the democratization process in Honduras 1954–63. The Honduran case adds novel insights, but generally supports the secondary literature on the role of the armed forces in that country's democratic collapse (Euraque 1996; Funes 1995; Schulz and Schulz 1994). In contrast, the Costa Rican case shows how the absence of a military caused something not to happen, namely a democratic breakdown. This is an explicit counterfactual argument: if Costa Rica had not abolished its military, democracy likely would not have survived.[1] The evidence to support this claim challenges many conventional views of the democratization process in Costa Rica, especially the well-accepted belief that democracy was consolidated in Costa Rica soon after the 1948 Civil War. Therefore, the Costa Rica chapter requires more evidence and will be somewhat more detailed than the Honduran case.

Due to a paucity of research on the politics of Costa Rica in the 1950s,[2] the evidence for the post-1949 period is based

1. The use of counterfactuals and the criticism of that strategy have been around for generations (see Tetlock and Belkin 1996 for a full discussion).

2. The limited research on Costa Rican politics in the 1950s focuses primarily on individual events and includes Acuña (1977), Aguilar Bulgarelli (1977), Ameringer (1978, 1996), and Kantor's pro-Figueres study of the 1953 election (1958). One excellent source for Central American politics in the 1950s is Martz (1959). González Vargas (1990) and Long-

extensively on primary research. The two key sources of this research are newspapers and elite interviews. I read *La Nación* from January 1948 through June 1958. *El Diario*, *La República*, and *La Hora* were also consulted, but not over the entire time period. I selected *La Nación* as the principal newspaper source, as it was the most comprehensive newspaper in Costa Rica during the time period.[3] The second principal primary source is the elite interview. When José Figueres took control of the government in 1948, the members of his junta were very young; most were in their thirties. For this reason, many important political actors from the 1948–58 period are still alive. Some had never been interviewed and were relieved to tell their story and share a cup of coffee over their scrapbooks. These interviews confirmed and clarified reports, documents, and speeches from the newspapers and often led to follow-up interviews or interviews with others. By combining this primary research with two good sources of U.S.-Costa Rican relations for this time period (González Vargas 1990; Longley 1997), important conclusions can be reached about the

---

ley (1997) provide excellent accounts of U.S.-Costa Rican relations for this time period. Costa Rican scholars have, in personal interviews with the author, provided many hypotheses for the lack of scholarship on Costa Rican politics in the 1950s. One explanation offered by Jorge Rovira Mas is institutional; sociologists study the period from 1960 forward and historians study the period before 1950, and political science has been a largely professional degree in Costa Rica. This is a plausible explanation, although I would add that this period has been ignored in part because the results of such a study may question the democratic myth of the country and may paint a less than favorable impression of revered political leaders from both major political camps. The aftermath of the 1948 Civil War is still dangerous academic territory. When a commission announced plans to hold a symposium on the 1948 Civil War and the results of that event, former and future presidents (Echandi and Rodríguez) wrote that such an academic event may be risky for the "unity and tranquillity of the Costa Rican family" and that as it would merely awaken hatred, it is better to look to the future and forget the past (Rodríguez, 1997). In contrast to the 1950s, many excellent works have been produced on the 1940s in both Spanish and English. Some of the best are Aguilar Bulgarelli (1978), Bell (1971), Lehoucq (1992, 1996), Lehoucq and Molina (forthcoming), Rojas Bolaños (1986), and Salazar (1995).

3. *La Nación* represents the most conservative elements of Costa Rican society and has always been highly partisan. In contrast to the other papers, however, *La Nación* was a reasonably comprehensive source of news (many days containing over one hundred pages). While biased in editorials and reporting, *La Nación* regularly printed rebuttals from opponents, carried advertisements from all major political parties, printed major political speeches and pronouncements in their entirety, summarized important articles from other local newspapers, and presented lengthy interviews with major political actors from all political camps. Booth notes that "[p]aid newspaper advertisements are a major form of political discourse in Costa Rica" (1989, 401) and *La Nación* had both the largest amount and most varied advertisements. Quite simply, *La Nación* was and continues to be the newspaper of record for the country.

timing and process of the consolidation of democracy in Costa Rica and the role of demilitarization in that process.

Costa Rica

Twice each day, the Hotel Del Rey provides a free tour of San José. The charming and knowledgeable tour guide eagerly explains the exceptionalism of Costa Rica—the lack of an army, the European manner of the people, the long democratic tradition, and an enduring culture of egalitarianism and compromise. An impressive feature of the tour is the Bella Vista Fort, a massive military structure just east of downtown, perched majestically on a hill. It was here, the guide explains, that the great democrat José Figueres dissolved the military in a memorable ceremony, smashing a sledgehammer onto the fort's walls, proclaiming that the military budget would go to education, and decreeing that the Bella Vista would no longer house soldiers, but would be transformed into the national museum. As the bus approaches the imposing fortress, hundreds of bullet holes become visible in the walls. A furious battle, the guide reveals, was fought here by the Figueres-led National Liberation Army to overthrow the communists and restore democracy in 1948.

A few blocks away from the Bella Vista, Miguel Ruiz Herrera is hanging his paintings in an exposition on the tenth-floor gallery at the state-owned National Insurance Institute (INS). Blind in one eye, the painter and poet is being assisted by two state workers to hang and adjust the lights. Pleased to have a captive audience, even of two, Ruiz begins to tell them part of the history of his poems and paintings. "These paintings were done in the early 1960s when I was in exile in Nicaragua," he states. The elder of the two workers asks, "Exiled from where? Guatemala or El Salvador?" "No," retorts the old painter, "from Costa Rica! Figueres found a bunch of weapons in my house that we were going to use to overthrow him and I had to escape in self-imposed exile. They didn't catch me because I crossed the border into Nicaragua dressed as a woman." The two workers laugh, certain that the painter is a lunatic. Ruiz continues, "In the 1970s we had five hundred men ready and Guatemala was going to give us the weapons and we were going to kidnap Figueres and the government leaders and force them to quit being communists. Some bastard betrayed us and I was thrown in jail that time. Figueres threw me in jail in 1955 for forty-six days—it was solitary confinement without ever seeing the light." The workers suddenly realize that they are speaking with an obvious madman and move on. One smiles at the other and says, "Loco."[4]

The history memorized and rehearsed by the tour operator and believed by tourists and locals alike is largely inaccurate. The 1948 Civil War, though violent and bloody, did not include major battles in San José. The bullet holes are real and a desperate battle was waged at the Bella Vista fort—the future of the country hinged on the outcome. In that 1949 battle, José Figueres was on the outside and *compañeros* of Miguel Ruiz Herrera, former head of intelligence for Figueres's National Liberation Army, painter and poet, were on the inside trying to overthrow Figueres. Ruiz himself actively participated in the *Cardonazo,* the last military-led coup in Costa Rica. As for the stories of the painter that were discarded by educated Ticos as the rantings of a madman, they are true. Such is the history of Costa Rica and our understanding of the consolidation of democracy in this small but theoretically important country. Myths, propaganda, selective memory, and a chauvinistic view of Tico exceptionalism have led to an inaccurate portrayal of the democratization process.[5]

I argue that democratization was not consolidated soon after the 1948 Civil War, but was only consolidated after 1958.[6] The crucial period for this consolidation includes the almost never studied 1953–58 period. An examination of this period clearly demonstrates that the weakness of the military was a crucial component of democratic survival, as it strongly impacted the three power relations that matter for democracy—state, class, and transnational. Democracy did not naturally and automatically flow out of cultural and structural conditions of the eighteenth and nineteenth centuries. Though these traditional explanations for democratization are partially correct and useful, to fully comprehend Costa Rica's impressive democratic success in the later half of the twentieth century, one must understand the domestic and international dynamics of the 1948–58 time period, dynamics that were shaped by the militarization variable.

4. The author witnessed and overheard this conversation while waiting for an interview with Ruiz. The author also took the Del Rey tour of San José.

5. For an excellent overview of scholarship of Costa Rica pre-1990, see Edelman and Kenen (1989).

6. Jorge Rovira Mas (1990) is one of the few to posit that democratic consolidation was difficult and that it did not arrive until after the 1958 elections.

Conventional Views of Costa Rican Democracy

In October 1989, Costa Ricans celebrated one hundred years of democracy in an international event attended by U.S. President George Bush and all the presidents of Central America.[7] There are very few countries that can rightly claim a full century of democratic rule, and Costa Rica is not one of them. In his excellent 1951 book, Obregón details every military coup, attempted coup, rebellion, and war involving the Costa Rican armed forces from the first Civil War of 1823 through the last attempted military coup in 1949. Obregón lists 115 military and political conflicts during this period and suggests that Costa Rican political development up until 1948 had more similarities with other Latin American countries than Costa Ricans like to admit (1951, 3). Lehoucq (1992), Salazar (1995), and Salazar Mora (1990) describe a political system typically of a republican and civilian nature but one in which power was gained through fraud, intrigue, single-party power, and outright imposition of presidents by their predecessors. Despite electoral reforms, it is difficult to argue that things were getting better instead of worse. Rafael Angel Calderón Guardia was imposed by his presidential predecessor León Cortés in 1940 and gained 84.3 percent of the vote (Salazar 1995, 202). An educated and charismatic caudillo, Calderón had a fierce rupture with Cortesismo soon after and in 1944, Calderón handed the presidency to Teodoro Picado in highly suspect elections in which Picado defeated León Cortés with 66 percent of the vote (Salazar 1995, 231). The period 1940–48 is replete with violence, ethnic persecution of Ticos of German, Spanish, and Italian heritage,[8] assassination attempts, electoral fraud, U.S. concern with com-

7. In an interview with the author, Oscar Arias admitted that he knew that Costa Rica was not a democracy for one hundred years. He exaggerated the significance of the event in order to pressure George Bush to attend an event with Daniel Ortega of the ruling Sandinistas in order to further the Central American peace initiatives.

8. The original dispute between Figueres and Calderón, which culminated in the 1948 Civil War, emerged from the treatment of Germans, Spaniards, and Italians. The Axis-Allies fracture may have more to do with the development of civil strife in Costa Rica than social policy. León Cortés had undeniable leanings towards the Axis powers. Calderón accepted U.S. pressures to confiscate some German properties and to deport some Costa Rican citizens to detention camps in the United States. Soon after Calderón broke with Cortés, the Nazis torpedoed a United Fruit Company ship, the *St. Paul*, near the Costa Rican port of Limón. The boat sank and twenty-four workers drowned. The police watched as a mob responded by looting businesses owned by Germans, Italians, and Spaniards. One of the damaged buildings belonged to José Figueres, the son of Spanish immigrants. Figueres, who had never before participated in politics, was outraged and on 8 July 1942 gave a radio address lambasting the government for its inability to maintain public

munist power, strikes, riots, abuse of state and police power, rumors of palace coups, plots to overthrow the government, terrorist activities, and dangerous class tensions (see Cañas 1982; Cardona Quirós 1992; Lehoucq 1992; Martz 1959; Rojas 1986). Lehoucq, who may be the most informed scholar on Costa Rican political history 1900–1948, also disputes the democratic nature of Costa Rica pre-1948. "Since 1882, outgoing presidents have imposed their successors on at least six different occasions. During the same period also, opposition movements have launched twenty-six rebellions against central state authorities—three of which succeeded in installing a new incumbent in the presidency. . . . The use of violence and fraud to capture state power only declined in the aftermath of the 1948 civil war," a violent conflict with between two thousand and four thousand deaths (1996, 334–35).[9]

The second half of the twentieth century has been quite different from the first; Costa Rica has been a stable democracy with healthy party competition and impressive respect for political rights (Biesanz, Biesanz, and Biesanz 1998; Booth 1998; Chalker 1995; Lehoucq 1997; Wilson 1998; Yashar 1995). This is a remarkable accomplishment for a poor country located on an isthmus plagued by war and instability. Costa Rica stands alone in Latin America as a democracy for this entire period. The country's democratic exceptionalism has been explained with various theories and approaches.

The National Myth and Extant Theories of Costa Rican Democratization

If one sits down in the *Plaza de la Cultura* and strikes up a conversation with a friendly Tico about Costa Rican political development, one would likely hear an explanation that due to many cultural features of *Costarri-*

---

order and protect private property. During the speech, the police arrested Figueres and forced him into exile in Mexico. The Calderón government threatened to close down all radio stations if they continued to let "poor devils" and "unknowns like Figueres" speak. "We should not permit that an ignoramus and unknown degrade the name of the republic" (Vargas 1993, 445–46).

9. Samper (1988) was one of the first to demonstrate empirically the extent of electoral fraud and foul play in Costa Rica. Lehoucq and Molina (forthcoming) will soon publish a detailed account of fraud and electoral processes in the country.

cences or *Ticos*, the country was predestined to be democratic. Ticos are by nature hardworking, egalitarian, democratic, honest, white, forgiving, nonviolent,[10] and consensus-building.[11] These cultural traits form part of the highly developed sentiment of exceptionalism. These cultural and structural explanations for democracy are often repeated in guidebooks and general surveys of the country.

> Costa Rica has always been unique in Central America. It was a small, relatively prosperous white nation of small property-owning farmers in a region of extremely backward, deeply divided countries with very large Indian and mestizo populations which were dominated by tiny elites of rich landowners. It has been consistently ruled by civilian, democratic governments, while all its neighbors have spent the greater part of their histories under military rule. . . . The sole episode of military dictatorship in the country's history occurred from 1870–1872, and no soldier has been elected to the presidency since 1917. . . . The main reason for these striking differences is that the entire country was settled by immigrants from the Galicia and other parts of northern Spain. . . . The immigrants settled down to become a homogeneous society of peasant farmers. (Dyer 1979, 150)[12]

Dyer's account is full of blatant factual errors[13] but the core argument of a cultural connection between Costa Ricans and democracy has a long and impressive pedigree. Eugenio Rodríguez Vega, a leading political and intellectual force in the National Liberation Party (PLN), provides the

10. Feminists and others in Costa Rica often question the pervasive characterization of nonviolence, given shockingly high rates of domestic violence.

11. Although many older Ticos complain that something has happened and the youth and modern politicians have gone astray.

12. Contrast this commonly accepted account with that of Martz (1959, chapter 6), in which he examines Costa Rica in the 1950s and accurately reports that "Costa Rica differs but little from the supposed norm" of Central America. "Elections are only partially honest, and the results are not always observed"; and "it is far from the well-seasoned government of democratic practice prevalent among the more advanced members of the Western world. Costa Rica today is in a position to slip back just as its neighbors show signs of awakening to the more advanced precepts of democratic government" (210–11).

13. We have already discussed that Costa Rica was not always democratic. The claim that military dictatorships ruled only for two years is bizarre. Tomás Guardia ruled as a military dictator from 1870 to 1882. In addition, the Tinoco brothers ruled the country in a military dictatorship for two and a half years from 1917 to 1919.

quintessential statement: "Democracy is not for Costa Ricans merely a political structure of government: it is, before all else, a deep feeling that has endured alive and palpable for our entire history as an independent nation" (1954, 14). It is part of a "national myth" that has enough threads of truth to be convincing to the casual observer. Indeed, the country has not been racked by a long series of violent civil wars and civilians have often resided in the presidential palace. But the connection between culture and democracy is tenuous at best and in the case of Costa Rica has never been established in any causally convincing fashion.[14]

Just below the surface of the cultural argument in Costa Rica lies a widespread belief among Costa Ricans that they are racially exceptional and by blood have a democratic nature because they are white or of pure European descent. Creedman refers to the overall Costa Rican democratic myth as a "white myth" or "*leyenda blanca*," which "portrays Costa Rica as an idyllic democracy without violence or poverty, a so-called 'Switzerland of Central America'" (1977, x).[15] Racial explanations of Costa Rican exceptionalism are usually only implied in scholarly works and are closest to the surface in Harrison's controversial cultural account of development (1985, chapter 3).[16] Recent genetic and historical research has reached the quite undeniable conclusion, however, that the overwhelming majority of Costa Ricans are Mestizos—or of mixed blood from European, African, and indigenous ancestors (Mairena 1995).[17] Yet, while the racial make-up

14. The most influential work on political culture in recent years has come from Inglehart and his colleagues and has caused a heated debate (see Granato, Inglehart, and Leblang 1996; Jackman and Miller 1996). Inglehart and Carballo (1997) use survey research to support the proposition that Latin America has a distinct political culture.

15. My classmates in the history graduate program at the University of Costa Rica boasted that they could define Costa Rica's perceived exceptionalism in three words: *blanco, democrático, y pacífico* (white, democratic, and peaceful).

16. Busey (1958, 644–45) and Seligson (1980, 156–62) argue that ethnic homogeneity has helped maintain stability in Costa Rica. Seligson contends that the lack of a significant Indian population is important, as the peasants are not ethnically distinct from the elites, and that where ethnic distinctions co-vary with class differences, elite repression and peasant revolts are more likely. The ethnic issue challenges two case comparative studies of Costa Rica and Guatemala.

17. When the evidence was reported that even the whitest of Ticos were of mixed blood, many went into denial and continue to maintain the myth of the pure European. Local Mormons told the author that Costa Ricans are loath to do genealogy for fear of discovering that they have black or Indian blood. According to University of Costa Rica researchers, as a result of elite Spaniards having numerous offspring with slaves and Indians early in the colonization of the country, the blood is equally mixed at any socio-economic level. The Costa Rican blood composition is 61% Caucasian, 29% Amerindian, and 9%

of the country is complex and little understood, it is also true that the mere belief in a homogeneous and exceptional population may have been an important component in building a national identity (Paige 1997, chapters 7–8; Palmer 1995). However, many countries have developed a strong sense of nationalism, ethnic homogeneity, and exceptionalism, and have had democratic breakdowns, such as Argentina and Uruguay.

The second part of the national myth is economic and structural and is highly intertwined with the cultural exceptionalism explained above. There are many variants of the explanation of how economic forces combined to pave the way for democracy (some of the better argued comparative studies are Mahoney [2001], Pérez Brignoli [1988], and Williams [1994]). Some link democracy with a particular land-tenure system and the particularities of the development of the coffee industry. This causal linkage is in part unconvincing given the uncertainties and debates about the historical reality of Costa Rican landholding patterns (see Gudmundson 1986, 1–20). Aguilar Bulgarelli and Alfaro Aguilar (1997) have now even challenged the long-held view that forced labor was relatively unimportant for early agriculture in Costa Rica. The authors document the introduction of some three thousand slaves and make the claim that the economic and political elites that have dominated the country since colonial times (see Stone 1975) gained their dominant economic position through the surplus value of slave labor. In spite of the historical uncertainties, the vision of the yeoman farmer as the centerpiece of the development of a rural democracy endures and is strongly associated with democracy in Costa Rica in the post-1948 period.

Gudmundson (1986) questions the equality of the colonial period and provides a compelling case that the myths served the political purposes of the very authors who propagated them, a charge Molina (1991) brilliantly illustrates. According to Molina, beginning in the 1940s the history of Costa Rica was reinterpreted through a social-democratic lens. The principal scholars of this period were Carlos Monge, Monge's student Rodrigo

African (Mairena 1995, 12). The vast majority of Costa Ricans are Mestizos. The genetic evidence has recently been supported by historical work. Aguilar Bulgarelli and Alfaro Aguilar (1997) have convincingly demonstrated that slavery was much more common than Costa Ricans had previously imagined. Some three thousand slaves were brought to Costa Rica when the overall population of the country was in the thousands. Some families had in excess of two hundred slaves. Interracial breeding was very common and African blood can be genealogically traced to many of the country's most important political and economic families.

Facio, Eugenio Rodríguez, and Carlos Meléndez. The definitive word on the yeoman farmer and the classless society sprang forth from Monge:

> As the central figure of our political, social, economic, and cultural history, the yeoman farmer emerged, and is deeply rooted, in the eighteenth century. . . . He was the genuine product of Costa Rica's curious colonial history. Because of the economic conditions in our country, social classes or castes did not arise. . . . A great history of democracy lies in his soul. . . . In those early times, he was distant from commerce, society, and politics, attached to his land like a mollusk to his shell. But after the eighteenth century, new institutions arose in which he could participate and he engaged actively in the political process that began in 1812. To understand the special concern for liberty that Costa Ricans have always shown, the respect for the country's leaders for law and for human life, one must know the yeoman who labored upon the land. (Monge 1989, 12)

Monge, Facio, and Rodríguez were principal actors in the social-democratic movement and in the Figueres governments. Their interpretation of Costa Rican history emphasized the egalitarian nature of pre-coffee Costa Rica and the economic stratification that resulted from coffee and capitalism. The social-democratic state would be required to restore the egalitarianism that was fundamental to Costa Rican exceptionalism. For Molina, after 1930–40 the historians made a new evaluation of the colonial legacy—the social-democratic version—adopting the essential elements of the liberal version, but accentuating the economic and social equality. From an ideological point of view, this image, far from legitimizing the Costa Rica of the coffee oligarchy, condemned it. The forceful conclusion of Molina's study is that interpretations of the colonial legacy have been much more an ideological instrument than an academic exercise (36).[18]

Empirical investigations of land distribution have spurred a great debate. Writing in 1958, Kantor notes that scholars regularly claimed that

18. As evidence of misusing history to justify a point, Molina presents the case of Governor Diego de la Haya. Diego writes in 1719 that the people of Costa Rica were so poor that the governor himself had to plant and harvest his own food or perish. What greater evidence of the utter poverty and equality in colonial Costa Rica! Citations of poor Governor Diego struggling to eke out an existence to support the egalitarian thesis are ubiquitous. Yet, Molina decries this as selective and biased research since Governor Diego admits, in the same document, that labor was provided by Indians (32).

land-holding patterns were highly equitable in Costa Rica (7) but that the agricultural census of 1950 showed that land-holding patterns were highly stratified. Seligson (1980) contends that the advent of coffee production resulted in the demise of the family farmer and the emergence of large estates and a landless proletariat, a position seconded by Winson (1989) and many others. In contrast, Hall (1982) argues that small-holders have dominated coffee production and landownership, a position supported by many, including Torres-Rivas (1975).

More recent empirical studies have not settled the debate. Samper (1994) presents one of the most sophisticated analyses of land-holding patterns in Costa Rica, a comparative study with El Salvador. By 1950—the period when Costa Rica democratizes—the average size of a coffee finca in "egalitarian" Costa Rica is similar to that in "highly stratified" El Salvador and the holdings of "medium-sized" coffee fincas are also similar. Samper's comparative research results in several conclusions: (1) the reality of coffee holdings differs substantially from the image of an agricultural society dominated by medium-sized coffee farmers (155); (2) "Costa Rican democracy in the first half of this century, plagued by fraud and other mechanisms of manipulation of the still-masculine vote, was not a mechanical reflection of a supposed egalitarian rural economy" (186); (3) in both Costa Rica and El Salvador in the first half of the twentieth century, the coffee elite governed in a more or less direct form and controlled their countries unchallenged by electoral processes (200).[19] Samper does emphasize one important distinction between these two countries in the 1930s. Because of more mini-farmers in Costa Rica and a larger population in El Salvador, a much higher percentage of the Costa Ricans owned coffee fincas than did the El Salvadorans. Samper estimates that in the 1930s, 5 percent of the Costa Rican rural population owned a finca, compared to only 1 percent of rural Salvadorans (138).[20] While both percentages are small, one could argue that the larger percentage of landowners in Costa Rica—even if the plots were generally too small to sustain a family—impacted the political dynamic. It is unwise to carry this argument

19. Winson uses a different source of coffee tree distribution—*Informe Sobre la Situación del Café* for 1935—and reaches conclusions that support Samper. The largest 1% of farms had more coffee trees than the smallest 75% combined (Winson 1989, 16–23).

20. A separate issue is the role of the rural peasantry in social movements. For Central America, see for example Brockett (1987, 1991), Edelman (1999), and Kincaid (1987, 1989).

very far, as Samper's data also shows that by the early 1950s, the number of fincas in El Salvador had grown to 31,815 while the concentration of fincas in Costa Rica had reduced the total number to only 15,222, resulting in a very similar percentage of coffee finca owners in the population of each country (1994, 140–41). All in all, one is much more impressed by the remarkable similarities in coffee land distribution in these two countries than by any distinctions. One crucial difference between Costa Rica and El Salvador through the middle of the twentieth century is that due to its small size, El Salvador had no agricultural frontier.

Paige (1997) examines different data and reaches different conclusions. He finds that land distribution was considerably more equitable in Costa Rica (1955) than in El Salvador (1940), Guatemala (1967), and Nicaragua (1957). However, most of the small Costa Rican farms were land-poor sub-family plots and were not large enough to contain a yeoman farmer. Indeed, in 1955 there were a mere 1,775 family-sized coffee farms in Costa Rica, a smaller number than in Nicaragua. While it is possible to say that large coffee estates were less influential in Costa Rica than in Guatemala, El Salvador, and Nicaragua, there is no evidence to portray Costa Rica as a slice of Iowa transplanted to the Central American isthmus. It is an undeniable fact that land was highly concentrated in Costa Rica long before competitive and fair elections emerged. Brockett (1992) develops an alternative measure, the Relative Rural Disruption Potential Index. This index combines a number of land and rural population data and finds that Nicaragua (score of 52) and Costa Rica (59) have the lowest rural disruption potential, El Salvador (100) and Guatemala (99) have the highest potential, with Honduras (87) in the middle.

Another type of equality may have existed that encouraged democratization—income distribution. As we will see shortly, Costa Rica was very poor at the midpoint of this century. For there to have been the sizable middle class that dominates images of the country, income distribution would have to have been highly egalitarian. Many scholars have observed a positive relationship between equality and democracy, including de Tocqueville and Dahl. Muller (1988, 1995a, 1995b) and Simpson (1990) have argued with statistical evidence that more egalitarian countries have a greater likelihood of sustaining democracy.[21] The rationale for this claim

21. Bollen and Jackman (1985, 1995) and Nielsen and Alderson (1994) assert that Muller and Simpson are wrong and that inequality and democracy are unrelated net of industrialization.

is "grounded in the theoretical proposition that extreme inequality generates intense, irreconcilable class conflict that is incompatible with a stable democracy" (Muller 1995b, 990). Even if Muller is correct, the sequence of the causal argument does not work for Costa Rica. Costa Rica's democracy was consolidated and stable soon after the 1958 elections. Until 1961, Costa Rica had a concentrated level of income inequality similar to that in Brazil and one in which the top 20 percent of the population received 60 percent of the national income. Costa Rica achieved an improvement in income distribution only by 1971 (Bowman 1997, 133).

It is also argued that economic development is positively related with democracy (Bollen 1983; Bollen and Jackman 1985; Burkhart and Lewis-Beck 1994). Seligson argues for a "minimal threshold" of economic development for democracy in Central America and argues that Costa Rica was the only country in Central America well above the minimal GNP per capita of $240 in 1957. Seligson also claims that Costa Rica was above the necessary but insufficient literacy threshold of 50 percent (1987, 173–77). The minimum threshold argument for economic development and democracy is tenuous for the Costa Rican case. The most widely used comparative data for macroeconomic indicators are available in the Penn World Tables project (Summers and Heston 1984). According to Mark 5.6 of the Penn World Tables, per capita GDP of Costa Rica was unimpressive, even in comparison with the rest of Central America. Other Latin American countries were much wealthier than Costa Rica and yet did not have the same democratic experience, even those with high literacy rates such as Argentina and Uruguay.

It is interesting to note that Guatemala had a higher per capita GDP in 1950 than Costa Rica. The Summers and Heston data are corroborated with newspaper reports in *La Nación*, praising the economic vitality and potential of the Guatemalans in comparison to Costa Rica.[22]

In sum, in 1948 Costa Rica was a highly inegalitarian, poor, dependent country. "Along with a concentration of wealth in few hands, an extensive mass of dispossessed formed. There were problems of various types: the quality of life of the worker could not have been more deplorable; the campesino was malnourished, shoeless, uneducated, in a precarious condition" (Brenes 1990, 20). "The Electric Bond and Share, the American and Foreign Power, the Northern Railway Company and the United Fruit

22. 18 January 1948, p. 8.

Table 4.1 1950 per capita GDP in 1985 U.S. purchasing parity dollars[1]

Costa Rica	Guatemala	El Salvador	Nicaragua	Honduras
$1,457	$1,525	$1,207	$1,152	$921
Argentina	Chile	Mexico	Uruguay	Venezuela
$4,032	$2,431	$2,192	$3,451	$4,799

1. These data are from Mark 5.6 of the Penn World Table, which displays a set of national accounts economic time series that extend in some cases from 1950–92. The unique feature of the PWT is that its expenditure series are denominated in a common set of prices in a common currency so that real international quantity comparisons can be made both between countries and over time. The PWT is derived from benchmark United Nations pricing studies that produce Purchasing Power Parity. The price parities and PPP's are used to convert the countries' national currency expenditures to a common currency unit, thus making real quantity comparisons across countries. For more information, see Summers and Heston, 1991. These data were downloaded from HTTP://WWW.NBER.ORG/PWT56.HTML. Data from Bulmer-Thomas (1993) present a similar but slightly different portrayal of 1950 Central America, with PCGDP of $282 for Costa Rica, $193 for El Salvador, $248 for Guatemala, $209 for Honduras, and $191 for Nicaragua (in real 1970 $U.S.).

controlled as monopolies major portions of the economy. We were a Banana Republic" (Vargas Araya 1993, 108). As late as 1954, *La Nación* reported statistics that claimed that 80 percent of *Costarricences* were barefoot.[23]

Elections were fraudulent and politics were controlled by the coffee elite. In the mid-1940s, when total votes fluctuated between 100,000 and 130,000, between 40,000 and 60,000 false voter identification cards were in circulation (Lehoucq 1996, 348). The 1940s witnessed an increase both in electoral irregularities and in many manifestations of political violence and class warfare, culminating in the Civil War of 1948 and two thousand to four thousand deaths. Democracy was not the automatic destiny of Costa Rica.

Seligson is correct in noting one exception for Costa Rica; literacy levels may have approached 80 percent by 1950 (176). Human capital has long been higher in Costa Rica than in the rest of the isthmus, and the potential positive benefits of human capital are enormous. While this is important, one should not romanticize education in Costa Rica. In 1956, only 14 percent of students who had previously entered first grade had made it to sixth grade and other scholars claim that barely half of the adult population was literate in 1950 (Céspedes and Jiménez 1995, 8).[24] Another

23. 10 September 1954, p. 3. Iván Molina suggests that peasants went barefoot out of preference and not poverty (personal communication).

24. *La Nación*, 24 October 1956, pp. 1, 5.

factor that is often pointed to as facilitating democracy in Costa Rica was the absence of ethnic divisions and forced labor. This is essentially true but not enough to assure democracy; ethnic division and forced labor were also minor factors in Honduras.

This discussion of the Costa Rican democratic myth was essential, given the enduring belief in the predestination of democracy for this country. For if Costa Rica's democratic success was predestined by colonial heritage, political culture, structural factors from the nineteenth century, or socioeconomic conditions in 1950, then the militarization variable is irrelevant. Certain factors in Costa Rica were beneficial for democracy. The state quite early had the capacity to build a trans-isthmus railroad, to construct schools, to collect taxes, and to extend hygiene to the popular sectors (Palmer forthcoming). State capacity was likely enhanced by the concentration of the population in the *meseta central* around San José and the isolation of the country from Guatemala and El Salvador, whose meddling in Honduran politics was a constant threat to stability. Elections, for all their defects, were common and civilians were often in the presidential palace. Forced labor did not dominate the agricultural sector, which is crucial as it lowers the potential costs of democracy for the oligarchy.[25] Ethnic divisions were limited. The country was not wracked by the series of wars that were so destructive in many other Latin American countries. And Costa Ricans believed that they were exceptional and democratic and middle class. Perhaps most important of all, literacy was relatively high given the level of economic development. Despite these conditions, democracy was not guaranteed and, I argue, would have been less durable without the proscription of the military.

Explanations for Democracy Centered on the 1940s

In recent years, scholars of Costa Rica have discounted the mythical explanations of democracy and focused instead on actors and events of the 1940s as the immediate causes of democratization. They have generated

25. Forced labor was extensive in El Salvador and Guatemala and also in parts of Nicaragua. This factor makes comparisons between Costa Rica and these countries difficult. In contrast, there was little forced labor in Honduras.

various hypotheses for the outcome.[26] I will focus on two, one centered on elite pacts and the other on institutions.[27]

The Pacted Costa Rican Democracy. The importance of pacts as a process in democratization has been discussed by Burton, Gunther, and Higley (1992), Di Palma (1990), Higley and Gunther (1992), and Karl (1990). "At the core of a pact lies a negotiated compromise under which actors agree to forgo or under-utilize their capacity to harm each other by extending guarantees not to threaten each other's corporate autonomies or vital interests" (O'Donnell and Schmitter 1986, 38). Colombia and Venezuela are two important examples from Latin America where explicit formal pacts between the major political parties for the sharing of power and spoils accompanied long periods of regime stability.

Unlike Colombia and Venezuela, no long-term formal elite pact was agreed upon in Costa Rica after the 1948 Civil War.[28] Proponents of elite pacts, most notably Peeler (1985, 1995, 1998), assert that a tacit elite pact was reached by the social democratic forces led by Figueres and the more conservative forces led by Ulate. While the pact was not formal, it was nonetheless "conscious and explicit" in the Costa Rican case (Peeler 1985, 44).[29] Compromises were reached in redrafting the constitution of 1949. Figueres gave up power to Ulate in 1949 and Ulate in turn handed power back to Figueres after the elections of 1953. Bitter political enemies made

26. None of the authors, myself included, ignores that Costa Rica did have certain preconditions that were more or less favorable for democratic government. Rather, these arguments are dynamic in claiming that initial conditions were not enough to ensure democracy, but that process and contemporary events and conditions matter.

27. There are other explanations. One recent attempt comes from the noted scholar of Central America, Jeffery Paige (1997). Paige compares Costa Rica, El Salvador, and Nicaragua and argues that democracy flows indirectly out of leftist insurrections; "the key blow that fractured the agrarian agro-industrial alliance of the coffee elite was provided by the armies of the left" (321). The civil wars, coupled with changes in the demand for agricultural exports by the world system, led to the decline of the reactionary agrarian elite and the rise of a more democratic agro-industrial elite. Paige's is a powerful book, although the implication that the Figueres forces in the 1948 Civil War were leftist is debatable. More important, the Honduran case creates challenges for Paige's study. Honduras exhibits Paige's outcome (electoral democracy at the end of the twentieth century) without his purported cause (leftist insurrection).

28. As will be detailed, Figueres agreed to many pacts. But these were short-term agreements and not at all comparable to the more permanent power-sharing arrangements of Colombia and Venezuela. In addition, Figueres was quite willing to renege on these pacts.

29. Booth (1998, 197) also argues that elite pacts are an important explanatory variable for Costa Rican democracy.

and subsequently lived up to agreements and mutual tolerance soon evolved into stable democracy. The difficulty with the elite pact as an explanation in the Costa Rican case is that it was informal, and while "conscious and explicit" to Peeler, it is not obviously explicit to others. In addition, it is very difficult to establish a causal process with elite pact explanations, as the arguments to date are tautological or circular: *the elite pact is often identified as the cause of democratic consolidation even as democratic consolidation is identified as evidence of an elite settlement.* In contrast to Peeler, O'Donnell and Schmitter (1986, 76) identify Costa Rica as an exception to the pacted democracy path in Latin America: "This regime suggests that pacted democracies may not be the only safe path"; they identify demilitarization as the secret to Costa Rica's democratic endurance. I will present evidence in this chapter to support O'Donnell and Schmitter's contention that no pact existed in Costa Rica. What impeded the enemies of Figueres from overthrowing the regime was not the will, but the way.

Yashar (1997) also relies on a modified elite pact or compromise to explain why the social democrats after 1948 were not overthrown by the elites. Yashar defines the 1940–48 period as a democratizing period and the 1948 Civil War as a counter-reform revolution that "marked an end to a decade of popular sector mobilization, social reforms, and democratic participation" (210). Yashar anticipates the obvious question: if the elites overthrew Picado/Calderón in 1948 in a reaction to policies adverse to their interests, why didn't they also overthrow Figueres? Figueres hit the ruling elite in a way never dreamed of by Calderón and Picado. The social policies enacted by Calderón were watered down to limit any negative effects on the agricultural elite, as the labor code did not apply to agricultural workers. In contrast, Figueres nationalized the banks and decreed a 10 percent tax on the well-to-do in an overt frontal assault on the established coffee oligarchy. Yashar argues that elites permitted Figueres to continue because they understood his "bitter" reforms to be "bounded" (one-time) while the more moderate Calderón/Picado reforms were "unbounded" (218). How does one know that the oligarchy in 1948–49 had a high level of confidence that the reforms were bounded? No evidence or explanation is offered except that they did not overthrow Figueres, so they must have had confidence that no more reforms were coming. Historical evidence is clear, however, that Figueres pushed through many other reforms in 1948–49 after the "bitter" decrees, and again in the post-1953 period, that angered his enemies and redistributed resources. Figueres's enemies feared that the social democrats were leading the country on an incremental path towards socialism. Yashar herself discounts the importance of the "boundedness" and identifies the real key for regime stability: the elite was furious with Figueres and felt threatened "but with no army could provide no credible threat to force the junta to reverse the decision" (189).

Institutional Explanations. Lehoucq (1992, 1996, 1997, 2000) takes cultural and structural arguments to task and argues that an understanding of Costa Rican democratization must be focused on the microfoundations—the decision calculus and actions of individual political actors (both politicians and political parties). Lehoucq starts from the proposition that it was far from inevitable that democracy would emerge, consolidate, and survive in Costa Rica. The source of democratic stability is institutional. The battle that mattered for democracy was that fought for control of political power. Politicians and parties are rational actors whose principal motivation is gaining and holding office. Electoral reform that gives political actors confidence in the electoral game will improve the chances for democracy, and Lehoucq identifies the 1946 electoral reforms as one source of future electoral probity and democratic stability.

Wilson (1998) also develops an institutionalist explanation for democratic success, based on institutions developed after the 1948 Civil War. These institutions flowed out of the 1949 constitution and such developments as the abolition of the military, the prohibition of presidential reelection, and the enactment of mechanisms to ensure transparent fairness in the electoral system.

Extant explanations for democratization in Costa Rica—cultural, economic-structural, elite pact, and institutional—all share the conviction that democracy was in place and consolidated soon after the 1948 Civil War. I argue against the conventional wisdom, positing instead that one can only begin to speak of stable democracy in Costa Rica after the 1958 elections.[30] An examination of the 1948–58 period greatly enhances and in some cases challenges the extant theories. The impact of demilitarization on three power relations—class, transnational, and the state—was crucial to the democratization process. This process eventually led to a stalemate between Figueres and his enemies. The historical section that follows details the consolidation of democracy in the decade after the 1948 Civil War.

30. One exception is Rovira Mas (1990).

The 1948 Civil War and Its Aftermath

There are many good accounts of political events in the 1940s and I will not dwell on them. A quick introduction of the cast of characters and a brief overview of the major political events is useful. Costa Rican political parties lacked coherent ideologies and were personal vehicles of the coffee elite. The coffee oligarchy, both the large growers and the processors/exporters, was the dominant political actor for the one hundred-year period ending in 1950. Labor began flexing its muscles in the bakeries, shoe factories, and print shops around the turn of the century. The Costa Rican Communist Party was founded in 1931 and quickly gained strength among urban artisans and in banana plantation labor camps. The Banana Strike of 1934 involved some ten thousand striking workers and was violently repressed by the army.

León Cortés was president from 1936 to 1940 and was very popular in rural areas for expanding public works. Even today, citizens of Costa Rica will tell you about the probity and work habits of Cortés: he would get up early and show up at the post office to make sure that government employees were starting work on time. As with others who had reputations for making the trains run on time, Cortés had pro-Axis sympathies and worked diligently to repress labor unions. Cortés imposed Calderón Guardia, a medical doctor, as his successor in 1940. This marked the third consecutive landslide victory for the National Republican Party and there were clear indications that this would become a hegemonic party of the Costa Rican oligarchy. The near unanimous support for Calderón splintered quickly (he won more than 80 percent of the vote). According to Lehoucq (1992, 164–67), Calderón's refusal to name Cortés's son, Otto, as president of the national assembly and the subsequent sacking of Cortés's relatives from government jobs infuriated Cortés and led to a bitter split. This split intensified with a series of measures from December 1941 through June 1942, when President Calderón issued decrees against Costa Ricans with German, Italian, Japanese, and Spanish connections. Properties were seized, citizens were sent to internment camps in Costa Rica and Texas, and important trade with Germany was halted. Many Costa Ricans, including León Cortés, had strong pro-German loyalties. Calderón's anti-Axis policies were encouraged by the United States and provided the means for purging the government of Cortés loyalists (Schifter 1986, 107–8). Thus, less than two years after gaining the presidency with the unified support of the coffee oligarchy, the support of his popular predecessor, and 84.3 percent of the vote, Calderón had managed to turn his patron into an enemy and seriously weaken his domestic support.

In one of the greatest of Calderón's many blunders, security forces seized the politically unknown and diminutive José Figueres as he criticized the government in a radio speech on 11 July 1942. Figueres was sent into exile in Mexico; a political star was born. He did not return to Costa Rica until 1944 (Vargas Araya 1993, 446–47).

The split with Cortés and the persecution of citizens with German, Italian, and Spanish connections spawned serious political crisis in the country. The crisis was deepened when Calderón responded by forming an alliance with the Manuel Mora-led communists and with the progressive Archbishop of the Catholic Church, Monseñor Sanabria, who relied on papal encyclicals such as *Rerum Novarum* to argue for social policies to foster spiritual *and* temporal well-being.[31] Together, this unlikely trinity pushed through a labor code, social security, and social guarantees. To be sure, with farm laborers and small businesses exempt from most of the provisions, these social reforms were more style than substance. In fact, with coffee prices high and the United States taking all the *café* that previously was exported to Germany, the agricultural elite did not suffer. Add to this the economic incentives and tax relief provided by Calderón and the coffee farmers never did better (Schifter 1986, 107–8). The coffee elite saw exports of the golden bean nearly double from $3,989,310 in 1939–40 to $7,488,761 in 1944–45 (Rojas Bolaños 1986, 47; see also Bulmer-Thomas 1987, 91).

Despite the minimalist substance of the reforms, the social legislation victory was seen as enormous for the communists, who were very influential in the union movement and on the banana plantations. Communist participation in the government was an easy target for *Cortesistas* still stinging over their treatment by Calderón, and Cortés himself ran for the presidency in 1944 against the Calderón-anointed attorney Teodoro Picado. The campaign was heated and turnout for the vote heavy; some 137,806 votes were cast in 1944 versus 108,136 in 1940 and 99,369 in 1948 (Salazar 1995, 313). Picado defeated Cortés with some 66 percent of the vote in an election widely believed to have been marred by fraud. Workers appeared to have voted en masse for the Picado-Communist electoral bloc (*El Bloque*

31. For a discussion of the church in Costa Rica, see Backer (1978).

de la Victoria) in support of the social reforms and against the fascist influence associated with Cortés (Salazar 1995, 233). The ensuing Picado years can be characterized as moderate. He enacted no further social or labor reforms; he tried to distance himself from the communists and strengthen ties to the United States (Salazar 1995, 234).

Despite Picado's moderation, tensions continued to mount after 1944. Protests against the regime were met with violence, which led to more violence. "The confidence in the political system began to evaporate and terrorist bombs in the principal cities became a normal event" (Molina and Palmer 1997, 12). In June 1946, the *Almaticazo* marked the first attempt at revolution against Calderón-Picado. Financed and planned by coffee baron and *Cortesista* Fernando Castro Cervantes, a small group seized the Alma Tico radio station and was soon captured (Rojas Bolaños 1986, 122). Among them was Edgar Cardona, who three years later would be minister of defense and would lead a coup against Figueres. Figueres sought out Cardona and other youthful participants in the *Almaticazo*, applauded their courage, ridiculed the *Almaticazo* as amateurish, and challenged them to join him in an organized overthrow of the regime (interview with Edgar Cardona, 20 December 1997, Moravia, Costa Rica).

Otilio Ulate, the leader of the opposition, wrote that "The country is in a dilemma; either it must abandon the suffrage or have a civil war to restore honor and integrity to the public" (*New York Times*, 4 February 1947). One man, José Figueres Ferrer, was hard at work preparing for the civil war. In a radio address on 31 August 1946, Figueres argued that traditional methods could no longer be used to preserve liberty and suffrage in the country (Vargas Araya 1993, 448). A month after this speech, León Cortés unexpectedly died and a scramble ensued to gain the leadership of the opposition.

In July 1947, the country experienced a bitter capital strike known as the Sit Down Strike (*Huelga de los Brazos Caídos*). Yashar argues that this strike resulted from a proposed income tax (1997, 117–19). Martz portrays the strike as a response to increased violence on the part of security forces and the growing discontent over Calderón and Picado's monopolization of political power (1959, 211–13). Security forces were under serious stress as terrorism and violence increased, including bombings of military headquarters. The government tolerated extreme uses of force on the part of the police. *Cortesistas* complained of the dreaded "*cinchas*," sword-like weapons with dull blades that police used to beat opponents (Cardona

1992, 8). The brutality reached a breaking point on 20 July 1947 when government forces attacked crowds in Cartago, killing two and wounding many others. Otilio Ulate, the leader of the opposition, helped organize a business strike. Within days the capital was paralyzed and businesses of all types were shut down. Frustrated, the government sent armed thugs into the streets to destroy and loot unopened stores. Martz asserts that Picado was hoping for an all-out confrontation and attempted revolution, but the opposition remained calm, forcing Picado to seek a negotiated resolution (1959, 214). Conversations between the representative of the opposition, Ricardo Castro Beeche, and the government began on 1 August and an end to the crisis was agreed to and signed on 3 August (Obregón Loria 1951, 115). The agreement addressed political and not economic issues (placing in doubt the claim that taxes were the cause of the strike). What the opposition wanted was the power to oversee the electoral processes in 1948. This was granted when Picado agreed to let the opposition have an equal number of delegates on the Electoral Tribunal and to name the very powerful position of president of the Electoral Registry (Obregón Loria 1951, 115; Yashar 1997, 118–19). These 1947 agreements and especially an improved Electoral Code in 1946 were measures that Picado used to "regain his adversaries's confidence in electoral institutions" and to ease tensions that might lead to an armed overthrow of his regime (Lehoucq 1997b, 16).

Figueres continued with plans for the overthrow of the government and was loath to accept any peaceful resolution. Figueres continued preparations for war on two fronts. In Costa Rica, he continued to recruit young men who participated in acts of sabotage, terrorism, and even an attempted assassination of Calderón Guardia (*La Tribuna*, 23 October 1947; Cardona 1992, 17–28; LaFeber 1984, 101). In addition to Cardona, Miguel Ruiz Herrera became a trusted Figueres ally whose value to Figueres was enhanced because his father was an honorary consul for Portugal. His automobile with diplomatic plates was used to transport arms for the revolution that Figueres was hell-bent on launching (Ameringer 1996, 64; interview with Miguel Ruiz Herrera, San José, Costa Rica, 3 December 1997).

"You can't make chocolate without cacao," and Figueres was frustrated because he couldn't make a revolution without arms (Figueres quoted in Ameringer 1978, 26). Figueres had been busy at work securing weapons since his exile in 1942. While exiled in Mexico, Don Pepe met with two leaders of the anti-Somoza movement, the Nicaraguan Rosendo Argüello and Professor Edelberto Torres, who were both actively involved in the Central American Democratic Union (UDC). Figueres convinced Argüello that violence was the only way to oust the dictators and that the "struggle should begin in Costa Rica because it was the weakest link in the dictatorial chain" (Ameringer 1996, 64). In 1946, Figueres and Argüello raised $60,000 for arms that were seized in Mexico shortly before being sent out of the country; the Mexican authorities also threw Torres and Argüello in jail (Ameringer 1996, 64). By 1947, it was an open secret that Figueres was planning a revolution and acquiring arms. Costa Rican communists worked in Mexico to stop the weapons flow and may have contributed to the debacle with Argüello and Torres (interview with Eduardo Mora Valverde, San José, Costa Rica, 16 December 1997).

In the summer of 1947, a fighting force of 1,200 men gathered on the puny Cuban island of Cayo Confites to prepare for an armed overthrow of Dominican dictator Rafael Trujillo. The United States and Trujillo pressured the rebels' patron, Cuban President Ramón Grau, to stop the rebel movement and he reluctantly yielded, seizing the men and the weapons (see Ameringer 1996, 27–60). Guatemalan President Juan José Arévalo stepped into the vacuum caused by Grau's humiliation to become the new patron of the antidictatorship movement in the Caribbean Basin. Arévalo transported the cache of arms from Cuba to Guatemala, and Guatemala City was quickly flooded with dissidents and exiles from the Dominican Republic, Honduras, Nicaragua, and Costa Rica. A battle soon ensued over who would get to use the guns and Figueres was the winner, but only if he would sign a pact with rebels from Nicaragua and the Dominican Republic. The Caribbean Pact was signed on 16 December 1947 and was an agreement for a supranational body to press the antidictatorial struggle. Costa Rica was singled out as the easiest country to take; once the Caribbean Legion destroyed Calderón and Picado, Costa Rica would be used as a base to overthrow the Three T's (Tacho Somoza in Nicaragua, Trujillo in the Dominican Republic, and Tiburcio Carías in Honduras).[32]

By late 1947, the race for the 1948 presidential elections was set between Calderón and Ulate. San José was tense, as fraud was expected from both sides and violence was becoming the norm. El Salvador's *El Diario de Hoy*

32. Ameringer (1996, 66–67) points out that Figueres did not have access to the weapons immediately after the signing of the Caribbean Pact and that Arévalo and Juan Rodríguez wanted to wait to see if Calderón was really going to steal the 1948 elections.

reported that everyone had improvised some type of weapon and the majority had prepared Molotov cocktails (2 February 1948). The U.S. ambassador to Costa Rica reported in October 1947 that neither of the candidates was what Costa Rica needed and that both were willing to resort to arms if they did not win the election (Schifter 1986, 226). Even though the United States knew that Figueres was busy acquiring weapons abroad, the United States continually refused to grant Picado's requests for arms for the Costa Rican security forces and even used pressure to hinder Picado from purchasing weapons from third countries (Schifter 1986, 220–30).[33]

The 1948 elections were controversial and so fraud-ridden that to this day no one knows who actually won; a mysterious fire that destroyed many ballots adds to the difficulty. It must be noted that the opposition, due to the agreement made after the *Huelga de los Brazos Caídos*, controlled the Civil Registry and had strong representation on the Electoral Tribunal. On 9 July 1948, the director of the Civil Registry reported that the country should have 175,000 voters but the number had been inflated with 40,000 defective inscriptions (*La Nación*). According to *Calderonistas*, the Civil Registry was used to purge Calderón supporters from the voting rolls. In electoral campaigns through the 1950s, newspapers would print large lists of the citizens that supported a particular candidate or party. Supposedly, if an impressive list of people publicly supported a party, this would generate even more support. These lists, according to *Calderonistas*, provided the opposition-controlled Civil Registry (directed by Figueres ally Benjamín Odio) with the names of potential Calderón supporters and thousands of names were eliminated from the official roles. People would go to vote and would be denied that right, leading to huge protests in San José and the provinces. *Calderonistas* screamed, "We want to vote!" (Bakit 1990, 21–22; interview with Oscar Bakit, San José, Costa Rica, 26 November 1997; Aguilar Bulgarelli 1983, 247–56). Ambassador Nathaniel P.

33. Costa Rica wanted to purchase planes for an air force and other weapons. U.S. Ambassador Donnelly finally did approve the purchase of twenty-five guns, which in the end were insufficient to battle the Figueres forces (Schifter 1986, 228). In the ensuing Civil War, U.S. policy was a determining force for Picado's defeat, as they were determined to destroy the government's ally, the communist *Vanguardia Popular* (LaFeber 1984, 102–4). Picado's trump card was military assistance from Somoza's potent National Guard and Somoza was more than eager to help, as he saw Arévalo's Caribbean Pact as a direct threat to his rule. Ambassador Davis and the United States cut Somoza off at the pass and helped force Picado's surrender to Figueres (LaFeber 1984, 102–6; Longley 1997, chapter 4). Olander (1996) argues against the thesis that U.S. action shaped the outcome of the Civil War.

Davis reported that thousands of Costa Ricans were unable to vote, but in his opinion the addition of these voters would not have changed the election outcome (Schifter 1986, 257).[34]

The vote count favored Ulate, with 54,931 votes, while Calderón garnered 44,438 votes (receiving less than half the votes that Picado earned in 1944). The three-member Electoral Tribunal voted 2–1 to proclaim Ulate the victor, but the congress subsequently annulled the elections (Aguilar Bulgarelli 1983, 257–91). It could not have been a better outcome for Figueres, who was now able to say "I told you so" to Arévalo and Argüello and count on arms and support. It was now insured that cooler heads would not prevail and violence would be used to select the next leader of Costa Rica.

Figueres began that war on 12 March 1948 in a brilliant move by sending Max "Tuta" Cortés and thirty men to seize the unprotected airport at San Isidro in southern Costa Rica. By noon, three TACA (Central American Air Transport) planes had landed at San Isidro and had been hijacked. Nineteen flights shuttled between San Isidro and Guatemala to pick up the weapons used by General Rodríguez in the failed Cayo Confites campaign and eighteen officers, including Argüello and the very experienced Rodríguez (Ameringer 1996, 70). These officers and the weapons sent by Arévalo were keys to the victory (LaFeber 1984, 102). Many young Costa Ricans fought bravely and would play important roles in future events. Among them were two relatives of León Cortés, Max "Tuta" Cortés and Fernando Cortés. Edgar Cardona had been participating in terrorist activities with Figueres and became the security minister at age thirty-two. Edgar Cardona brought Frank Marshall into the Figueres war band. Marshall was only twenty-three years old when he was named a general during the Civil War. His valor and daring led Figueres to name him *Jefe de Estado Mayor* when the war ended. Part of that valor may have resulted from the fact that Marshall's stepfather, Ricardo Steinvorth, was one of the Germans persecuted by Calderón; Marshall himself was educated in Germany and had strong pro-Nazi tendencies. Miguel Ruiz Herrera, who studied business administration and finance at UCLA in the mid-1940s, was named head of intelligence for the Liberation forces. Tuta Cortés, Edgar Cardona, Frank Marshall, and Miguel Ruiz were

34. In their excellent study on Costa Rican elections, Molina and Lehoucq argue that the fraud was sufficient to alter the outcome of the election and that Calderón probably won (1999, Chapter 15). Aguilar Bulgarelli (1983, 255) argues that the fraud contributed only to the margin of victory.

the closest thing to a military caste that existed in Costa Rica after the Civil War. For Figueres, their predilection for playing army would produce many close calls for his regime.

Figueres took power on 8 May 1948 after agreeing to four different pacts. The first was the Caribbean Pact with Arévalo and others to now use Costa Rica as the base to topple dictators in the region. The second was the Pact of the Mexican Embassy, brokered largely by the U.S. ambassador, which included the surrender of Picado's government and the respect of life, liberty, and property of the losing forces (Aguilar Bulgarelli 1986, 387–90). The third was the Ulate-Figueres Pact, signed on 1 May 1948. Figueres had no intention of giving power to Ulate when he began the war of liberation (Aguilar Bulgarelli 1986, 395). Figueres himself had stated unequivocally that "You are wrong if you believe that I come to hand the presidency to Ulate, nor to any other corrupt politician, I come to transform this country" (quoted in Shifter 1986, 274). Nevertheless, Figueres was pragmatic enough to understand that the United States and most Costa Ricans expected Ulate to gain the presidency that he had "won" in the election. The Ulate-Figueres Pact provided that: (1) the revolutionary junta would govern for eighteen months with a possible extension of six months; (2) elections in December 1948 would select a constitutional congress to produce a new constitution; (3) the junta would recognize and declare that Ulate was the legitimate winner of the previous election and would take power after the junta's mandate expired (Aguilar Bulgarelli 1986, 396–97). The fourth agreement was the Ochomogo Pact agreed between Manuel Mora and Padre Núñez, a leading figure in Figueres's movement (Ameringer 1978, 62). This agreement called for the communists, who had thousands of armed men ready to defend San José, to allow Figueres to waltz into the capital unopposed in exchange for a guarantee to uphold the social guarantees and to respect the rights of the party and its members. These four pacts were incompatible with each other and forced Figueres to walk a tightrope during the eighteen months of the revolutionary junta of the Second Republic.

The Revolutionary Junta

There are many excellent works that cover the eighteen months from the end of the war to the inauguration of Otilio Ulate on 8 November 1949.[35]

35. The classic study of this eighteen-month period remains Gardner (1971). See also Aguilar Bulgarelli (1975) and Rovira Mas (1988).

I will only detail certain events and developments that deal directly or indirectly with militarization and democracy. It is clear that powerful domestic economic sectors felt threatened by the Figueres regime and that they did not view his economic project as "bounded" or a single bitter pill to swallow.

When Figueres and his group of young ministers (all between age thirty and forty-five) took power, they were caught in the contradictions of their pacts and quickly moved to backtrack on many of them. In complete disregard of the Pact of the Mexican Embassy and the Pact of Ochomogo, the junta began a brutal and sweeping persecution of communists and noncommunist supporters of Calderón and Picado. A powerful and feared Tribunal for Immediate Sanctions was created, charged with seizing the properties of members of the previous two administrations (Muñoz Guillén 1990, 150; Quirós V. 1989). Properties were seized (*La Nación*, 12 May 1948), citizens were jailed, *Calderonista* students in the university and law school were purged (Bakit 1990, 158), some communists were murdered in cold blood,[36] and many thousands were soon in exile in Nicaragua, Honduras, and Mexico. Figueres seemed intent on ferreting "out all elements that might stage a counterrevolution" (Martz 1959, 225). The communists were outlawed in a decree on 18 July 1948 and the party was not legalized again for more than two decades. According to long-time communist leader and two-time legislative deputy Eduardo Mora Valverde, Figueres was completely responsible for the ban on the *Vanguardia* party. Even though the party suffered and Mora spent time in prison, Mora is convinced that Figueres was personally against the action but politically astute enough to carry it out:

> Figueres is the person responsible for our being banned. But at the same time, Figueres was not in agreement. Figueres was above all pragmatic and he acted because he was pressured. He was forced to ban *Vanguardia* because of U.S. Ambassador Davis and pressures that came from the United States. . . . Ambassador Davis had told him that the United States would never permit him to become president of Costa Rica and rule for eighteen months if he honored the Pact of Ochomogo or did not ban the Communist Party. . . .

36. Mora Valverde (forthcoming) details many atrocities and murders of communist sympathizers. One of the most infamous is the *Codo del Diablo* incident, where various imprisoned members of the *Vanguardia* party were taken out by security forces, murdered, and dumped at a location known as the Devil's Elbow (see also Bakit 1990).

> The truth is that Figueres was a very progressive and advanced man. He did not fight the Civil War and destroy Picado to end the social guarantees but rather to use Costa Rica as a base to destroy the other dictators in the region, because Picado was the weakest government in Central America. He wanted to defeat Picado, Somoza, Carías, and Hernández Martínez in El Salvador and establish a socialist republic. This idea was a dream. This was crazy. The United States would never allow this. (Interview with Eduardo Mora Valverde, San José, Costa Rica, 16 December 1997)

Figueres was, indeed, a most difficult man to understand.[37] In 1959, Martz asked the question that to many remains unresolved: was he a "democrat or a demagogue" (241)? On his coffee farm he practiced what he called socialism—five hundred sharecroppers benefited from guaranteed prices, sanitary houses, free milk for their children, a communal vegetable farm, and medical and recreational benefits (Martz 1959, 242). Yet he allied with the most conservative elements—including neofascists—to oppose Calderonism. He had a reputation for being frank and very honest in discussions, yet had no problem reneging on the many pacts that he and his representatives had signed. The following letter illustrates the enigma of the violently "anticommunist" Don Pepe. Less than two months before banning the Communist Party, Figueres sent this personal message to Professor Edelberto Torres, his friend from his days in exile in Mexico and co-conspirator in obtaining arms for the revolution and in the struggle against dictators.

> First of all I would like to clarify that I am not interested in maintaining power in Costa Rica, rather in the possibilities to help you

37. The following two anecdotes about Figueres and Fidel Castro are illustrative. In the late 1950s, Marcial Aguiluz, a member of the security forces and later an active member of the communist party, was sending arms to Huber Matos, one of Fidel's men in the Sierra. Marcial was at the airport loading a plane with government arms to send to Matos. Figueres arrives at the airport, sees Marcial, and asks him: "What the devil are you doing?" Marcial responds, "I am sending weapons to Fidel." Figueres looks at him for a moment, takes off his coat, and helps him load the plane (interview with Eduardo Mora Valverde, 16 December 1997, San José, Costa Rica). In 1959, Figueres went to Cuba to give a speech. He was interrupted by some Cubans for being too supportive of the United States. Figueres often used this speech as proof of his pro-American, anticommunist philosophy. After this speech, he was often consulted by American officials on attempts to kill or destroy Castro. Figueres would then telephone Fidel and pass on all the information (interview with Adolfo Chacón, 8 December 1997, San José, Costa Rica).

and the cause in whose name I have been supported. . . . In regards to the immediate assistance that you ask of me, I am sorry to admit that my government is weaker than it appears; the arms that you and Chendo obtained for me are those that maintain power, because what I found in the barracks is old and totally inadequate for any military campaign, even more so for a revolution in Nicaragua, where you would have to confront a well trained and prodigiously armed military. . . . Therefore, to proceed in the proper order, we should divide our plans in stages: The first should be, logically, the consolidation of my government, as without assuring the base that will be Costa Rica, a campaign in Nicaragua even if it is done with sufficient force would be overly exposed. . . . Meanwhile, I am gathering the necessary funds for two items: The first is to pay the Dominicans that helped us, who are essentially mercenaries. . . . Here, they come every day with rumors and intrigues of every sort, claiming rights that they have not acquired as I only have fundamental agreements with you, Don Rosendo, and Chendo. . . . Let me repeat, if I am in the presidency resisting pressures and sabotage of every type, it is only because I want to fulfill my pact with you (to use Costa Rica as base to overthrow Somoza) which when finished, I think I will retire as the only justification for this war is what is derived for the good of Nicaragua and Central America. Now I plead with you, for the benefit of our cause, that you and Rosendo adopt another tactic in certain things: let me explain. Last night in the home of Alex Murray Jr., Rosendo said to the U.S. military attaché Colonel Hughes, that the United States should rectify with actions their policies in Latin America. . . . He told him that the first step should be to terminate the Chamorro-Bryan Treaty, which was humiliating for all Central America and unbecoming for a country which called itself democratic as it was a reflection of the abuse by the strong of the weak. The Yankee, although brutal, is at its core a child that one should obligate to do what one wishes through deception. I have dealt with them often in business, and it is easy to do with them as you wish if guile is used. In politics I am using this tactic. I have no reason for opposing the Marxist philosophy . . . but I do not commit the stupidity of Manuel Mora of directly combating the Yankee and capitalism. I will achieve economic reforms more radical than Mora and all his

> party, and I will gain more battles against the Yankee imperialist in a brief time than these people have gained in twenty years, simply by means of the tactic. . . . You should appease all the politicians that could be useful to you, without showing them your true goals until after the triumph. . . . It is necessary to destroy the capitalist to destroy the reactionary. Our first great battle should consist of the liquidation of the capitalist forces in Central America, since these have been the most serious enemies of the Central American Union and have been the support of all of the dictators.[38]

Figueres made good on the claim to go further in changing the economy and attacking capitalism than Mora and the communists. Indeed, in one single day, the junta landed a greater blow to the oligarchy than Calderón and Picado did in eight years. On 19 June 1948, Figueres announced the nationalization of the banks and an extraordinary tax of 10 percent on all capital over 50,000 colones (about $8,000).[39] Of the 10 percent tax, Martz writes:

> For less prosperous citizens or small businessmen with a yearly income of less than ten thousand dollars, the levy meant nothing. The wealthy were hit hard by the law, however, for the 10 percent levy took a sizable chunk from even the most affluent businessmen. The tax went into effect in November, 1948. A month before another junta decree had announced drastic import restrictions. "Private" importations were forbidden, with future imports to be made through junta control. A 50 percent tax was declared on the c.i.f. value of luxury merchandise, and 30 percent on semi-luxury goods. New panic broke loose in business circles. Importers were dazed. (1959, 226)

While the tax decree caused panic and dismay, the nationalization of the banks was even more despised by the oligarchy. The banks served the

38. Evidently Figueres also used guile and deceit with Rosendo Argüello and Edelberto Torres. Argüello published this letter from Figueres to Torres in his scathing 1951 book, *Quiénes y Cómo nos Traicionaron* (*Who Betrayed Us and Why*, 126–30).

39. The decrees for bank nationalization and taxes were given a day after the junta suspended civil guarantees. Street manifestations, violence, and threats of counterrevolution were the purported reasons for the suspension (*La Nación*, 19 June 1948; Brenes 1990, 31), although the suspension may have been more for fear of a backlash to the new decrees. The suspension of individual rights was lifted on 16 July 1948 (*La Nación*, 17 July 1948).

interests of a very small sector of society, the agricultural and commercial elite; the Gini coefficient of credit likely approached 90 percent in the large private banks (*Proyecto Estado de la Nación*, 1995, 25). Jorge Rovira Mas, the noted Costa Rican sociologist, sums it up best:

> From our contemporary perspectives, it is difficult to appreciate the magnitude and significance of the bank nationalization in Costa Rica in 1948. The capitalists screamed to high heaven. They had reason to do so. In one swift stroke, nationalization of banking liquidated the political and economic power base of a major capitalist sector: finance capital. The government junta's action, possible only because of extraordinary power, with one blow banished the bankers—one of the most reactionary groups in the bourgeoisie—from the economic scene. . . . There were other repercussions. Nationalization lessened the economic power of other groups among the large capitalists, particularly the commercial-importer sector, heavily reliant on bank credit. From then on, loans were granted according to diverse new criteria, principally to the various sectors and economic activities the government hoped to stimulate. . . . The conscious intent of nationalization was to weaken, at its economic roots, the principal segments of the dominant class. (Rovira Mas 1989, 129)

In his speech announcing these radical new decrees, Figueres added insult to injury for the large landowners by proclaiming a 10 percent increase in the minimum wage for coffee and sugarcane laborers. Figueres and his allies were a new generation who envisioned a new Costa Rica with an activist state and a new division of the economic pie. Those poised to benefit were new bourgeois groups. It is not hard to imagine who would be opposed, even violently opposed, to this reorientation of the economy. "For the principal sector of the dominant class, rooted in the agroexport system dating from the previous century, this change meant a loss of supremacy and the unmistakable beginning of its disappearance as the primordial force in Costa Rican society" (Rovira Mas 1989, 129).

La Nación, the voice of the most conservative elements, had exhibited a cautious stance towards Figueres for the first two months of the ruling junta. After the decrees of 19 June, the gloves came off and the attacks were brutal. The brunt of the attack was aimed at Alberto Martén, the

Ministro de Economía y Comercio who developed the idea of the bank nationalization. *La Nación* exclaimed on 24 June that after the nationalization of the banks, "realized in less than the seven days that God needed in the Genesis, the voice of him that understands and even of the neophyte is of alarm, of panic." On 30 July, the newspaper announced that the nationalization was the ruin of the country and that an "exodus" of deposits had flowed out of the country. By 6 October, *La Nación* asked whether the Figueres-Martén economic plan should be characterized as "fascist corporatism" or "falangist syndicalism," and complained that with the new economic system the owner would be nothing more than another worker. Martén boldly responded to the challenge from the newspaper with a series of eight articles entitled "Political Democracy and Economic Democracy." The first article carried the openly threatening title "*El Capitalismo está Condenado a Muerte*" (Capitalism is condemned to die), in which the use of Marxist dialectic was transparent (*La Nación*, 7 July 1948): The thesis is capitalism; the antithesis is communism; and the synthesis is solidarity, which "consists of the nationalization of activities."

La Nación not only printed domestic attacks, but also sought to buttress its argument that Figueres, Martén, and Labor Minister Padre Núñez were socialist and dangerous by reproducing a series of remarks by former Undersecretary of State Sumner Welles. Welles was a respected hard-line voice on communism and Latin America who had served as the Latin American advisor of Secretary of State Charles Evans Hughes in the 1920s and who had extensive experience in Central America.[40] On 29 June 1948, just days after the controversial decrees, *La Nación* featured Welles attacking the Figueres government as dangerous. On 2 July, Foreign Relations Minister Benjamín Odio, the former and controversial director of the Civil Registry, responded directly to Welles's charge that "Nazis, fascists, and communists occupy key positions in the government of the Second Republic." *La Nación* of 5 October carried the front-page report of "Sumner Welles's New Attack on Costa Rica." According to the former diplomat, Guatemala, Venezuela, and Costa Rica "have assumed the right to overthrow the governments of Nicaragua, Honduras, and the Dominican Republic." He added the labels "dictator" and the "extreme left" to his former derogatory characterizations of Figueres.

40. "The Calderón problem would never be understood in the State Department as long as Sumner Welles was there. As long as Sumner Welles was in the State Department, the department was going to be Calderonista. When Sumner Welles left, it was a new era" (interview with Alberto Cañas Escalante, 12 December 1997, San José, Costa Rica).

The evidence is at odds with Yashar's conclusion that the elites in Costa Rica viewed Figueres's economic project as "bounded" and restricted to the decrees of June (1997, 218).[41] The junta continued to issue decrees that threatened old money (detailed in Rovira Mas 1988). On 4 November 1948, *La Nación* expressed the frustration of the ruling elite: "It is not a secret that Minister Martén counts with the unanimous opposition of commerce in the country, which has felt heavy on its shoulders a series of dispositions and tributes that each day are made more difficult to comply with." On 9 November, the headline was a plea for a return to pre-Figueres days and an interview with Manuel Francisco Jiménez, who clearly stated the panic of the dominant economic class: "Everyone expects a new surprise every morning, a new decree or law that can substantially modify the norms of work and initiative."

The fear of counterrevolution in this period was constant. Martén, in fact, argued in later years that one of his principal motivations for nationalizing the banks was to "take from the discontents the banks' resources for financing a counter-revolution" (quoted in Brenes 1990, 32).[42] Ulate

41. Yashar notes that a "weakened but politically incorporated elite proved auspicious for democracy. The junta achieved this balance in the context of factional divisions within the elite, rapid but bounded redistributive reforms, and signals that the elite would be allowed to assume political office and participate in policy debates. These last two elements were lacking when the prior reform coalition governed from 1942–1948" (1997, 220). This is a poor description of Costa Rica in the period 1948–49. The redistributive reforms were not seen as bounded and rapid, but rather like a slippery slope towards the ruin of the agro-export elites. The elites were completely unified against Figueres. The capitalist class was indeed divided, but the oligarchic capitalist families and big capital remained fiercely anti-Figueres and highly unified. "The group of capitalists that supported Figueres was very, very small. The support of some capitalists for Figueres arrived in the 1970s when they finally gave up the vision of overthrowing him: if you can't lick them, join them. They only did this because they saw that they could not sack him" (interview with Alberto Cañas Escalante, 12 December 1997, San José, Costa Rica.)

42. There are many explanations for why the junta nationalized the banks. After the war, of course, the government was desperately short of funds. A reading of the definitive work (Brenes 1990) leaves one with the strong impression that Martén and Figueres thought that monopolized capital had too strong an influence on investment decisions. Miguel Ruiz Herrera, who went to protest to Figueres when the decree was announced, told the author that Figueres told him that he did not care if the decree made economic sense or not, he wanted to wrest power away from the handful of dominant families that totally controlled capital (interview 3 December 1997, San José, Costa Rica). Figueres, who often had a sarcastic answer for important questions, once gave the following explanation: "I nationalized the banks in 1948 because a journalist, Isberto Montenegro, published on the front page of the *Diario de Costa Rica* an editorial which said that the junta didn't do anything. I had to demonstrate that we had lots of plans. Thus, it occurred to me to nationalize the public deposit" (quoted in Brenes 1990, 29).

used his newspaper, *Diario de Costa Rica,* to accuse Figueres of opening new wounds with his decrees and of endangering the country by openly plotting the overthrow of Somoza. "By September, several embassy officials warned that the situation presented 'dangerous possibilities'" (Longley 1997, 92).

In addition to headaches and threats from the *Calderonistas,* the communists, and the agro-export oligarchy, the Caribbean Pact was beginning to cause Figueres no shortage of trouble. Mercenaries and revolutionaries from throughout the region arrived in San José seeking money and arms from Figueres. The junta's "uninterrupted attempts to disrupt peace in the region by aiding the Nicaraguan exiles" upset many Costa Ricans and U.S. officials (Longley 1997, 102). Hundreds of revolutionary members of the Caribbean Legion were soon housed in the *Cuartel de la Artillería* in downtown San José and on fincas owned by Figueres. Ticos constantly complained of violence, drunkenness, and confrontations between these foreign soldiers and local soldiers. Minister of Security Edgar Cardona and other officials sent a letter to the junta asking for the immediate deportation of the mercenaries. One of those most infuriated with the armed foreigners in Costa Rica and the use of Costa Rican resources to invade other countries was Frank Marshall, the twenty-three-year-old war hero and *Jefe del Estado Mayor.* In June 1948, Marshall attempted a coup against the government that was quickly put down by Cardona; Marshall was forced to resign (Cardona 1992, 41–47; interview 20 December 1997, Moravia, Costa Rica).

By the early fall of 1948, less than six months after Figueres's smashing victory, the founding junta of the Second Republic was under siege. Conservatives and *Ulatistas,* communists and *Calderonistas,* certain U.S. officials, and a militarily superior neighbor named Anastasio Somoza all had Figueres in their sights.

Reports circulated of mysterious trips by Figueres to Guatemala (*La Nación,* 3 August 1948). Figueres was battling with the Dominican General Juan Rodríguez and other "officials" of the Caribbean Legion; Arévalo tried in vain to resolve the disagreements. For Figueres, the first priority was keeping the leftover weapons from the Civil War—which still belonged to the Dominican Rodríguez—as the junta was unable to purchase replacement arms. In November, Figueres announced the disbanding of the Caribbean Legion and tried to gently push them out of the county. The founding junta of the Second Republic gave General Rodríguez

$125,000 for the weapons lost or destroyed in the war and kept those that remained (Ameringer 1996, 86).

The Abolition of the Military

On 1 December 1948 José Figueres Ferrer, leader of the founding junta of the Second Republic of Costa Rica, took a sledgehammer to the walls of the massive Bella Vista military fort and announced the proscription of the Costa Rican military. The following year the military was constitutionally abolished. What were the antecedents of this act? Answers to this question are not as straightforward as they at first appear. Part of the problem in assessing these issues is that many scholars in Costa Rica who have written on the military are also active in partisan politics. For pro-Figueres scholars such as Cerdas A. and Vargas C. (1988) and Vargas A. (1993), Figueres was a visionary and his heroic act of demilitarization was transcendental for the country. For anti-Figueres scholars such as Urcuyo (1990), the military had slowly disappeared between 1900 and 1948 and the abolition of the military merely formalized the reality.[43] It is therefore useful to discuss the formal demilitarization process. I argue that, while it is true that the military was extremely weak in December 1948, the proscription of the armed forces as a permanent institution was transcendental for the country; it insulated Costa Rica against the military build-up that the United States oversaw in the region in the 1950s and 1960s (such as in demilitarized Bolivia). The comparison with Honduras in the following chapter makes this point clear.

The first half-century of Costa Rican independence (1821–70) witnessed instability, invasion from U.S. filibusters, internal and external war, and eleven successful *golpes de estado* (Obregón 1951). Military leaders tied through family and personal holdings to the coffee elite were the arbiters of power during much of this period, especially after the successful war in 1856–57 against William Walker. A pair of generals—Blanco and Salazar—allied to the Montealegre *cafeteleros*, called the shots from 1859 to 1869, after which they were unexpectedly forced to resign by President Jesús Jiménez. The Montealegres were unwilling to watch their political power disappear and in 1870 selected General Tomás Guardia to oust

43. See also Høivik and Aas (1981).

Jiménez after Blanco refused to head the coup (Salazar Mora 1990, 24). Guardia ruled the country for twelve years, breaking loose from the Montealegre family. Guardia built state power, abolished the death penalty, closed the congress, oversaw the creation of a liberal constitution, carried on an intense personal rivalry with Guatemalan President Barrios that nearly led to war, and greatly enhanced the power of the military as an institution. Guardia built a navy around the purchase of three battleships and during this time period Costa Rica was a military power on the Central American isthmus: Guardia even sent the battleships to discipline the military-less Hondurans (Funes 1995, 49). The 1870–90 period was the golden age of militarism in the country. Beginning in 1870, the military began to gain a sense of institutional purpose and autonomy. Guardia augmented the military budget, professionalized the army, opened military academies, issued a military code in 1871, and provided generous salaries to high-ranking and permanent military officials (Solís and González 1991, 71).

Scholars disagree sharply over the timing and reasons for the decline of militarization in Costa Rica. Fallas Barrantes (1984) and Umaña Aglietti (1978) both argue that there was a steady decline in the power of the military from the exit of Guardia in 1882 until the constitutional proscription in 1948. Umaña posits that with the disappearance of traditional external enemies, the military lost its purpose and simply wilted away (109–10). Fallas believes that the military decline was due to the transfer of military budgets to education (111). Both authors also support the cultural belief that Costa Ricans are antimilitary by nature.[44] Urcuyo also claims that the military slowly disappeared, starting at the end of the nineteenth century, and that the constitutional proscription in 1948–49 was in effect merely the coup de grace that put the institution out of its misery (1990, 239).

The best scholarship on the Costa Rican military quite convincingly disputes the claims of an early decline in the institution. Muñoz (1990) details, among other findings, that: (a) there is no linkage between declines in military spending and increases in education spending at the end of the nineteenth century; (b) the decline in military power is not as early as

44. Fallas states that Costa Ricans are idiosyncratic in being fierce enemies of anything that smells of militarism (111) and Umaña posits that in colonial Costa Rica there were no social classes and everyone was equal, which led to a unique antimilitary society (xiv). This of course does not hold up well to empirical evidence.

others believe, but rather begins after the Tinoco dictatorship and the war with Panama in 1921; and (c) the United States plays a key although indirect role in the unfolding demilitarization of Costa Rica and in the weakness of the institution before the 1948 Civil War by enacting an arms blockade against President Picado in the 1944–48 period. In 1995, Román published a new time series of Costa Rican central government finances for the 1870–1948 period, which unequivocally ends the debate. Costa Rican security expenditures did not fall dramatically either in total outlays or in percent of budget until after 1922. It was only thereafter that education spending regularly surpassed security expenditures (Román 1995, 81). The argument that declines in military budgets resulted in larger education budgets in pre-1920 Costa Rica is unsustainable.[45]

While Costa Rica's increase in education spending at the end of the nineteenth century was not a result of reductions in military budgets, the evidence does show that militarization during the Tinoco dictatorship led to massive education cuts. Between 1916 and 1919, the percent of national spending going to the military increased from 13.3 percent to 35.3 percent, while education spending plunged from 13.9 percent to 5.1 percent.[46]

The total permanent number of soldiers remained at 1,000 until 1918, when it rose dramatically to 5,000 (Muñoz 1990, 31, 104). In 1918, the Costa Rican armed forces had more permanent soldiers than the rest of Central America combined, according to Muñoz (1990, 167). By 1921, the number of soldiers had fallen suddenly and drastically to 500, which remained constant through 1940, when the total number of full-time soldiers was 544 (Muñoz 1990, 104). What accounts for the sudden increase in the number of soldiers in 1918 and the reversal in 1921? The key to understanding the decline in the military institution in Costa Rica is found in the political events from 1913 to 1919.

The Costa Rican elections of 1913 were significant in that they were the first direct elections; for the first time the voters would directly select the president. As in many other Latin American counties of the period, the electoral system suffered from the defect of requiring an absolute majority for a victory—if no candidate received an absolute majority then the congress would select the victor. This process often led to backroom deals,

45. This is an appealing—but in the end erroneous—argument made by many, including Fallas (1984), Físchel (1990), and Mahoney (2001, chapter 6).

46. It is no wonder that teachers led the local opposition to the Tinoco regime.

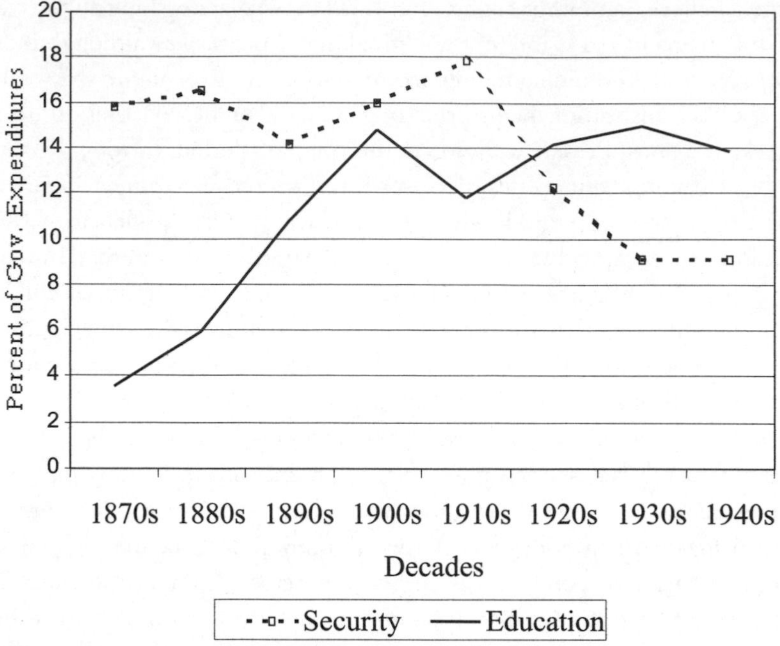

Fig. 4.1 Security versus education budgets by decade, 1870s–1940s

violence, and coups. The 1913 elections featured three candidates and the campaign was typical for Costa Rica, with "arguments by the candidates, insults, slanders, and complete disregard of principles and platforms" (Salazar Mora 1990, 232). Máximo Fernández of the Republican Party was the leading vote-getter in the 7 December balloting, with 42.1 percent or 27,094 votes. Due to infighting among the major parties, the congress was unable to select a president. The country continued without a president-elect through the end of April 1914. At that time, leading politicians and the military conspired to place Alfredo González, who had not even been a candidate, in the presidency. The military installations were placed at the command of Don Alfredo at midnight on 28 April and on 1 May the Legislative Assembly—at the end of a barrel—selected González to be the president effective 8 May 1914. The comedy of previous Costa Rican elections was now a farce, as the results of the first elections with direct ballots resulted in the selection of a president who did not receive a single vote.

President González's partner in this coup was Federico Tinoco, a politician and military officer who led the taking of the military installations by pro-González forces. In exchange, Tinoco was given the positions of minister of war and navy, commander of the San José commandancy, and chief of police. Alfredo González, who, unbeknownst to his patrons was a believer in greater state intervention, soon upset the coffee elite by proposing direct income taxes and taxes on uncultivated lands based on the principle that "the rich should pay as the rich and the poor should pay as the poor" (quoted in Salazar 1995, 49). A national investment bank for state investment was also proposed. These proposals challenged the nation's oligarchy for the first time in the country's history. The reaction was swift and firm. On 27 January 1917, Minister of War Federico Tinoco ousted President González in a military coup.

The reaction from the "democracy loving" Costa Ricans was pure jubilation. "Tinoco was a very popular man, supported by illustrious intellectuals, bankers, coffee growers, and the clergy. He was also able to obtain public support from the most prominent and respected politicians, including five ex-presidents" (Físchel 1992, 121). In addition, Tinoco had unwavering support from Minor Keith, founder and president of the United Fruit Company (UFCO), whose banana holdings controlled large tracts of the Costa Rican lowlands. Tinoco greatly increased military spending, increased the number of soldiers fivefold, employed a host of spies and thugs to ensure control, pushed through his own constitution, and was elected president. With political, public, business, and international support, it appeared that Costa Rica was well on the way to establishing a long-term military dictatorship.

International timing, however, did not favor Tinoco. Had his coup occurred ten years earlier or ten years later, his stay in office likely would have been a long one. His seizure of power unfortunately coincided with President Wilson's policy of nonrecognition for nonelected leaders in Central America. Despite Tinoco's bending over backward to satisfy Wilson, the U.S. president would not budge. As Murillo (1978, 1981) so clearly demonstrates, Tinoco supported U.S. foreign policy and declared on the side of the United States in World War I, held elections to legitimize his rule, and had the support of the Costa Rican elite and U.S. businesses in the country. Secretary of State Lansing strongly advocated the extension of recognition to Tinoco and sent his nephew, John Foster Dulles, on a fact-finding mission, which concluded that recognition should be granted. Nevertheless, Wilson was bull-headed and U.S. actions led to a severe recession in the country. Finally, in 1919, after two and one-half fruitless years of trying to gain recognition, Tinoco was forced out of power when the United States sent warships to both the Pacific and Caribbean coasts. Costa Rica's experiment with military dictatorship was over and, coupled with an embarrassing display by the military in a brief war with Panama in 1921, the military institution was completely discredited and lost influence in politics.[47] The demonstration effect was powerful. Military regimes bring problems and suffering.

Even with a shrunken military in the post-Tinoco period, it would be incorrect to characterize the Costa Rican army as uniquely small within the Central American context. The fact is that Central American nations all had very few permanent soldiers during this time period. Central American militaries never were in preparation for continental warfare and by the early twentieth century were largely internal repressive organs, which requires fewer soldiers. The large build-up of Central American militaries occurred during the Cold War. In 1922, when Costa Rica's number of soldiers was at an all time low, on a per capita basis Costa Rica's number of soldiers was very similar to the other, more populated Central American republics. The oddity was not Costa Rica but rather Honduras, which was the least militarized nation of Central America 1850–1950.

How is it possible that the Costa Ricans constitutionally abolished the

Table 4.2 Number of soldiers in army, circa 1922

Country	*Population*	*Soldiers*	*Soldiers per 1,000*
Costa Rica	430,000	300	.70
El Salvador	1,220,000	900	.74
Guatemala	1,370,000	1,000	.73
Honduras	770,000	300	.39
Nicaragua	650,000	500	.77

SOURCE: Muñoz 1990, 167; SALA 22, 67–72. Mahoney (2001, chap. 5) gives much higher numbers than Muñoz for El Salvador and Guatemala. Perhaps some of the discrepancy is in the difficulty in differentiating part-time reservists from full-time professionals (Costa Rica had 49,200 men in military militias in 1900, but only about 1,000 full-time soldiers [Muñoz 1990, 31, 104]). Schirmer argues that in "pre-1944 Guatemala, as in the rest of Central America, the military was a ragtag army" (1999, 10), a depiction seconded by Jonas (2000, chap. 1).

47. LaFeber (1984, 55–58) argues that Wilson refused to recognize Tinoco because Tinoco had signed an oil agreement with a British company. The fact that Secretary of State Lansing and other high-ranking officials advocated recognition calls LaFeber's assessment into question.

armed forces? After the Civil War of 1948 and the collapse of the government, the military was decimated. Why didn't Figueres rebuild a military with loyal forces?

There are many theories about the causes of the proscription of the armed forces. Figueres's supporters, such as Cerdas A. and Vargas C. (1988), present Figueres as a visionary who knew that militarization would stunt social development. However, in 1948 Figueres could not have predicted the shift in U.S. policy to support militarization in the region and the development of the Doctrine of National Security that would accompany the Cuban revolution in 1959. It is more likely that immediate political incentives led Figueres to abolish the armed forces. Figueres had several incentives. It is difficult to determine which of these factors influenced Figueres or in what combination. By December of 1948, Figueres faced the following challenges:

- Mercenaries and revolutionaries from throughout the Caribbean Basin participated in the Civil War of 1948 and hundreds of exiles flowed into the country immediately after the Figueres victory. The United States was extremely displeased with a large army of antidictatorial revolutionaries training in the country. Costa Rica's proximity to the Panama Canal added discomfort to the relationship, as the United States was unwilling to tolerate instability so close to this vital U.S. security interest (Muñoz 1990). Due to pacts with the revolutionaries, Figueres had a difficult time getting rid of them once his use for them was over.
- An election for the Constitutional Convention was scheduled for the first week of December 1948. Support for Figueres appeared to be weak.
- Counterrevolutionary forces were poised to invade the country from Nicaragua. Anastasio Somoza was Figueres's enemy and had the forces to easily defeat him.
- Figueres and his ruling junta had infuriated the conservative agro-export elite in the country with the nationalization of the banks and a 10 percent tax on assets of more than about US$8,000. They were also aware that the armed forces were often used as an ally of the oligarchy to reverse progressive policies, as they had in Costa Rica with the *golpe de estado* against Alfredo González in 1917. "If an army existed here, it would have dumped us. We predicted this. . . . The military could have been a force to unite the opposition. With a military, the calculus is completely different. For this reason, we were totally against the milita-

rization found in the rest of Central America" (interview with Gonzalo Facio Segrada, San José, Costa Rica, 1 December 1997).

With these serious threats to Figueres's regime and his social democratic program hovering over the country, the minister of security, Edgar Cardona, proposed a plan to abolish the armed forces. According to Cardona:

> I spoke to Figueres about the dissolution of the army. I could not speak publicly because it was not proper for an official of the armed forces. I told him, "Look, Mr. President, the press is attacking us and the minister of education for spending too much money on education; we should spend even more. We can tell them that it is necessary to spend money on education in the country and with the abolition of the army we can spend even more money on education. Let us abolish the military, for with a civil guard we have sufficient security. Figueres thought for a while, and he said yes, it seemed like a great idea. (Interview with Edgar Cardona, San José, Costa Rica, 20 December 1997)

Once Figueres had decided that abolishing the military was desirable, the actual act was simple, as the junta ruled by decree, the career military officers had been trounced and exiled during the Civil War, and there was no organized opposition to the idea. The *Book of Official Acts of the Founding Junta of the Second Republic* notes on 14 November 1948 that "The plan of the suppression of the army, presented by the Minister of Security, is authorized and accepted" (Cardona 1992, 49). On 1 December 1948, the decision to abolish the military was announced to the country in the ceremony at the Bella Vista. The speakers were Cardona, Minister of Education Gámez, and Figueres. This abolition became part of the constitution in 1949.[48]

While the formal proscription occurred in 1948, the actual demilitarization process was more gradual. After a coup in April 1949, the military disappeared rather quickly. Figueres clearly understood quite early the

48. In his speech Cardona stated that "there have been attacks on the Ministry of Public Education for having too large a budget. This is from every point of view unjust and demonstrates ignorance about the meaning of education for a people such as ours" (quoted in Cardona 1992, 52).

threats of a military caste. In order to safeguard against a military caste emerging in the police forces, the security forces had not been highly professionalized and Costa Rica had traditionally exhibited very high turnover in the security forces after elections. Figueres also appreciated the value of military superiority and kept a cache of weapons for several decades, just in case arms were deemed necessary to protect his project.[49]

The formal dissolution of the military served various political purposes. First, it gave Figueres the potential excuse to break his various pacts and promises and finally rid the country of the Nicaraguan, Dominican, and Honduran exiles who were living in the barracks, though all of the exiles were not asked to leave for several months. Second, there was hope that it would boost the Figueres forces in the December elections, which in the end was unsuccessful in that the Social Democrats were humiliated, winning only four out of thirty-four seats (*La Nación*, 10 December 1948 and 4 January 1949). Third, Figueres was able to portray the country as defenseless against the heavily armed Somoza. In the ensuing wars with Somoza-supported counterrevolutionaries, the "military-less" Costa Ricans were able to generate significant international support and intervention by the Organization of American States. Fourth and finally, the lack of an autonomous military institution left the conservative opposition without a means to overthrow the Figueres regime and reverse his political project.

Threats to the Ruling Junta

Calderón and his followers saw the dissolution of the military and the anti-Figueres vote as an opportunity. Somoza had been assisting the training and arming of a counterrevolutionary force for several months and a force of some three hundred invaded Costa Rica on 12 December 1948. The invasion was a disaster from the beginning. There was no surprise in the attack (*La Nación*, 11 December 1948). Figueres quickly rearmed the combatants from the Civil War and the six hundred members of the Caribbean

49. The levels of militarization of Costa Rica's police force (for years known as civil and rural guards) vary over time. During the Arias administration (1986–90), the formal use of rank was forbidden, police could not spend the night in the station, and officers wore uniforms designed by schoolchildren. Ranks returned under Calderón Fournier (1990–94) but have disappeared again under Rodríguez (1998–2002).

Legion still in the country (Longley 1997, 97) and the *Calderonistas* soon bogged down.

Calderón expected a mass uprising within Costa Rica to get rid of the "insensate" Don Pepe. After his defeat, he complained of being betrayed by "many people in San José, who had promised to rise up and join our forces as soon as the troops had crossed the border" (*La Nación*, 21 December 1948). Calderón miscalculated on several fronts. While he did have thousands of loyal supporters inside the country, local opponents to the regime were unlikely to put up a fight unless the invading force made significant headway and won some important battles. First, the Social Democrats' disastrous December election results gave many the hope that Figueres would soon be nothing more than a footnote in history. "Tacones" had no public support.[50] There was a chance that he would be gone in a matter of months without the need of war. And second, those who fought most valiantly in the war against Figueres, the communists, refused to support any plan that involved Somoza (interview with Eduardo Mora Valverde, 16 December 1997, San José, Costa Rica). Ulate, who had long given up any semblance of a pact with Figueres, demonstrated unity with the junta as soon as he realized that no internal uprising would occur. The junta took no chances either, quickly arresting *Calderonistas* (Longley 1997, 98).

On a separate front, Figueres immediately sought international assistance through the Organization of American States. The fact remained that Figueres could not defeat Calderón *and* Somoza's National Guard. On 14 December the Organization of American States (OAS) invoked the Rio Treaty's Article 6, which called for mutual defense in the case of the attack on a member nation.[51] An OAS commission rebuked both sides, charging that Somoza had assisted the invaders but also pointing a finger at Figueres for housing the Caribbean Legion. The fighting ceased and Figueres was pressured to finally get rid of the last of the Dominicans, Nicaraguans, and Hondurans.

The importance of this little war has often been ignored. The fact that the OAS would intervene quite rapidly and halt the fighting gave Figueres and his chief advisors confidence that they really could fully dissolve the

50. Figueres was very self-conscious about his physical stature and wore elevator heels to add a couple of inches to his 5 ft. 4 in. frame. *Tacones* (heels) was one of the nicknames that his enemies used in derision.

51. For more on the Rio Treaty, see Schoultz (1987, Chapter 5).

military and free ride on the United States.[52] They greatly feared a strong internal military as *the* force that the conservatives could use to halt their project and oust them from power; at the same time they faced a credible threat in Somoza. Article 6 of the Rio Treaty and the "test run" of the December 1948 invasion made the military-less state highly attractive. "I was convinced that a military was unnecessary because in those days I had greater faith that with the Inter American Treaty of Mutual Assistance of the OAS we could halt any invasion. It certainly saved us on two occasions. That treaty really helped us get through some very difficult years. . . . It was much riskier to have an army than to not have an army and rely on the OAS" (interview with Gonzalo Facio Segrada, 1 December 1997, San José, Costa Rica).[53]

The military, however, would have its swan song, an uprising on 2 April 1949 known as the *Cardonazo.* This was a very serious attempt that ended with nine dead and thirty wounded. The plotters controlled the majestic Bella Vista Fort, and gave a short list of demands that included a revocation of the bank nationalization and the 10 percent tax and a purge of the "leftist" ministers Martén and Núñez from the junta (*La Nación,* 2 April 1949). One of the grand old names in Costa Rican politics, General Jorge Volio, hurriedly sent a message to coup leader Cardona that he could send a large group of men to help overthrow Figueres if Cardona would merely provide them with arms.[54] "Volio did not request anything in exchange for the help. What he wanted, with all his heart, was to get rid of the governing junta and seek, perhaps, the possibility of a return to the past with Calderón Guardia and with Picado" (Villegas Hoffmeister 1986). Guillermo Villegas Hoffmeister investigated the *Cardonazo* for fifteen years

52. Urcuyo (1990, 8) confirms the idea that from the positive international reaction to invasion in December 1948, the Costa Ricans relied on the inter-American system for defense despite being surrounded by dictators who wanted to oust Figueres.

53. Gonzalo Facio was one of the closest advisors to Figueres and perhaps the closest of those still living. He was justice minister of the founding Junta, was the president of the congress in 1953, and has been foreign minister, ambassador to the United States, and ambassador to the United Nations. After his failure to secure the PLN's presidential nomination in 1978, he left the PLN and later served as ambassador to the United States under the Unity Party regime of Calderón Fournier, the son of Figueres's enemy, Calderón Guardia.

54. Jorge Volio Jiménez was a Catholic priest, soldier, philosopher, and university professor who had a propensity to use force to get his way. He was also vice president from 1924 to 1928 and served eleven years in the Legislative Assembly (Creedman 1991, 291–92).

and has concluded that the coup would have succeeded except that the young warrior Frank Marshall betrayed his friends and co-conspirators and saved Figueres (1986).[55] "If Marshall would have stayed with us, the whole thing [Figueres] would have ended right there and the history of Costa Rica would have been different" (interview with Miguel Ruiz Herrera, 3 December 1997, San José, Costa Rica).

There were many individuals involved in the attempted coup and perhaps more than one motive. The "straw that broke the camel's back" was Figueres denying a government position to a relative of León Cortés, *dejá vu* for Calderón's decision to pass over a Cortés for head of the congress, which contributed to the political crises of the 1940s (Cardona 1992, 70).[56] Max "Tuta" Cortés—who was one of the original seven to join Figueres's army, and who was the Costa Rican counsel in New York and the nephew of León Cortés—was appointed to be police chief by Cardona.[57] Figueres refused to allow the appointment and immediately thereafter the coup attempt occurred. It is hard to believe, however, that a group would attempt a coup merely over the naming of the police chief. There were many other more important reasons. Cardona denies that the "Tuta" affair was the major cause, instead charging that Padre Núñez, the labor minister, and Martén were leftists and too brash (1992, chapter 11; interview 20 December 1997). Villegas argues in the definitive study that the two principal reasons for the *Cardonazo* were the 10 percent tax and the perceived communism of Martén and Núñez (1986, 37–38).

Miguel Ruiz Herrera seems to have been the intellectual author of the *golpe*. Ruiz was from one of the elite families in the country; his father was honorary counsel for Portugal and a banker. Ruiz himself served as a director of intelligence for the Army of National Liberation but withdrew his support for Figueres over the nationalization of the banks and spent three decades trying to overthrow him. Ruiz is adamant that the coup

55. Miguel Ruiz explains that the reason for this betrayal was a falling out between Cardona and Marshall after an affair between Cardona and Marshall's sister (interview 3 December 1997).

56. The original break between Cortés and Calderón, and arguably an important component of the way the 1940s unfolded, came when Calderón sacked Cortés's relatives from the government payroll and refused to allow Otto Cortés to gain the presidency of the legislative assembly.

57. *La Nación* reports that "Tuta" Cortés had returned from New York because the communism of Padre Núñez was so extreme that he was known in the United States as "Manuel Mora with a frock" (11 May 1949).

occurred for one reason, the decrees targeting capital: We tried to overthrow Figueres precisely because "Figueres had nationalized the banks and they (the banking families) were very mad. He also imposed a 10 percent tax" (Interview with Ruiz, 3 December 1997, San José, Costa Rica). Figueres observed that "undoubtedly the military uprising was also stimulated by the disloyal campaign that certain oligarchic circles have been orchestrating against the governing junta, as a response and reprisal to our economic policy" (*La Nación*, 11 May 1949).

Brenes characterizes the *Cardonazo* as the first and most energetic of many attempts to restore economic power to the oligarchy. "Viewed within the big picture, this act (the *Cardonazo*) has profound consequences . . . they were delegates of the old capitalist sectors, although united with the social democrats during the juncture of 1948, they attempted to recuperate power in order to impose their own political project which obviously was opposed to the economic policy of the Junta" (1990, 68).

Luis Alberto Monge, who was a Figueres intimate in 1949 at age twenty-three and whose long career as diplomat, labor leader, and politician was capped with the presidency from 1982 to 1986, had this to say of the military and the *Cardonazo*:

> If there would have been a military here [in the 1950s], the opposition would have allied with it, as they did with Security Minister Cardona in 1949. The opposition was opposed to Padre Núñez and Alberto Martén. The first because he was labor minister and they thought he was a leftist and the second because he had written the decree to nationalize the banks. The reactionaries made contact with the military through individuals at the Union Club. . . . The opposition wanted to use these people to effect a *golpe de estado*. (Interview 8 December 1997, Pozos de Santa Ana, Costa Rica)

Between the attempted coup and the inauguration of Ulate in November 1949, tensions were reduced but still continued. Bombs occasionally went off. Figueres and Ulate continued to make threats and counterthreats. The participants in the *Cardonazo* were pardoned. The Constitutional Assembly rejected the Figueres-supported constitution calling for an activist state and instead settled on a revised version of the 1871 magna carta. There were some important changes. Women and blacks were given political rights. The legislative assembly was strengthened vis-à-vis the presidency. An enhanced Supreme Electoral Tribunal had more power and autonomy to oversee honest elections (see Gardner 1971; Wilson 1998).

Two constitutional details are particularly salient for our purposes. The first and most transcendental was the constitutional proscription of the armed forces: "The army is proscribed as a permanent institution. For the vigilance and conservation of public order there will be the necessary police forces."[58] In addition, the *fuero militar*, or a separate justice system for crimes committed by members of the security forces, was abolished (*La Nación*, 14 July 1949). The *fuero militar* continues to be a point of contention in other Latin American countries where members of the military are judged and punished—usually extremely mercifully—by their own for crimes such as murder, rape, and even attempted coups. The *fuero militar* has long undermined legitimacy of the justice system in Latin America and enhanced the autonomy and strength of the armed forces, often placing the military caste above the law.[59]

In October, elections were held to choose deputies for the legislative assembly to serve with Ulate. Again, the Social Democrats performed miserably, gaining only three seats. The citizens of Costa Rica and U.S. officials let out a massive sigh of relief when the unpredictable and brash Don Pepe turned over power to Ulate. The most difficult moments, however, were yet to come. Figueres "returned to power in 1953 with more radical policies that tested the United States in a period characterized by heightened problems with a correlation between communism and nationalism. Nevertheless, the country would receive a brief respite from the upheavals of the preceding decade during the four years of Ulate's presidency" (Longley 1997, 108). The fact that the military was proscribed, weak, and nondeliberative contributed to the survival of Figueres in future years and the ultimate consolidation of democracy in the country.

The Ulate Presidency and the Elections, 1949–1953

In the four years of his presidency, Ulate "accomplished no major innovations" (Longley 1997, 111). Ulate was popular and conservative and

58. *Constitution*, Title 1, Article 12.

59. Like the abolition of the military, the termination of the *fuero militar* did not become institutionalized immediately. In 1952 a crisis developed; President Ulate resigned after the Legislative Assembly investigated an incident in which the police attacked and beat members of the *Unión Cívica Revolucionaria* party. Ulate and the police thought the

brought a sense of stability to the country. The newspaperman was an old-style Liberal whose connection with the most conservative forces in the country was solidified in 1917 when he organized street *fiestas* in San José to celebrate the military coup and the overthrow of progressive president Alfredo González (Brenes 1990, 96). During Ulate's four years, two private banks were established and "Figueres's pet scheme, the 10 percent capital levy, was ignored" (Martz 1959, 233).

During these four years, Figueres and his supporters were busy trying to regroup from their two electoral disasters. In 1951, the National Liberation Party (PLN) replaced the Social Democrat Party as Figueres's electoral vehicle. The PLN was a programmatic party with a very specific platform and was soon organized throughout the country. The party supported strong state intervention to spread economic benefits and to curtail the power of foreign capital. The party also supported the replacement of dictatorial governments with democracies and the enhanced authority of the OAS (see Kantor 1958, 44–48).

Figueres knew that he must also develop support within the United States and he spent a great deal of time traveling and giving speeches. Don Pepe had spent some years in Boston in his youth, read the *New York Times* daily, had an American wife, and could quote Jefferson and Locke. He could charm many U.S. officials but with his blunt talk could cause others to bristle. Figueres ended up with strong supporters: "To those Americans who believe in José Figueres, and they are legions, he is the Blessed Trinity" (Bonilla 1975, xxvii). Figueres developed allies in the U.S. Senate, in the American Federation of Labor (AFL), with the important liberal group Americans for Democratic Action (ADA), and with some members of the State Department. Some officials in the CIA and the State Department, however, were highly dubious.[60] Figueres's speeches and writings could often be interpreted as anti-American and anticapitalist. At Grinnell College in 1952 he announced that "We do not want foreign investment. Foreign investment in an important sector of the economy or of the territory of a country constitutes economic occupation. This is not a fantasy. I

matter should only be investigated by the security forces. After a couple of weeks, Ulate returned to office after the Assembly's investigation cleared the police commanders (Martz 1959, 237).

60. I am grateful to Mitchell Seligson for pointing out that the relationship between Figueres and the CIA is somewhat unclear. There is evidence that he collaborated with the CIA in anticommunist activities, although with Figueres one never knows how many sides and angles he was playing at any given time.

know of what I am speaking. I am a citizen of a banana republic" (quoted in Vargas Araya 1993, 137–38). Figueres also raised a few eyebrows when he criticized U.S. foreign policy: "Militarism and graft are perfectly acceptable to the U.S. in our relationships with you as long as your men in power pay lip service to our side in the world struggle and see to it that foreign investments are properly respected" (quoted in Longley 1997, 120). By 1951, Rosendo "Chendo" Argüello had concluded that Figueres had used the Caribbean Pact for his own purposes and turned against Don Pepe, publishing a blistering attack that included the letter from Figueres to Professor Torres (above). The UFCO expressed concerns over Figueres after he stated in a 1952 public interview that long-term contracts could be broken if doing so served the interests of the country (Longley 1997, 126). The State Department Office of Intelligence assessed the "probable position of José Figueres" in August 1953. "Figueres will not voluntarily become a communist puppet, but his nationalist program is, in some ways, similar to that in Guatemala and for that reason, communist capacity in Costa Rica will possibly grow. . . . The probability of a confrontation with the new president of Costa Rica will be constant as he always fights to augment the negotiation power of the small undeveloped countries vis-à-vis the large country manufacturers" (quoted in Vargas Araya 1993, 139).

Despite the meager showing of the Social Democrats at the polls and the ascendancy of Ulate to the presidency, many of the country's elites viewed Figueres as a continual threat. Indeed, Don Pepe looked so bad that Calderón no longer looked like an enemy, but a potential ally. As early as January 1950, a movement began "to unite Ulatistas and Calderonistas against Pepe Figueres" (*La Nación*, 11 January 1950). Alejandro Aguilar Machado, who had served as secretary of state under many different governments and represented some of the most conservative forces, publicly asked for a united front of Calderonism and Ulatism as the only way to destroy Figuerism (*La Nación*, 11 January 1950). By February, representatives of Ulate were meeting with ex-President Picado in Nicaragua (*La Nación*, 23 February 1950). The rivalry between Ulate and Picado and Calderón was still heated and a true united front would not be forged until after Figueres regained the presidency in 1953.

The elections of 1953 initially focused on three candidates, but then shifted to only two. Mario Echandi, the right hand of Ulate for many years, withdrew for reasons that are not altogether clear. This left a two-man race, Don Pepe with the organized PLN and Fernando Castro Cervantes of the *Partido Demócrata* (PD). Castro was a wealthy landowner and businessman who based his entire campaign on smears and attacks on Figueres; he was closely linked to reactionary elements and not opposed to using violence to take power. Castro had financed and planned the failed uprising in 1946 known as the *Almaticazo.* It is hard to imagine an election so divided along class lines. "Business interests were almost entirely behind Castro. They feared Figueres would launch a 'soak the rich' program to finance his development plans, and his avowed interest in socialist doctrine was another source of concern" (Martz 1959, 240). In contrast, the PLN laid out a specific program of improved education and living standards for the poor, government programs to improve housing and health care, rising wages, control of foreign investment, and support of democracy throughout the Caribbean Basin.

Conservative elements outside of Costa Rica viewed the strong-running Figueres as a communist and a threat to regional stability. U.S. officials in Nicaragua strongly supported Somoza and made charges to the State Department that Figueres was a leftist. In March 1953, Adolph A. Berle Jr. was sent by the State Department to Nicaragua to learn of the charges and then to Costa Rica to assess Figueres. Berle concluded that Figueres was exactly the type of leader that Central America needed and he ridiculed the U.S. officials in Managua for their lack of professionalism and inability to even speak Spanish. Berle, one of the most influential men in Washington, became a close friend of Figueres and a staunch supporter—one that Figueres would later need to survive. Berle introduced Figueres to other important intellectuals such as Arthur Schlesinger Jr., Adlai Stevenson, and Dean Rusk (Longley 1997, 122–23).

Castro's trump card was communism, and he tried furiously to make the charge stick to Figueres. This onslaught began in earnest in March 1953, some three months before the elections. Looking back from today, Castro's attacks seem juvenile and ridiculous. Yet this was the height of the Cold War and these types of attacks were not altogether unsuccessful at the time, even in the United States with McCarthyism. In the six months leading up to the election, Castro and *La Nación* called Figueres a liar, a thief, an assassin, a Marxist-Leninist, and uninformed about soccer. A sampling of the Castro campaign tactics in *La Nación* includes:

- Death of Stalin, the colleague and supporter of Figueres (7 March 1953)
- Democrat Party ready to take up arms to defeat Figueres (10 March 1953)[61]
- Reprinting of the letter from Figueres to Professor Torres, in which Figueres admits to liking Marxist philosophy and to deceiving the United States (11 March 1953)
- Reprints an article detailing the ten points needed to identify a communist and shows how Figueres meets all ten (9 April 1953)
- Claims that since Figueres is a Marxist, he is the enemy of the Catholic Church and of the Costa Rican woman (30 April 1953)
- Figueres is a communist and the proof is that he did things (10 percent tax and bank nationalization) that Manuel Mora would never even propose (16 May 1953)

It is interesting that for all his charges that Figueres was communist, it was Castro who made a pact with the still-underground communists to get their votes (Kantor 1958, 38). Despite the fact that Castro Cervantes was reactionary and Manuel Mora had publicly supported the bank nationalization and the 10 percent tax (*La Nación*, 17 February 1949), the communists agreed to vote for the *Partido Demócrata*.[62] Enthusiasm for Castro among the communists was low, however, and many of them simply refused to vote. Turnout was low considering the fact that women were enfranchised for the first time. Figueres won 121,509 votes compared to 66,874 for Castro (Kantor 1958, 64). Luis Alberto Monge, PLN official and president of Costa Rica from 1982 to 1986, summarizes the 1953 elections:

> I don't believe that there was fraud or irregularities in 1953 that could have altered the results of the elections. What did exist, and we showed it in studies, is the great abstention of *Calderonismo*. *Calderonismo* did not show up to vote. And they did not like the

61. Both sides claimed that the other was purchasing weapons and preparing to use violence to gain power. The PLN's *La República* (16 April 1953), for example, charged that Castro loyalists were training on the *finca* "El Coyolar." *La Nación* charged that the Caribbean Legion was preparing to use force to give Figueres the presidency (6 May 1953).

62. When I questioned Eduardo Mora Valverde about this bizarre agreement, he responded: "We voted for Castro Cervantes because we reached an agreement with him. He promised us certain things. To vote for Figueres would be to vote for those that had just murdered our *compañeros*. Besides, Castro Cervantes did not have a chance of winning. The only one that could win was Figueres. To vote for Castro Cervantes was to reduce the votes of Figueres" (Interview 16 December 1997).

> candidate that Dr. Calderón wrote that he supported, Señor Fernando Castro Cervantes. Fernando Castro Cervantes was the most authentic representative possible of the Costa Rican *latifundia* [large estates], and the most conservative. (Interview 8 December 1997, Pozos de Santa Ana, Costa Rica)

To nobody's surprise, with their defeat the Castro camp immediately cried foul. The first evidence pointing to fraud and one that would be mentioned for years was the "jeep incident." "The election was certainly not completely free. In fact, a jeep wrecked on the road to Puntarenas a few days before the elections. Spilled in the crash was an already sealed ballot box containing five thousand ballots, almost all for Figueres. Such shenanigans indicate that the election was far from honest and above board" (Martz 1959, 254). The Democrat Party analyzed 59,944 ballots and found 14,000 were fraudulent. Lightly veiled threats were made by anti-Figueristas such as Congressman Venegas Mora: "I believe that we are again approaching cloudy days for the tranquillity of Costa Rica" (*La Nación*, 14 October 1953). While the extent of fraud or irregularities was probably not enough to have changed the outcome, the opposition believed that Figueres wanted power and would resort to fraud and irregularities if needed to maintain power.[63] *La Nación* (16 October 1953) reprinted some of the important speeches from the Legislative Assembly, which included: "A political party can do nothing when the electoral organisms are co-opted by one group. I believe that Don Otilio Ulate had more electoral guarantees in front of Calderón than the anti-Figueristas in the previous election." *La Nación* also published the "Manifesto of the National Independent Republican Party," the current party vehicle of still-exiled Calderón Guardia. The manifesto praised Calderón and blasted the recent elections as a fraud and a *golpe de estado*.

The Crisis for Figueres, 1953–1958

José Figueres Ferrer, a political unknown just a decade earlier, now came to power in a special 4.5-year term, with an overwhelming electoral man-

63. Gonzalo Facio Segrada, who was a founder of the PLN, a major in the war, president of the Legislative Assembly (1953–58), and diplomat, admitted that "Yes, there were problems in this election. . . . Liberation would have won no matter what, the irregularities would not have made a difference. But yes, there were voting irregularities that were the result of us creating a new, completely different system of voting and not because we were

date, a well-organized party, and two-thirds of the deputies in the Legislative Assembly (thirty of forty-five seats). "On that day, 8 November 1953, the stormiest and most controversial figure in contemporary Central American politics assumed power" (Martz 1959, 241). Figueres already had serious enemies, both domestic and international. Thousands of *Calderonistas* and communists detested Figueres both for the war and for the atrocities, exiles, and seizure of property after the Civil War. The business elite considered Figueres a socialist and feared creeping statism and new measures that would reduce their share of the economic pie. Pérez Jiménez in Venezuela, Somoza in Nicaragua, and Trujillo in the Dominican Republic all vowed to destroy him and were all much better armed. And powerful elements within the United States, particularly in the CIA, viewed Don Pepe as a deceitful and dangerous leftist.[64]

In this section, I will show how events in the 1953–55 period strengthened the opposition to Figueres. By 1954, all of the leading voices in Costa Rican politics—Calderón, Picado, Ulate, Echandi, the communists, and Castro Cervantes—reached the conclusion that force must be used to oust Figueres. There was no elite pact for democracy. Costa Rican culture did not inhibit a violent uprising. Institutions did not channel preferences towards support of ballots over bullets. Figueres was able to survive for one reason—without a military the opposition did not have the means to overthrow him. To illustrate the crisis that Costa Rica experienced in these years and the causal mechanism between militarization and democracy, events will be analyzed in chronological order.

If anyone thought that Figueres would be a more moderate and cautious president than leader of the junta, they were quickly disappointed. One month after taking office, Figueres sent a letter to U.S. Ambassador Robert Hill calling for a new contract with the UFCO: "In addition, my government considers that the contracts that the United Fruit Company operates under in Costa Rica are a vestige of colonialism employed by other countries in past epochs" (*La Nación*, 23 December 1953). The UFCO argued that they had a contract that was valid for another twenty years and sought assistance from the State Department. Figueres was mas-

---

intentionally planning to carry them out" (interview, 1 December 1997, San José, Costa Rica).

64. In 1955, conservative American columnist Robert Johnson stated what many conservatives in the United States thought: "Pinkos sound the same in any language. Communism thrives in Figueres" (quoted in Longley 1997, 128).

terful at keeping the Americans off guard and in promoting his nationalism as better than what Arbenz was offering in Guatemala. For all the conservative U.S. congressmen and diplomats who charged Figueres with being a leftist and a threat, there were other groups in the State Department, the Senate, in labor, and in academia that strongly supported Don Pepe (see Longley 1997, 131–36). In the end, Figueres won the battle against the UFCO. In June 1954, a new contract was signed that gave Costa Rica nearly 50 percent of all profits from the powerful multinational (*La Nación*, 5 June 1954).[65]

Upon taking power, Figueres also sent a clear message to wealthy Costa Ricans: They would be expected to share their wealth with the many less fortunate who voted for the PLN (*La Nación*, 8 November 1953). By March 1954, the PLN economic plan was clear—high tariffs, higher wages, and state-directed industrial expansion. In May 1954, agricultural workers sent a letter to the Labor Ministry decrying minimum wages in the agricultural sector as "an excess of socialism" (*La Nación*, 13 May 1954). The opposition deputies in the Legislative Assembly, led by Mario Echandi, and the commercial elite were strongly opposed to such measures (*La Nación*, 10 March 1954). Accusations that Figueres was a closet socialist and was planning dangerous military adventures against Somoza and Trujillo were ubiquitous in San José.

Of all his audacious political actions, Figueres's decision to boycott the Caracas Conference of the OAS was probably the most ill advised. Secretary of State John Foster Dulles called the meeting to condemn communism in general and Arbenz in particular. Figueres immediately refused to attend because the Pérez regime in Venezuela was dictatorial and a number of political prisoners were in jail. Adolph Berle, former Ambassador Davis, and then U.S. ambassador to Costa Rica Robert C. Hill all pressured Figueres to attend. Figueres was firm even when members of his own cabinet pleaded with him to reconsider, as this would be ammunition for those who already charged Don Pepe with being soft on communism. Costa Rica was the only no-show at the Caracas Conference and Dulles

65. The invasion of Castillo Armas to overthrow Arbenz began less than two weeks later. I believe it is highly likely that Figueres and his high taxes were palatable to the UFCO and the United States only because the expropriation of Arbenz was seen as the alternative. Costa Rican historian Victor Hugo Acuña told me that Figueres was the Martin Luther King who was only tolerable because of the more threatening Arbenz, who was likened to Malcolm X.

was furious. Ambassador Hill called Figueres a "chameleon" and used the Professor Torres letter to argue that Figueres was trying to fool the United States and establish a leftist government in Costa Rica (Longley 1997, 137). On 1 March 1954, the *Miami Herald* reported from Caracas that Figueres had provided a victory to the communists and that the senior observers of the region suspected that the regime of President Figueres was pro-red, pro-Russian, and opposed to cooperation in the hemisphere (reprinted in *La Nación*, 4 March 1954). The enmity between the Dulles brothers and Figueres was now cemented.

> We knew that we had a permanent enemy in John Foster Dulles. And we knew that Foster Dulles was a friend of Pérez Jiménez, a friend of Somoza, and friend of Batista, and a friend of Trujillo. (Interview with Alberto Cañas Escalante, 12 December 1997, San José, Costa Rica)

> Everyone associated with the Dulles brothers and with the CIA was hostile to Figueres. And they believed that they could liquidate Figueres. (Interview with Luis Alberto Monge, 8 November 1997, Pozos de Santa Ana, Costa Rica)

The heated rivalry between Ulate and Figueres turned into open warfare in May and June 1954. The 1949 constitution stated that a president must wait eight years to run for an additional term.[66] During his tenure as president, Ulate held a successful plebiscite to change the wait to four years, which would mean that Ulate could run again in 1958. However, in May 1954 the PLN-controlled Legislative Assembly voted against the measure and the constitutional change was rejected. Ulate supporters rioted in the streets and violence erupted in the Legislative Assembly. The public spat between Figueres and Ulate was intense. Figueres gave a speech after the riots and proclaimed that "I am tired of saving Ulate" (*La Nación*, 3 June 1954). Ulate countered, in a bold front page story headlined "Figueres and Mora are closer each day," that Figueres "wanted the communists to collaborate in his government" and read letters from communist leader Manuel Mora that the only difference between Mora and Figueres was that Figueres liked to do things faster. In addition, Ulate

66. The Constitution was later amended to prohibit any second term for the president.

charged that Figueres was dangerous and would lead Costa Rica into war and destruction: "the ambitious Señor Figueres sees himself as Simón Bolívar" (*La Nación*, 3 June 1954). The opposition saw the congressional action as a blatant attempt to eliminate the most popular opposition candidate in the next election and as more evidence that the PLN would use whatever tactic possible to maintain power. From this moment on, Ulate worked tirelessly to enlist domestic and international support to oust Figueres via his two newspapers and trips to the U.S. to meet with John Dulles and U.S. newspaper editors. "There was a great crisis when Ulate wanted us to change the constitution. But Figueres knew how to handle the situation; and there were no military and colonels to deal with" (interview with Alberto Cañas Escalante, 12 December 1997, San José, Costa Rica). "Ulate was going to Nixon and the *New York Times* and Dulles and whoever would listen and tell them that Figueres and Liberation were communists. Yes. This was a very violent period. And it fell to me to preside over a Legislative Assembly that was very violent. . . . This whole period can only be qualified as extremely violent" (interview with Gonzalo Facio Segrada, 1 December 1997, San José, Costa Rica).

Like water torture, PLN legislation continually battered the wealthiest sectors in the country. In June 1954, a new corporate tax of 30 percent for profits over 250,000 colones was passed. The ninety largest companies in the country would see their taxes increase from 5 million colones a year to 14.5 million colones a year (*La Nación*, 13 June 1954). The response from the mouthpiece of the oligarchy was predictable: it is "unacceptable, as it is unjust and contrary to all that is convenient for the nation, that they fall in the error of blocking the productive sources of national wealth. . . . This leaves the impression that there exists a hostile sentiment and an eagerness to persecute private capital" (*La Nación*, 13 June 1954). Added to additional banana taxes and new tariffs, the government was now sucking an additional 53 million colones from capital: "Private initiative is over if businessmen go to work only to benefit the state" (*La Nación*, 13 June 1954).

Within Costa Rica, 18 June 1954 was a day of fear for many and a day of hope for others. The U.S.-supported invasion to topple the elected progressive president of Guatemala, Jacobo Arbenz, had begun. For Figueristas, there was fear that Somoza, the Dulles brothers, and the opposition would try the same action in Costa Rica. For the enemies of Figueres, there was growing confidence that Figueres's days were numbered. The

CIA-inspired invasion of Guatemala is one of the sorriest chapters of U.S. actions in the Caribbean Basin. Many Central Americans still clearly remember the event and the day as clearly as many Americans remember the assassination of President Kennedy. Costa Rican sociologist Manuel Rojas Bolaños recalls the day Arbenz fell. He was in typing class. In those days a horn went off if there was an important announcement coming over the radio. The horn sounded and the typing teacher went to find out the news. He came back and gleefully announced that Arbenz had fallen: "They got one communist. Now it is Figueres's turn!" (interview, 13 October 1997).

In fact, preparations to oust Figueres were soon underway. On 19 June 1954, one day after Castillo Armas invaded Guatemala, *La Nación* reprinted a wire service map of Central America that carried a short blurb in English on each country. The blurb for Costa Rica was: "José Figueres's government is puzzling. To some he is an anticommunist leftist, trying to improve living conditions. Others say he is more of a communist than anyone in Central America." The conservative newspaper misleadingly translated only one side of the story: "the president of Costa Rica, José Figueres, has been accused of being more communist than any other person in Central America." Venezuela's Pérez Jiménez, still smarting over Costa Rica's snub at the OAS conference, sent planes to San José that dropped leaflets with a caricature of Figueres and the Venezuelan progressive Betancourt as homosexuals (*La Nación*, 23 June 1954). In a threat to the government, *La Nación* reported that 250 Costa Ricans participated with Castillo Armas in Guatemala, including known *Calderonistas* such as Rodolfo Quirós Quirós and Mariano Fournier (1 July 1954).

In the latter half of 1954, all the newspapers of Costa Rica were full of reports of planned rebellions, charges of communism, anger on the part of the business elites, plans by the government to try to get weapons, and accusations between Figueres and Somoza. On 17 July, Fernando Castro Cervantes warned of an upcoming civil war and begged the still-fractured opposition to unite forces to destroy Figueres: "I am a political enemy of Señor Figueres" (*La Nación*). No one was fanning the flames any more than Ulate himself, whose newspapers gave constant warnings of invasions and war (*La Nación*, 18 July 1954). Everyone, including the communists, knew that "Echandi, Castro Cervantes, Ulate, and Calderón were conspiring to use force to overthrow Figueres" (interview with Eduardo Mora Valverde, 16 December 1997, San José, Costa Rica).

At the end of July, a group of twenty armed men assaulted the telegraph office in the northern town of Sarapiquí and took a pair of hostages. Government forces arrived and gave battle, and the rebels escaped into Nicaragua (*La Nación*, 24 and 27 July 1954). The crisis was so deep that calls were made for Figueres to resign. Ulate admitted with feigned shame that he always knew deep down that Figueres was a communist sympathizer, now willing to call together a Junta of Notables to solve the country's many problems (*La Nación*, 30 and 31 July 1954). As usual, the bank nationalization was employed to verify the leftist tendencies of the government: "Only Russia and Costa Rica have a nationalized bank. . . . The idea of a bank at the service of the socialist super-state comes from Karl Marx" (*La Nación*, 11 September 1954).

Mario Echandi, the leader of the opposition in the Legislative Assembly, joined Ulate and Castro Cervantes in predicting that Figueres was losing control of the country "before a fiscal voracity without limits, before an avalanche of taxes that choke the people" (*La Nación*, 1 October 1954). In fact, Echandi had joined Calderón, Castro Cervantes, and Ulate in "asking for direct support from Castillo Armas in Guatemala to take out Figueres" (interview with Gonzalo Facio, 1 December 1997, San José, Costa Rica).

The month of November 1954 began with headlines that high officials in the government of Costa Rica had been implicated in a plot to assassinate Picado (*La Nación*, 3 November 1954). The hatred for Figueres and the desire of the major players to overthrow him helped to unite the once factionalized opposition. Castro Cervantes had been meeting with Calderón and a headline announced what was once thought impossible: "ULATE ALLIES WITH CALDERON GUARDIA" (*La Nación*, 16 and 19 November 1954). Ulate made this new alliance public in Washington, D.C., announcing that he had no other choice to combat the tyranny that ruled in Costa Rica. It is clear that Picado, Calderón, Echandi, Castro Cervantes, and Ulate were in agreement that nondemocratic means should be employed to get rid of *Tacones* and save the country from socialism.

The government was certainly aware of the thickened plot. In a Figueres speech, the president admitted that "the government knows perfectly well that confabulations of four or five groups that are disputing for power are thinking to take power through an assault on the Costa Rican institutions" (*La Nación*, 19 November 1954). Figueres mentioned that the government had detained Miguel Ruiz Herrera at the airport because they knew that he was the intermediary between the revolutionary groups. This is the same Miguel Ruiz who was director of intelligence for the Army of National Liberation, who turned on Figueres after the bank nationalization, who masterminded the Cardonazo, and who now paints and writes poetry. The government later disclosed that some four hundred Ticos had fled into Nicaragua to join the revolutionary movement (*La Nación*, 23 November 1954).

Ulate and Figueres were both waging a tireless battle to gain the support of the United States in the now-unavoidable counterrevolution. Figueres sent the leader of the Legislative Assembly, Gonzalo Facio, to Washington and New York to lobby for support. "Many people feared an invasion with U.S. support. . . . I renounced the presidency of the Legislative Assembly to become ambassador to Washington, as I had various contacts. The United States did not have great sympathy for us" (interview, 1 December 1997). Ulate went himself to lobby the United States to restrict arms from going to Figueres and provided the following statement to the wire services: "In order to reveal the communist affiliation of Señor Figueres I will soon turn over to the appropriate authorized international organization the proof of the identity and ideas that President Figueres shares with Marxist philosophy, including an unpublished article written by a North American woman journalist who visited my country at the end of 1953, and to whom Figueres declared that an invasion by the Soviet Union of Alaska would be healthy because it would galvanize the American continent" (*La Nación*, 27 November 1954).

As tensions were building in Costa Rica, some three hundred to five hundred Costa Rican counterrevolutionaries were training in Nicaragua.[67] The United States' role in the training and preparation of the rebel forces is not fully known. The United States Ambassador to Nicaragua, Tom Whelan, toured the rebel training area in Coyutepe and reviewed the troops that were preparing to invade Costa Rica (Ameringer 1989, 238). Whelan was a close friend of Somoza and Sumner Welles and sympathetic to the Calderón cause (Acuña 1977, 35). Costa Rican authors claim that the CIA was actively involved in preparing the invasion; they termed the invasion against Guatemala "Plan G" and that against Figueres "Plan C" (Acuña 1977, 39; Vargas Araya 1993, 140–43). Longley (1997, 145–46)

67. Note that this is a much larger force than the one that accompanied Castillo Armas (see Gleijeses 1991).

points out that greater access to CIA files is needed to determine the extent to which the CIA was involved in assisting the rebels, but that it is clear that the CIA had at least prior knowledge of the attack and the insurgents' plans. Ameringer adds that

> [Figueres] accused the CIA of aiding Somoza in the attack upon Costa Rica in repayment for his support of the CIA-sponsored invasion of Guatemala. "The same North American mercenary aviators who took part in the attack upon Guatemala," Figueres asserted, "later came from Nicaragua and machine gunned eleven defenseless towns in our territory." Figueres was referring especially to Jerry DeLarm, a North American adventurer, who flew for Castillo Armas and the CIA and who was related to Calderón by marriage. This charge presents a paradox of U.S. policy, with its covert side trying to topple Figueres, and its overt side rescuing him. (Ameringer 1989, 238–39)

What is quite clear is that on 11 January 1955, Miguel Ruiz Herrera, Carlos Tinoco Castro, and various others started the war by capturing the small Costa Rican city of Ciudad Quesada. The next day the other rebels invaded from Nicaragua (*La Nación*, 12 and 13 January 1955).[68] Figueres had used a very successful propaganda ploy since 1954—a well-armed dictatorship against a defenseless democracy. Somoza had just purchased twenty-five P-51 Mustangs from Sweden and was in a position to annihilate Costa Rica (Martz 1959, 193). The key for Costa Rica was invoking the nonaggression pact of the Rio Treaty that required the conflict to be characterized as an aggression of one country against another. Both sides knew that. The opposition tried to demonstrate with the seizure of Ciudad Quesada that this was an internal affair. Figueres and his lobbyists tried fiercely to portray the war as an invasion from Nicaragua. Costa Rica immediately asked for intervention from the OAS and combat airplanes for self-defense (*La Nación*, 16 January 1955). The OAS sided with Costa Rica, invoked the Rio Treaty, and requested that the United States provide four P-51s for Costa Rica, which the United States sold for $1 each to the beleaguered country. Commercial pilots were given a crash-course in flying the prop-driven warplanes and by January 17, army-less Costa Rica

68. The definitive study of the 1955 revolution is Acuña (1977).

had an air force flying sorties against the aggressors. "The new aerial presence was pivotal, and within a week the rebel pilots surrendered to Nicaraguan officials" (Longley 1997, 146).[69]

For the second time, the Rio Treaty of the OAS saved Figueres. *Calderonistas* claim—perhaps accurately—that their movement was every bit as domestic as the 1948 Civil War led by Figueres and armed by Guatemala. Alvaro González Vargas argues that without the CIA-supported Castillo Armas invasion against Arbenz, the United States would not have saved Figueres. After the fall of Arbenz, when the U.S. denial of involvement was discovered to be false, the United States was heavily criticized in Washington, Europe, and throughout Latin America. America's commitment to democracy was challenged. The United States could not watch a second elected president fall with CIA complicity (1990, 207–70). And if one had to choose between which of the two to save, Figueres was more palatable than Arbenz.

Two months before the invasion, Miguel Ruiz was involved in a most bizarre episode. He very publicly turned over a sealed letter to Archbishop Ruben Odio with instructions that the letter should be made public upon his death or when the prelate deemed appropriate. The expected revolution came on 11 January 1955. On 29 January 1955, after the hostilities had largely ceased, Archbishop Odio made the document public and it was published in its entirety in *La Nación*. The document is remarkable in that it details ex ante the machinations and intrigue against Figueres. The following points are unambiguous:

- Those involved in the invasion were intimate with Castillo Armas and the two invasions were well coordinated, supporting contentions that the CIA was involved in both movements.
- Fernando Castro Cervantes, Calderón Guardia, and Mario Echandi had been trying for some time to create a unified "movement to overthrow Figueres."
- Ruiz Herrera was the principal liaison between Calderón, Castro Cervantes, and Echandi to try and unify the movement.
- The attempt to unify a revolt failed in the end for one reason—they had

69. Another crucial element for the defeat of the rebels was the decision of Frank Marshall to once again take up arms and combat his friend (Miguel Ruiz) and support Figueres. Some three hundred ex-combatants of the Civil War agreed to go and fight the ground troops of Picado if Marshall was in charge (Acuña 1977, 82).

the will to overthrow Figueres but they did not have the way. The oligarchy and opposition politicians were in the same dilemma that Yashar describes for the opposition to the nationalization of the banks: the opposition wanted to overthrow Figueres, "but with no army could provide no credible threat" (1997, 189). With no army to ally with, the opposition was forced to rely on support from Somoza. Somoza was willing and eager to help destroy Figueres, but with a small hitch. Teodorito Picado Jr., the son of the former president, had been Tachito Somoza's companion at West Point and a friend of the family. Somoza would provide arms and training only if Teodorito were the leader of the revolt. This was too much for Echandi and Castro Cervantes to accept, as it gave Somoza too much control.[70] With Somoza as patron of the movement, the communists also refused to participate in an internal revolt (interview with Eduardo Mora Valverde, 16 December 1997, San José, Costa Rica).

Had an autonomous and powerful military existed in Costa Rica, the opposition would not have needed to ally with Somoza for the force. Figueres would not have been able to seek help from the OAS. The CIA might even have used allies in the military to topple Figueres. Costa Rica by 1955 was experiencing a crisis of truly massive proportions. At the height of the Cold War, the president was portrayed as a communist, big capital was unified against him, the CIA was his enemy, and the four major political factions were in agreement that he must go by force if need be. There was no elite pact, no consolidated democracy, and no faith in elections. What saved Figueres and led to the eventual consolidation of democracy was simple: the lack of an army to do the deed. "If there were a military here, the events would have played out differently. There would have been a force to unite the opposition. With a military, the calculus is completely different" (interview with Gonzalo Facio, 1 December 1997, San José Costa Rica). "If we had our own military caste and did not need to get weapons from Somoza, it would have been simple to unify the opposition and overthrow Figuerismo in 1955" (interview with Miguel Ruiz Herrera, 3 December 1997, San José, Costa Rica).

70. Edgar Cardona, who led the coup in 1949, was also involved with Echandi. "I had become a great Echandista and was in El Salvador getting ready to go to Coyutepe to train for the 1955 revolution. I got a message from Echandi instructing me not to go" (interview 20 December 1997, Moravia, Costa Rica).

The end of the war did not bring peace to Costa Rica. Two members of the Legislative Assembly, Guillermo Jiménez Ramírez and minority leader Mario Echandi, were suspended from the congress for having participated in the rebel movement. The revelations made by Ruiz, disclosed by the Archbishop, and printed in their entirety by *La Nación*, established without question that Echandi had conspired to overthrow the government and Jiménez had participated in acquiring arms for the rebels. The deputies were charged with "conspiring to overthrow the legitimate government of Costa Rica . . . according to documents that the indicted Miguel Ruiz Herrera placed in the hands of the Archbishop of San José." The vote to suspend them was thirty-one to ten. Mobs reacted angrily to the charges, burning Echandi's law office; Echandi was beaten and nearly lynched (*La Nación*, 2 and 4 February 1955). Ulate, whose hatred of Figuerismo was now tangible whenever he spoke or wrote, attacked the government in his newspapers. *El Diario* announced that the "Government has unleashed an era of violence in Costa Rica," charging that the *Liberacionalistas* had sent mobs to destroy *El Diario* and had sent nothing less than three hundred agents to eliminate Mario Echandi. Ulate even blamed the recent war on Figueres, charging that he meddled too much in the affairs of others and tried to prop up Arbenz, Haya de la Torre, and Betancourt (2 February 1955).

Opposition deputies in the Legislative Assembly were furious with the suspension, called Figueres a dictator, and stormed out of the congress. Constitutional rights were suspended and the situation was nothing less than chaotic. Amidst the chaos, Vice President Richard Nixon arrived in San José to try and arrange a truce between Figueres and Somoza. The division between the PLN and the opposition was so sharp by this time that to Nixon it must have appeared that two different governments existed. Nixon gave a speech to the Legislative Assembly, attended only by PLN deputies. Then he met separately with opposition deputies who "affirmed that the crisis in the country was because the regime had never issued an amnesty (since the 1948 Civil War) and that the regime had taken a totalitarian course to perpetuate itself in power" (*La Nación*, 23 February 1955).

Nixon met with Figueres and then met in private with Ulate. Given the tone of *El Diario* in the days before the meeting with Nixon, it is not hard to guess what Ulate told the Republican vice president. Two days before the meeting, *El Diario* published a full-body picture of former president

Ulate and a fiery speech that accused Don Pepe of being a dictator, totalitarian, violent in speech similar to Adolph Hitler, and a murderer of young Costa Ricans who fought in his war against Calderón. Worst of all, Figueres did not listen to Ulate when he was willing to mediate the conflict and avoid war (20 February 1955). Nixon left the country convinced that Figueres was dictatorial and communist. "After meeting with Ulate and the opposition deputies, Nixon went on to say that communism had been transferred from Guatemala to Costa Rica. Years later, I met with then-President Nixon and he laughed and told me that he used to think that we were communists" (interview with Gonzalo Facio, 1 December 1997, San José, Costa Rica).

From March 1955 until the elections of 1958, the major political controversies in the country revolved around five issues. First and foremost was an amnesty for all participants in the civil violence from 1948 through 1955. The nonconfrontational and conciliatory political culture often invoked when people talk of Costa Rica was not evident in the mid-1950s. Not only had the Figueristas exiled and jailed thousands, they had seized properties with the Tribunals of Immediate Sanctions—"a kind of Nuremberg," according to the defendants (interview with Oscar Bakit, 26 November 1997, San José, Costa Rica). Seven years later, an amnesty and a healing had never occurred. Amnesty did not come until 1958.

> There were many pressures from people who had suffered under the other governments, people that had been jailed and mistreated, and people that had been killed for defending the election tables. And these people put on lots of pressure to form a hard line [against an amnesty]. . . . The amnesty was also postponed because of the two invasions. We were talking of an amnesty when the invasion of 1948 occurred. Then when we were considering an amnesty again there was an invasion. . . . The hardliners around Figueres were saying: "How can we pronounce an amnesty if they are invading the country. They are not willing to contend with us in the electoral arena, only with force, they want to take power with force." (Interview with Luis Alberto Monge, 8 December 1997, Pozos de Santa Ana, Costa Rica)

A second major political issue was electoral reform. The PLN recognized that people still had the perception that elections were fraudulent.

The 1955–58 period was full of commissions and plans to change electoral procedures and improve confidence in the elections. The opposition regularly charged that Figueres was going to perpetuate PLN control of power. An event in 1956 lent credence to the charges of fraud that were constantly leveled by Castro and the opposition. The Supreme Tribunal of Elections found incontrovertible evidence that PLN money in the 1953 elections had gone to officials in the Civil Registry. "Just what difference the bribed officials made in the elections is speculative. It is obvious that the PLN paid them to help ensure its overwhelming victory" (Martz 1959, 254). The opposition was fearful that Figueres would use similar means to win the next election.

A third political issue was the suspension of Echandi and one other opposition deputy from the congress and the open warfare between the two blocks. The suspension was lifted after six months and the Legislative Assembly returned to nervous normalcy in October 1955 (*La Nación*, 4 October 1955). Tensions at the Legislative Assembly remained high, and heated discussions and violent outbreaks occurred. For example, in August 1957 Figueres announced a plan to sell the Manzana de Artilleria (a large plot of land belonging to the security forces) to build a central bank building and a plan to tear down the National Assembly to build a new one. The opposition used this as a pretext to send mobs to riot at the National Assembly, leading to widespread destruction and the shooting of six people. Figueres accused Miguel Ruiz Herrera of organizing the fracas. Ruiz Herrera responded that he was proud to have tried to overthrow Figueres and proud to keep trying (*La Nación*, 20 August 1957). Bombings, terrorist acts, and planned acts of violence were regular features in the press.

The fourth important and continuing political element was the charge against the government of statism, international adventures, class warfare, higher and higher taxes, and abuse of power (for example, *La Nación*, 26 April 1957). Attacks on government policy were mixed with personal attacks against Figueres: "Figueres has been attacked by his enemies as have few men in Costa Rican history . . . no insult is too far-fetched. The President also was criticized for his two marriages with North American women, the first ending in divorce in 1953. People bitterly muttered about his apparent unwillingness to marry a Costa Rican" (Martz 1959, 257). It is difficult to find a derogatory term that his enemies had not used to characterize Figueres. Frank Marshall, who fought valiantly and perhaps decisively for Figueres on four occasions (Civil War, Invasion of December 1948, Cardonazo, Invasion of 1955), started his own anti-Figueres ultra-rightist party—the Revolutionary Civic Union—and invoked a new characterization referring to Don Pepe as a new Louis XIV (*La Nación*, 29 March 1957).[71]

The fifth and final major political issue dominating political discourse and the newspapers was the internal dispute between the two major political blocks leading up to the 1958 elections. The PLN was trying to maintain unity and the opposition was trying to unify. The PLN eventually split into two factions; lifelong Figueres friend and Public Works Minister Francisco Orlich ran as the Liberation candidate and Finance Minister Jorge Rossi broke off and ran as the candidate of the Independent Party. After much haggling and a convention in the soccer stadium, most of the opposition united behind Mario Echandi as the candidate of the *Movimiento Democrático Oposicionista* (MDO). In Costa Rican elections, voters can split their vote for president and the party list for congress. Calderón Guardia, still in exile, headed the party list for the Republican Party but exhorted his many followers in advertisements to split their vote and support Echandi for the presidency: "Our Goal, Mario Echandi for the presidency of the Republic and many Calderonista Deputies in the Congress!" (*La Nación*, 10 January 1958).

Rumors of revolts and fraud were constant. Frank Marshall pulled a major public relations coup by publicly shaming the three major candidates—Echandi, Orlich, and Rossi—into signing a pledge to accept the verdict of the Supreme Tribune of Elections as final and to use legal norms to appeal claims of fraud (*La Nación*, 14 January 1958). This pledge was important, as the PLN had recently threatened to use force if the election did not go their way. In Costa Rican elections, votes were cast at tables and all registered parties had officials at each table—this group of officials would determine if a person could vote or not. The opposition registered "phantom" parties to stack the voting tables and the PLN responded with

71. The reactionary paramilitary force named the "Free Costa Rica Movement" arose from Marshall and his party. Financed by the Taiwan government, the *Movimiento Costa Rica Libre* (MCRL) was officially organized in 1961 and railed against communist threats and Cuba (Honey 1994, 8). In addition to Marshall, Ruiz Herrera and Cardona were linked to the organization that planned coups against Figueres and other PLN leaders through the 1970s (interview Miguel Ruiz Herrera, 3 December 1997, San José, Costa Rica). In fact, Edgar Cardona was once president of the MCRL (interview with Edgar Cardona, 20 December 1997, Moravia, Costa Rica). The United States later financed the MCRL to battle pro-Sandinista elements in Costa Rica (Honey 1994, 558–59).

a full-page ad in *La Nación* titled "The Invasion of the Tables." The ruling party charged that these new parties were phantoms that the opposition had invented to commit massive fraud against the PLN. "Look carefully, Costa Rican. Look at what is happening. Be alert. Remember that concessions such as these were what fortified Caldero-Communism in Costa Rica. We must cut out the infection now, or within a few short years we will have to resort to the means that we employed in 1948" (15 December 1957).

The results of the peaceful and orderly 2 February 1958 elections were as follows: 102,528 votes for Echandi, 94,788 votes for Orlich, and 23,920 votes for Rossi. Echandi did not get 50 percent of the vote but did receive slightly more than the 40 percent needed to avoid a run-off and was declared president (*La Nación*, 5 March 1958). Echandi owed his success to support from Calderón and the rift in the PLN. In the vote for the Legislative Assembly, Liberation won twenty deputies and the Independents gained three. Combined, the twenty-three deputies of the ruling party won a slight majority in the forty-five-seat congress. Of the other twenty-two seats, Calderón's party won eleven, showing the continual appeal of the caudillo. Echandi's party gained only ten seats and the final seat went to Frank Marshall (*La Nación*, 1 May 1958).

The PLN did not immediately recognize the results. Orlich complained that the registry was deficient and that the party "estimates that at least 40,000 supporters were unable to vote" (*La Nación*, 6 February 1958). The party asked that the votes from three hundred voting tables be annulled (*La Nación*, 14 February 1958). Indeed, a major battle emerged within the PLN over the course of action to take. The regime won more than 50 percent of the vote if the two parties were combined! The only reason they lost was because two official candidates split the vote. For Figueres, it was a bitter pill to swallow to watch his archenemy, Mario Echandi, take hold of the reins of government. Mario Echandi, who had plotted to overthrow the regime and who had been beaten, nearly lynched, suspended from the congress, and whose office was burned by Figueristas, would now be president. "There were people within Liberation, fanatics who said how are we going to hand the government over to Echandi if we are the majority. Our two blocks received many more votes than they did" (interview with Luis Alberto Monge, 8 December 1997, Pozos de Santa Ana, Costa Rica). Indeed, one of those most opposed to handing the presidency to Echandi was José Figueres. "When Orlich lost the election, Figueres said, 'whoa, I am not going to recognize this election.' Many within Liberation did not want to give up power. Figueres did not want to surrender power. This would have been fatal for Costa Rican democracy" (interview with Gonzalo Facio, 1 December 1997, San José, Costa Rica).[72]

Fortunately, the losing candidate and long-time Figueres confidant, Francisco Orlich, was able to convince Figueres that this was madness. "Orlich was the one person who could put the brakes on Figueres. He was the one person who could bang on the table and make Figueres listen" (interview with Alberto Cañas, 12 December 1997, San José, Costa Rica). A childhood friend of Don Pepe's, Orlich saw no reason to gain the presidency through illegal means. The PLN still controlled the Legislative Assembly. He could easily win the 1962 elections if the party were unified (which he did). And without a military hierarchy, there was no force in the country powerful enough to keep the opposition in power and cheat the PLN out of winning in the electoral arena.

Echandi took office and the PLN and Independent deputies in the Legislative Assembly reunified under the PLN banner. Hope for true democratic consolidation and a commitment to wage political battles in the electoral arena were now possible. The Supreme Election Tribunal gained stature as an institution and as a guarantor of free and fair elections. In 1958, a general amnesty was finally pronounced and Calderón Guardia returned to the country after a ten-year exile. Thousands lined the Paseo Colón to greet him. He ran unsuccessfully for the presidency against Orlich in 1962.

72. The claim that Figueres was against respecting the elections of 1958 may be difficult to accept for many who see him as a combination of George Washington and the Holy Trinity. I asked two others who may have known about this to corroborate the information. Alberto Cañas and Luis Alberto Monge both said that they could neither verify nor deny the claim, but added that if anyone knew Figueres's response to the election, it would have been Gonzalo Facio. "At that time Gonzalo Facio was extremely close to power. He was an intimate friend of Figueres. He would know more than I" (Interview with Luis Alberto Monge, 8 December 1997, Pozos de Santa Ana, Costa Rica). The other person in the inner circle was Francisco Orlich, who is now deceased. Dr. Adolfo Chacón, who is finishing a study of Figueres based on hundreds of interviews and ten years of study, confirmed the Facio claim that Figueres initially refused to honor the election and told the author that an agreement to turn over power was only possible after Echandi agreed to name a security minister agreeable to the PLN leadership (Interview 8 December 1997, San José, Costa Rica). I could not confirm this deal, but historian Iván Molina Jiménez told the me that arriving at a mutually acceptable security minister was a common ritual in Costa Rican electoral deal making. Héctor Pérez Brignoli revealed in a personal communication that similar negotiations occurred after the PLN lost the presidency in tainted elections in 1966.

Conclusion

Democracy did not come to Costa Rica through an elite pact after the 1948 Civil War. The oligarchy did not view Figueres's reforms as bounded. The political culture of the Ticos did not guarantee peace and democracy. Structural variables are important for framing the process of democratization but do not fully explain either the process or the cause. And the electoral reforms of 1946 and 1949 were not enough for politicians to commit exclusively to the electoral arena. Democracy was consolidated after two decades of crisis and violence that eventually led to a stalemate. The PLN opposition, try as it might, could not topple Figueres through force. And Figueres and Orlich believed they were the dominant party and that when unified, they could gain and keep power through elections. Without a military caste, uncertainty is reduced and time horizons are lengthened.

Let us now look briefly at the impact of demilitarization on the three power relations introduced in Chapter 3. We are interested in the counterfactual question: if a powerful and autonomous military had existed, what would have been different? The first power relation is class. It is clear that reforms were seen as a direct threat by the oligarchy. Not only have we established that conditions were ripe for the elite to seek military allies and intervention if a military had existed, we have gone much further. Unambiguous evidence reveals that the opposition representing the conservative sectors of society made every attempt to find the force to overthrow Figueres. Without a domestic source of that force, they turned to the United States and to Somoza.

In addition, the absence of a military insulated centrists from extremist elements, facilitating class compromise. As in Guatemala and El Salvador, there were extremist anticommunists in Costa Rica. Many of them, such as Frank Marshall and Miguel Ruiz, were military officers who later formed the backbone of the Free Costa Rica Movement (*Movimiento Costa Rica Libre* MCRL), a reactionary group financed by Taiwan with ties to the Guatemalan military and death squads (interview with Miguel Ruiz, 3 December 1997). If Costa Rica had a military caste, it likely would be composed of people like Marshall or Ruiz, or at the very least friends of Marshall and Ruiz. If that were the case, their war games and attempted coups of the 1970s and 1980s would appear less comical and harmless, and could easily lead to the vicious cycle of violence that plagued other Central American countries.

The second power relation is transnational. When Figueres took power in 1948, the Costa Rican armed forces were very weak. This may cause some to argue that the abolition meant little because there was little to abolish. This assumption is erroneous; the weakness of the armed forces made it easier to abolish the army but did not make the decision less momentous for the future of the country. By the early 1950s, the United States was building up militaries throughout the region. Even a small autonomous military hierarchy would have been nourished and expanded until it would have been a powerful institution. This point cannot be overstated. Muller (1985) details the linkage between U.S. military aid, empowerment of militaries, and the collapse of democracy. Holden (1993) discusses how U.S. military power and assistance were an important aspect of the "elite counteroffensive" that occurred in Central America in the 1950–90 period. The proscription of a permanent military in Costa Rica not only inhibited the manifestation of U.S. military power in the country but had also eliminated possible allies of the CIA or other officials in Costa Rica. The United States knew that its power was limited in Costa Rica without a group of friendly colonels there.[73] "We received great pressure from the United States so that we would form a modern army here. They wanted to give us equipment and training and everything. We said no" (interview with Gonzalo Facio, 1 December 1997, San José, Costa Rica).

> The United States always tried to pressure Costa Rica into reinstituting a military. It actually got to the point that the United States was able to convince people like Carlos Andrés Pérez to tell us that the world had changed and with the problems in Central America, Costa Rica needed a small military to defend itself. We certainly dissented from the policies of the United States, which was to build up the militaries to contend against communism. And the United States thought that if we did not have a military here, how are we going to contain communism? This was a grave mistake in the foreign policy of the United States for years, during the entire Cold War process; to think that one could stop the advance of commu-

73. Not only has the United States used military allies to support conservative regimes and protect U.S. economic interests, it have used the generals as lobbyists. For example, when Oscar Arias was trying to put together a peace plan, "the Central American militaries were pressured very heavily by the United States to disrupt the Arias Peace Plan" (interview with Oscar Arias, 24 November 1997, San José, Costa Rica).

> nism with armies. Indeed, the armies became hated and guerrillas were armed not because of communism, but to seek refuge from the militaries and the trampling of human rights and elections and all those things. Therefore, the United States chose a despised ally in Latin America. (Interview with Luis Alberto Monge, 8 December 1997, Pozos de Santa Ana, Costa Rica)

> Here in Latin America we would have elections and the generals would say, "I don't like this president that won or is going to win, I will take power." Right? This occurred with the help of the CIA, with the help of the United States, with the satisfaction of the United States, with the United States looking the other way. Sometimes highly involved, such as the case of Castillo Armas in Guatemala, and other times less involved. (Interview with Oscar Arias, 24 November 1997, San José, Costa Rica)

With no generals in Costa Rica, no high command, and no military caste, this transnational dynamic was very different. It boded well for democracy. We will see the other alternative clearly in the Honduran case.

The third power relation of importance for democracy is the strength and autonomy of the state. In times of crisis in Latin America, a powerful professional military steps in to take charge in what may be called military tutelage. In Costa Rica, the crisis in the 1953–58 period was intense. However, state power resided wholly in civilian institutions. Instead of a military stepping in to solve the crisis and gain prestige, it was the Supreme Electoral Tribunal that took responsibility for ensuring a fair and free election in 1958. This state institution gained tremendous legitimacy as the autonomous enforcer of suffrage. If a military caste had existed, the development of other state institutions and state strength might have been compromised.

The evidence in this chapter is powerful, but we must remember that a counterfactual argument is probabilistic and not deterministic. Militarization does not by itself explain democratic consolidation in Costa Rica. History matters, as does state capacity, the absence of forced labor, the sense of exceptionalism and nation, electoral institutions, literacy levels, and other factors. The argument is that an autonomous military institution in Costa Rica during the Cold War would have significantly decreased the likelihood of stable democracy. The evidence thus far strongly confirms the argument. The next chapter will add the Honduran case to the comparative historical analysis in an effort to increase the causal inference.

When Bullets Trump Ballots

militarization and democratic collapse in honduras

5

"Every time that our country's name appears with profusion in the international press, it is because something bad has happened. Never, or almost never, are we mentioned for some positive action, for something that would really make us proud" (Meza 1981, 23). Two negative images have dominated popular press accounts of Honduras: the banana republic and the militarized state. During the first half of this century, popular magazines regularly referred to this country as the quintessential banana republic, and with good reason. Bananas dominated the country's exports and banana companies strongly influenced the country's politics. Political battles between Samuel Zemurrey (the Banana Man) and the United Fruit Company (the Octopus) often helped determine the country's president and led to wars and regular intervention of U.S. marines.[1] Domestic and international peace was only possible after the banana archenemies fused in 1929 (Pérez 1988, 119).[2] Heavy reliance on bananas has long been pointed to as a weakness for Honduras. Torres-Rivas observes that the banana is in many respects an inferior product to the coffee bean,[3] for it pays lower taxes and evolves into the classic enclave whose economic logic is "incomprehensible," as it leaves few longstanding benefits for the host country (1975, 60–66).[4] In

1. Barahona (1989) is an excellent and dispassionate account of U.S. political and economic influence in Honduras in the period 1907–32.

2. Zumurrey's Cuyamel Banana Company supported the Liberal Party and the United Fruit Company supported the National Party.

3. There are many explanations for the late development of the coffee industry (see Williams 1994; Euraque 1996). I would argue that the Honduran state lacked the capacity to simultaneously nurture coffee and banana production and they chose bananas by targeting state resources and foreign investment in that sector and by keeping property laws that discouraged coffee production. In the 1940s and 1950s, the Honduran government emphasized coffee and the country now produces an amount similar to that of Costa Rica.

4. There have recently appeared studies that contradict the notion that the banana enclave had only negative effects on the local economy

contrast to the earlier news reports, media stories in the 1960–90 period most often focused on an intransigent and antidemocratic military caste, the human rights abuses of the security forces, and the U.S.-Honduran military alliance against the Sandinistas.

Whether dominated by the banana companies or the generals, Honduras has always been portrayed as a hopeless case and a pliable and obedient dependent of the United States. The country has suffered from extreme instability, meddling from more powerful neighbors, poor soil, a dispersed population isolated by poor communication and transportation, slow development of national identity,[5] poverty, stifling debt,[6] and inadequate education. Democracy has not fared well in Honduras in the post-1950 period. Looking at the country's economic, political, and transnational challenges, it is easy to conclude that democracy never had a chance in the 1950–80 period.

This chapter argues that, in fact, Honduras did have a chance to develop a democratic polity in the post-1950 period. In the 1950s, there were many factors that favored democratic government: the country was finally relatively stable; there was no history of an aristocracy;[7] the landed

---

and that the decision to feature bananas as the prime export was illogical. Bulmer-Thomas (1993) shows that in the late 1920s and early 1930s, Honduras had more total exports than any other Central American country and double that of Costa Rica. In 1930, Honduras had the highest per capita GDP on the isthmus (Bulmer-Thomas 1993). Posas (1993, 117–23, 126) disputes the often held view that the Honduran elites traded favorable tax laws in exchange for bribes. Honduras always followed Costa Rica's lead in terms and conditions for the banana companies and many times was able to obtain more favorable conditions than the Costa Ricans. The Honduran officials believed that the benefits of banana capital would be shared with local banana producers and small industrialists. For example, banana lots were originally alternated between locally owned producers and the transnational banana companies so that the locals could benefit from transportation. The banana companies also diversified and invested heavily in local businesses. The Vaccaro Brothers founded many companies, including the most important bank in the country. Indeed, if an economist visited Central America in 1930, Honduras would be the success story. In addition to having the highest receipts from exports and the highest per capita GDP, it was also the only country paying its foreign debt. Honduras's banana miracle went sour with diseases and natural disasters that greatly reduced exports in the post-1930 period (Ellis 1983; Kepner and Soothill 1949). Euraque (1996) reveals how banana money led to the emergence of a progressive, pro-democratic, and dynamic petite bourgeoisie on the Honduras North Coast. Barahona also concludes that the banana companies had an overall positive and "dynamizing" economic effect for the country (1989, 239).

5. See Barahona (1991).

6. In 1888, Honduran debt was higher than the land value of the entire territory (Euraque 1996, 4).

7. During a mining depression in the seventeenth century, the wealthiest families abandoned Honduras. This is one of the principal factors for the lack of an aristocratic tradition

oligarchy was relatively weak; labor unions were flexing their muscles; forced labor was not a problem; a progressive and dynamic new business class was evolving on the north coast that had important pro-democratic effects; the military was nearly nonexistent; two traditional political parties existed; and small-holding coffee production was exploding, leading Stokes in the 1940s to envision "the development of a kind of rural, agrarian democracy" (1950, 24). While Martz's 1959 portrayal of the country is less than optimistic, he noted that there was no inherent or structural reason for the country to flounder. He also saw "promise of an improved and more enlightened approach to Honduran problems" after the first year of the Villeda presidential term (1959, 163).

Unfortunately, this promise would be dashed as the emergence of a powerful military institution after 1954 negatively impacted all three of the power relations important for democracy. This case is useful for our purposes as it is an excellent contrast to the Costa Rican example and spotlights the causal mechanism whereby militarization's impact on class, transnational, and state power relations affects democracy. When moderately progressive reforms were announced in the sexenio of President Ramón Villeda Morales, an alliance between the newly powerful military and the oligarchy tipped the democratic scales away from the emerging pro-democracy coalition of students, labor, and small capitalists. In Costa Rica, in contrast, the oligarchy did not have such an ally and was forced to seek an external military force such as Castillo Armas, Somoza, Pérez, or Trujillo. The United States and the United Fruit Company both nourished the expanding role of Honduran militarism and paved the way for the end of six years of civilian government. Try as it might, the United States was unable to build a professional military in Costa Rica. And finally, the Honduran case demonstrates quite clearly how the powerful and autonomous military can overwhelm the strength and autonomy of the state.

The Honduran case is also enlightening juxtaposed to that of Costa Rica because it provides an unambiguous answer to the often made proposition that the proscription of the military in Costa Rica was unimportant since the institution was weak and debilitated by 1948; the proscription merely formalized the situation. As we shall see, the military was much weaker in the Honduran case but in the environment of the Cold War and

in Honduras and the absence today of Spanish nobility family names that endure in other Latin American countries (Oquelí 1983, 8).

the Cuban revolution could grow rapidly into the dominant political actor in the country. We begin with a brief review of the Honduran military and Honduran politics.

Among Central American countries, Honduras has the longest tradition of two dominant parties—the Liberals and the Nationals. The Liberal Party was formed in 1891 by one of the country's most successful presidents, Policarpo Bonilla. The National Party was originally a breakaway group of Liberals led by Manuel Bonilla. Until 1948, the Nationals and the Liberals were the only official political parties in the country. The parties largely served as mechanisms for gaining power and distributing patronage and have not held distinct visions for governing the country, save that the National Party has been more stridently anticommunist. For many years, the two parties were aligned with rival North American banana companies; the Liberals with Cuyamel and the Nationals with United Fruit. The military has been strongly allied with the National Party. While Hondurans have shown displeasure with the corruption, nepotism, and failure of the principal parties, alternative parties have never captured a significant portion of the electorate. Among Central American countries, Honduras also has the strongest labor unions and organized peasant associations. As in Costa Rica, the Caribbean plains proved to be fertile not only for bananas but for organized labor. Labor and peasant organizations were largely wiped out under the rule of Tiburcio Carías (1933–48). By the mid-1950s, peasants and workers would become an organized force to be reckoned with; and the reckoning alternated between eras of cooptation/compromise (1958–62, 1972–75, 1990s) and eras of conflict/repression (1963–72, 1978–80s). As in Costa Rica, even the most progressive political leaders worked to weaken the more radical organizations (with even indirect links to communism) and replace them with anticommunist unions and peasant organizations.

One of the common errors committed by observers of modern Central America is to believe that these countries were always saddled with powerful and professional military institutions. Yashar and others single out Costa Rica as the exception in Latin America for having a small military as measured by soldiers per capita (1997, 53). In fact, in the first half of this century, Costa Rica had more soldiers per capita than Honduras; the military was also more institutionalized in Costa Rica than in Honduras (Muñoz 1990, 167). Unlike any of the other five Central American republics, the military institution had no political influence in Honduras 1900–1950. Indeed, in Honduran newspapers before 1954, it is difficult to find any mention whatsoever of the military. In Stokes's landmark 1950 study of the politics of Honduras that details all significant political forces, the armed forces are conspicuously absent from the discussion of important political actors. Honduras did not have an institutionalized and professional armed forces until the 1950s (Funes 1995; Ropp 1974; Salomón 1992). The lack of forced labor may have inhibited early militarization. "At any rate, the existence in El Salvador and Guatemala by the late nineteenth century of relatively strong military academies, supported by relatively solid financial ties with their respective states, permitted, generally speaking, more organic relationships between coffee oligarchies in these countries and 'their' governments. Such relationships resulted from the repressive police force and military necessary to sustain the exploitative labor relations" that did not exist in Honduras or Costa Rica (Euraque 1996, 49).

This does not mean that the country was free of militarist caudillos and civil war. Holden (1996) and Tábora (1995) document the high levels of violence in Honduras, much of it state-sponsored. There were 146 documented violent political engagements between 1870 and 1949, almost all having fewer than fifty to one hundred deaths (Euraque 1996, 45). These revolts were simple and fierce quests for political power that often resulted from the fact that winning presidential candidates rarely received the 50 percent of the vote necessary to win the elections. When the candidate with the most votes was denied office by the congress, a revolt often ensued. The opposing sides were *not* militaries but largely unorganized partisan (or paid) militias. The combatants were not professional soldiers, and are well described by a U.S. diplomat:

> Many, perhaps the majority of the men which made up the armies' litigants did not know why they fought. . . . On the other hand many were primarily interested, which is natural given the circumstances, in ending up on the winning side; and when the momentum of the battle shifted, desertion was complete. The commanders had no uniforms, just armbands. The soldiers were not liberals or conservatives but merely blues or reds. It was not uncommon that a blue soldier carried in his pocket an armband of the reds or vice-a-versa, and he did not hesitate in changing when the moment arrived. (W. Beauloc, quoted in Funes 1995, 115)

In the 1923 elections, an attorney, farmer, algebra professor, and long-time political militant named Tiburcio Carías was the National Party choice. An imposing figure with experience in many political rebellions, Carías won the election with 49,453 votes, compared to 35,474 for the runner-up. Unfortunately, Carías was some 3,681 votes short of an absolute majority and crisis resulted when Carías opponents refused to attend the congress, denying a quorum and a Carías victory. After intervention from the United States and months of civil violence, Carías agreed to let his running mate take the presidency. In 1928 Carías ran again, and was the surprise loser to the Liberal Vicente Mejía Colindres. Carías sent his congratulations to the new president and peace reigned in the country. In 1932 Carías decisively defeated his Liberal challenger, Angel Zúñiga Huete, and actually won more than the requisite 50 percent. The Liberals revolted and were quickly defeated. Carías remained in the presidency for the next sixteen years (see Argueta 1988).

Carías, who quickly gave himself the title of general, was a caudillo and a dictator who exiled his enemies, massacred protesters,[8] and clamped down on the press. He also built roads, balanced the budget, and brought a good deal of stability to the country. He saw little reason to build an army. "In a very deliberate manner, Carías was able to keep the military non-professional. . . . This was so, because he distrusted, and the facts tend to confirm it, an autonomous and well-organized military, with the requisite amount of power in its hands to become the arbiter of Honduran political life" (Argueta 1988, 123).[9] "Two famous phrases are attributed to Doctor and General Tiburcio Carías Andino. One makes allusions to loans and the other to the military. On the first he said that he was not interested in taking loans because in the end Honduras would be robbed. On the second he expressed that he was not interested in forming an army because . . . it would be dangerous" (Funes 1995, 145).

The stability enjoyed by Honduras and the charisma and hospitality of the caudillo led Stokes to paint an apologetic portrayal of Carías and ex-

8. Carías was much less repressive and violent than his counterparts in Guatemala and El Salvador. In 1944, one hundred protesters were massacred by the police in San Pedro Sula, which contributed to Carías leaving office in 1949 (Weaver 1994, 144). Argueta and Quiñónes posit that the subservient Carías—"If Carías sinned, it was in being overly loyal to North American interests"—was eased out by Americans, as the end of the World War II and the Cold War made support of dictators suddenly embarrassing (1983, 127). By 1949, however, the United States was again willing to support friendly dictators.

9. There was an air force with U.S. planes and U.S. pilots that Carías used to maintain order (Argueta 1988, 116). Carías also had contracts with the commercial airliners so that they would drop bombs instead of delivering the mail if he requested (Argueta 1988, chapter 9).

press high hopes for the political development of the country. The caudillo had set the foundation of stability and a rural democracy could now emerge (1950). When he left office in January 1949, his handpicked successor took over after an unchallenged election.

> Juan Manuel [Gálvez] is the most honorable and honest man in my government. He is the only one to whom I can confer the power to soften the bitterness caused by my long term in the Presidential House; he is going to grasp a hot coal in his hands, which he will have to put out little by little. This is the only way to save the democratic institutions, the interests of the country, the lives and belongings of all of you. This is why I have arranged for him to arrive without obligations to the Presidency of the Republic. You should respect my decision made for the good of Honduras. (Carías, quoted in Argueta 1990, 75)

The six-year Gálvez presidency brought great change to the country. Much more urbane and progressive than his predecessor, Gálvez allowed greater opposition, freer speech, labor organization, and oversaw the strengthening of the state apparatus with the founding of the Central Bank and a state investment bank, an income tax, agro-industrial entities, and a cotton gin (Argueta 1990, 76). He also paid off the onerous British railroad loan that had been on the books for over a century (Argueta and Quiñónes 1983, 128). Under Gálvez, "Honduras became more pluralistic and dynamic than ever before. New political interest groups developed among campesinos and urban laborers. And the army could do little about these changes because it was not yet a self-conscious, professional institution" (LaFeber 1984, 132).

In a daring and compelling interpretation of Honduran development, Euraque shows that by mid-century a strong commercial and industrial sector had emerged on the Honduran North Coast (1996). Rather than the enclave sucking out all capital and stifling local business dynamism, the banana companies of Samuel Zemurrey and others actually provided seed money and partnership for the development of new Honduran small industrialists independent of the established oligarchic landholders and the political families. These new forces were in many ways reformists who supported a modernized economy and democratic openings.[10] Coupled

10. This industrial group was immigrant-controlled, largely by Christian Arabs (Euraque 1996, 30–35). While successful in business and influential in politics, Hondurans of

with increased student and labor activism, a strong pro-democratic coalition existed in the country for the first time.

In the annals of Honduran history, 1954 will always be a critical year of watershed events that shaped the future of the country—the great banana strike, the use of Honduran soil to launch the invasion against Arbenz, and the signing of the Bilateral Treaty of Military Assistance with the United States. The great banana strike began on 2 May 1954 when a workers' spokesman was terminated for demanding extra pay for work on Sunday. Within days, some twenty-five thousand United Fruit workers and fifteen thousand Standard Fruit workers were on a strike that would last sixty-nine days and cost millions of dollars (Schulz and Schulz 1994, 20–23). Miners, brewers, and other workers soon joined the strike, letting loose pent-up frustration from the stifling Carías years; thus the modern Honduran working class was born. What is surprising is that many among the national bourgeoisie, and especially the North Coast emerging industrialists who had received seed money from banana companies, supported the striking workers. North Coast elites donated large sums of money to the striking workers and many commercial and manufacturing elites formed the Committee to Help the Banana Strikers (Euraque 1996, 92–94). The strike was finally settled through repression and incentives and a U.S.-assisted campaign to smear the strikers as communist collaborators of the Arbenz government. The resulting settlement was a disappointment, but the strike was a long-term victory as it resulted in the legalization of unions, an eight-hour day, paid vacations, and overtime pay (Schulz and Schulz 1994, 20–23).

The second important event in 1954 was that Gálvez permitted the use of Honduran soil for the U.S.-inspired invasion of elected President Jacobo Arbenz in Guatemala. The negative impact of Honduran involvement in this antidemocratic action goes far beyond the stain of shame for the country and the Gálvez regime. On 20 May 1954, in a quid pro quo for Honduran support for the Castillo Armas invasion and as a continuation of U.S. policy of military assistance treaties,[11] the United States and

Arab descent were long excluded from political office. In recent years this has changed drastically, and the 1997 election of Carlos Flores Facusse as president as well as several deputies of Arab descent point to the full integration of the Arab community into all activities.

11. In March 1950, State Department official George Kennan stated the three goals of U.S. policy in Latin America: the protection of "our" raw materials; the prevention of

Honduras signed a Bilateral Treaty of Military Assistance (Salomón 1992, 7). The agreement called for U.S. military aid in exchange for free access to any "raw and semi-processed materials required by the United States of America as a result of deficiencies or potential deficiencies in its own resources" (Ropp 1974, 504–28). The First Infantry Battalion was organized by the United States on 20 July 1954—less than one month after the fall of Arbenz—and remained under U.S. jurisdiction until August 1956 (Funes 1995, 160). With alleged communists in neighboring Guatemala and Leftists participating in the banana strikes, the United States wanted insurance for its many investments. In 1950, George Kennan detailed future U.S. strategy for Latin America in the face of communist threats: "The final answer might be an unpleasant one, but . . . we should not hesitate before police repression of the local government. This is not shameful since the Communists are essentially traitors. . . . It is better to have a strong regime in power than a liberal government if it is indulgent and relaxed and penetrated by Communists" (quoted in Smith 1996, 126).

The United States had previously encouraged militarization in the country. The Lend-Lease Program was used by Carías to improve the air force. In 1952, the United States helped found the Francisco Morazán Military Academy to train professional officers. And finally, at the height of the Cold War in Central America, U.S. actions in 1954 fully established a military institution capable of "repression of the local government" and "strong" enough to topple any "indulgent" "liberal government."

U.S. Ambassador to Honduras Whitting Willauer provided the following analysis of the 1954 agreement: "The Bilateral Treaty of Military Assistance, celebrated between Honduras and the United States, is important for achieving the peace. A country that relies on a weak military force can never carry forward a plan of internal and international security. What is necessary is an organized military power that can respond to the techniques and the exigencies of national and international security" (Willauer, quoted in Velásquez 1954).

By 1954, various new forces were emerging in the country that would translate into new power dynamics in the years to come. A new urban bourgeoisie was growing, demanding change, and flexing its muscles. In addition, in 1954, "two new forces entered the scene, both with extraordi-

---

military exploitation of Latin America by enemies; and the prevention of the psychological mobilization of Latin America against the United States (LaFeber 1984, 107).

nary energy, two actors called to carry out a very influential role in the political life of the nation: the Armed Forces and the Honduran working class" (Funes 1995, 160).

The Public Debate over Militarization

One widespread opinion is that modern states require an institutionalized military. This proposition is supported by two distinct strands of social science—one in the field of comparative politics/sociology and the other in the field of international relations. Comparativists interested in state formation and capacity often build on the Weberian proposition that states have a monopoly on the legitimate use of violence and effective control of a specific territory.[12] State building and war making are two sides of the same coin.[13] In recent years, Jeanne Kirkpatrick charged that Costa Rica was not even a legitimate state, as it had no military.[14] In the field of international relations, both realist and neorealist schools posit that states seek to increase military power vis-à-vis competitors or enemies.[15] Given the ubiquitous expectation that countries would naturally build military institutions during the process of state modernization, it is no surprise that scholars fail to investigate the forces that supported and opposed the emergence of military institutionalization and autonomy in developing countries. The next section details that in Honduras, there in fact existed a significant public opposition to militarization.

The Honduran press was liberalized greatly during the Gálvez regime and political debates in the various newspapers became common.[16] The

12. The classic work on the state is Evans, Rueschemeyer, and Skocpol (1985).

13. See Tilly (1990).

14. In 1981, U.S. Ambassador to the UN Jeanne Kirkpatrick informed Costa Rica that further U.S. economic aid would be predicated on the re-creation of a professional army (Black 1986, 186). Kirkpatrick chided the Costa Ricans, telling them that "Costa Rica is not a viable country because it has no military" (author's interview with Oscar Arias, 24 November 1997, San José, Costa Rica).

15. For a compelling discussion of this issue, see Escudé (1993).

16. *El Cronista* was a Tegucigalpa-based newspaper that was published regularly from 1953 to 1981 and had an estimated circulation of ten thousand. In the 1950s, Honduras was largely illiterate and *El Cronista*'s impact was mainly among Tegucigalpa's intellectual elite, literate rural merchants, and landowners. Nevertheless, this was the "dean" of Honduran newspapers, and is regularly used by scholars such as Funes to document the 1950s. It is also important to note that the paper provided both sides of the militarization debate an ample public forum over a three-year period and that the participants in the public dialogue were from as far away as Copán. For more on *El Cronista* and the Honduran press, see Gardner (1963) and Euraque (1986).

professionalization of the armed forces did not occur without a healthy public debate in the editorial pages and news columns. The level of sophistication of the arguments is at times quite impressive and at other times eerily prophetic. The total absence of news or commentary about the military ended abruptly with a piece about the military agreement with the United States:

> the spectacular notice that invites us to laugh that Honduras and the United States of North America will soon sign a military pact, and it makes us laugh because Honduras has never fought with anybody and has no one to fight with. . . . And to think that we could be invaded by the Russian Soviets, this causes even more laughter because truth be told . . . it is easier to believe that we will be invaded by those that are now making treaties to protect us. . . . We should seek another position . . . one misplaced comma can lead us to complete enslavement [by the U.S.]. (Antonio Gómez Milla in *Acción Democrática*, 22 May 1954)[17]

An official spokesperson for the Liberal Party provided a different opinion shortly thereafter: "among the stipulations figures or is specified the sending of an American military mission to Honduras with the goal of organizing a small army that truth be told, the country does not have outside of some militias under command of a few officials. . . . We believe that for some time the Honduran armed forces should be technically organized, with substantial modernization" (Andrés Brown Flores in *Acción Democrática*, 22 May 1954). A year later, the debate heated up with a long series of editorials and letters in *El Cronista* that appeared from May 1955 through June 1957. These commentaries well illustrate the absence of a military institution in the country and a keen understanding of the potential dangers of militarization.

> A few days ago I read in a certain newspaper from the capital something that appeared as a plan for a school of advanced military studies, which according to the announcement, should be established shortly in Honduras. In government circles and even amongst the public opinion it appears that there exists a favorable climate for

17. For an expanded account of the militarization debate in Honduras, see Bowman (2001).

> this new factory of creole "Junkers." This would be the masterwork of our ignorance. . . . It would be a stupendous measure if the government would eliminate the defense minister, and with him all the commanders and soldiers in the country and establish in their place an efficient civil guard, and a mounted police to insure individual security in a civilized manner. (Néstor Enrique Alvarado in *El Cronista*, 9 May 1955)

René Zelaya Smith, an army captain, responded with a phrase that would be heard for decades in the country: "If you want peace, prepare for war. . . . The armed forces are necessary to oversee the order and tranquillity of the country" (*El Cronista*, 30 May 1955).

Néstor Alvarado responded on 13 June with a most interesting argument, similar to the one made to this author some four decades later by Gonzalo Facio in Costa Rica. The United States is the hegemon in the region and Honduras would be safer and have more money in the bank if it would free ride on the United States and the security guarantees that the Panamerican system provided. After several more articles by Néstor Alvarado and defenders of the military, Andrés Alvarado Lozano, a schoolteacher from the Copán region, entered the fray.

> If there is one thing that Honduras has in common with Costa Rica . . . it is in the absence of a military caste which weighs on the politics of its people. . . . From this national army, from this military academy that Señor Alonzo asks for, there will emerge an insolent military clique, that over time will become the great headache for Honduras for many years. It is better to be like Costa Rica with an army of teachers than to expose yourself to the creation of a military caste, which has caused bitter tears throughout the Caribbean. (*El Cronista*, 7 July 1995)

Captain Juan Espinoza countered that modern militaries are not like those of old, but are pro-democratic and nonpolitical. And, added Espinoza, Costa Rica has twenty thousand well-trained men (*El Cronista*, 9 July 1955).[18] A few days later, another pro-military argument appeared, and

18. Andrés Alvarado responded that Costa Rica did not have a military and it only appeared to have lots of soldiers when teachers and volunteers took up arms to fight Somoza, Picado, and Calderonistas (*El Cronista*, 19 July 1955).

the key point would be echoed by Jeanne Kirkpatrick to the Costa Ricans some twenty-five years later.[19] "In Honduras a professional army is not only necessary but urgent. The truth is that we have no military. And since we have no military, it is doubtful that we have a state. This is the truth. The military does consume the budget. With a military other services will be reduced. But the military guarantees the state" (*El Cronista*, 12 July 1955). A week later, J. Simeon Alonzo of the military academy confidently expounded pro-military arguments that would prove fallacious:

> The Republic of Chile is one of the most civilized and cultured nations of South America, it has an armed forces that is a source of great pride, a complete democracy lives there, our first military mentors were from this exemplary nation and even today the teachings of the Chilean soldiers flow in our environment. If in Chile there has never been and there will never be the military caste that you so greatly fear, why can't Honduras structure a similar armed forces? (*El Cronista*, 18 July 1955)

Alonzo and other military proponents continued to promise that modern militaries do not meddle in politics and that they do not deliberate. Professional soldiers only fight external enemies. Colonel Armando Velásquez gave one of the first official military comments carried by the press. Velásquez, who had penned *La Fuerzas Armadas de Una Democracia* in 1954 (*The Armed Forces of a Democracy*) and had received special training at Fort Leavenworth, would quite ironically participate in various coup attempts in the coming years. In *El Cronista*, the colonel celebrated the emergence of a professional military institution and lauded the United States for assisting in its creation:

> We should give our most sincere gratitude to the members of the missions of the United States armed forces that have provided such ample cooperation to our government in this stage of the restoration of the military system. With their cooperation, diverse courses of information and capacitation were organized in which the officers received many teachings on modern war, unifying doctrines and knowledge. With these contingents of officials and courses we

19. For an excellent account of U.S. efforts to militarize Costa Rica in the 1980s, see Honey (1994).

> are able to give a start to the embryonic organization of our armed forces. (3 October 1955)

By 1956, the Honduran military was sending the defense minister to the U.S.-sponsored meetings of Central American War Ministers. These meetings would be institutionalized in 1963 as the *Consejo de Defensa Centro Americana* (CONDECA), a much-criticized creation of U.S. tutelage. With astute vision, a commentary in 1956 identified the future role of this military cooperation on the isthmus: the reunion of war ministers in Guatemala was "the final comedy performed in Central America. . . . In short, the recent meetings of Central American war ministers contribute nothing in support of the continental cause, neither for peace nor for the likely acrimony. . . . These councils have revealed the design of an especially strong egoism and support for the prolongation of dictatorships" (Hernán Robles in *El Cronista*, 3 October 1956). And Robles was absolutely right. CONDECA's focus dealt strictly with internal security measures and was an instrument of U.S. policy (LaFeber 1984, 151). The same Robles also warned Honduras that the United States was arming and supporting dictators in the supposed defense of democracy. Unfortunately, the people were ignoring the possibility that these same weapons of democracy would someday be used to put down those that exercise their democratic right to protest (*El Cronista*, 22 February 1956). In a commentary entitled "The Crisis of Democracy," *El Cronista* sharply criticized the United States and the militarization of the continent: "Instead of winning the support of our people with practical projects, they destroy the forces capable of defeating communism and opt instead for arming dictators with tanks, cannons, and planes. . . . Militarism is the wrong answer to Communism and Latin America will suffer for the U.S. policy" (6 April 1956). And finally in the following year, after the military had staged its first coup, which was greeted with widespread support, another wise Honduran scolded his fellow citizens for having too much faith in "*los gloriosos*," for the Latin American military and democracy are mutually exclusive (Humberto Rivera y Morillo in *El Cronista*, 26 June 1957). By this time, Honduras had a strong military institution that would soon get much stronger with the 1957 constitution. Honduras had chosen *los gloriosos* and democracy would be smothered by the same voices that so often promised that this was a new, pro-democratic, and nondeliberative force.

The public debate on the pros and cons of militarization confirms the claim by Funes (1995), Ropp (1974), and Salomón (1992) that Honduras lacked an institutionalized military at the midpoint of the twentieth century. It also reveals that the development of a professional armed forces did not happen unopposed and automatically. To have a strong military or to follow Costa Rica in having only a civilian-controlled police force was one of the dominant issues in the leading independent press in the 1954–57 period. The articulate and far-sighted opponents of militarization presented a sophisticated and well-founded defense of the then visible and viable Costa Rican model: a military consumes too many resources; the United States is the hegemon and little Honduras should free ride as the United States will not permit serious threats to regional stability on the isthmus; the Panamerican institutions such as the Rio Treaty can ensure the existence of the Honduran state; the founding of a professional military will evolve into a monster and will be a great headache for the country; and civilian leadership will never fully develop as it will be smothered by the power of the military. Looking back at these arguments forty-five years later, the opponents to the militarization project were absolutely correct. With the United States actively pushing the militarization project, however, the debate was moot and the development of a military caste forged ahead.

Political Development after Gálvez

In addition to providing room for an expansion of political, civil, labor, and economic forces in the country, President Gálvez oversaw a relatively free election in 1954. Martz, who disapproved of Costa Rica's Figueres, wrote that Gálvez "was one of the most democratic Central American presidents of recent years—one of the very, very few" (1959, 129). For the 1954 elections, the National Party selected the old caudillo, seventy-eight-year-old Tiburcio Carías, as their nominee. This split the party and the *Partido Reformista* resulted, which subsequently selected the former Carías vice president and the now archenemy, Abraham Williams, as its standard bearer. Ramón Villeda Morales, a pediatrician who had studied in Guatemala and Germany and who represented the pragmatic democratic Left, was nominated by the Liberals.

Villeda was cultured and well-read, and is often compared with José Figueres. A self-styled urban petty bourgeois reformer, Villeda Morales at times was even linked with the liberal radicalism of Víctor Raul Haya de la Torre of Peru, Luis Muñoz Marín of Puerto Rico, Jose Figueres of Costa Rica, Juan Arévalo of Guatemala, Ramón Grau San Martin of Cuba, Juan Bosch of the Dominican Republic, Rómulo Bétancourt of Venezuela, Germán Arciniegas of Colombia, Pedro Joaquín Chomorro of Nicaragua, and others.[20] In the 1950s, he was supported and befriended (like Figueres) in the United States by well-connected, anticommunist liberals like Adolph A. Berle,[21] later a policy advisor to the Kennedy administration (Euraque 1996, 70). Like other liberals such as Figueres, Villeda was often smeared as a communist. Just before the 1954 elections, for example, *El Espectador*, the voice of President Gálvez, repeatedly referred to the Liberal Party as the "Partido Liberal Comunista." In 1955, when Otilio Ulate was violently opposed to Figueres and was using all his energies to destroy him, his *Diario de Costa Rica* lumped Villedismo and Figuerismo in the same dangerous category—leftist and to be destroyed: "Doctor Villeda Morales is intimately connected with the regime of President Figueres in Costa Rica. This is because of the similarity of their ideas, because people of the same ideology travel back and forth between the countries. . . . The Honduran Liberal Party and the Costa Rican National Liberation Party share the same (leftist) destiny" (reprinted in *El Cronista*, 24 August 1955). The United States also feared some of the more radical views that Villeda had expressed and linked the Liberal Party with the Arbenz regime in Guatemala. The FBI was brought in to investigate charges that communism ran rampant in the Liberal Party. U.S. Ambassador Whitting Willauer, a constant meddler in Honduran politics, was highly suspicious of Villeda and worked tirelessly to forestall the 1954 elections that might, in his view, transfer the elected leftist problem from Guatemala City to Tegucigalpa (Cruz 1982).[22]

20. A remarkably large number of these men were at one time or another either deposed or exiled by the armed forces of their own countries. The exception of course is Figueres, who did not face a military. Villeda is often portrayed as identifying closely with Figueres and wanting to follow the path of Costa Rica; for example, see LaFeber (1984, 133). Villeda's desire to follow Figueres was so strong that he actually sent Don Pepe as the representative of Honduras to the Punta del Este Conference in Uruguay in 1961 to negotiate the Alliance for Progress principles (Vargas 1993, 457).

21. Berle played a crucial role in supporting and saving Figueres when counterrevolutionary forces were attempting his overthrow. Berle was unable to help Villeda when a sudden and violent military coup occurred in 1963.

22. Ramón Ernesto Cruz was a leading National Party official at the time and personally participated in meetings with Carías and Willauer. He was later elected president of the country in 1971 and was deposed in a coup in 1973. "Cruz was the pathetic example of the intellectual, with legal training, who participates in party politics without the capacity

In Honduras, the United States ambassador had always been extremely powerful. In 1954, that post was held by the consummate anticommunist, Whitting Willauer. Willauer had never set foot in Central America before he arrived in Honduras in February 1954. But he had long experience with communism, working for the CIA and the Chinese Nationalists in the late 1940s when Chairman Mao took power (Gleijeses 1991, 289). He did not want the same outcome in Central America. The new American ambassador had actually been originally nominated to go to Guatemala and oversee the overthrow of Arbenz but was switched to Honduras where he starred in a supporting role by keeping the Honduran government in line and providing the training of the Castillo Armas forces. The Great Banana Strike hit Honduras soon after Willauer's arrival and he saw "Pinkos" as the source of the trouble. In a letter to General Chenault of the Flying Tigers, Willauer wrote: "We have a helluva situation down here and unless really forceful action is taken we are going to have a little Commie Chine [sic] right in our own backyard" (Willauer quoted in MacCameron 1983, 58). He also "had evidence that the Liberal Party had been infiltrated with Leftist elements, that the Leftists had organized various communist cells within the Liberal Party and, in addition, with the fall of the Arbenz Guzmán government, it had been confirmed that the Liberal Party had been receiving financial assistance from said fallen regime" (Cruz 1982, 17).[23]

---

to establish his own style of political administration" (Argueta 1990, 52). Considered honest and legalistic, his testimony of the events of 1954 is used here to understand the role of Willauer and the United States. Cruz based his account on written notes of meetings with Willauer.

23. Of course the charge that Villeda was communist was absurd. Given the paranoia of the times, however, it was believed by many. Paranoia and the unfair fabrication of evidence against people like Figueres and Villeda are apparent in the following conversation from a U.S. Congressional Committee on Communist Aggression hearing in 1954. Patrick Hillings was a congressman, and John D. Erwin was the ambassador replaced by Willauer in 1954.

Mr. Hillings: Will you say that Morales (Villeda Morales), one of the leading candidates for the Presidency at the present time, has followed the Communist line in many of his statements and activities?

Mr. Erwin: I cannot say that because I heard none of his speeches during the campaign. I didn't see him quoted.

Mr. Hillings: Has he, as far as you know, in the past followed the Communist line on some issues where the Communists have taken determined stands?

Mr. Erwin: Well, he didn't hold political office, he was a doctor. He didn't have to vote on anything so it would be pretty hard to say about that. One thing I think helped him in his campaign, his wife was one of the first to champion women suffrage and

With the National Party split into Carías and Williams camps, the highly plausible election of Villeda at the head of a unified Partido Liberal made Willauer nervous. On 14 September 1954, the ambassador met with Carías in an attempt to guarantee that the liberal Villeda would fail. His plan was to get the caudillo to withdraw his candidacy and support a constitutional change for the *continuismo* of President Gálvez. In 1952, Gálvez had attempted to push reforms permitting reelection through the congress, but the measure lost. Now, Willauer argued that such a change was

---

this is the first year women have voted down there. Mrs. Morales [note the former ambassador's unfamiliarity with Spanish surnames even after serving two tours in Honduras] is a charming woman, daughter of a former foreign minister of the country now deceased—her father is deceased I mean—she was one of the people, one of the ladies who got out and organized the women voters of the country and Dr. Morales had quite a hand in it too.

Mr. Hillings: The fact that he supported women suffrage wouldn't mean he is a Communist?

Mr. Erwin: No. No. What I'm trying to get at there is in the elections he would naturally get a large block of women's votes—has nothing to do with Communism, of course.

Mr. Hillings: I don't know whether you are trying to evade my question or whether you just don't have any facts on it. You gave a definite inference in your statement that Morales may be a fellow that could be friendly to the Communists if he should be president of Honduras. That was the inference from what you said. I want you to tell me why.

Mr. Erwin: That is an impression I have.

Mr. Patrick McMahon: Could I ask you to clarify that?

Mr. Hillings: Just a minute. I want the witness to answer the question.

Mr. Erwin: I think most of his friends in nearby countries were all pretty much on the radical side. For instance, we don't know how his campaign is financed, but it was very well financed.

Mr. Hillings: Who were some of his friends in those other countries that you say are very radical?

Mr. Erwin: Well, we have some word that the President of Costa Rica [José Figueres]—Betancourt down there in Venezuela—

Mr. Hillings: . . . he was a former President of Venezuela; isn't that right?

Mr. Erwin: Yes.

Mr. Hillings: He was in effect kicked out of Venezuela?

Mr. Erwin: That is correct.

Mr. Hillings: Isn't he alleged to have made a speech one time in which he said, 'Yo soy Comunista'?

Mr. Erwin: That is right.

Mr. Hillings: Which means, 'I am a Communist'?

Mr. Erwin: So quoted.

Mr. Hillings: So that Betancourt has been a great friend of Morales?

Mr. Erwin: Whenever he went to San José to visit, which was often, we understood that he was usually in his company and was entertained by him.

(MacCameron 1983, 55–57)

necessary because the United States "desired to avoid that the Honduran political battle could result in the implantation of a regime like that recently deposed in Guatemala" (Cruz 1982, 16–17). Carías was opposed to a continuation of Gálvez and proposals to seek a unified candidate of the Reformist and National parties were fruitless given the extreme personal animosity between Carías and Williams.

In the weeks leading up to the elections, the country was inundated with floods that killed a thousand people and left many thousands homeless (*El Cronista*, 7 October 1954). The three contending parties asked for a postponement of the elections but Gálvez argued that the democratic process should continue without delay. Like so many other elections in Honduras, the election results provided both a clear winner and yet no winner. The final results were 121,213 votes for Villeda, 77,041 votes for Carías, and 53,041 votes for Williams. Villeda was a mere 8,869 votes short of the required majority and uncertainty ruled (Martz 1959, 140–48). Under Honduran law at the time, if no candidate received an absolute majority, the congress would decide the outcome by simple majority rule. Unfortunately, two-thirds of the deputies were required for a quorum to conduct business and when the National and Reformist deputies boycotted the proceedings in a ploy designed by Ambassador Willauer, a stalemate resulted (Argueta 1990, 110). The crisis deepened when Gálvez abandoned the country on 15 November, suffering from exhaustion and an apparent heart attack. On 6 December, an obscure vice president and former bookkeeper for the Rosario Mining Company named Julio Lozano seized dictatorial power. Lozano's ascent to the presidency was salutary for the "deathly ill" Gálvez, who was instantly healed and returned from New York on 8 December to assume the presidency of the Supreme Court (Funes 1995, 178).

Lozano was an inept president who became more and more repressive as time went on. In July 1956, several opponents of his regime, including Villeda, were exiled to Guatemala. They were soon exiled from Guatemala and ended up as Don Pepe's guests in Costa Rica. The move against Villeda sparked violent student demonstrations, business closings, and civil disobedience. In October, Lozano held one of the most fraudulent elections in the country's history. *El Cronista* announced the results under the title: "Although You May Not Believe It: May the People Be the Judge." The election results were as follows: the official National Union Party had 370,318 votes, the Liberals had 2,003 votes, and the National

Party had 41,724. In the Intibucá Department, the ruling party won all 13,616 votes cast (*El Cronista,* 19 October 1956). On 20 October, the military high command visited Lozano to warn him that they had detected a possible coup and that they would be flying air force planes around the capital in a show of support. Lozano was pleased. On 21 October, the planes began circling the skies of Tegucigalpa and the little dictator soon discovered that they were not there to support him, but to depose him. "I have been deceived" (Funes 1995, 186). The first military coup of the century had been executed.[24]

The country was ecstatic. This really was a new military at the service of the people. 21 October would be a national holiday and the new name of various communities around the country. Hernán Robles, who had previously warned of militarism, now used the pages of *El Cronista* to praise the honorable professional military: "The army will be the permanent custodian of the popular will" (10 December 1956). A three-man ruling military junta gave strong signals that this was a progressive and modern military.[25] The junta was composed of air force commander Héctor Caraccioli, ex-President Gálvez's son Roberto Gálvez, and commander of the military academy General Roque Rodríguez. They abolished the death penalty in early November (*El Cronista,* 3 November 1956), freed political prisoners, formed a cabinet with members from all political parties, and promised to stay in power only until a democratic government could be installed. On 11 November, the junta sent an air force plane to fetch Villeda from Costa Rica. Villeda's dignity in exile had made him a national hero and thousands greeted him upon his return. Villeda was soon sent to Washington as the country's ambassador, where he solidified friendships with progressives such as Adolph Berle and where he worked hard to rid himself of the "communist" tag.

While the ousting of Lozano was welcomed, it also ushered in the era of the military as the final arbiter of politics. The development of the institution was complete, going from nearly nonexistent in 1954 to the dominant institution only two years later. As Funes notes, the rapid

24. The first nonmilitary coup was in 1904 when Manuel Bonilla closed Congress and jailed some deputies, including Policarpo Bonilla (personal communication with Mario Argueta).

25. There were reactionary sectors within society and the military that viewed the junta as too progressive. Colonel Armando Velásquez Cerrato headed a coup attempt in May 1957. The attempt failed and the colonel found refuge in the Guatemalan embassy (Becerra 1983, 168).

growth of the military suddenly overshadowed civil society and political institutions (1995, 192–93).

The 1957 Constitution

The requirement of an absolute majority to win the presidency had led the country from electoral crisis to electoral crisis. The country needed a new constitution and elections for the Constitutional Assembly were held on 22 September 1957. The Liberal Party dominated in a clean and honest balloting, gaining 209,109 votes and thirty-six deputies, as compared to 101,274 votes and eighteen deputies for the National Party, and 29,489 votes and four deputies for the National Reformist Party (Becerra 1983, 168; Funes 1995, 193). On 21 October 1957, exactly one year after the ousting of Lozano, the Liberal Party-controlled Constitutional Assembly convened.

For our purposes, only two highly related results of the assembly need be discussed: the autonomy of the military and the selection of Ramón Villeda Morales as president. Everyone in the country knew who would win a presidential election. Villeda was as popular as anyone had ever been. The ruling junta had often declared that after the Constitutional Assembly met, a new election would be held to select the president. Dr. Villeda himself wanted the legitimacy of a direct election, and scoffed at the idea that the Constitutional Assembly could select the president (*El Cronista*, 24 September 1957).

On 14 November 1957, the ruling military junta and the Liberal Party suddenly reversed course and decided that there should be no direct election and that Villeda should be declared president. The armed forces decreed that "due to the difficult circumstances that affect the country, it has not been possible to strictly comply" with our promise to hold a second election (Oquelí 1981, 3). One member of the ruling military junta—Roberto Gálvez—resigned in protest and was replaced by Oswaldo López Arrelano, who quickly became the strong man of the armed forces. The Liberals publicly argued that Villeda had won the two previous elections and that the country could not afford to have another election when the outcome was already known (Becerra 1983, 169).

For Villeda to agree to become president without a presidential election appears to be completely irrational. He was wildly popular and revered almost as a saint by the majority of the people. Pictures of the bookish doctor with thick horn-rimmed glasses appeared on newspaper front pages and were hung on the walls of homes throughout the country (interview with Matías Funes 12 December 1995, Tegucigalpa, Honduras; interview with Ramón Oquelí 24 July 1997, Tegucigalpa, Honduras). And before the sudden move to have him declared president, Villeda had unequivocally and publicly declared that he would not take the presidency without a direct election by the people (*El Cronista*, 24 September 1957). What happened? A deal was made between Villeda and the military junta, the details of which remain a shrouded mystery of secret meetings, threats, and backroom deals. Most scholars believe that a deal involving the U.S. State Department, the United Fruit Company, the Honduran military, and the Liberal Party resulted in the naming of Villeda.[26]

"What happened is very simple: military officers and Liberal Party officials held various secret meetings and agreed to various important agreements" (Funes 1995, 194). But, these were not the only actors involved. Ambassador Whitting Willauer, executives of the United Fruit Company including company president Kenneth Redmond, and other State Department officials reportedly met at the UFCO's plush Blue Waters Villa and agreed to the "Pacto del Agua Azul" (Natalini de Castro, Mendoza, and Pagan 1995, 144–54; Funes 1995, 194–97; MacCameron 1983, 97–98). This pact called for an exchange: the military and the United States would support the declaration of Villeda as president of the country, and in return Villeda would grant the military immense constitutional autonomy and power.

This explanation, however, remains unconvincing. Again, Villeda could easily win a direct election that would provide legitimacy that a selection by the Constitutional Assembly would not. Ramón Oquelí, the noted Honduran scholar and journalist, and an objective and dispassionate fountain of information on the country, provides one possible explanation. Ac-

26. "Various commentators have noted a meeting on 9 November 1957 attended by Ambassador Whitting Willauer, local executives of the United Fruit Co., State Department representatives, and Villeda Morales. . . . Only access to State Department archives or testimony of alleged participants will clarify this issue. However, State Department records later recognized that 'although the military supported the advent of power of the Villeda Morales regime, they did so with reluctance and only after being accorded special constitutional status making them semi-independent of the President'" (Euraque 1996, 176 n. 64). I attempted to arrange an interview with Oswaldo López Arellano, who is rumored to possess a copy of *el Pacto de Agua Azul*, but was unsuccessful.

cording to Oquelí, the arrangement was masterminded by the calculating strongman of the military, Oswaldo López. López had previously declared to the people that "on one day not very far off, the (armed forces) will become the maximum representation of the national conglomerate" and that the "armed forces could no longer be considered a fleeting phenomenon in the institutional life of the country" (Funes 1995, 92–93). To make this dream a reality, López tricked Villeda by telling him that the very popular Roberto Gálvez Barnes of the military junta would be the unified candidate of the military, the Nationalists, and the Reformists if a direct election were held. He also warned Villeda that the military would not be able to guarantee a clean and fair election. Villeda was left with no better option than to accept the deal. After the deal was consummated, Roberto Gálvez Barnes left the ruling junta to protest the decision to forego the presidential elections. In a conversation with Villeda, Gálvez told him that he had never contemplated plans to run for the presidency. Villeda discovered the trick, but it was too late (interview with Ramón Oquelí, 24 July 1997, Tegucigalpa, Honduras).

Whether Oquelí's account is accurate or not, we are certain that a quid pro quo of monumental proportions was agreed to. The prize for Villeda was enormous, a six-year term as the president. The payback to the military was even greater. The Liberals pushed through Title XIII of the constitution by a vote of thirty-two to seventeen, which gave the armed forces "more freedom of action [for a Latin American military] than any document since Paraguay's constitution of 1844" (Johnson 1964, 162).

> Article 318: The Armed Forces will be under the direct command of the Chief of the Armed Forces; *through him* the President of the Republic will exercise the constitutional function that belongs to him respecting the military institution.
>
> Article 319: The orders that the President of the Republic imparts to the Armed Forces, through the Chief of the Armed Forces, must be adhered to. *When a conflict arises, it must be submitted to the consideration of Congress*, which will decide by a majority vote. This resolution will be definitive and must be adhered to.[27]
>
> Article 321: The Chief of the Armed Forces, upon taking charge

27. In the constitutions of 1894, 1906, 1924, and 1936, the president had direct control over the armed forces.

> of his position, will issue before the National Congress the following solemn oath: 'In my name and the name of the Armed Forces of Honduras, I solemnly swear that I will never resort to instruments of oppression; *even though our superiors command it*, we will not respect orders that violate the spirit or letter of the Constitution: that we will defend the national sovereignty and integrity of our land . . .
>
> Article 330: The administration of funds assigned to the Defense Branch, will be controlled by the Bursar of the Armed Forces.

Article 330 led to a secret budget, completely shielded from civilian oversight. The constitution of 1957 allows the chief of the armed forces to disobey the president merely by claiming that the president's orders are against the spirit of the constitution, and indeed directs the soldiers to obey the military chief when he is in disagreement with the president. In addition, Title XIII of the 1957 constitution provided for the armed forces to determine promotions and control the naming of the commander in chief of the armed forces.[28] "It is obvious that the autonomy conferred to the Armed Forces in 1957 converted the army into a sort of uncontrollable Frankenstein" (Funes 1995, 318). Even at the time, the implications of these concessions were obvious. Deputy Horacio Moya Posas characterized Article 319 as "a time bomb that will always be placed within the organization of the Government" (quoted in Oquelí 1981, 3). It was only a matter of time before the time bomb exploded. Democracy was now destined to fail.[29]

It is highly plausible that the handwriting of the constitutional provision for the armed forces to disobey the president if they disagreed with him was that of Ambassador Willauer. If Villeda turned out to be a replay of Arbenz, Willauer wanted weapons to work with. In 1954, the ambassador had first attempted to deny a presidential victory to Villeda by pushing for a continuation of Gálvez, and when that failed he urged the National and Reformist deputies to block Villeda's ascent to the presidency in 1954

28. This section is drawn from *La Gaceta* (Honduras, 20 December 1957), *El Cronista* (1957), Johnson (1964, 162–63), Funes (1995), MacCameron (1983, 94–95), and Becerra (1983).

29. The contrast between the Honduran 1957 constitution and the Costa Rican 1949 constitution is stark. The Costa Rican article dealing with the military states: "The army is proscribed as a permanent institution. For the vigilance and conservation of public order there will be the necessary police forces."

by preventing a quorum in the National Assembly (see Cruz 1982; Oquelí 1995, 155). In 1957, the embassy approved Villeda, but only after "Whitting Willauer was the composer of Article 319" of the constitution (Oquelí 1995, 342).

The Sexenio of President Villeda

Villeda was an admirer of Figueres and would become a great admirer of Kennedy (Funes 1995, 230). Upon taking office, he began an ambitious program of school building and infrastructure development. He would also propose an ambitious program of land reform that challenged the oligarchy and the international banana barons (Woodward 1985, 255–56). He walked a political tightrope between those who accused him of being leftist and those who accused him of being reactionary. With the United States leery, he, like Figueres, took every opportunity to demonstrate his anticommunism, outlawing subversive material and breaking diplomatic relations with Castro's Cuba. Villeda and Figueres had very similar lists of enemies: during his term, Anastasio Somoza and Rafael Trujillo would both be involved in plots to overthrow Villeda (Euraque 1996, 112) and from the moment he took office, "the ultraconservative groups . . . never abandoned their conspiracies and plans" to overthrow him. In his first year, reactionary groups used bombs and a clandestine radio station—Liberation Radio used the march from *Bridge over the River Kwai* as its theme—in an attempt to destabilize the country (Becerra 1983, 170).

The pediatrician turned president also inherited a basket case. The economy and the budget were in shambles (Martz 1959, 161–63). And as Villeda often proclaimed, Honduras was the "country of the 70s"—70 percent illiteracy, 70 percent illegitimacy, 70 percent rural population, and 70 percent avoidable deaths. Given the circumstances, his work as president was impressive. Like his mentor Figueres, Villeda saw the state as the tool to build a new bourgeoisie. Villeda's priority was education (Posas and del Cid 1983, 176). During his tenure, the number of elementary education students rose from 146,000 to 259,000 and the number of teachers nearly doubled from 4,600 to 8,800 (Natalini, Mendoza, and Pagan 1985, 85). The average annual increase in elementary schools was 30 schools per year from 1950 to 1957, and during the Villeda presidency exploded to 232 new schools per year from 1958 to 1962. The percentage of the budget assigned to education rose from 8 percent in 1950 to 16 percent in 1963 and Villeda provided 50 percent more money for the public university in his six years than had his predecessors in twenty-four years (Posas and del Cid 1983, 176–77). As a doctor, Villeda also had a clear vision of the state of health services, and the number of health centers more than doubled from twenty-nine to sixty-three in his six-year term (Natalini, Mendoza, and Pagan 1985, 87). The country also had a notable diminution in infant mortality (Argueta 1990, 187).

With the assistance of the Alliance for Progress,[30] Villeda oversaw the improvement of public services, the extension and paving of the highway system, reforms of the judicial system, and the first stages of industrialization. For example, the state opened a cement factory in 1959 and cement consumption rose from 600,000 bags to 1,046,000 bags in four years (Natalini, Mendoza, and Pagan 1985, 72). Human capital and infrastructure, the building blocks of sustained economic development, were being addressed as never before in the country.

Villeda also introduced a Labor Code in 1959. Copied largely from Costa Rica and Mexico, the Labor Code was met with protest from the representatives of the oligarchy and the banana companies (Posas and del Cid 1983, 177–78). The 1961 creation of the National Agrarian Institute, mandated to oversee agrarian reform, was anathema to the landed oligarchy, who had "continued conspiring the entire duration of the Villeda Morales government" (Rojas 1993, 130). Villeda and democracy, however, were now supported by a burgeoning civil society, including the strongest labor movement in Central America,[31] an active student movement that benefited greatly from Villeda's budgetary commitment to education and

30. Honduras was the first Latin American country to qualify for development money under the Alliance for Progress. "By the fall of 1961, the government had formulated the mandatory four-year development program which, among its general social and economic goals, included agrarian reform, resource development, and highway construction" (MacCameron 1983, 112).

31. Honduran labor organizations arrived late, even by Central American standards. The Honduran Workers Union was formed in 1921 (Acuña 1993, 283). Fed largely by labor organizing on the North Coast banana plantations, labor grew rapidly and "Honduras developed a much larger and politically more potent organized work force than other Central American countries" (Booth and Walker 1993, 48–49). For example, data for 1973 reveal that Honduras had more union members than any other Central American country and many more agricultural union members than the rest of the isthmus combined (Euraque 1996, 99). The best study of the labor movement in Honduras is Meza (1991), who argues the expansion and consolidation of the syndicate movement in the country occurred during the Villeda years (chapter 5).

personal support of university autonomy, a free press, an emerging urban middle class, and—as Euraque so convincingly demonstrates—a pro-democratic small business and industrial sector on the dynamic Northern Coast. In addition, Villeda had emerged as the poster boy of the Kennedy administration's commitment to the Alliance for Progress and its hope for democratic government. The domestic oligarchy, especially the large landowners and the National Party, were strongly opposed to *Villedismo*, but by themselves were far too weak to challenge the progressive changes occurring in the country. As Euraque states: "up to October 1963 it seemed that perhaps Villeda Morales's presidency finally could assert that it was a maximum expression of the progressive changing time" (1996, 120). Honduras was poised to finally emerge from its long morass and make strides in its quality of governance and its living standards.

Class, transnational, and state power relations would have strongly favored the emergence of democracy, except for one important caveat. The growth of the military after 1954 and the constitutional powers granted to the institution in 1957 placed the Honduran armed forces at the intersection of all three of the power relations that Rueschemeyer, Stephens, and Stephens (1992) have identified as important for the emergence and durability of democracy. The military negatively affected all three power relations.

Villeda and the Military, 1957–1963

After 1957, it soon became apparent to the Liberal Party that the constitutional prerogatives and power provided to the Honduran armed forces were incompatible with democracy. The military made constant demands on the civilian government, including requests for changes in the cabinet (*El Cronista*, 7 April 1958). Flagellations and even the shooting of civilians by security forces occurred, and with the constitutional independence of the military, no civilian charges could ever be brought. The press began to question the "constant brutality" committed by soldiers (*El Cronista*, 27 February 1959). The murder of two students at the hands of the military in 1959 resulted in a surge of protests (Oquelí 1981, 4). In May 1959, Francisco Milla Bermúdez, then magistrate of the Supreme Court and designate to the presidency—and one of the leaders of the Liberal Party who actively participated in the constitutional deal-making that granted near omnipotent powers to the military—declared to the *Miami Herald* that the best thing for Honduras would be the dissolution of the armed forces. The armed forces, added Milla, consumed too great a part of the budget and the army was politically aligned with enemies of the government (*El Cronista*, 11 May 1959).

The generals were furious with the Milla statement. The general public was not. In an article entitled "The Popular Opinion Says That We Suppress the Army," *El Cronista* reported that the public response to the Milla comments was completely unexpected; the people wanted the soldiers to abandon the barracks and "seek other more dignified means of daily sustenance" (*El Cronista*, 14 May 1959). The university students also seconded Milla's proposal. *El Cronista* reproduced a declaration from the UNAH (Universidad Nacional Autónoma de Honduras) that "applauded" Milla and added that the students were neither supporters nor adversaries of Villeda's "Government of the Second Republic," but that they were "enemies of the military caste, because when this OGRE grows dictatorships result" (15 May 1959). Milla responded that he was not the enemy of the military, but that he did aspire to follow the lead of Costa Rica and replace barracks with schools (Funes 1995, 222).[32] Of course, the genie was already out of the bottle and the United States would never have permitted the demilitarization of Honduras.

On 12 July 1959, Villeda faced his first military coup attempt. Colonel Armando Velásquez Cerrato, who in 1954 wrote so eloquently about the new, nondeliberative, and apolitical military, led the rebellion—his second in two years.[33] Velásquez, who was closely associated with the National Party, Somoza in Nicaragua, and the most reactionary forces in the country, was supported above all by the National Police.[34] The coup was violent, leading to many dead and injured. For the first few hours of the coup,

32. In this time period, there are many references to following the Tico example and going *sans armee*. In April 1958, Costa Rica attempted to push a proposal through the Organization of American States for the disarming of all of Latin America. The proposal was voted down (*El Cronista*, 18 April 1958).

33. This is the same Velásquez who attempted a right-wing coup against the "progressive" military junta in May 1957. The most conservative forces in the country did not approve of the progressive rhetoric of the young colonels (Becerra 1983, 168).

34. The most conservative elements of both the National Party and the Reformist Party gave support and even organized right-wing guerrilla groups to aid Velásquez (Natalini, Mendoza, and Pagan 1985, 117).

the "loyal" members of the armed forces stood on the sideline waiting to see if the coup would gain momentum. Students and other members of the civil society rushed to Villeda's defense and fought valiantly against the rebels; UNAH students saved Villeda. When the coup produced no quick victory, the head of the military stepped in and arranged for an end to the attempt and permitted Velásquez to flee the country (Becerra 1983, 172; Oquelí 1981, 4).

The impunity of the armed forces, the coup against democracy, and the belated defense of the government by the head of the military resulted in a backlash against the armed forces. Efforts to curb armed forces power emerged on two fronts. One occurred in the National Congress when Liberal Deputy Ildefonso Orellana Bueso introduced a motion to reform Title XIII of the 1957 constitution.[35] Orellana's perspicacious speech included the following statements:

> This group of individuals clustered with the pompous name of "Armed Forces" wants to convert themselves into a privileged and all-embracing caste, shielding itself to reach its goals in Title XIII of our fundamental law, from whose trench they are preparing to stab the back of the Honduran people, having now been converted not only in the devouring octopus of the national budget, but also in a real social threat, in an imminent danger for our own security, and in an enemy of the functioning democracy in which we have dedicated our faith. . . . When we established Title XIII of the Constitution, we did not have the right to toss the dominion of the bayonets on the patriotic people that loves its institutions and knows how to defend them. A people that knew how to throw themselves on the battlefield in the instant of danger, knowing how to heroically fight for its rights when they were trampled on. It is therefore an obligation for us, as legitimate representatives of the people, to return the peace and tranquillity that they enjoyed before the implantation of the dictators. If we do not make this change, we are leaving open a great crack, an open door, and through this crack or this open door, a caste that longs to perpetuate itself in power can enter. . . . This can be seen even by the blind

35. The Orellana speech was reproduced in its entirety in *El Cronista* from December 16–19, 1959.

> and by the children. We are on the verge of a military dictatorship. The country has been left to the law of the bayonets . . . after a series of individual and collective murders. . . . The country breathes blood everywhere. We repeat: Never has a tyrant dared to so challenge the citizenry! Not Tiburcio Carías Andino with his team of delinquents! Not Julio Lozano Díaz with his gang of gunslingers! (*El Cronista*, December 16–19, 1959)

Orellana provided a list of 117 soldiers and officers who had committed serious crimes but who were protected by the military tribunal. His motion called for the substitution of the words "armed forces" for "army" and the constitutional elimination of the autonomy of the military that created a "state within a state." The military would, under Orellana's motion, be controlled by elected civilians, soldiers would not be protected from the courts for common crimes, and the army's budget would be administered by the executive branch. Finally, all promotions and leadership positions would be determined by the president. *El Cronista* supported the motion, stating that the future of Honduran democracy depended on the approval of the bill (16 December 1959). The Orellana bill ended up generating a great national debate, and the bulk of the citizenry supported it according to press reports, but the armed forces were far too powerful for such a law to pass (Funes 1995, 227).

President Villeda knew that he could not at this moment weaken the power of the armed forces, and so he opted to create a neutralizing force. Within a week of the Velásquez coup and the participation of the military-controlled National Police, Villeda began to organize a civil guard that would be under complete control of the president.[36] The National Police was disbanded. The civil guard and the armed forces were constant rivals and violent episodes between the two forces were common. In March 1961, the army killed nine civil guards after the army had lost a soccer game to them. The soldiers were evidently upset when the goal that tied the game was annulled (Funes 1995, 229). In September 1961 at Los Laureles, the civil guard massacred eleven soldiers and civilians who were caught in a coup attempt against the government (Becerra 1983, 173).

36. Hernández Martínez in El Salvador, Ibáñez in Chile, and Leguía in Peru also created police forces to counterbalance the army. See Loveman (1999).

Land Reform

Like Costa Rica, Honduras never faced a problem of the landed dispossessed before the middle of this century. By the 1950s, the agricultural frontier and the escape valve for those seeking land was disappearing. Throughout Central America, the transition to export agriculture with an emphasis on cattle ranching and cotton was adding to tensions, as large numbers of peasants were being dislodged from their lands (Brockett 1987, 1991; Kincaid 1987, 1989; Williams 1986).

In Honduras, the landless problem was compounded by an influx of Salvadoran immigrants and the dismissal of thousands of banana workers who were now seeking land for subsistence farming. The growth of the coffee industry based on small farms was able to ameliorate but not resolve the land problem. Agrarian conflict soon emerged as a national powder keg and land invasions increased in frequency and violence.

In response, Villeda set up a colonization program that distributed 75,000 acres of national and *ejidal* (communal) land between 1958 and 1960 (Schulz and Schulz 1994, 29). In 1962, the government sponsored a new peasant union, the National Association of Honduran Peasants (ANACH). These measures would not alone solve the nation's land problems. The Liberal Party had, since 1953, supported "the principle of expropriation for reason of public utility and necessity" and was committed to "limit land concentration in the hands of the *latifundistas*" (Liberal Party Platform, quoted in Euraque 1996, 103). In 1961, in direct response to the mandatory four-year development program of the Alliance for Progress, the government had targeted land reform as a priority (MacCameron 1983, 112). The three goals of the 1962 Agrarian Reform Law were: (1) a more efficient use of farmland by requiring large landowners to put their idle lands to use or lose them to expropriation, (2) to clarify the legal ownership of disputed lands, and (3) to provide an escape valve for the growing mass of landless peasants (Schulz and Schulz 1994, 29).

The landed oligarchy, the UFCO, and certain U.S. officials were furious. As had happened since Villeda took office and as would happen for decades when land reform was discussed in Latin America, his enemies accused him of being a closet communist and an ally of people such as Castro. "Every time that the agricultural question pushes its way to the top of priorities and the government gives indications of being willing to put a land reform law into effect, outside attacks of an imminent 'communist infiltration' in our country intensify. The trick is old, but nevertheless has remained no less effective: to smear as 'communist' all intents of social transformation" (Meza 1981, 71). The UFCO was outraged by the fact that they did not receive, as was their custom, an advance copy of the law and an opportunity to veto the points that they did not like. On 7 September 1961, the president of UFCO, Thomas Sunderland, sent a note to Edwin Martin, assistant secretary of state:

> The events of today indicate that the situation in Honduras is growing more serious with the passing of time. In spite of the affirmations made by President Villeda Morales in the presence of the American Ambassador that a copy of the proposed law would be shown to us today, Honduran government officials have declined to show the bill. . . . We urgently need action by the State Department through the American Ambassador with the goal of obtaining a copy of this proposal before it is too late to take action to defend American interests. (Quoted in Meza 1981, 8)

The State Department and UFCO allies in the U.S. Senate went quickly to work. A debate on the floor of the U.S. Senate quickly devolved into flag waving and threats against Honduras. Senator Hickenlooper, the author of the Hickenlooper Amendment that punished countries that expropriated or nationalized U.S. properties, was not opposed to using the communist smear: "Last Sunday, yesterday, the Agrarian Reform Law was signed at a large ceremony. There was a large number of speeches with references that the Hondurans were going to confiscate American property and that this belonged to the people of the country. Apparently one of the speakers had recently returned from Castro's Cuba" (quoted in Meza 1981, 8).

Two months after signing the Agrarian Reform Law, Villeda was summoned to Washington to meet with Kennedy at the White House. After this meeting, Villeda removed the progressive director of the National Agrarian Institute (INA) and "agrarian reform shifted drastically from expropriation of private property to colonization or resettlement projects upon state-owned land" (MacCameron 1983, 113; also see Brockett 1991). Villeda had seen what happened to Arbenz when the CIA and the UFCO decided that he was a threat. Land reform continued in a watered-down version and the country headed into the 1963 elections.

The 1963 Elections and the End of Honduran Democracy

The National Party entered the electoral season in crisis. Due to the support given the Liberals by the peasants, the working class, the emerging middle class, and the North Coast industrialists, the Liberal Party looked strong going into the election. Ramón Cruz defeated Gonzalo Carías Castillo, the son of the old caudillo, by only three votes in the National Party Convention. Gonzalo Carías proceeded to form his own party, splitting the Nationalists. The Liberal Party selected Modesto Rodas Alvarado even though Villeda favored another candidate. Villeda and most of the party maintained unity. Roque J. Rivera, a leader of the Tegucigalpa conservative elite who was expelled from the Liberal Party in 1962 for denouncing the "communist infiltration" in the Villeda government, organized the Orthodox Republican Party but it did not gain many adherents from the Liberal ranks (Becerra 1983, 174).

Rodas was the charismatic and intelligent former president of the Constitutional Assembly that wrote the 1957 constitution. Some argue that he had fought the provision granting autonomy to the armed forces (MacCameron 1983, 116; Schulz and Schulz 1994, 31). He later supported attempts by Orellana and Bueso to restore civilian control over the armed forces. By 1963, he campaigned in front of large and animated crowds largely on the demilitarization platform. The debate on militarization had never really ceased for the entire decade 1954–63. The demilitarization platform was apparently popular with the Honduran masses, as Rodas was the clear favorite and huge crowds cheered his demilitarization speeches. At the height of the campaign season, Costa Rican Foreign Minister Daniel Oduber visited the country with an endorsement for demilitarization: "The communist threat is banished with laws that benefit the peasants. I don't believe that the Armed Forces are even necessary in our countries" (*El Cronista*, 7 September 1963).

In the months leading up to the elections, as in the 1953 election in Costa Rica, the oligarchy and the most conservative forces continued to smear the government with charges of communism. Monseñor Héctor Enrique Santos, the Archbishop of Tegucigalpa, gave a series of masses in September asking God and the heavenly hosts to stop the communist infiltration that was gnawing away the foundation of the nation (Funes 1995, 236). Rumors of an impending coup had circulated since the spring (*El Cronista*, 9 and 23 April 1963). The United States was well aware of the coup plans and publicly denied the possibility of a military overthrow of Villeda: "Honduras represents a case of significant and true progress towards the stabilization of democracy and institutional maturity. A government democratically elected is getting ready to finish its six-year term, during which the military forces have been distinguished by its loyalty to the Constitution and the democratic regime" (Secretary of State Dean Rusk on the *Voice of America*, *El Cronista*, 28 September 1963). Privately, the State Department and the embassy knew differently. Latin America had witnessed a number of coups in 1962 and 1963 and the Kennedy administration did not want to see one of their favorites—Villeda—be the victim of yet another embarrassment for the Alliance for Progress.[37] Then-Ambassador Burrows actively discouraged the coup, warning López Arellano that President Kennedy would suspend economic aid if the *golpe* proceeded.

On 3 October 1963, a mere ten days before the election, the military staged a preemptive coup. Cognizant of the support of civil society and students in the previous coup attempt, the military unleashed one of the most violent coups in the history of Central America. Scores of civil guards were killed as they slept and violence against civilians continued for days. Attempts by students and Liberal Party supporters to challenge the overthrow of democracy were met with brutal reactions by *los gloriosos.* One of the first actions of the armed forces was to bring the national police functions under complete military control; between 1963 and 1998 there was virtually no difference between military and police training (Salomón 1995, 42). The United States immediately withdrew diplomatic recognition.

In many declarations, the military claimed that the primary reason for the coup was to protect the country from communism. Oswaldo López, the strongman of the military, declared to Nicaragua's *La Noticia* that "The North American Embassy in Tegucigalpa informally inspired the coup, frequently complaining that the Villeda Morales government overtly tolerated communist activity in Honduras" (19 November 1963). When López went ahead with the coup, his conservative allies scoffed at the threatened suspension of U.S. aid and a break in diplomatic relations:

37. In March 1963, President Kennedy held a summit in San José, Costa Rica, with the presidents of Central America (including Panama). In what must have been a great embarrassment for Kennedy and the Alliance for Progress, of the six countries on the isthmus, only Costa Rica and Honduras had democratic regimes. For a complete transcript of the speeches, including that of Villeda, see *Combate* (May and June 1963).

The United States "would be back in six months." The U.S. threat was hollow. Numerous democratic presidents were ousted in 1962 and 1963 and all of them were friends of Villeda. Coups in Argentina, the Dominican Republic, Ecuador, El Salvador, Guatemala, and Peru were followed closely in the press and the conservative opposition in Honduras could track the pattern: the United States in every case suspended relations, publicly exclaimed support of democracy, and then quickly renewed relations with the generals. The pattern would be no different in Honduras. The United States would wait barely two months after the violent and repressive coup to forget their tough discourse and crawl back to the generals and recognize the military regime on 14 December 1963. The embarrassing fact was that the U.S. commitment to democracy was secondary to U.S. support for a militarized response to real and imagined communist threats.

The United States chose poorly when in the early 1950s it staked the future stability of Latin America on increased militarization.[38] The long march towards military responses to social issues received an additional boost after the Cuban revolution in 1959 (Wright 1991, chapter 4). Official American action and rhetoric encouraged the strengthening of military institutions and the elimination of progressive regimes with ideologies similar to that of Figueres in Costa Rica. The bilateral military treaties of the 1950s and the introduction of the doctrines of national security in the early 1960s tilted power relations away from democracy. "Between 1961 and 1966, the military overthrew nine Latin American governments, including Guatemala's and Honduras's in 1963. In many cases, civilian conservatives urged the military to act before elections brought undesirable liberals to power, or before planned Alliance programs threatened the oligarch's interests. The School of the Americas became known as the School of the *Golpes*" (LaFeber 1984, 152). Above all, the strong military served as the great equalizer for the conservative oligarchy that was now threatened by the growth of progressive and democratic social and economic forces. "In conclusion, the military coup d'état of 3 October 1963 should be understood as a conservative and brutal reaction of the imperialist banana bourgeoisie and their political allies, the traditional landed elite, that view with great concern the transformative political pressure. . . . At this

38. "A more recent lesson, this time from Southeast Asia, was that Washington's tendency to militarize issues—to solve problems by shooting people—is often counterproductive" (Schoultz 1987, 327).

juncture, the army undoubtedly acts as the armed ally of the landed oligarchy and of imperialism" (Posas and del Cid 1983, 193–94).

The 1963 coup finalized the assent of the Honduran armed forces as the dominant political actor in the country and buried the opportunity for political and social progress in the country. The next three decades of development in Honduras are "a tragedy irredeemably converted into farce" (Meza 1981, 128), detailed in the works of Euraque (1996), Funes (1995), Schulz and Schulz (1994), and Salomón (1992).[39] In the 1980s and after the dramatic shift in U.S. policy described in Chapter 3, electoral democracy returned to Honduras in a strange hybrid regime in which the military still called the shots and human rights violations surged.[40] Nearly two hundred students and labor leaders were "disappeared" by U.S.-trained Honduran soldiers during the "lost decade" of the 1980s (Amnesty International 1988).[41] By 1982, when "democracy" returned to Honduras, the military institution had grown to such a degree that

> for reasons of "National Security," the Honduran Armed Forces are in charge of the police, the merchant marine, customs, immigration, civil aviation and airports, and also the national telephone company. The military exercises administrative control of extensive regions in the interior of the country. Military officials constitute a power elite, with their own government, their own judicial court, and in a growing manner their own economic sector. Making use of the resources of the Military Pension Institute (IPM) . . . the military institution has accumulated a large group of holdings: their own bank (that offers a credit card to the public); an insurance

39. In 1972, a short-lived reformist military regime emerged, led by the ever-unpredictable Oswaldo López Arellano (see Sieder 1995). "The timid appearance of a reformist military on the national scene was reason enough so that the dumb, in an excessive and condemnable extirpation of enthusiasm and optimism, easily forgot the political past of the army and began to elucidate diverse theoretical interpretations of the new role of the Armed Forces in Latin America. . . . They pretended to see in the army an ideologically reformed body. . . . This error inevitably led to other more serious errors and thus there emerged a whole chain of erroneous interpretations, divorced from reality and based more in desires than in facts" (Meza 1981, 173).

40. The Honduran military is explored in greater detail in Chapter 7.

41. In 1996, what many observers had long believed was confirmed: The United States was training Latin American military officers to use execution, torture, blackmail, and other forms of coercion against civilians (*Washington Post*, 21 September 1996). Two hundred "disappeared" may appear low next to numbers for Argentina and Chile, but is very high in the Honduran context.

> company; many factories, including the largest cement factory in the country (which was purchased from the civilian government as part of a "privatization". . .); a car distributorship; a radio station; a public relations firm; large tracts of coastal properties designed for tourism development; and—in an ironic example of what an economist would call "vertical integration"—a first class funeral parlor. (Comité de Abogados por los Derechos Humanos 1994)

Conclusion

These two chapters employ comparative historical data and methods to assess the relationship between militarization and democracy. The differences between quantitative and qualitative measures of militarization are noteworthy. According to the MPR quantitative data used in Chapter 3, Honduras had levels of militarization about twice as high as Costa Rica. The qualitative data establishes that the gap is much greater.

Outside of militarization, the similarities between Costa Rica 1948–58 and Honduras 1954–63 are notable. Figueres and Villeda both serve six years during this time period as moderate and pragmatic social democrats. Figueres's National Liberation Party received two-thirds of the vote in 1953 and Villeda's Liberal Party received two-thirds of the vote in 1957. Both men were supported by an emerging small industrial class, peasants, noncommunist labor, and a growing middle class. Both had spent time in the United States, were well read, could be charming and cultured, and had strong allies among the progressive wing of the State Department, among academic circles, and within the Democratic Party. Their list of enemies was also similar. The landed oligarchy, the United Fruit Company, the CIA and the Dulles brothers, and conservatives within the U.S. government mistrusted both leaders and wondered if they were closet communists. The Somozas and Trujillo were willing to give assistance to those who wanted to oust the two social democrats. Figueres and democracy endured in Costa Rica while Villeda and democracy were crushed in Honduras.

The comparative historical chapters argue that, contrary to the conventional wisdom, Costa Rican democracy was not consolidated soon after the 1948 Civil War. Democracy did not result from an elite pact, from cultural and structural preconditions from the nineteenth century, or from institutional measures. In the mid-1950s, all of the political factions in the country and the societal forces that they represented were seeking a way to employ force to oust Figueres. Ulate, Castro Cervantes, Echandi, Calderón, and the communists had given up on democracy and were seeking a violent end to Figueres. The will to oust Figueres existed, but not the way. The abolition of the military as a professional and deliberative body changed the calculus of the opposition and left them with no better option than to seek assistance from Somoza in Nicaragua. This split the opposition and the 1955 counterrevolution failed.[42]

In contrast, the opposition to democracy and progressive reforms in Honduras was able to enlist the support of a powerful internal military caste to oust Villeda and democracy when the oligarchy's interests were threatened. The Honduran case is especially useful as it demonstrates how a near nonexistent military institution could grow with U.S. support into the arbiter of national politics in a very short period of time. The same could have occurred in Costa Rica.

Timing, however, is critical. Costa Rica constitutionally abolished its military in 1948–49. By the early 1950s, U.S. policy to build up military institutions in Latin America as a bulwark against communism dramatically altered U.S.-Latin American relations and resulted in rapid militarization of the region. After the Cuban revolution in 1959, militaries were further empowered and doctrines of national security gave those militaries license to torture civilians, harass labor organizers and academics, and overthrow progressive governments. The U.S. commitment to democracy is superficial at best in the face of the military-led anticommunist paradigm. Looking at the legacy of militarization in Honduras and demilitarization in Costa Rica, we can only conclude that the United States chose poorly in designing an anticommunist strategy for Latin America. "The end of the Cold War presented the United States with a new foreign policy opportunity in Latin America. The United States no longer needs to bolster the militaries to stop communism and has begun focusing more efforts on promoting economic and political freedom" (U.S. General Ac-

42. The findings in this chapter dovetail nicely with Mares's (1998b, 243) argument that "three factors could lead to a failure to consolidate democracy: the inability of political institutions to produce compromise among competing political groups; civilians willing to utilize extra-constitutional means to bring about change or defend the status quo; and a military willing to play an active role in political battles." Honduras had all three conditions, while Costa Rica was missing the final one.

counting Office, 1996). Had the United States chosen to promote political freedom, democracy, and social progress instead of massive "militaries to stop communism" during the Cold War, Costa Rica might have been the norm and not the exception.

This section began with a theoretical framework that militarization negatively impacts the three power relations important for democracy. The comparative historical analysis confirms the expectations. The differing levels of militarization in Costa Rica and Honduras altered class power relations. The oligarchy was empowered by militarization in Honduras and was able to enlist the repressive arm of the state to halt progressive reforms. In Costa Rica, Figueres was able to push through reforms such as the nationalization of the banks and other measures that the oligarchy disdained and survive. The different levels of militarization also affected transnational power relations. The United States had a different impact in Honduras because of militarization. Indeed, U.S. Ambassador Willauer was a major player in granting the military unequaled constitutional autonomy and independence as insurance against the possibility of another Arbenz regime. U.S. encouragement and support of the military and criticism of Villeda encouraged the 1963 coup. The United Fruit Company also had a powerful ally to help protect its interests. In Costa Rica, in contrast, the United States and the United Fruit Company were forced to deal with civilians, as the security forces had no deliberative role. U.S. attempts to build a military in Costa Rica were unsuccessful. Finally, levels of militarization altered the capacity and autonomy of the state. In Costa Rica, with no military to arbitrate, civilian institutions were able to develop and mature. The Supreme Electoral Tribunal emerged after the 1958 elections as the independent and autonomous body that would determine who would hold the reigns of power. In Honduras, military power became so dominant that civilian institutions wilted. By 1963, the armed forces had erected a state within the state and democracy in the 1980s was under the tutelage of *los gloriosos.*

The results of the comparative historical research add insight to the quantitative results in Chapter 3. Militarization may not strongly impact the incidence of transition to democracy, but it may alter the quality of that democracy by restricting the autonomy of civilian government. Militarization does impact the incidence of democratic collapse. Therefore, there may not exist a linear relationship between level of militarization and democracy for any given year. Over time, however, where militarization was strong in Latin America during the Cold War era, sudden declines of democracy result. Even in the most highly educated countries with the longest histories of consolidated democracy—Chile and Uruguay—very large military institutions led to authoritarianism and repression.

When I started this section, I had theoretical expectations that the comparative historical analysis would reveal that the probability of democratic consolidation would have been lower in Costa Rica and higher in Honduras if their levels of militarization were switched. The evidence is overwhelming and surpasses the expectations. It is difficult to imagine Figueres surviving the 1953–58 presidential term with Oswaldo López Arellano and a strong autonomous military in the country. It is equally easy to imagine that Villeda would have finished his term had the United States and Hondurans heeded the advice in 1955 of Andrés Alvarado Lozano, the humble schoolteacher from Copán:

> If there is one thing that Honduras has in common with Costa Rica . . . it is in the absence of a military caste which weighs on the politics of its people. . . . From this national army, from this military academy that Señor Alonzo asks for, there will emerge an insolent military clique, that over time will become the great headache for Honduras for many years. It is better to be like Costa Rica with an army of teachers than to expose yourself to the creation of a military caste, an institution which has caused bitter tears throughout the Caribbean. (*El Cronista*, 7 July 1955)

guns versus butter

militarization, economic growth, and equity

PART

Guns Versus Butter

a quantitative analysis of militarization and material development

6

This chapter tests the hypothesis that militarization negatively affects economic and social development in Latin America. I examine the effect of militarization on two separate dependent variables, equity (calorie consumption) and economic growth.[1] The evidence clearly demonstrates that large militaries negatively impact both economic growth and equity in the region. In addition, these two relationships illustrate the very different effect of militarization on development in different regions of the world, regions that have very different military trajectories and missions.

Scholarship on the relationship between militarization and development has its roots in the 1960s modernization school, which posits that militarization plays an important role in the development process (Andreski 1968, Inkeles 1966, Janowitz 1964, Johnson 1964, Levy 1966, and Pye 1964).[2] In contrast to the modernization scholars, observers of Latin America claim that militarization is inversely related to political development (Arias 1991, 1994), social spending (Ames 1987), citizen well-being and social development (Escudé 1993; Sivard various), democracy (Bowman 1996), and food consumption (Arias 1987). In addition, a host of Latin American scholars point to the military as a negative force for development in individual cases (for ex-

1. I combine these two dependent variables in a single chapter because many important quantitative studies similarly combine these variables and apply similar theoretical arguments. See, for example, Bullock and Firebaugh (1990), and Weede (1983, 1986, 1992, 1993).

2. At least many scholars claim that these authors support the proposition that large militaries lead to modernization in LDCs. As shown in Chapters 1 and 2, many of these authors identified Latin America as a unique region in which militarization would not lead to greater modernization. Andreski, who has written the clearest theoretical expectations for the argument that militarization leads to reduced social stratification, argues that Latin America is the exception (1968, 210–11). Pye's influential article deals only with new nations and not Latin America (1962). Janowitz's (1964) work is applicable only to developed countries.

ample, for the Honduran case see Salomón various; Funes 1995; Ruhl 1997; Oquelí various; Schulz and Schulz 1994). Scheetz, Pape, and Kulikowski (1997) examine the effects of military spending on economic growth for the Guatemalan case and show that for every 0.43 percent increase of GDP spent on the military, the GDP declines by 1 percent over a quarter century. The strength of the case study evidence is such that in recent years the World Bank, Japanese aid officials, and even State Department officials have accepted the position that militarization inhibits social development and have pressured for drastic downsizing (see IMF 1992; and FBIS 8/19/94). It would appear that the modernization school's assessment of the Third World militaries' ability to facilitate development has been soundly discredited.

Yet, another group of researchers—the large-N cross-sectional quantitative scholars—has been publishing impressive work on the militarization/development relationship. Many studies directly measure the relationship between militarization and equity/economic growth, the so-called "guns versus butter" debate. Numerous cross-national studies document a positive and significant relationship between relative size of the military force (number of soldiers per thousand inhabitants or MPR) and material development (Chan 1989; Weede 1983,1986, 1992, 1993; Weede and Tiefenbach 1981a, 1981b).[3] These studies rely on the modernization literature of the 1960s to explain/predict the results of their regressions; high military participation ratios lead to discipline, technical prowess, social mobility, and literacy, which in turn lead to better equity or faster economic growth. Dixon and Moon find that MPR makes a positive contribution to welfare performance in LDCs and use a modernization framework to explain the relationship: MPR has a "largely positive influence . . . derived from the individual benefits of military training and the modernizing effects of mass armies" (1986, 675). Kick and Sharda (1986), and Kick et al. (1990), examine the effect of social and economic militarization on various social indicators and find a significant positive impact of MPR on social development that they theoretically explain with the seemingly resurrected modernization rubric. Using a sample of sixty-six market economy LDCs from 1960 to 1980, Bullock and Firebaugh (1990) directly assess the guns versus butter relationship and conclude that military par-

3. Weede's 1993 study finds the relationship between MPR and economic growth to be positive and significant; the relationship between MPR and equity is positive but just missing the 0.1 significance level with a sample size of 53.

ticipation ratios positively and significantly affect economic growth and food consumption. In their multivariate model, MPR is the most important indicator of improved calorie consumption.

The dean of the militarization and development research is Erich Weede. In a host of studies, Weede finds that large militaries are positive forces in developing countries, leading to both economic growth and equity. Weede suggests the following causal mechanisms:

> How to make sense of the proposed link between threats to national security and better growth rates? First, one may argue that threats to national security have a sobering impact on the ruling classes. Where ruling classes feel threatened, they become interested in a thriving economy to support a strong army. Second, threats to national security promote conscription and high military participation ratios. Then, most young men will be affected. The military may become something like 'the school of the nation.' The main characteristic of this 'school' seems to be that of patriotism, discipline, and taking orders pervade the military curriculum. Military training contributes to mass discipline. Mass discipline and the readiness to fit into some hierarchical social order may be regarded as a special kind of human capital, if seen from the perspective of the ex-conscript or his prospective employer, or the results of military training may even be regarded as social capital, if seen from the perspective of society and the national economy. (1993, 243)

In sum, of the dozens of large-N quantitative studies that use MPR as the causal variable and some manifestation of development as the dependent variable, the results are near unanimous that large militaries (in number of soldiers) are good for development and equity in the Third World.[4] These studies reach the rather awkward conclusion that what LDCs presently need are militaries with lots of soldiers and little expenditure and that current demilitarization efforts in the Third World will have negative consequences for social development and economic growth.[5]

What then is the relationship between militarization and material de-

4. Bowman (1996) is an exception in finding a negative relationship between MPR and democracy in a study limited to Latin America.

5. This preference for large militaries with small budgets contrasts with preferences of those such as Huntington, who claim that democracies in the Third World are more likely to endure with small, well-funded militaries.

velopment? Were the 1960s modernization scholars right all along? Have the qualitative scholars been less than objective and influenced by the political correctness of promoting demilitarization? The vastly disparate results found by the large-N cross-national researchers and the qualitative, case study, or regional researchers who blame militarization for a lack of development presents a major intellectual puzzle. This is an important contemporary policy issue given the widespread debate on reducing military burdens in LDCs and the shrinking militaries in Latin America. In this chapter, I argue that the puzzle can be solved by looking more closely at LDC militaries as institutions and asking the simple question: are militaries from different regions of the world similar enough institutions for the MPR indicator to have any use in large-sample cross-regional studies, or is this a variable that does not travel well and can only be used to generate highly bounded explanation? I argue for the latter in detail in Chapter 2. Without carefully assessing the historical and geopolitical trajectories of militaries as institutions, many large-N quantitative scholars have made a serious mistake by treating all LDC militaries as the same variable. I contend that the Latin American military during the Cold War is not comparable to other LDC militaries and that the relationship between militarization and material development (equity and growth) in Latin America will be substantially different than that found by the myriad studies that found a positive relationship.

Chapter 2 presents a lengthy discussion of the distinct qualities of Latin American militaries in comparison with those in other regions of the Third World. The major point developed in that chapter is that the Latin American military institution is different because of: (1) the long historic tradition of security forces as an institution with an almost spiritual calling to battle progressive internal threats; (2) the influence of the United States during the Cold War to enhance the introverted nature of the Latin American military; and (3) the fact that Latin American countries do not wage major wars on each other. In sharp contrast, in the early 1960s when Latin American militaries were very powerful political institutions, the forty-odd entities of Sub-Saharan Africa were either nonexistent or very fragile (Coleman and Brice 1962, 359). A third group of countries includes Taiwan, South Korea, the Asian sub-continent, and the Middle East, which have serious external enemies and very large militaries. As posited in Chapter 2, these Latin American distinctions invert the expected effect of militarization on development proposed by Andreski and others.

Theoretical Issues

The theoretical expectations are quite elementary. Both economic and organizational resources are scarce in Latin America. These resources are necessary for long-term economic growth and social development/equity. Militarization absorbs scarce resources. Therefore, there is a trade-off between militarization and economic development over the long term.

This type of opportunity-cost argument is certainly not new. Commenting in 1963, Lieuwen alleged that "One of the chief impediments to real economic progress in nearly all Latin-American countries, whether the regime was military or not, was the inflated demands the armed forces made on government revenues. Traditionally, since the turn of the century, the armed forces' reported share of the national budget has averaged about twenty to twenty-five percent annually in most Latin American countries" (157). This point is echoed by Nordlinger, who notes that on average a Third World country only has 16 percent of GNP available for capital formation. An LDC that spends 4 percent of GNP on defense is thus restricting capital available for investment by 25 percent (1977, 166).

A second related theoretical basis for the negative relationship between militarization and economic growth is political and relates to government focus. The larger and more powerful the Latin American military, the less focus the government (civilian or military) can ration for design, implementation, and staying power of long-term development policies. The causal mechanisms between militarization and economic growth are explored in depth in the comparative historical chapter that follows (Chapter 7).

The negative relationship between militarization and development hinges on the assumption that states are important actors and state capacity is correlated with developmental success; with the proper resources and organizational ability, the LDC state can promote social development and economic development.[6] Militarization (be it in personnel or budget) in

6. Many studies confirm this assumption and Ali and Adams (1996, 1790) reveal that food programs can significantly improve food consumption and can have a significant positive impact on income distribution.

Latin America negatively impacted two sources of state capacity, one economic and one political.[7] There are serious economic and political opportunity costs of large militaries. First, state capacity requires economic resources. It takes money to develop the infrastructure and human capital required for better paying jobs. Social development requires huge investments in schools, health clinics and hospitals, vaccination campaigns, agricultural and nutrition programs, and housing programs. Every percent of the budget going to the military is one percent less that can go to social spending. Ames (1987) uses a rational choice framework to come to the same hypothesis that there is a trade-off between social spending and military spending. His empirical research strongly supports this hypothesis. Arias also notes this trade-off in spending and has demonstrated that military spending during the Cold War inhibited needed spending on education, health, and social programs in Central America.

Perhaps more important, when policymakers are looking over their shoulders for the next coup to appear, the long-term focus and coherence necessary for development are undermined. Development requires much more that just money; lots of money with little policy coherence will not lead to social development. Similarly, if governments are engrossed with national security and destroying union leaders, academics, and progressives, they will be unable to dedicate the time, energy, and focus that successful development policy requires. They may not even want to. Large militaries may well be an indicator of the oligarchy or the middle class trying to forestall redistribution. In the Third World, almost by definition government expertise and focus are scarce resources. Dedicating them to fending off generals, clinging to power, tinkering with civil/military relations, or terrorizing your own people are poor investments. Any organization must prioritize its goals. For example, Latin American governments who place militarization above social welfare will have a limited organizational capacity in meeting the basic needs of their citizens. Large powerful militaries in Latin America will correlate with reduced time horizons and increased uncertainty, resulting in more stopgap and short-term policies and less of the medium and long-term policies necessary for success in human development.

The final reason why we would expect larger militaries in Latin America to lead to lower performance on the part of the state deals with

7. For a discussion of assessing state strength and capacity, see Huber (1995).

accountability. Large militaries in this region are an indication of perceived internal threats. The larger the military during the Cold War, the greater the degree of anticommunism. When anticommunism became the dominant political theme, governments and politicians were able to focus on this as an issue and deflect other issues such as improvement of living conditions. This made it difficult for citizens to demand improvements from the government. Leaders can always say that they are fighting for "freedom" or "liberty," and can bring up anticommunism as the common good and a national emergency when people are hungry and jobless and human rights are regularly abused. Not only individual governments but entire governing elites are less accountable when they can shift attention to security issues. Politicians are off the hook if they can argue that a national Armageddon is underway, with communism or socialism or anything "leftist" built up as the principal threat to family, God, and *Patria*. For example, in Costa Rica, which had a low degree of militarization, communism declined substantially as an election issue by the late 1950s and electoral discourse revolved around citizen-centric themes and improvements in living conditions. In contrast, in Honduras, which had a higher degree of militarization, anticommunism remained a dominant electoral theme until the early 1990s, and the threat of communism was used as a pretext for military incursions into politics and for the halting of equity-enhancing programs such as land reform.

We have two competing hypotheses based on very different theories: the hypothesis put forward and supported by the published quantitative studies that due to a modernizing dimension, social militarization (the number of soldiers variant) leads to social and economic development. In contrast, my hypothesis based on state capacity, resource/organizational scarcity, and accountability posits that militarization negatively affects both social development and economic growth in Latin America. The following sections will graphically present the relationship between militarization and equity and between militarization and economic growth.

The Findings

A. Militarization and Equity

Because of the lack of comparable longitudinal income distribution data, in this analysis I employ changes in calorie consumption as an indicator of equity. Reliable longitudinal data for a large number of developing countries over a similar time period are just not available. Deininger and Squire assess the existing data and create an exhaustive new dataset for income distribution, which reveals that even economically advanced LDCs such as Argentina and Uruguay not only have no acceptable longitudinal data, but also have no acceptable income distribution data for any single year (1996). Indeed, only nine of the twenty Latin American countries have "acceptable quality" longitudinal income distribution data. In this study, I have opted for an alternative indicator—change in calorie consumption per person per day. Not only is food consumption an important dependent variable in its own right, this indicator also fits the admonition of Sirowy and Inkeles (1991) of seeking alternative measures of social welfare that capture an element of distribution for studies on equity.

Change in calorie consumption per person per day is an indicator that possesses many desirable qualities. First of all, Paul Streeten (1981) has led the intellectual charge that development should focus on "first things first" and a basic needs approach. There is nothing more basic than food.[8] We cannot brag about democracy and economic growth and literacy rates if large numbers of children go to bed hungry. The centrality of food for a large number of inhabitants in the developing world is captured by John Mellor of the Food Policy Research Institute.

> Food is emotional, political, life threatening. Naturally, it fills the cultural outlook and colors the life for the half-billion rich people in the world. But the quest for food and the worry as to how that quest will fare bear with terrible immediacy on well over 1 billion people, the hungry and the undernourished. It is central to the worries of another billion or two who are at risk of falling into the ranks of the hungry or who, having only recently reasonably ensured their departure from those ranks, remember hunger all too well. (1999, ix)

Malnutrition is the leading killer in the world and undernutrition is the principal malnutrition problem (Foster and Leathers 1999, xiv). And,

8. I am quite cognizant of the fact that a mere increase in calories does not translate directly into improved health and nutrition. Nevertheless, I maintain that almost all the countries in this study had a large number of inhabitants in 1960 that were undernourished in numbers of calories. And undernutrition is the single most important indicator of hunger and malnutrition.

while protein deficiency can and does occur, evidence shows that even poor people who consume sufficient calories adapt their diets to consume adequate grams of protein. Therefore, it is common to find people with both calorie and protein deficiencies and with calorie deficiency but not protein deficiency. Yet, it is difficult to find people with a protein deficiency without a calorie deficiency (Foster and Leathers 1999, 28). Therefore, calorie consumption is a single indicator that captures the hunger, undernourishment, and malnutrition that plagues a billion people.

Second, change in calories per person per day captures an element of distribution; it may be argued that it is an indicator of the distribution of an important resource—food. The wealthy are always going to eat. However, unlike income, they can generally only eat so much, so the indicator has a declining marginal utility. Therefore, to have high calories per person per day (a mean average) for a country, the working class and popular sectors must also consume a relatively high number of calories. If 30 or 40 percent of the population is undernourished, it will bring down the average number of calories for the entire country no matter how rich the rich get. Since food consumption for the upper quintile of the population is assumed to be relatively stable, change in average number of calories per day will be a result of changes in the food consumption for the rest of the population. If the average number of calories per person per day is increasing, the lower quintiles are eating more and approaching food equity with the higher quintiles. If the average number of calories is decreasing, then the lower quintiles are eating less and the gap between calories consumed by the rich and those consumed by the poor is widening. This would provide some indication of an unequal distribution of resources/income. At least in the case of Chile, data revealing a surprising decline in the number of calories per person from 1969 to 1989 preceded and, I would argue, predicted the later disclosure of a shocking deterioration in the distribution of income over the same time period (Psacharopoulos et al. 1993; Schneider 1993). Foster and Leathers (1999, chapter 9) also document the strong relationship between income distribution and food consumption. And Reutlinger and Selowsky (1976, 20) reveal a direct linear relationship between income share and food consumption in Latin America.

Third, we have comprehensive data for calorie consumption for a large sample of LDCs for a period of time that captures enduring and not merely transient change. This same series of data is unavailable for income distribution. Studies using income distribution as a dependent variable are often forced to use "snapshot" cross-sectional studies that are highly susceptible to simultaneity and spuriousness problems and have produced misleading confidence in the Kuznets U-Curve for LDCs (Bowman 1997, 128–29). In contrast, the FAO provides comparable data on food consumption in comparable years for a large sample of LDCs and with enough data points over time to capture change.

Fourth, governments should be able to enact policies that assure improved nutrition for the majority of its citizens. If large numbers of children go to bed hungry in modern Latin America, for example, there is something wrong with the long-term quality of government. While nutrition and food consumption is a complicated issue, experts understand the "processes which in a generation can abolish hunger and undernutrition" (Mellor 1999, x). Yet hunger is a reality in all Third World regions. Some 50 percent of Central Americans do not eat enough food to meet minimal nutritional requirements (Barry and Preusch 1986, 140). Even in Latin America's wealthiest country, Argentina, the face of hunger caused national embarrassment when the international press showed videos of poor families grilling cats and complaining of hunger. There are many policy alternatives for improving food consumption, and a debate on these policies is well beyond the scope of this study.

Fifth and finally, food consumption is a dependent variable in one of the most important studies of the relationship between militarization and equity (Bullock and Firebaugh 1990). Bullock and Firebaugh found a positive relationship between MPR and food consumption, and I show that these findings disappear when we account for the regional effect of militarization.

First, let us examine the relationship between number of soldiers per thousand inhabitants and change in calorie consumption in Latin America in the 1963–89 period as presented in Figure 6.1. As this bivariate scatterplot clearly shows, there is a rather remarkable negative correlation between militarization and food consumption in Latin America, with a Pearson's correlation of −0.845 (substantively, for every additional soldier per thousand inhabitants, daily per capita calorie consumption declines by 88). Indeed, this is about as strong a relationship as we find in the social sciences. Especially noteworthy is the high level of significance ($p = 0.000$) with only eighteen cases. The finding goes directly counter to previous statistical studies that find a positive relationship between MPR and social indicators such as food consumption, precisely as hypothesized here and in Chapter 2.

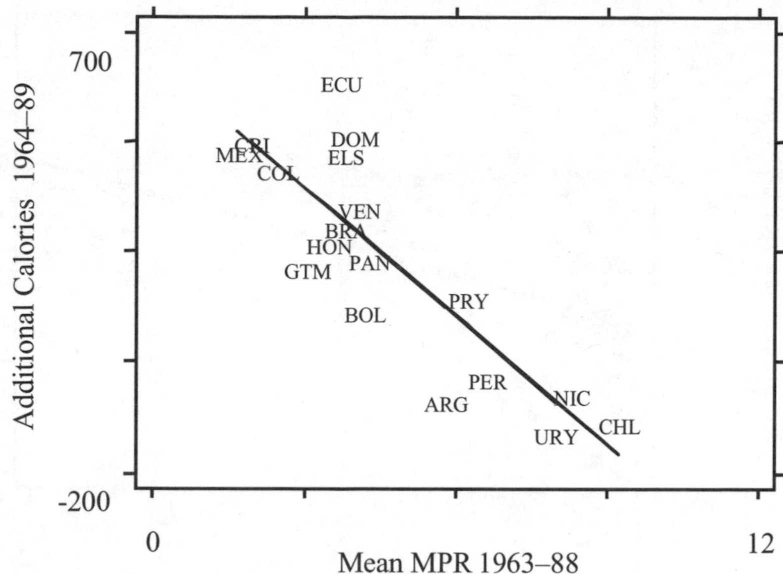

Fig. 6.1 The relationship between MPR and additional calories in Latin America (N = 18; r = −0.845; p = 0.000)

Yet, we must highlight that extant studies on the militarization/equity relationship examine a much larger sample of LDCs. Let us now repeat the bivariate scatterplot with a universal sample of seventy-six developing countries, presented in Figure 6.2. The variables are identical to those illustrated in Figure 6.1; the only difference is that the sample size is increased. The change in the relationship is dramatic.

These two simple graphs present our puzzle. Why is the relationship positive in the universal sample and negative in Latin America? In Chapter 2, I provided the theoretical argument that would predict such a finding. We can explore this relationship further with bivariate scatterplots for other regions of the world. Figure 6.3 presents the relationship for twenty-five cases in the Middle East, North Africa, and Asia, and for the thirty-one cases in sub-Saharan Africa.

THE DIFFERENCES BY REGION

The solution to our intellectual puzzle—cross-national scholars find that large militaries are good for LDC development even while regional and case study scholars find the opposite—is provided by our scatterplots. There are three groups of LDC militaries that are not the same variable.

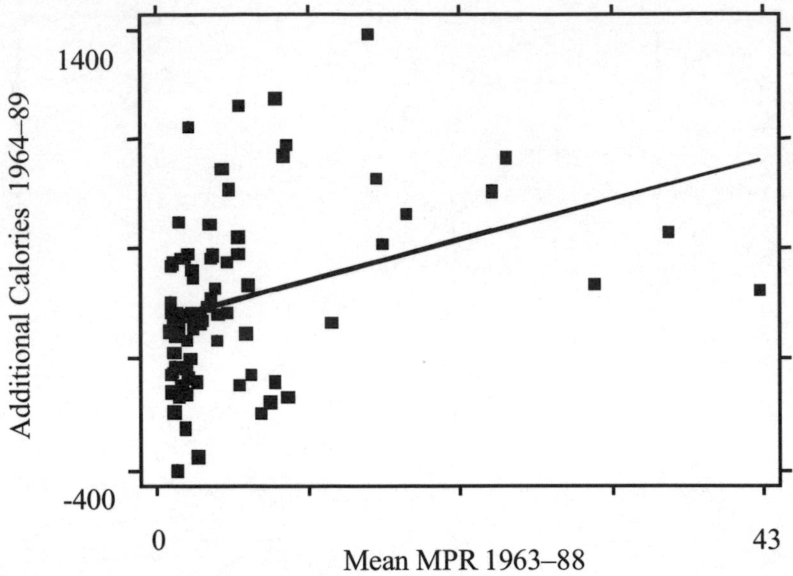

Fig. 6.2 The relationship between MPR and additional calories in seventy-six LDCs (N = 76; r = 0.290; p = 0.011)

The first group includes those in sub-Saharan Africa that in general have small, fragile, or nonexistent militaries and have performed quite poorly on development indicators during the time period of study. The second group consists of Latin American militaries that are too small for external wars and too large for police forces (Andreski 1968, 212). As a group, Latin American militaries are medium-sized and the region had moderate

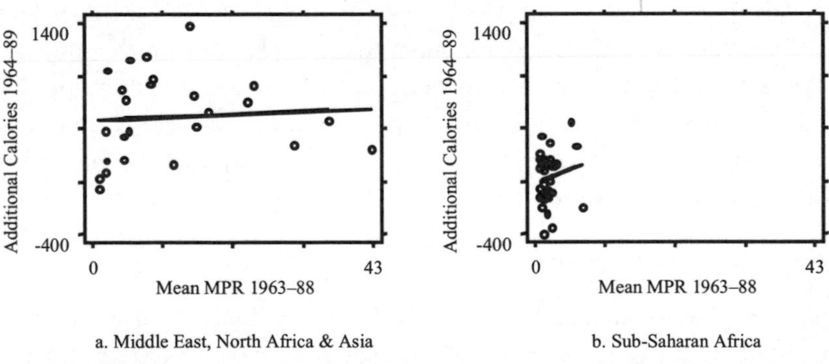

Fig. 6.3 MPR and additional calories outside of Latin America

performance on development indicators during the Cold War. A third group consists of countries from the Middle East, East Asia, and the Asian sub-continent that have very large militaries due to serious external threats of war. These cases also had excellent economic performance in the 1964–89 period (many countries in this group are oil producers and many received large amounts of external aid during the Cold War).

The correlation between MPR, additional calories, and region is summarized in Figure 6.4. Given this figure, it is no surprise that Bullock and Firebaugh (1990) find a positive relationship between MPR and food consumption. But of course, the relationship is spurious, as both ADDCALS and MPR are correlated by region. We can see that even within the Sub-Saharan cases and the Middle Eastern, North African, and Asian cases presented in Figure 6.3, there is no relationship between militarization and additional calories. The only region with a significant relationship is Latin America, and that relationship is negative for the reasons we previously discussed. One may question these bivariate relationships and wonder if they hold up with control variables in multivariate analysis. The short answer is yes. MPR is significant and negative in Latin America in multiple regression models that include original level of calories, initial

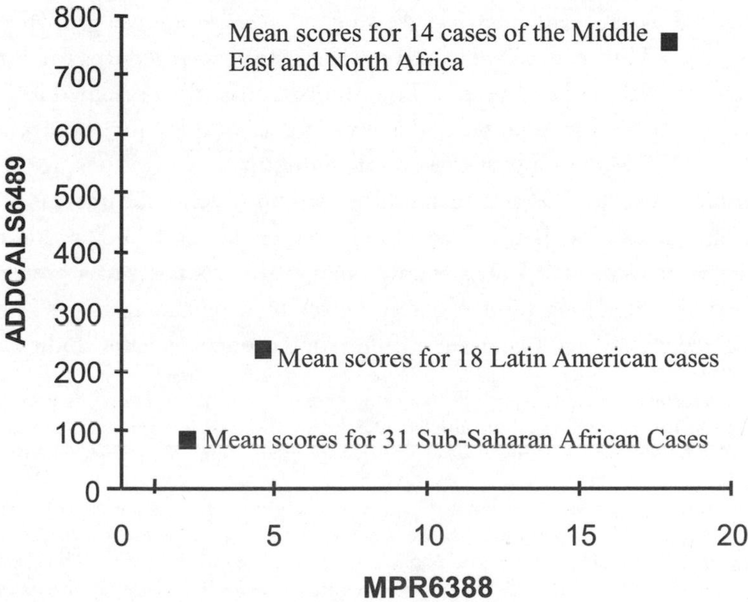

Fig. 6.4 Mean MPR and ADDCALS scores by region

level of GDP per capita, economic growth, and the openness of the economy as control variables. The results and a discussion of the methodology are presented in the appendix.[9] The substantive effect is staggering. For every additional soldier per 1,000 inhabitants, on average every man, woman, and child in a Latin American country would consume 52 fewer calories per day; and for every percent of GDP spent on the armed forces, each inhabitant would consume 80 fewer calories per day (holding constant the four control variables).

B. Militarization and Economic Growth

This section examines the relationship between militarization and economic growth, both in Latin America and throughout the developing world. As noted above, a host of studies have documented a significant positive relationship between MPR and economic growth. I argue that due to the difference in trajectories, histories, missions, and internal versus external threat environments, one should actually expect the logic of Andreski and others to be inverted in Latin America. That is, in this region we hypothesize that large militaries reduce economic growth.

In this analysis, the dependent variable—economic growth—is operationalized as the econometrically estimated average annual growth rate 1963–89.[10] This method is favored by economists, as it reduces the influence of the selected end-points. The results are visually presented in Figure 6.5. Figure 6.5.A presents the bivariate scatterplot for seventy-two LDCs. The results support the extant studies that report a positive relationship between MPR and economic growth in LDCs—the effect is positive and significant. If we stopped here, we could reach the "awkward" policy conclusion that LDCs should build larger militaries as a prescription for greater long-term economic growth. This conclusion is "awkward" because it goes counter to numerous country-specific studies and

9. One may also raise questions about simultaneity of the direction of causation. This is addressed at length in the Appendix. Finally, the negative relationship between militarization and development is similar when military spending is employed as the causal variable.

10. The econometrically estimated growth rate is a fitted regression line of a logged gdp time series. This is the least arbitrary operationalization of economic growth, as other measures such as point-to-point compound rates or average growth rates can be strongly affected by the end points and can lead to "dishonest motives that can make the statistics appear good or bad as needed" (Kasliwal 1995, 35–37). The GDP data are from the Penn World Table, Mark 5.6.

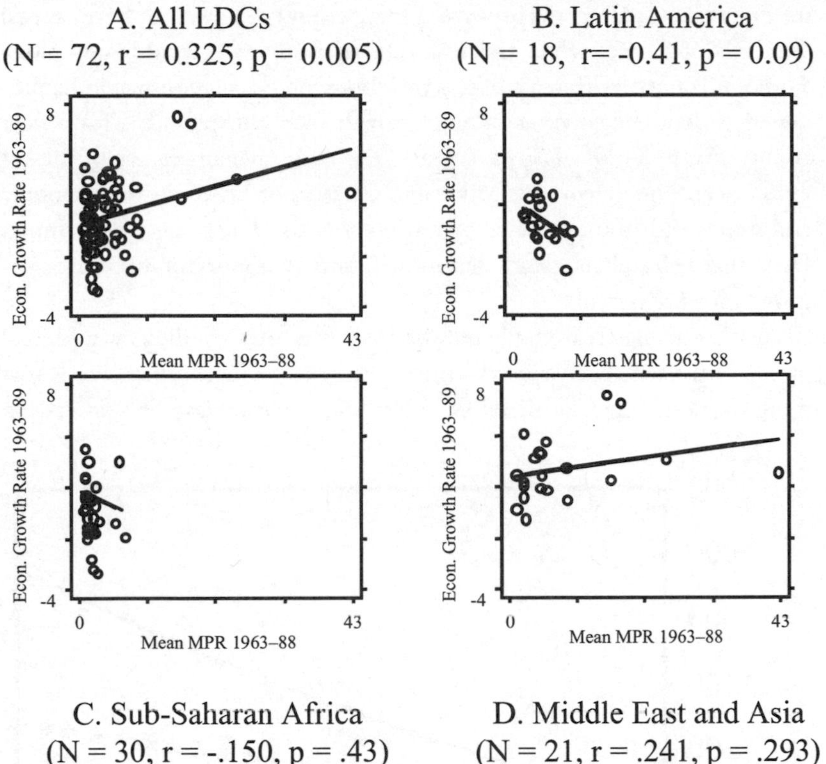

Fig. 6.5 MPR and economic growth rates by region

because it is spurious. A clearer picture develops when we look at particular regions.

As expected in Latin America, the relationship is inverted from that of the universal sample. As shown in Figure 6.5.B, the relationship is negative and significant. The larger the MPR, the lower the annual growth rate. In fact, for every additional soldier per thousand inhabitants, the annual growth rate declines by 0.253 percent. To further illustrate the effect of militarization on economic growth in Latin America, we can easily calculate the expected rate of economic growth over the 1963–89 period. Let us assume that countries X, Y, and Z all had a real per capita GDP of $1,000 in 1963. Let us further assume that country X had an average MPR of 2, country Y had an average MPR of 5, and country Z had an average MPR of 10 over the1963–88 period. What predicted impact will MPR have on per capita GDP over a quarter century? The effect is illustrated in Figure 6.6. After twenty-five years, country Y would have a real PCGDP of $1756, while the PCGDP in country Y would only reach $1286. A country with ten soldiers per thousand population would be predicted to have negative economic growth over the period, with a year twenty-five PCGDP of $939. Oscar Arias and other observers of the region are absolutely correct. Militaries are a major brake on the economy and impoverish the countries of Latin America. The policy prescription from this research is clear: demilitarization is important for economic growth for the region.

Again, one may reasonably question whether these findings would hold up in multivariate analysis with control variables. The short answer is that militarization, operationalized as either military spending or soldiers per

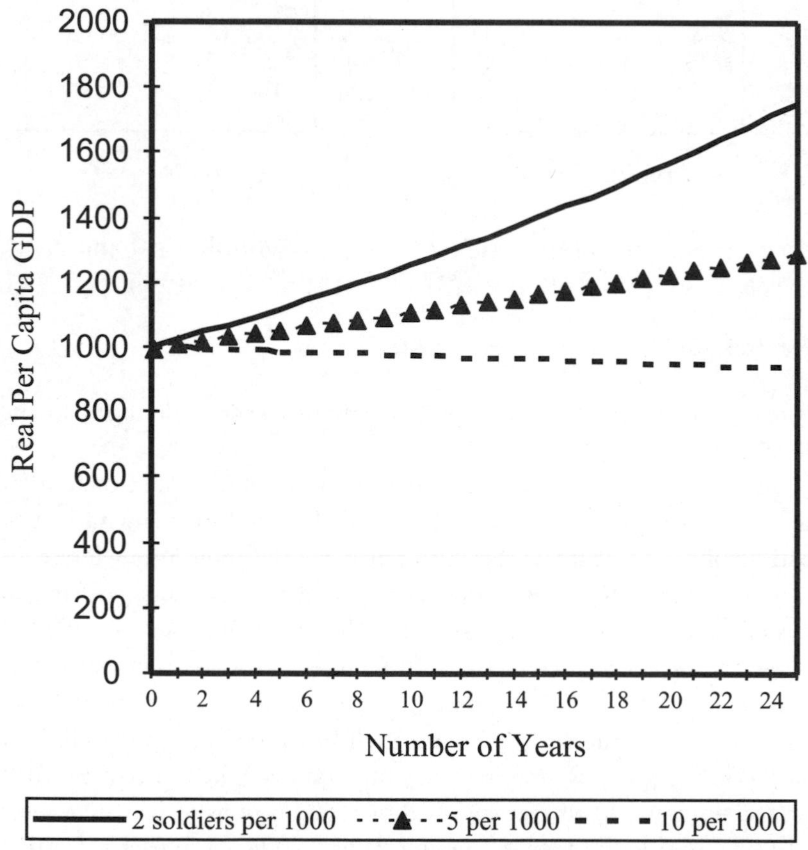

Fig. 6.6 MPR and economic growth rates in Latin America

thousand inhabitants, negatively effects economic growth in Latin America when employing initial level of PCGDP, democracy, instability, education, government spending, and investment as control variables. The full table of results is presented in Table 6.3.

Conclusion

Two competing hypotheses were tested in this chapter. The first, based on modernization theory and extant statistical studies, is that large militaries positively impact food consumption and economic growth in LDCs. The second, based on state-capacity and opportunity cost theory, is that large militaries negatively impact food consumption and economic growth. It is also argued that due to unique features of the Latin American military and geopolitical history, one should not expect militarization to have the same effect in both Latin America and among all LDCs.

The results of this chapter confirm the state-capacity theory for Latin America that large militaries—measured by either budget or number of soldiers—had a strong, significant, and negative effect on both calorie consumption and economic growth during the Cold War. The militarization variable, even with only eighteen cases, has a robust, highly significant, and negative effect on calorie consumption and growth. The greater the concern for national security doctrines, the lower the capacity of the state to design and implement long-term policies to elevate the living conditions of the citizenry.

The vast difference between the militarization/development relationship in Latin America and a universal sample of LDCs is also dramatically revealed. Our discipline is currently undergoing a debate on the value of area studies and regional knowledge. Some social scientists argue that area studies contribute little to theory building or hypothesis testing. At the other extreme, some argue that understanding individual cases is the ideal and that the quest for generalizations is naïve. I do not want to enter too directly into this polemic, but these results can make a small but important and positive contribution to the discussion. Area scholars believe that "researchers in the area-studies tradition do not seek generality of explanation, because they hold that the 'context' in which politics gets played out is highly determinative of the outcomes" (Laitin 1995, 456). Area scholars also claim that it is dangerous to interpret relationships without any historical knowledge of the cases. These two claims are supported by the results of this chapter. It is clear that LDCs are remarkably heterogeneous. It is also clear that applying the results of a universal sample of LDCs on individual countries or regions may be dangerous, especially at the policy level. It may be misleading and inefficient to throw as many LDCs as possible into the statistical pot without first very carefully considering that the total sample may be made up of various smaller samples that may have very different slopes. My research supports the middle position that regional and area expertise is fundamental for generating and testing hypotheses. In this case, an area expertise in Latin America helps us to untangle and rebuff the puzzling findings of quantitative scholars that large militaries are positive forces for Third World development. Understanding area-specific nuances helps us develop more sophisticated explanations and to reconcile extant qualitative and quantitative findings.

Appendix

Design and Methodology for Militarization and Food Consumption Analyses

In these analyses, I use longitudinal change score models. Allison (1990) assesses models that measure the dependent variable at two points in time, which he characterizes as "powerful tool(s) for making causal inferences with nonexperimental data," as they greatly reduce threats of spuriousness. Quinn notes that the longitudinal cross-sectional regression model used by Barro and others "has been well-examined in the literature and is appropriate for studying long-run trends" (1997, 536). I use change scores over a twenty-five-year period (2 data points). Two separate models are employed. The first is the *change score method* where $Y_2 - Y_1$ is regressed on X. The second is the *regressor variable method*, where Y_2 is regressed on both Y_1 and X. The *regressor variable method* is computationally equivalent to regressing $Y_2 - Y_1$ on both Y_1 and X, producing identical coefficients for X and the same standard error and t-score. Therefore, in the *change score method*, Y_1 cannot appear as an independent variable (Allison 1990, 94). How does one select the proper statistical analysis? Allison makes some suggestions that lead me to select the *regressor variable method* for the analysis, but he adds that "arguments about model choice are notoriously difficult to resolve" and that "there may be no recourse but to do the analysis both ways and to trust only those conclusions that are consistent across methods" (110). To improve confidence in the robustness of my posited relationship, I use both the *regressor variable method* and retest the key equations with the *change score method.* I report only the regressor variable method regressions here, though the effect of militarization is similar when using the change score method. The results are presented in Table 6.1.

Simultaneity and Direction of Causation

The theoretical linkage posited between militarization and food consumption and equity dictated operationalizing the variable as the mean average

Table 6.1 Calories, 1989, regressed against MPR and MLSP for eighteen Latin American cases

Dependent Variable		*Calories 1989*	
Intercept	−681.99	−94.72	123.07
Calories per person, 1964	.549***	.743***	.558***
	(4.83)	(6.83)	(5.19)
PCGDP, 1963	214.58***	125.30*	151.99**
	(3.31)	(1.80)	(2.42)
Economic growth, 1963–88	450.61***	258.38**	254.31
	(4.28)	(2.23)	(1.54)
Openness of economy	2.65	2.13	.463
	(1.01)	(1.01)	(0.16)
Mean MPR, 1963–88		−52.10***	
		(4.58)	
Mean MLSP, 1963–88			−79.94*
			(2.07)
R^2	.836	.910	.878
F prob.	.000	.000	.000

***$p < 0.01$, two-tailed test, **$p < .05$, *$p < .10$

White's heteroscedasticity-consistent robust standard errors employed; beta coefficients in first cell rows; *t*-ratios in parentheses

Variables:

Calories 1989	Number of calories per person per day, 1989 (from FAO)
Calories per person 1964	Lag of dependent variable, calories consumed per person per day, circa 1964
PCGDP 1963	Log per capita GDP in constant purchasing power parity dollars (from PWT)
Economic Growth 1963–88	Percent change in PCGDP (PWT)
Openness of Economy	Mean average (exports + imports)/gdp, 1963–88 (from PWT)
Mean MPR 1963–88	Mean average number of soldiers per 1,000 inhabitants (SALA)
Mean MLSP 1963–88	Mean percent GDP spent on military (SALA)

of MPR or MLSP over the period 1963 to 1988. This is, however, problematic for the issue of simultaneity. This section aims to establish the direction of causation between changes in food consumption and the militarization variables. There are three plausible theoretical arguments about the causal effect of change in calorie (or protein) consumption on the militarization variables. First, one may argue that increased calorie consumption is due to an improved economy and that a growing economy provides for larger militaries; one may point to some of the oil-producing countries as examples. This argument does not threaten our findings for Latin America, as we find the opposite relationship—increased calories are associated with small armies. Second and third arguments are potentially more damaging. One may argue that where low calorie consumption existed in 1964, the government expanded the military over time for fear of unrest over living conditions. That is, low levels of CALS64 lead to increases in levels of MPR from 1963 to 1988. In addition, one may posit that as living conditions deteriorate or fail to improve over time, the government feels threatened and increases militarization. That is, CALS89–CALS64 is inversely related to changes in MPR (or MLSP) levels from 1963 to 1988. If these alternative explanations are empirically supported, then the theoretical explanation for the findings in this study are potentially weakened.

Fortunately, because we have data on change we can quite easily conduct an evaluation of these alternative explanations with simple correlations. First, we examine the correlation between nutrition in (CALS64) with subsequent change in the two militarization variables from 1963 to 1988 (CHMPR6388 or MPR88–MPR63; and CHMLSP6388 or MLSP88–MLSP63). Then we examine the correlation between change in food consumption 1964–89 (ADDCALS) and simultaneous change in the two militarization variables (CHMPR6388 and CHMLSP6388). These correlations are presented in Table 6.2. None of these alternative explanations based on simultaneity or reversed causation is very compelling, as none of the relationships are significant at even the 0.10 level. In an additional test of simultaneity, I ran the key equations substituting the militari-

Table 6.2 Test of simultaneity

Variables	*CALS64*	*ADDCALS*
CHMPR6388	r = −.29; p = .25	r = −.09; p = .74
CHMLSP6388	r = −.06; p = .82	r = −.34; p = .17

zation variable as an average from 1963 to 1972 instead of 1963 to 1988. While the explanatory power was slightly reduced, the militarization variables remained negative and significant. There is no empirical support for a reversed direction of causation or for problems of simultaneity.

Design, Methodology, and Regressions for the Militarization and Economic Growth Analyses

In this analysis, I want to examine the effect of both military spending and military participation ratios on economic growth for Latin America. Robert Barro provides a useful starting point for an econometric model. Barro's research has focused on the determinants of economic growth (1991, 1995, 1997) with special attention to the positive impact of human capital (education) and the negative impact of big government (government consumption). Barro's 1991 article seeks to explain why the results of many studies are inconsistent with the convergence theory that poor countries should have faster growth rates than rich countries. According to Barro, the answer to this puzzle is that convergence holds only when human capital is controlled for. Barro uses school enrollment rates as proxies for human capital. This landmark study looks at growth over the long-term with simple cross-sections of ninety-eight countries over a twenty-five-year time period. The important variables for economic growth are (1991, 437):

- initial level of GDP is negative when school enrollment rates are held constant
- human capital as measured by school enrollment is positively related to growth
- government consumption is negatively related to growth
- political instability is inversely related to growth
- democracy is positively related with economic growth in small doses and negatively related with economic growth in large doses (Barro 1997)

Despite the employment of a host of independent variables, Barro was unable to explain growth in Latin America and Africa with his models: "Of course, if the nature of being in Africa or Latin America is already held constant by the other explanatory variables, continent dummies would be insignificant in equations for growth, fertility, and investment.

Thus, the finding of significant coefficients on these dummies indicates that some regularities are missing from the model" (1991, 435). "Finally, the results leave unexplained a good deal of the relatively weak growth performances of countries in sub-Saharan Africa and Latin America. That is, the analysis does not fully capture the characteristics of the typical country on these continents that lead to below-average economic growth" (437). I do not know why Barro's model is less than satisfactory for Africa. As for Latin America, the results show that militarization is an important variable to be included.

In addition to the control variables identified by Barro (1991), I also include investment in the regressions. This variable was strangely missing from Barro's groundbreaking study, yet Levine and Renelt (1992) show that of the more than fifty variables that have been found to be significantly correlated with economic growth, only share of investment to GDP is robustly correlated with economic growth. My regression models include both military spending and MPR as separate causal variables to double check the findings. The first two equations of Table 6.3 are for Latin America, while the last two equations are for fifty-two LDCs. Both militarization variables are significant and negative for Latin America, and positive for all LDCs in multivariate regressions (significant for MPR).

Table 6.3 Real PCGDP growth rates, 1963–1989, regressed against military participation ratios and military spending in Latin America and all LDCs

N-Size *Dependent Variable*	*Latin America 18 Growth Rate 1964–89*			*All LDCs 52 Growth Rate 1964–89*	
Intercept	−0.34	1.42	1.25	2.44	2.02
PCGDP 1963	−.0007***	−.0006**	−.0007***	−.0005***	−.0005**
	(5.22)	(3.25)	(5.62)	(2.78)	(2.49)
Democracy	.020	.010	.008	.010	.009
	(0.69)	(0.35)	(0.37)	(0.40)	(0.38)
Instability	1.065	−.188	1.15	.064	.550
	(0.47)	(0.09)	(0.73)	(0.04)	(0.29)
Primary education	.028	.039*	.027*	−.016	−.017
	(1.51)	(1.89)	(1.90)	(1.16)	(1.12)
Secondary education	.025	.107	.060	.039	.047
	(0.70)	(1.82)	(1.63)	(1.15)	(1.16)
Government consumption	−14.855*	−13.929**	−14.42**	−11.33**	−10.410*
	(2.22)	(2.37)	(2.42)	(2.22)	(1.87)
Investment	.209**	.119*	.168**	.119**	.139**
	(2.59)	(1.88)	(2.86)	(2.35)	(2.71)
Mean MPR 1963–89		−.347*		.064**	
		(2.05)		(2.09)	
Mean MLSP 1963–89			−.646***		.048
			(3.50)		(0.68)
R^2	.615	.763	.837	.442	.413
F-ratio prob.	.008	.028	.004	.001	.008

***$p < 0.01$, two-tailed test, **$p < .05$, *$p < .10$

White's heteroscedasticity-consistent robust standard errors employed beta coefficients in first cell rows; *t*-ratios in parentheses

Variables:

PCGDP 1963	From Penn World Table (PWT)
Democracy	Number of years, 1963–88, with free elections
Instability	Instability measure (Barro-Lee dataset on floppy)
Primary education	Percent total pop. with primary education 1960 (Barro-Lee)
Sec. education	Percent total pop. with secondary education 1960 (Barro-Lee)
Gov. Consum.	Ratio of real government "consumption" expenditure to real GDP (Barro-Lee dataset)
Investment	Mean percent GDP investment, 1963–88 (PWT)
Mean MPR 1963–89	Soldiers per 1,000 inhabitants (ACDA)
Mean MLSP 1963–89	Military Spending as percent of GDP (ACDA)

Escaping the Lost Decade

militarization and economic growth in costa rica and honduras

7

The previous chapter established the strong negative effect of militarization on both equity and economic development in Latin America. In this chapter, I reexamine the relationship between militarization and economic growth in a comparative analysis of Costa Rica and Honduras. The comparative historical analysis opens the black box of the relationship established in Chapter 6, illuminating the causal mechanism and establishing sequence and agency. The qualitative data show precisely how militarization undermines state capacity, reduces time horizons, dilutes state focus, and depletes accountability, which in turn leads to reduced material development. To clearly demonstrate how militarization negatively affected economic growth in Honduras and how demilitarization enhanced economic growth in Costa Rica, I focus on the post-1980 period and the response of these two small and highly dependent countries to the economic crisis of the 1980s and the challenges of globalization.

After relatively impressive economic growth rates from 1950 to the late 1970s, Latin America suffered what economists regularly call the "lost decade" in the 1980s. Eleven out of the eighteen Latin American countries in this study had lower levels of real PCGDP in 1990 than in 1979; some nations such as Argentina and Venezuela suffered a 25 percent drop in PCGDP over this time period.[1] A combination

1. Data are from Mark 5.6 of the Penn World Table. Although the Penn World Table has greatly advanced our confidence in GDP data, there still exists considerable room for improvement. For example, the Costa Rican Central Bank recently discovered that previous data on Costa Rican GDP were underestimated by around 30%. Previous calculations of GDP were based on adjustments to the 1966 structure of the economy. The new calculations are based on the 1991 structure of the economy. Since so many things have happened since 1966 (three structural adjustment programs, the rise of tourism, export processing sectors, and a different and much bigger financial sector), it is to be expected that the previous numbers were incorrect. But a 30% change is dramatic and alters a great many data. For example, percent of GDP spent on educa-

of high levels of foreign debt, high interest rates, low prices for primary export products, and a drastic increase in energy prices ravaged the economies of Latin America and led to a widespread belief that the entire economic and productive structure needed to be overhauled. According to international lending institutions and USAID officials, and even to many economists within Latin America, import-substitution industrialization (ISI) was outdated or "exhausted," and success in the new global economy required an economic opening and export-led growth (ELG) of new or nontraditional products. The transition from ISI to ELG entails extraordinary economic change and dislocation. A successful transition requires government focus, policy flexibility, and financial resources.

I posit that militarization undercuts two pillars of the state capacity required to design, implement, and sustain successful economic policies. First, militarization undercuts capacity by absorbing scarce economic resources needed for investment. Indeed, in 1989 Honduras (mis)spent 8.4 percent of GDP on the armed forces, a higher figure than any other country in Latin America save Cuba and Nicaragua (SALA 32, 343). Honduras, one of the poorest countries in the hemisphere, spent US$3.77 billion 1985 dollars on the military from 1978 to 1990.[2] Indeed, Honduras could nearly wipe out its entire foreign debt with this money. It is difficult to imagine that this money could not have provided better police forces, more effective justice, citizen-centric security, and a sizable investment in human capital and economic infrastructure.[3] Second, militarization and

---

tion (the law requires 6%, which obviously was not being met after the upward adjustment), on health, on the military, etc., have all been overstated (personal communication with Costa Rican economist José Cordero Peña). In this book, I use the lower GDP figures (from the Penn World Table). Had the higher figures (that show greater economic growth after 1966) been used, the study's argument would only be strengthened.

2. Military spending data from *SALA* 32, Table 1206, and PCGDP figures from the Penn World Table, Mark 5.6.

3. One of the tragedies is that all of this money spent on the military may have had a negative impact on security. As Isacson astutely notes: "Individual members of the military, as well as some aspects of the armed forces as an institution, must be considered among Honduras' security threats. The corruption and continued human-rights abuse of many members of the military-controlled security forces are threats of the first order, both to individual security and to Honduran hopes for democratization and development. On the institutional level, the armed forces continue to threaten Hondurans' security by maintaining routine checks over civilian power, monopolizing fiscal resources, and continuing to enjoy impunity. Through such activities as the maintenance of secrecy regarding military expenditures and private-sector investments, the failure to turn over fugitive officers required to stand trial for human rights abuses, or the provocative statements of its leadership, the Honduran military, as an institution, impedes the development of democracy and

military power and autonomy undermine political and organizational capacity and irrationally shifts priorities away from development to national security. This claim is difficult to support with quantitative data but can be clearly demonstrated in a comparative analysis of Costa Rica and Honduras. It will be shown that in the 1980s and early 1990s, when these countries needed to respond quickly and effectively to major economic challenges, the Honduran state and civil society were consumed with issues of civil military relations and military power. Crisis after crisis involving the military became priorities that pushed aside other important issues and policies. By the early 1980s, Honduras was not a country with an army but an army with a country and the long and difficult task of wresting prerogatives and sectors of the state back from the colonels expended valuable political and organizational capital.[4]

After a brief discussion of the economic crisis, this chapter will have three foci. The first is a discussion of Honduran military power in the 1980–95 period.[5] It is impossible to understand the causal mechanism linking militarization with material development without a basic overview of the power and autonomy of the armed forces. The discussion is comprised of two sections. The first is a description of the overwhelming power of the military after the 1963 coup and the continual series of crises that resulted from efforts to limit that power, which resulted in a sharp reduction of state capacity to govern effectively. This is followed with a discussion of the military's emergence as a major economic actor and the problems associated with military capitalism.

After a description of the Honduran military, we look directly at the question: how did the militarization variable impact economic recovery in

---

the rule of law. As such, it must be considered a threat to civilian security in Honduras" (1997, 141).

4. This point can be illustrated with recent events in the United States. On the day that a major scandal involving President Clinton hit the news, the price of tobacco stocks dropped. Financial experts argued that the latest scandal would divert White House attention from the tobacco settlement to crisis management. Without focus and a sense of priority, the U.S. executive branch would have a much lower chance of successfully managing a resolution of the tobacco settlement. In Honduras, the relative political crises in the 1980s were much higher and the initial levels of capacity much lower, making it extremely difficult for the Honduran government to handle important economic issues. In July 1997, during a visit by this author to the country, not a single day went by without a major newspaper story on military impunity, disrespect of civilian authority, or criminality associated with the armed forces.

5. For a discussion of recent issues of civil-military relations in Honduras, see Becerra (1994), Bowman (1999), Rosenberg, (1990), Ruhl (1997), and Sieder (1998).

Costa Rica and Honduras? We begin with an examination of U.S. economic assistance. The 1979 victory of the Sandinistas in Nicaragua and the ensuing war between the Reagan administration and Managua provided both challenges and opportunities for Nicaragua's neighbors in Costa Rica and Honduras. The United States was willing to spend previously unimaginable sums of money to further its geopolitical goals and billions of dollars flowed into the region. There was a major difference as to the type of aid each country received. The United States uses aid to pursue its own short-term goals. In its fight against the "leftist" Sandinistas, aid was used to build and strengthen allies. In Honduras, the military was an obvious choice for an alliance and the Honduran generals were very adept at claiming a large share of the aid—the $400+ million received by the military could have gone to much better use. In contrast, almost all of the aid going to Costa Rica was economic. This money was critical for Costa Rica to reorient its economy towards export-led growth with minimal dislocation and no increase in poverty levels.

A second comparative focal point is tourism. I contend that Honduras has a greater tourism endowment than Costa Rica and should have been able to capitalize on the tourism and eco-tourism boom of the late 1980s and early 1990s. Instead, Costa Rica had a tourism explosion while tourist receipts in Honduras stagnated. Why? Militarization is a key explanatory variable for two reasons. First, Honduran civilian officials were paralyzed by civil-military crises during this time period and were unable to enact simple legislation to spur the industry. Second, the antimilitary image of Costa Rica and the Nobel Peace Prize were powerful draws of eco-tourists to Costa Rica, while the international image of Honduras as a land-based battleship (the U.S.S. Honduras) was a powerful deterrent.

The Economic Crisis and the Beginning of the "Lost Decade"

When the economic crisis struck in 1979, Costa Rica and Honduras had very similar exports. The two leading foreign exchange earners were bananas and coffee; other primary products such as wood, cotton, and meat made up the rest of the merchandise exports. In 1980, Costa Rica had exports of some $1 billion dollars, while Honduran exports totaled $891 million. Neither of these figures is particularly impressive, though on a per capita basis, Costa Rica was considerably higher at $438 per capita compared to $226 per capita merchandise exports in Honduras (SALA vol. 32, 704, 711).

The Latin American debt crisis struck earlier and perhaps deeper in Costa Rica than in any other Latin American country. The depth of the crisis and the fears of disaster are best summed up by Marc Edelman, who reviewed the situation in 1983, just as the economy was bottoming out:[6]

> Costa Rica, long considered a model of stability, political pluralism, and prosperity in the turbulent and impoverished Central American region, has recently experienced a turbulent and dramatic economic decline. After maintaining a stable currency for seven years, the Costa Rican government decided in September 1980 to float the colón. Within twelve months, a de facto devaluation of over 450 percent took place. Prices, which in 1980 had risen a mere 18 percent, rose 65 percent in 1981, giving Costa Rica the third-highest rate of inflation in Latin America after Brazil and Argentina. Inflation is currently running at an annual rate of close to 100 percent, which may put Costa Rica in an unenviable first place among Latin American countries. Per capita gross national product measured in colones declined 1.5 percent in 1980 and 5.5 percent in 1981; in dollar terms, however, Costa Rica's per capita income of 1,540 dollars, by far the highest in Central America, fell to less than 300 dollars. Unemployment, relatively low in the 1976–79 period, has doubled since 1980 to 9.2 percent, but the rapidity of this change and the high, but less easily measured, levels of underemployment magnify the official jobless rate, despite its appearing low in comparison with many Latin American countries. The country's foreign trade, with chronic imbalances exacerbated in recent years by rising petroleum costs and declining coffee prices, has deteriorated to the point where the deficit in 1979 and 1980 was over one-half of total export earnings. The public-sector foreign debt has surpassed three billion dollars, giving Costa Rica one of the highest levels of per capita indebtedness in the world and forcing the government to declare a moratorium on payments of interest and principal. A 1982 estimate claimed that if the debt service schedule

6. For more on the beginnings of the Costa Rican crisis, see *Cuadernos Centroamericanos de Ciencias Sociales* (1981).

> had not been renegotiated, interest obligations alone would have absorbed more than all the country's export earnings. To complete this summary of indicators of Costa Rica's grave economic situation, the government deficit has risen to unprecedented proportions, forcing a partial dismantling of the extensive state-sponsored social-welfare apparatus. This action in turn has further contributed to lowering the living standards of the population. (1983a, 166–67)

Like Costa Rica, Honduras was saddled with high foreign debt and low prices for exports.[7] Honduran real PCGDP peaked in 1979 and dropped by more than 10 percent before bottoming out in 1983.[8] Between 1979 and 1983, the Costa Rican real PCGDP collapsed, falling by more than 19 percent. The economic challenges facing both countries were daunting. The world economy was changing, and to flourish economically, each country would need radical reform. According to Katzenstein (1985), small countries are both highly vulnerable to changes in the world economy and often more maneuverable and flexible in meeting those economic shifts and dislocations. Smallness alone does not translate into flexibility and response to economic crisis, however.[9] For the two Central American countries in this study, levels of militarization directly affected both the response time and the quality of response to the economic challenge.

The Honduran Military and Crises, 1980–1996

By the 1980s, the power of the Honduran military in both political and economic spheres was immense. Except for a brief interruption in 1971, the military controlled the government for two decades.[10] Even when civilians took de facto control of the reins of government in 1982, important sectors were retained by the armed forces. The turf wars waged between

7. For more on the Honduran economy in the 1980s, see del Cid (1991) and Murga (1985).

8. Figures from Mark 5.6 of the Penn World Table.

9. For the small European democracies, Katzenstein (1985) argues that corporatist arrangements, democracy, and export-oriented market competition leads to economic flexibility and political stability.

10. López was selected president after fraudulent elections in 1965 (Funes 1995, 247–49).

civilian politicians and civil society against the armed forces have now continued for nearly two decades. An exhaustive examination of all of the problems that militarization caused during this era would fill a book.[11] In this section, I will review several of the most challenging: control of the state apparatus and threats to civilian rule; human rights violations and impunity; and military capitalism.

Control of the State Apparatus and Threats to Civilian Rule

Military Chief Oswaldo López Arellano ruled from the coup that ousted Villeda in 1963 until 1971 and again from 1972 to 1975, ruling in the first period as a reactionary and in the latter period as a moderate populist. The second López Arellano military administration was incapacitated by "Bananagate" and was subsequently challenged and replaced by a younger group of officers.[12] The new military power elite replaced the Superior Council of National Defense with the Superior Council of the Armed Forces (*Consejo Superior de las Fuerzas Armadas*—COSUFFAA); internecine battles for the control of COSUFFAA would largely determine control of the country. This coup d'état by the military against the military began the custom in Honduras in which later cohorts of military academy graduates, "promotions," banish their elder officers and seize the reins of the armed forces, along with the accompanying power, prestige, and opportunity for material gain. The only rule for officer jockeying was the agreement that no armed forces chief would remain for more than one four-year term.[13] Given the unequaled power that Honduran military chiefs hold, the selection process for the most powerful figure in the coun-

11. Schulz and Schulz (1994) have done an excellent study of the 1980s. For more on the Honduran military in recent years, see Funes (1995), Salomón (1992, 1995), and Isacson (1997).

12. "Bananagate" was the term for the 1975 scandal in which United Brands was caught paying US$2.5 million to the Honduran economic minister in exchange for a tax reduction that would save United Brands some US$7.5 million in the first year alone. Bananagate not only led to the fall of López, but also led Eli Black, the chairman of United Brands, to jump to his death from the forty-fourth story of his Manhattan office as the payout became public (Schulz and Schulz 1994, 42–43).

13. In 1992–93, commander in chief General Luis Alonso Discua used his political skill—threats, betrayal, intimidation—to have the Congress revoke Article 32 of the Constituent Law of the Armed Forces, which prohibited the reelection of the commander in chief, and succeeded himself for a second term beginning in early 1993 (Schulz and Schulz 1994, 300–303).

try could be stated as "no suffrage, no reelection."[14] In 1975, Colonel Juan Alberto Melgar Castro became the new military leader, a position from which he went on to become chief of state. The conservative Policarpo Paz García was named military chief.

In August 1978, Paz García led a military coup against Melgar Castro. The immediate cause of the coup appears to have been military involvement in organized crime and drug running. General Paz was co-owner of a ranch with Juan Ramón Matta Ballesteros, the head of Honduran organized crime and a major drug figure.[15] In 1977, a scandal broke over organized crime and drugs, and Paz "resented the president's failure to prevent press reports of his involvement in a series of drug and bribery scandals" (Schulz and Schulz 1994, 48).

In September 1979, just two month before Managua fell to the Sandinistas, U.S. officials met with General Paz and informed him that Honduras was to become the new Nicaragua, a dependable ally supported by U.S. economic and military assistance (Schulz and Schulz 1994, 57). The deal, however, required a democratically elected government in the country and a return of the colonels to the barracks. In April 1980, a Constituent Assembly was elected, which subsequently decided to keep General Paz as interim president until direct presidential elections could be held. It is notable that after years of military rule, elected civilians were unwilling to seize the reins of government and instead handed executive power back to

14. General Mario Hung Pacheco became the latest armed forces chief in January 1996. In September 1997, President Reina announced that Hung would be the last armed forces chief and that beginning in 1999, the defense minister would be a position of power and not merely decorative, and that this post would be held by a civilian. While Hung has publicly agreed with the elimination of the armed forces chief and the transfer of power to the defense minister, other officers have publicly grumbled and asserted that the armed forces will continue to select their own commander in chief.

15. By the mid-1980s, senior military officers had formed an alliance with Matta to turn the country into a transshipment point for cocaine. Matta was accused of participating in the 1985 torture-murder of U.S. DEA agent Enrique Camarena in Mexico. The United States wanted Matta extradited, but extradition was against Honduran law. It is reported that in 1988, Elliot Abrams sent a memo to the Honduran embassy, threatening to release the names of Honduran military officers involved in drug trafficking unless Matta were turned over. Whether this story is true or not, in April 1988 one hundred elite Honduran troops broke into Matta's mansion, arrested the drug kingpin, and sent him to the Dominican Republic, from where he was flown to the United States and jail. Hondurans were enraged, many for the attack on sovereignty and others because Matta was considered a kind of Robin Hood. Rioters torched part of the U.S. embassy, causing $6 million in damage and the death of two persons (see Schulz and Schulz 1994).

the military.[16] In November 1981, presidential elections were held and some 78 percent of the eligible voters went to the polls and elected the Liberal Party's Roberto Suazo Córdova as the country's president.

By the time of the transfer of political power from the armed forces to the elected officials, military power was intertwined with many sectors of the state. The military controlled the telephone company (HONDUTEL), the merchant marine, customs, immigration, and commercial aviation. The armed forces diverted large sums of money from these entities to personal bank accounts or to military coffers. For example, in the administration of Carlos Roberto Reina (1994–98), the Honduran merchant marine was finally pried loose from military administration. The military had been reporting that the merchant marine was generating US$200,000 per year, yet in the first six months under civilian control the merchant marine generated US$2 million (Díaz 1996, 105).[17] This demonstrates in part why budget data for military spending are so problematic. The military books were secret and never audited. How much money was the military siphoning from the national telephone company or from customs? No one will ever really know. For this reason, experts plausibly estimate that the actual military budget is up to three times higher than the official budget.

16. After years of military dominance, it was difficult for the civilians to be weaned from military tutelage. In 1985, after one presidential election and five years of the new Congress, the major political parties were unable to select their own candidates for the presidential elections. President Suazo began machinations to extend his term, a move that was vetoed by the United States. To avoid a major crisis, the generals were called upon to solve the politicians' ineptitude. The solution, known as the Air Force Pact, or Option B, was surreal. Option B stated that since the parties were unable to select their nominees, multiple candidates from each party would appear on the general election ballot; the candidate receiving the most votes for each party would become the nominee (similar to the former system in Uruguay). Each party's nominee would subsequently receive all of the party's combined votes. What followed was a campaign that pitted candidates simultaneously against their party and the opposing parties. Fourteen people died in pre-election brawls. As one part of the circus atmosphere, President Suazo borrowed a U.S. military helicopter to drop flyers on a Callejas political rally, charging the candidate as a "sodomite with AIDS." The final results of the balloting gave 42.6% to the National's Callejas and 27.5% to the Liberal's Azcona. But the combined total of the multiple Liberal candidates was 51.1% and Azcona won. When asked about the election, U.S. Ambassador Cresencio Arcos responded, "the Marxists may have taken Nicaragua but the Marx brothers took Honduras" (quoted in Schulz and Schulz 1994, 131).

17. The income generated from the Merchant Marine comes from the registry of commercial ships.

The entire repressive apparatus of the state was also under military control. When the military ousted Villeda Morales in 1963, one of the first actions was to eliminate his civil guard and replace it with the military-controlled Public Security Force (FUSEP). Intelligence and crime investigation were also under the armed forces umbrella. Civil society and many government officials believed that the prerogatives of the armed forces should be reduced, especially in a fledgling democracy. The battle lasted through the 1990s and is finally being won. The telephone company, the merchant marine, customs, and civil aviation were demilitarized in the 1990s and the process of creating a new civilian police force is under way. The battle has been strenuous. The armed forces were totally uncooperative and on many occasions made open threats to leave the "tiger" alone.[18]

Forced conscription was brutal and hated by the population, but considered nonnegotiable by the military. President Reina (1994–98), who was a former justice on the Inter-American Court on Human Rights and former political prisoner, campaigned on a platform of reduced military power and the end of conscription. In 1994, after twelve years of civilian rule and four presidential elections, when Reina and the congress pushed through the end of forced conscription, the response was direct and forceful. "The military command has demanded that President Reina allow it to recruit young men by force and increase the Army's complement. If this is not allowed, they will not send soldiers to guard the street" (FBIS, 17 August 1994). After months of public battle and private pleading for crime control, the president cried "uncle" and reauthorized the military draft in October 1994 (FBIS, 12 November 1994). President Reina saw his home bombed, presumably on orders of the military, and a soldier "accidentally" dropped a grenade near him during a public speech.[19] In

18. Hondurans refer to the military as the "Tiger" and the military itself uses the term to threaten society and politicians. For example, when the military forcefully conscripted four hundred students from a single high school in 1990, the parents and several congressmen protested and pleas for an end to conscription were heard. General Arnulfo Cantarero, the armed forces chief, condemned the protests as a crusade by leftists and in a clear threat warned, "Don't annoy the tiger" (Boudreaux 1990)

19. Ruhl (1997) discusses the problems and challenges of reining in the military in Honduras and notes that "Military officers angry with what they perceive as the persecution of the armed forces under Reina are suspected by many to have been behind a series of bombings in 1995 and 1996 that have targeted the president, the Congress, the Supreme Court, and human rights activists. Several of the judges in human rights cases have received death threats and a number of potential witnesses have died mysteriously. The high com-

September 1997, the *Miami Herald* and Costa Rica's *La Nación* reported that a group of Honduran military officials and Cuban exiles residing in Honduras had mounted a campaign of terror against Reina. The military detested Reina for wanting to reduce the power of the armed forces and the Cubans viewed Reina as pro-Castro and "wanted the gratitude of the military and to receive permission to utilize Honduras as a secret operations base against the Cuban regime" (*La Nación*, 29 September 1997). In August 1994, a group of leading Honduran professionals, educators, and political authorities issued a statement claiming that "The threat of coup d'état is a latent condition in our country that is curbed only by international pressures" (FBIS, 17 August 1994). Despite these and other threats, through grit and determination the president was able to finally end forced conscription in 1996. As late as July 1997, the military launched new threats at Reina when the armed forces chaplain, a former military officer from Colombia, daringly stated at a public mass—attended by leading politicians and the press—that "the Armed Forces are cornered and could use their arms to defend themselves from those that are attacking them" (*El Heraldo*, 20 July 1997). Again, the point is that it is difficult for the government to focus on governing when crises with the military dominate the agenda and the media. Time horizons are reduced; one is more concerned with surviving one's term than in long-term development.

Human Rights Violations and Impunity

1981 not only signaled the return to democracy and the election of President Suazo, but also witnessed the election of Ronald Reagan and a new emphasis on anticommunism in the region. Honduras was surrounded by the Sandinista regime to the south and civil-war-torn El Salvador and Guatemala to the west. U.S. injections of military aid and antiterrorist training, and unconditional public support by the U.S. embassy for the actions of the armed forces, were akin to pumping large doses of steroids into the neighborhood bully. The result was quickly expanding strength and a feeling of invincibility on the part of *los gloriosos* that, when combined with a self-perceived spiritual calling to save the country from progressives, resulted in a marked increase in human rights violations.

---

mand no longer has a credible military coup threat to use against civilian authorities because of the certain opposition of the United States."

The commander in chief of the Honduran armed forces from 1982 to 1984 was General Gustavo Alvarez Martínez, a vehement anticommunist who had been trained at the infamous School of the Americas in Fort Benning,[20] the Superior War College in Peru, and the National Military Academy in Argentina. Alvarez clearly favored the Argentine "dirty war" style and dubbed U.S. experts an "army of tourists" (Franco 1994, 2).[21] In the late 1970s, Alvarez founded the Intelligence Battalion 3-16, the ruthless death squad comprised of elite U.S.-trained soldiers that recruited ex-soldiers and prisoners from the central penitentiary for some of the dirtiest jobs. Working closely with the Contras, who were "secretly" based in Honduras, Battalion 3-16 also employed Contras to "disappear" subversives (*Desaparecidos*, 1993, 8). Battalion 3-16 has been implicated in a host of disappearances and extra-legal executions. Student and labor leaders, peasant organizers, Sandinista and FMLN alleged supporters, and political activists were the usual targets. In the first twenty-six months after the return to "democracy," 128 disappearances were registered, and during the 1980s some 200 individuals were "disappeared."[22] For the period January 1988 to July 1989—long past the height of the abuses—the Committee for the Defense of Human Rights (CODEH) documented 13 forced disappearances, 322 assassinations, 470 cases of torture, and 2,058 illegal arrests. The military and the military-controlled police were implicated in most of the abuses (Central America Update, 1992)

This degree of violence on the part of the repressive apparatus of the state was new to Honduras and led to a response from civil society. Two organizations were founded: the Committee of Relatives of the Detained/Disappeared in Honduras (COFADEH) and the Committee for the Defense of Human Rights (CODEH). As with the open secret that Honduras

20. The School of the Americas (SOA) was established in 1946 in Panama and moved to Fort Benning in 1984. Dubbed "School of the Dictators," the "Coup School," and the "School of the Assassins" by human rights activists, the alumni of the school include a large list of military dictators and human rights abusers. In El Salvador alone, SOA graduates have been implicated in the assassination of Archbishop Romero, six Jesuit priests, U.S. Church women, and one thousand civilians in the El Mozote massacre (Colombus and Bourgeois 1994, 3).

21. This section is based heavily on monthly reports from the Centro de Documentación de Honduras (CEDOH), Funes (1995), Schulz and Schulz (1994), and my experience in Honduras.

22. A thousand-page document produced by the Honduran Human Rights Commission, *The Facts Speak for Themselves*, details the military involvement in human rights abuses during the 1980s.

was a base for the Contras, the government and the armed forces vigorously denied that the "tiger" had any involvement with the murders and disappearances of labor leaders, peasant organizers, student activists, and intellectuals. The truth has slowly emerged, however, especially after former members of the Battalion 3-16 defected and testified before courts and investigators (*La Tribuna*, 8 July 1997). The efforts of the human rights organizations were Herculean and dangerous, as the armed forces resented investigations into its past and present actions. Judges, journalists, and relatives of the human rights activists have been threatened, arrested, and murdered (CEDOH, December 1996).

Despite mounting and unambiguous evidence against the military and individual officers in gruesome crimes, justice has not been served, in large part because of the power of the military and the weakness of the judiciary. On 4 July 1987, a Supreme Court justice, Mario Reyes Sarmiento, was shot dead by police officers near a roadblock. A FUSEP agent was charged with the shooting and sent to the penitentiary to await trial. The armed forces removed the agent from jail, claiming that the military justice system had jurisdiction. "The inability of the civilian judiciary to act on the Reyes Sarmiento case, despite the publicity it received and the fact that the victim was a Supreme Court judge, is an indication of the powerlessness of the civilian judiciary when crimes are committed by military personnel" (Amnesty International 1988, 13).

During the period 1980–90, the United States regularly defended the Honduran military and dismissed the charges made by human rights activists as communist-inspired and unsubstantiated (charges that turned out to be largely correct). The United States needed the Honduran military as an ally in the Contra war and not only regularly ignored or denied evidence of human rights abuses, but openly "advocated executions, torture, blackmail, and other forms of coercion" in U.S. Army intelligence manuals used to train Latin America military officers (*Washington Post*, 21 September 1996). The United States helped to make *los gloriosos* untouchable and completely above the law. Once the Sandinistas left office, U.S. officials were quick to abandon the unsavory agents they had financed and trained. The degree of the reversal of U.S. policy is illustrated through the actions of Cresencio Arcos, who, as a U.S. embassy official in Tegucigalpa in the early 1980s, helped establish the secret basing of the Contras in Honduras and the transfer of huge sums of military aid to the Honduran armed forces. In the mid-1980s, Arcos was Elliot Abrams's deputy for

Central America and was the State Department expert on the Contras (Schulz and Schulz 1994, 260). In 1990, Arcos was sent back to Honduras as ambassador, reportedly with the instructions that "You were at the creation of this fucking mess. Now you can go back and shut it down" (direct quote of Arcos from Schulz and Schulz 1994, 261).

Arcos accepted this 180-degree turn in U.S. policy with enthusiasm and effectiveness. Less than a decade after building up the power, autonomy, and resources of the military, Arcos pushed hard for a dismantling of the very Frankenstein that he had helped to create. While in the 1980s the U.S. embassy continually smeared human rights activists as leftists, in the 1990s Arcos and U.S. officials began to decry the security forces' excesses and impunity. In 1991, eighteen-year-old student Ricci Martínez went to a military base to inquire about her forcefully conscripted boyfriend and ended up tortured, mutilated, raped, and murdered by military officers. Ambassador Arcos complained of the impunity of the armed forces and the lack of justice, and in a public denouncement of the military stated that justice "should not be turned into a viper that only bites the barefoot . . . so those that wear boots are immune" (quoted in Farah 1993). Justice in Honduras has long been undermined by Article 90 of the Honduran constitution, which recognizes military justice for military crimes. Until 1991, every crime committed by a soldier was considered a military crime (see Levitsky 1992).[23] Arcos and civil society fought for a year to have the officers tried in civilian courts and were eventually successful, resulting in the first conviction of military officers for serious civil crimes.[24]

The battle for justice has been lengthy and debilitating. More than a dozen military officials have been charged with disappearances and murders and the Supreme Court has ruled that civilian courts have jurisdiction. Evidence has been gathered, cases have been built, and a daring judge named Roy Medina has endured threats on his life and bombings of his office to oversee the case and order the arrest of the officials. The weak

23. Some claim that the biggest barrier to foreign investment in Honduras is the inadequate judicial system (Luxner 1993, 6). The impunity of the armed forces is a major cause of the weak judicial system.

24. One of the witnesses in the Ricci Martínez case, a humble ice cream vendor, was murdered in 1997, one month after receiving death threats from two military officials. The death of the key witness occurred a month before the court date of an appeal for Colonel Angel Castillo, who was convicted of the student's rape and murder (*Honduras This Week*, December 1997).

link in the case, of course, is that no one will arrest the suspects; the military not only goes to great lengths to shelter them, but also continues to pay them even though they have been fugitives from the law for years (*El Heraldo*, 20 July 1997).

Military officials are heavily involved in illicit drugs, auto theft, bank robberies, land theft, and other serious crimes. "By 1986–1987 the trafficking was completely out of control. Senior officers, primarily associated with the navy and military intelligence, had formed an alliance with Juan Ramón Matta Ballesteros to turn the country into the main drug transshipment point between Colombia and the United States" (Schulz and Schulz 1994, 205). Journalists and human rights activists are often the only ones who seriously investigate such crimes—often harassed, threatened, or forced to leave the country—as the military has had until recently total control of all police and investigative agencies in the country. Military impunity goes far beyond major crimes; perhaps the less publicized issues have a greater negative impact on society. For example, the owner of a restaurant told me that a soldier did not want to pay his bill and shot bullets through the windows. What recourse did the proprietor have? None.

The enormous power of the military, coupled with the Cold War fervor for protecting the *Patria* from progressive forces, led to impunity, human rights abuses, and criminality on the part of security forces in Honduras. While the absolute levels of human rights abuses were much lower than in Chile or El Salvador, in Honduras these crimes were still significant and sadly accompanied the redemocratization of the country. A great deal of energy has been expended by civil society and some politicians in an effort to restore justice and tame the tiger. This has been a priority now for two decades. The continued salience of these issues involving the military has often pushed other priorities to the back burner. Unfortunately, the battle to suppress the armed forces occurred at the same time as the economic crisis, and an effective policy response to global economic change was essentially postponed while military crises continued.

From the War-Room to the Boardroom: Military Capitalism in Honduras

"Healthy civil-military relations . . . require that the military has only one permanent function: the defense of national territory and sovereignty" (Isacson 1997, 22). One of the functions of the Honduran military that has raised concerns and that deals directly with the economy is the direct incursion of the armed forces into legal moneymaking activities, which fall under two general categories: the Military Pension Fund (*Instituto de Previsión Militar* IPM), and other activities.

The IPM was created in 1972 as an aid for veterans and a pension fund.[25] The board of directors of the IPM is comprised of the chief of the armed forces, the commanders of the army, air force, navy, and public security, and other leading officials. Two-thirds of IPM funds are provided by the state, while the other third is generated by co-payments of 9 percent of members' salaries. The IPM owns and operates the following business ventures: BANFFAA, which is one of the largest banks in the country; PREVISA, an insurance company; Inversiones Bursátiles, an investment company; PREVICARD, a credit card company; El Zodiaco, an advertising and printing company; SEEISA, a financial consulting firm; Stereo Concierto, an FM radio station; AGROINVASA, African palm plantations and an oil factory; HONDUFARMS, a shrimp farm; PERCASUR, a crustacean exporter; and Funerales San Miguel, a funeral home and cemetery that are seen by some Hondurans as ironic examples of vertical integration, given the military's involvement in assassinations and disappearances. In a bizarre example of privatization, the Honduran government privatized the Honduran Cement Company (INCEHSA) by selling it to the military at a low price of $22 million and with highly favorable terms of only $80,000 down (Funes 1995, 398). The military also owns shoe factories, clothing factories, a car dealership, a barbed-wire company, munitions and arms companies, real estate concerns, land for possible tourism developments, and the abandoned Sheraton-Tegucigalpa hotel project. The IPM has become the nation's fifth largest corporate conglomerate, with annual profits estimated at US$40 million.[26]

In an effort to shield the military's power from declines in U.S. largesse, the military sought self-sufficiency in staple grains for the soldiers. By 1990, military farms employed some ten thousand peasants for US$1 per day, and grew rice, beans, and other grains (Funes 1995, 400; Schulz and Schulz 1994, 282).

25. The discussion of the IPM and other military economic initiatives is taken from Funes (1995), Díaz (1996), and IPM (1993).

26. In the past few years there have been considerable rumors of economic difficulties in the military businesses.

What are the objections to the military's interest in economic goals?[27] How could economic activity have a negative impact on economic growth? Unfair competition and reduced security are two of the main problems that surfaced in Honduras when the military became a player in the private-sector economy.

Economic development is helped by fair competition and transparent rules of the game. Entrepreneurs in Honduras have complained loudly that military capitalism is unfair and counterproductive. Credible reports have been made that the armed forces have exploited their control of the telephone company for industrial espionage (*Comité de Abogados por los Derechos Humans* 1994, 4). In addition, the armed forces—and individual officials—have received free telephone services, duty-free imports (they have controlled customs and immigrations), tax benefits, and free electricity. And as many businesspersons have noted, how does one collect from a military business if they refuse to pay? In addition, the military-owned businesses have an advantage in securing lucrative contracts from the state (Funes 1995, 398). Given that military budgets have been secret, the armed forces can also employ various shell games to subsidize businesses that compete in the economy. These factors make competition with military businesses difficult and lead to uncertainties. "Civilian businesspersons have complained that the military's growing intrusion into the private sector constitutes unfair competition and that it erodes the spirit of free enterprise in the country. So far, docile civilian leaders, long accustomed to seeing top military officers use their posts to gain wealth, have done little to curb the expansion of the military's business empire" (Merrill 1995, 235).

The military's quest for personal and institutional enrichment has drastically hindered security. Article 6 of the Organic Law of the Armed Forces provides that all security falls within the monopoly of the military. Therefore, even security guards have been controlled by the armed forces. Until 1997, when the laws were changed to allow private security firms, a visitor to Honduras was often surprised to see official FUSEP agents deployed as security guards in banks, shops, and supermarkets. These businesses were required to pay expensive fees to the armed forces for security, while the poor police officer or security guard continued to receive a regu-

27. The economic goal is to make every colonel and lieutenant colonel a millionaire upon retirement (interview with Matías Funes, 4 December 1995, Tegucigalpa, Honduras).

lar low salary. Not only has this widespread practice enriched armed forces' officials, but more important, it has led to increased levels of crime. Security forces that should be on the streets maintaining order and fighting criminal activities are busy acting as armed guards for private businesses. For example, at an elementary school in a marginal neighborhood, several rapes had occurred as students entered or left class. The school principal called the police and pleaded for a police officer to patrol the entrance for one hour in the morning and one hour in the afternoon. The response from the military was that they would be more than happy to send the police officer if the school would prepay the bill (interview with Leticia Salomón, 7 December 1995, Tegucigalpa, Honduras). The military even bills the Honduran government large sums for guarding dams and overseeing elections.

On 2 March 1993, the U.S. government's *Voice of America* radio program pronounced that Honduras was no longer a country with a military, but a military with a country (Villeda 1993, 46). The *Voice of America* accused the military of human rights abuses, of drug trafficking, of unfair business practices, of impunity, and of continual disregard for civilian authority. These conditions made it difficult for the Honduran government to give the requisite attention to the economy without first restricting military autonomy. The process has been slow and painful.[28] Beginning with the term of President Reina (1994–98), much has been accomplished. Reina campaigned on an explicit demilitarization platform and his overwhelming victory gave tremendous legitimacy to the declawing of the Tiger. The U.S. policy shift from strong supporter of the military to strong critic of the armed forces, as well as the growth of civil society, coincided with Reina's election and opened an unexpected space for measures to reduce the army's power. Forced conscription was ended, the police were transferred to civilian control, an independent prosecutor's office was established, military budgets were reduced, human rights organizations and journalists gained the courage to criticize the Tiger, and international actors (mainly the United States) no longer embolden the colonels but acted to reduce their strength and omnipotence.

Much work remains to be done. Sadly, the dominance of civil-military problems in Honduras contributed to the "lost decade" of the 1980s and

28. The military fought even limited encroachments on its power. For example, when the National Congress took the Merchant Marine from the military, several deputies received death threats (Funes 1995, 399).

the government's slowed response to economic and human development in the 1990s. The *Houston Chronicle* aptly summarized the Reina administration: "Carlos Roberto Reina of the Liberal Party took over as president in January 1994 with promises to fight corruption and end military influence over civil society. Reina has had some success, establishing an independent prosecuting attorney's office and a new police force that is mostly free of military control. But Reina's administration has only recently begun to control the country's massive economic problems" (7 November 1997). Costa Rican officials had energetically addressed the economic crisis in the early 1980s. Hondurans were focused on a more pressing crisis.

Sandinista Neighbors: Economic Challenges and Opportunities

On 17 July 1979, the same year that the economic crisis began in Costa Rica and Honduras, longtime U.S. ally Anastasio "Tachito" Somoza abandoned Nicaragua for exile in Miami and then Asunción, Paraguay. His refuge, granted by longtime dictator General Alfredo Stroessner would be brief, terminated in September 1980 when Argentine guerrillas blasted his car with a bazooka. As Somoza fled Nicaragua, Sandinista (FSLN) leaders were being flown from San José, Costa Rica, to Managua on the Mexican presidential jet (Wright 1991, 187). On 17 July 1980, precisely one year to the day after Somoza abandoned Nicaragua, Ronald Reagan accepted the Republican Party's nomination for the presidency. Reagan campaigned against American weakness abroad—the humiliation of hostages in Iran, the cowardice of giving the Panama Canal back to Panama, and the weakness of accommodating communist aggression. Soon after taking power, the Reagan administration had drawn a line in the sand in Central America: one way or another, the Sandinistas would have to go.[29]

Within months of taking office, Reagan and his hawkish team of foreign policy players decided that an undeclared war would be waged on the Sandinistas. Contras would soon be heralded as the "moral equivalents of our founding fathers" and the junta in Managua portrayed as a gang of totalitarian demons and part of an international communist conspiracy

29. There are many works on U.S. policy towards Nicaragua and the Contras. They include Booth (1985), Dickey (1987), Honey (1994), Kornbluh (1987), Morley (1994), Pastor (1987), Robinson and Norsworthy (1987), Sklar (1988), and Walker (1987).

that threatened the southern border of the United States. The zeal for destroying the Sandinistas resulted in irrational U.S. policy, the Iran-Contra scandal, and embarrassment for Washington. For Costa Rica and Honduras, the Contra war caused severe long-term damage and dislocation. U.S. policy resulted in threats to sovereignty, economic dislocation, and savage crimes committed by the Contras in border communities. When the U.S. secured its objectives, it quickly and unceremoniously abandoned the Contra soldiers, leaving them with nothing but dangerous weapons, terrorist training, and a belief that they were above the law. Many former Contras still terrorize northern Costa Rica and southern Honduras with violent crimes and arms dealing, and many citizens are maimed yearly by the mines left behind by U.S. agents.

U.S. obsession with the Sandinistas also presented a golden opportunity to Nicaragua's neighbors. Just as Costa Rica and Honduras sank toward economic disaster, the United States came calling for allies and was willing to pay a steep price. In addition to wanting to contain and challenge Managua, the United States thought it would be a psychological setback to have pro-U.S. economies deteriorating in Costa Rica and Honduras. For the first time since the Alliance for Progress, the United States was willing to send large amounts of grants, not just loans, to Central America.[30] Compared with U.S. largesse in the 1980s, the Alliance for Progress was loose change.

The flow of grants to Central America occurred after the Reagan administration had shifted foreign assistance priorities to emphasize U.S. national security and an explicit linkage between economic policy and good standing with the region's hegemon. Elections, free and open markets, and anticommunism became the new mantra, replacing an emphasis on human rights. The priority in Central America was security and U.S. assistance was designed accordingly. "Unlike the Carter administration, which publicly espoused basic human needs in foreign assistance but actually shifted to security concerns, the Reagan administration sought to restore economic assistance to what it regarded as its traditional role as an instrument of national security policy" (Ruttan 1996, 121).[31]

Did different levels of militarization in Costa Rica and Honduras im-

30. Total grants to Honduras for the thirty-five-year period 1946–80 totaled $169.15 million; those to Costa Rica totaled $331 million over the same period.

31. There is considerable debate as to the effectiveness of U.S. international assistance in Central America. See Barry and Preusch (1982), Hellinger (1988), and Weber (1993).

pact the type of grants received and the effectiveness of those grants for the revitalization of the respective economies? The answer is an unambiguous yes.

The first issue centers on the types of grants and the amounts received. Costa Rica and Honduras are about equidistant from Managua, and the United States worked diligently to assault the Sandinistas from both the northern and southern fronts (Edelman 1983b; Honey 1994). One might expect that the United States would use aid as a tool to pay for basing the Contras and that a strong relationship would exist between cooperation and aid. Yet the relationship was much more complex. Until the late 1980s, Honduras was a very willing partner in the Contra war. Honduran government officials denied that the Contras were based on Honduran soil well after everyone knew that they were lying. U.S. troops were welcomed into the country to build bases, hold a series of joint exercises with the Honduran military, and even train the soldiers of Honduras's rival and enemy, El Salvador. In contrast, Costa Rica was much more defiant, especially after the transfer of power from Luís Alberto Monge to Oscar Arias in 1986 (Honey 1994).[32] The Costa Ricans exposed a secret U.S. base, declared Oliver North persona non grata, and regularly embarrassed U.S. officials in pushing a diplomatic solution to the crisis. Yet Washington was under intense pressure to make success stories out of democratic capitalism, and a government collapse in democratic and relatively prosperous Costa Rica would have had a serious negative demonstration effect. With these dynamics at work, the countries began to negotiate for assistance.

Table 7.1 presents total grants, economic grants, and military grants to each country for the period 1981–89. Costa Rica and Honduras received unprecedented amounts of assistance. Note that both countries received similar amounts of total grant money per capita, $330 per person in Costa Rica and $268 per person in Honduras. Yet, while Costa Rican grants went almost exclusively to economic ends, a large chunk of the Honduran grants—in excess of $400 million—were earmarked for the military. The result was that per capita economic grants to wealthier Costa Rica were 78 percent higher than those for Honduras, even though Honduras was the most loyal ally that the United States has ever had in Latin America.

32. Although Arias was clearly more independent than Monge, he was also in a much better economic position to bargain. Even Monge was uncomfortable with U.S. demands to militarize Costa Rica and rebuffed U.S. plans to militarize the country with a "Neutrality Proclamation" in September 1983. Honey contends that the United States retaliated by suspending USAID loans (1994, 301).

Table 7.1a U.S. grants to Honduras and Costa Rica during the Lost Decade (in $US millions)

	1981	*1982*	*1983*	*1984*	*1985*	*1986*	*1987*	*1988*	*1989*
Honduras									
Total	12.65	31.5	84.4	134.1	261.6	167.1	230.9	173.1	111.2
Economic	12.60	19.2	45.1	56.7	194.2	106.0	169.7	131.9	70.1
Military	.05	12.3	39.3	77.4	67.4	61.1	61.2	41.2	41.1
Costa Rica									
Total	5.3	11.1	52.5	109.1	199.1	139.1	151.1	105.2	122.2
Economic	5.3	9.0	47.9	100.0	187.9	136.5	149.4	105.0	122.0
Military	0.0	2.1	4.6	9.1	11.2	2.6	1.7	0.2	0.2

Table 7.1b Cumulative grants, 1981–1989 (in $US)

	Honduras	*Costa Rica*
Total grants	$1.2 billion	$895 million
Economic	$805 million	$863 million
Military	$401 million	$32 million
Total grants per capita	$268	$330
Economic grants per capita	$178	$318

How does one explain why Honduras received the short end of the aid stick? Why did Costa Rica receive mostly economic assistance while Honduras received economic and military assistance? I posed these questions to Eduardo Lizano, who, as Costa Rica Central Bank President from 1984 to 1990, was intimately involved in the negotiations.[33] His comments were direct and perspicacious:

> What you had in Central America was a chess game between East and West and we [the Central Americans] were in many respects the pawns. After the Sandinistas took over, the United States sought out alliances in each country to contain them and confront them. The United States wants foreign aid to serve its own purposes and during the 1980s this was anti-Sandinismo. Now, one must make alliances with those that have power. In Honduras the military had the power, so strong alliances would be formed with the armed forces and U.S. assistance would include significant military aid. In Costa Rica, there is no military power whatsoever, so

33. Lizano, one of the most respected economists in the country, was recently named the Central Bank president in the Pacheco administration (2002–2006).

the United States must seek other alliances. Political power in Costa Rica is held by the two main political parties.

In the 1980s, there was a consensus among U.S. officials and officials in both political parties that the priority in Costa Rica was to restructure the economy to favor nontraditional exports and to reduce the size of the state bureaucracy. The first part required huge sums of money to build up a private banking system. Funds for the private banks were cannibalized from USAID and used to push nontraditional exports. In addition, U.S. foreign aid set up CINDE[34] and funded other organizations to attract foreign investment. . . . Actually, there was tremendous agreement among U.S. officials and Costa Rican economists about the goals of the assistance. And the results were clearly successful with economic growth 1984–1994 of close to 4–5 percent per year, and enormous growth in nontraditional exports and foreign investment. (Interview with Eduardo Lizano, San José, Costa Rica, 2 October 1997)

The total package of money and goods that flowed into Honduras to bolster the U.S. alliance with the colonels in the 1980s was massive. In addition to the $400 million in military grants approved by Congress, the United States was able to skirt congressional oversight and use alternative means to feed the Honduran Tiger (Merrill 1995, 235). Huge joint military training exercises were held in 1983, 1984, and 1985 (Big Pine I, II, and III) involving a total of twelve thousand U.S. military personnel and dozens of warships. And in 1987, a mock invasion of Nicaragua coined Operation Solid Shield involved more than seven thousand U.S. soldiers. Not only were these exercises held to intimidate the Sandinistas, but also to deliver goods to the Contras and the Honduran military, as large quantities of arms and supplies were left behind after the end of the operations (interview with Matías Funes, 4 December 1995, Tegucigalpa, Honduras; Schulz and Schulz 1994, 153).

The Honduran military was also able to cash in on covert aid going to the Contras, by selling them arms, uniforms, and supplies at highly inflated prices. Finally, the United States built various military bases, radar

34. *Coalición Costarricense de Iniciativas para el Desarrollo* (CINDE) is a private and autonomous organization, created with USAID money and support to attract foreign investment to the country.

stations, and training centers throughout the country. The largest was the Palmerola Air Base (renamed the Enrique Soto Cano Air Base in 1988) located some 60 miles north of Tegucigalpa. The initial cost of Palmerola likely exceeded the $400 million in approved military grants and the annual upkeep alone was $50 million (Merrill 1995, 240), placing construction and upkeep costs over the 1983–98 period at over $1 billion. The base is the property of the Honduran government and on temporary loan to the United States. The location of Palmerola highlights the irrationality of military spending in Central America. Tegucigalpa is in desperate need of a better runway to replace the dangerous and antiquated Toncontín Airport. The United States built a first-class landing facility in the country but too far from the capital to serve as a commercial airport. So when the Americans abandon Palmerola, the Honduran military will lay claim to a first class air base to station their first-class wing of twelve advanced F-5 fighter jets acquired in 1987, while the capital will still suffer from an antiquated airport.

If all U.S. military expenditure in Honduras were added up—and due to the subterfuge this would be difficult—the total would easily surpass the total economic grants provided to the country. The fact is that the United States spent much more in Honduras than in Costa Rica during the 1980s, but because of different levels of militarization, the Costa Ricans received more economic grant money and much more economic assistance on a per capita basis. This money was critical for Costa Rica's eventual economic revitalization. In the words of Eduardo Lizano: "If Honduras had no military and Costa Rica did, the United States would have provided military aid to Costa Rica and nonmilitary aid to Honduras and the crisis in Costa Rica would have been much more dramatic and lengthy. It would not be the same country today" (interview with Eduardo Lizano, San José, Costa Rica, 2 October 1997).

Even with enormous injections of military money in Honduras, the country still received a large amount of economic aid. One of the principal contentions of this book is that militarization during the Cold War and an obsession with national security resulted in a loss of state capacity to pursue economic and social development due to misplaced priorities and inadequate focus. Any organization must prioritize its goals and for the Honduran democratic government in the 1980s, sustainable economic policies took a backseat to anticommunism and surviving military threats. Honduran presidents had one eye on the military and one eye on the U.S.-

Contra dynamic throughout the 1980s, leaving precious little focus for responding effectively to the serious economic crisis. Indeed, President Azcona (1986–90) regularly responded to concerns of economic depression and widespread immiseration with, "no hay crisis, no lo veo" (there is no crisis, I don't see it) (Funes 1995, 347). Not only were security issues grabbing the attention of Honduran officials, but they also dominated the agenda for the U.S. embassy and AID officials. Many Hondurans considered U.S. Ambassador John Negroponte to be the ambassador to the Contras instead of the ambassador to Honduras.

> Critics "charge that United States support for the Honduran military, including direct negotiations over support for the Contras, actually worked to undermine the authority of the elected civilian government. They also blame the United States for tolerating the Honduran military's human rights violations, particularly in the early 1980s. They claim that the United States obsession with defeating the Sandinistas in Nicaragua and the FMLN in El Salvador resulted in Honduras's becoming the regional intermediary for United States policy—without regard for the consequences for Honduras. *Indeed, some maintain that the United States embassy in Tegucigalpa often appeared to be more involved with the Contra war effort against Nicaragua than with the political and economic situation in Honduras.*" (Merrill 1995, 200; emphasis mine)

The USAID's *Country Development Strategy Statement for Honduras, 1992–1996* admits that the country has been painfully slow to respond to the economic crisis. "There has been a reluctance to . . . [pass legislation] to facilitate new investments in highly productive areas like shrimp farming, tourism, and banking" (USAID 1992, 10). Legislation favoring export-led growth did not arrive until 1990. The report gives clues as to the source of the inertia: "Yet Honduras' political culture continues to be defined by its authoritarian history and by the dominance of a few special interests. *There is a strong tradition of military control and influence over the government. National interests are not always pursued objectively*" (USAID 1992, 12, emphasis mine).

The U.S. General Accounting Office's 1989 report on assistance to Central America is also illuminating. The report notes that the Reagan administration adopted the Kissinger Commission recommendation "to focus U.S. aid on security goals" (1989, 17) and that "Past U.S. policies in the region appear to have been driven largely by the threat of an increasing Soviet bloc influence in the region" (1989, 25). The emphasis on a military solution to political and social problems had serious downsides, as "the process of modernizing Central American militaries . . . may also have increased their power to the detriment of civilian governments" (25).[35] The report also states that "U.S. policymakers should squarely face the *tradeoff* between the goal of economic policy reform needed to consolidate economic recovery in El Salvador and Honduras and political and military objectives" (61). Why? Because "*If political and military objectives are primary, then the process of economic and policy reform may have to be slower*" (61, emphasis mine). Militarization slowed effective response to economic crisis when actors were fixated on Cold War security dynamics.

The GAO report also discussed the direct impact of U.S. assistance in Costa Rica and Honduras. Note the difference in critical ESF (Emergency Stabilization Funds) assistance and the direct link between militarization and economic reform.

> The United States has provided $815.0 million in ESF assistance to Costa Rica through fiscal year 1988. Because of the close cooperation between the United States, IMF, and the World Bank and a commitment to reform on the part of the Costa Rican government, which had the support of its population,[36] a degree of economic stability was achieved by 1984.[37] (1989, 39)

35. The excessively militarized focus of U.S. assistance to the region is illustrated in the following: "some country officials indicated that U.S. training does not always fill their needs. For example, Costa Rican officials said that they did not need infantry training but rather instruction in investigative techniques, refugee management, and border patrol" (USGAO 1989, 26).

36. The claim that the Costa Rican population generally supported U.S. and IMF economic policy is an exaggeration and the issues of privatization and economic opening remain contentious in the country (see Honey 1994). Polls regularly show that some 90% of the population oppose privatizing the utilities. The population did embrace export-led growth.

37. The GAO report's view of the positive impact of U.S. economic assistance is seconded by a 1992 USAID report: "With over $1.3 billion in U.S. assistance during the 1980s, Costa Rica recovered from the severe regional recession that so adversely affected Central America beginning in 1978. Economic growth rates, which were negative in the early 1980s recovered and averaged 4.5 percent from 1986 through 1990. . . . Overall trade grew sharply since 1986, particularly nontraditional exports, which were a central focus of the U.S. economic assistance program through the 1980s" (1992, 3).

> Until late 1986, the situation in Honduras in some respects paralleled that of El Salvador. The U.S. need for the Honduran government's support of the Nicaraguan contras became a higher priority than economic reforms and reduced AID's leverage to encourage economic reform measures in Honduras. The United States provided Honduras with over $555 million in ESF assistance during fiscal years 1982–88. (1989, 42)

It is important to note that neither USAID, USGAO, nor I assert that militarization is the only variable that contributed to a strong response in Costa Rica and a pitiful response in Honduras. Certainly, militarization dovetailed with other factors, such as the high level of human capital in Costa Rica and a somewhat tentative business community in Honduras. Levels of militarization played a significant role.

As acknowledged by Lizano (above), U.S. economic assistance and a concerted effort on the part of U.S. officials, Costa Rican policymakers, and the Costa Rican business community resulted in not only a stabilization of the Tico economy but also impressive economic growth led by nontraditional exports.[38] As detailed by Clark (1995, 1997), Edelman and Monge (1993), Itzigsohn (2000), Rovira (1989), and Wilson (1998), Costa Rican exports are one of the great success stories in Latin America. One of USAID's pet projects was CINDE[39] (Costa Rican Investment and Trade Development Board), an autonomous and well-financed organization that led the charge for private banks, legislation to benefit nontraditional exports, and foreign investment. In essence, CINDE was a U.S. taxpayer-supported recruiter of jobs and investment from the United States to Costa Rica. With nearly unlimited resources, offices in San José, Miami, and New York, and a large and well-paid professional staff, CINDE has been wildly successful. As of September 1997, CINDE had lured 240 multinationals to invest in Costa Rica, including Baxter Healthcare, DSC Communications, ACER Computers, Sawtek, Sarah Lee, Conair, Pfizer, and Lucent Technologies. The crown jewel for CINDE was the successful

38. The Costa Ricans were concerned with security issues and the Contras, and the attention given to security by the Monge and Arias administrations was significant. Yet the security crisis in Costa Rica was a mild distraction compared to the situation in Honduras.

39. CINDE is not without controversy. There have been charges of corruption and critics claim that CINDE is a tool of U.S. hegemony, as it not only seeks foreign investment but is active in trying to influence public opinion and legislation to support privatization and austerity measures.

recruitment of INTEL to invest $500 million in Costa Rica. By 2001, INTEL will have produced 25 percent of its computer chips in Costa Rica, generating some four thousand direct jobs and $3.5 billion in annual exports. These investments and exports were only possible due to the economic aid provided by the United States during the 1980s crisis. Honduras received the largest military runway in the region; Costa Rica got INTEL.[40]

Even without factoring in INTEL's future exports, Costa Rica's record is impressive. By 1997, total merchandise exports reached $4.1 billion, quadrupling the 1980 figure and leading the region in per capita exports at $1,171 (*La Nación*, 23 February 1998). By 1999, exports reached $8.2 billion or $2,108 per capita. For comparison, per capita exports in 1999 for other selected Latin American countries are: Argentina = $771, Brazil = $332, Chile = $1,294, Honduras=$367, and Mexico = $1,526 (ECLAC 2000, 96; UNDP 2001, 154–57). Costa Rican and Honduran exports 1980–96 are presented in Figure 7.1. Both countries began the period with similar export totals but diverged sharply as Honduran officials and the U.S. embassy in Tegucigalpa were fixated on military issues and anticommunism, while Costa Rica and the USAID office in San José orchestrated a focused, well-financed, and sustained campaign to respond to the economic crisis and shift from ISI to export-led growth.

Costa Rica's export dynamism and Honduras's slow economic recovery are in part explained by the militarization variable. Due to heightened militarization in Honduras, the Hondurans (and U.S. officials stationed in the country) had neither the level of economic resources nor the priority and focus found in Costa Rica to respond effectively to the economic crisis and shift to export-led growth. The differences in levels of militarization also had an important intangible impact on foreign investment—country image. During the 1980s, Honduras was portrayed in the international

40. The linkage between foreign investment and militarization goes beyond the aid issue. According to CINDE official Sigrid Miller, Costa Rica cannot compete with Honduras, Nicaragua, and El Salvador in labor, electricity, and production costs. "In the region, Costa Rica is very expensive. But what many businesses are interested in is stability and with no military—and the military being a major cause of instability and uncertainty in the region—the lack of a military is a major selling point. Many of the multinationals that decide to locate here mention the lack of a military as one reason. The political climate along with the level of education are the two main reasons that companies locate here. The lack of the military gives long-term certainty in political stability and if INTEL is going to invest $500 million it wants to be sure about long-term factors" (interview with Sigrid Miller, 22 September 1997, San José, Costa Rica).

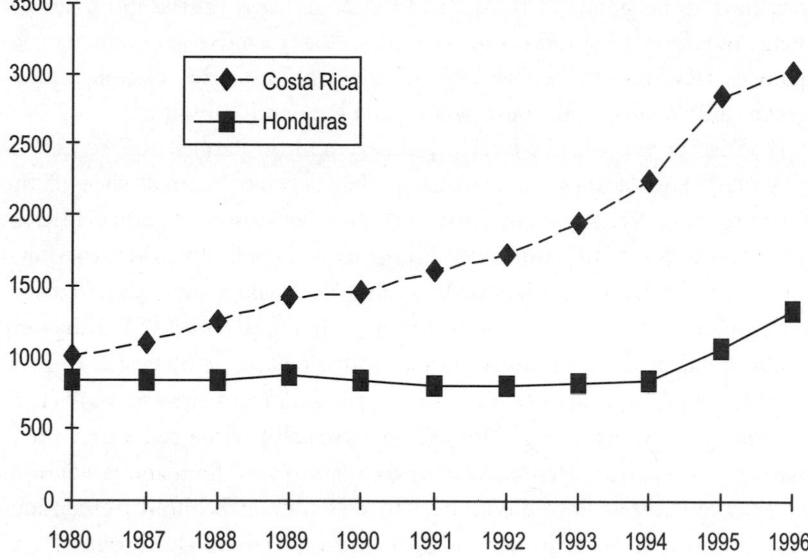

Fig. 7.1 Merchandise exports in $US millions

press as a land-based aircraft carrier (the U.S.S. Honduras) with no rule of law and short time horizons. Costa Rica promoted the lack of a military as a sign of stability and long time horizons. The Costa Rican Ministry of Foreign Trade and the Export and Investment Promotion Center (CENPRO) publish and distribute an impressive directory to attract foreign investors to Costa Rica, in which they list the advantages of producing in and exporting from Costa Rica. The first three advantages are "political stability, peace and democracy, no army" (CENPRO 1996, 10).

A Comparative Examination of Militarization and the Tourism Industry

In the first section of this chapter, I discussed the power held by the Honduran military and the resulting crises that occurred 1980–96 as a fledgling democracy and emerging civil society attempted to wrest power and prerogatives from the armed forces. The second section discussed the differing responses to the economic crisis in Costa Rica and Honduras. In order to more clearly demonstrate the charges that (1) "If political and military objectives are primary, then the process of economic and policy reform may have to be slower"[41] (GAO 1989, 61), and that (2) the international image of a repressive and powerful military has negative economic consequences, this final chapter section will concentrate on the relationship between militarization and tourism in Costa Rica and Honduras.

Tourism is the world's largest industry and the largest source of employment. For decades, Latin America has received a small slice of the world tourism pie. In recent years, a number of factors have provided an opportunity for Latin American countries to benefit from international tourism.[42] Tourism experienced a worldwide boom from 1980 to 1996, with annual expenditure increases of more than 9 percent. U.S. travel expenditure abroad, the largest source of tourism revenue by far for Central America, doubled from $29 billion to $57 billion from 1987 to 1998 (U.S. Bureau of the Census 1997, 268). The 1980s also witnessed a new niche market—ecotourism. Ecotourism, or tourism to view flora and fauna or to experience nature, allowed countries to seek tourism without tremendous investments in five-star hotels and golf courses. Archeological tourism and scuba diving also flourished in the 1980–96 period.

Costa Rica and Honduras are both blessed with an endowment of natural destinations for adventurous tourists. Having spent considerable time traversing both Costa Rica and Honduras, I agree with Ricardo Martínez, executive director of the Honduran Institute of Tourism (IHT), that Honduras has a greater tourism resource endowment than does Costa Rica (*Tourism 2000*, 6–7). According to the IHT, there are five attractions that bring tourists to Third World countries that are presented in Table 7.2, and to which I add surfing and fishing.[43]

The above rankings are not only shared by this author and Honduran tourist officials, but by many Costa Ricans as well. As early as 1956, José

41. Kevin Casas Zamora, Costa Rican scholar and former program officer at the Arias Foundation for Peace and Human Progress, told me that his research indicated that civilian governments in countries with large militaries often opted to do nothing in policy areas that might even have the most remote possibility of upsetting a fragile status quo with the armed forces (10 September 1997, San José, Costa Rica). This contributes to hesitancy in addressing important policy issues.

42. Tourism also has its dark side. Costa Rica has received unfavorable reports for sex tourism and a related crisis in the increased incidence of pedophilia.

43. Costa Rican surfing is growing in international fame and Playa Grande was featured in the surf movie *Endless Summer II*. Currently 3.7% of visitors list surfing as the principal reason for visiting the country. Only 2.8% of visitors list fishing as the principal reason for visiting Costa Rica, but it is widely accepted that fishing generates large sums of dollars per tourist (data provided by UNIMER survey firm).

Table 7.2 Tourism endowment in Costa Rica and Honduras

Attraction	*Costa Rica*	*Honduras*
Beaches	Good	Good (better)
Scuba	Average	Excellent+
Flora and fauna	Excellent	Excellent
Pre-Columbian sites	None	Excellent
Colonial heritage	None	Some
Fishing	Excellent	Good
Surfing	Excellent	Poor

Figueres noted the challenges for attracting tourists to Costa Rica. Unlike other countries such as Honduras, Figueres admitted that Costa Rica lacks pre-Columbian people and ruins, colonial architecture, and cultural souvenirs. In addition, the country has the most severe rainy season in Central America (Figueres 1956, 101). Honduras has the resources to at least match if not surpass the increases in tourism revenues achieved in Costa Rica.[44] Tourism revenues are presented in Figure 7.2.

As shown in Table 7.2, tourism revenues have increased tenfold in

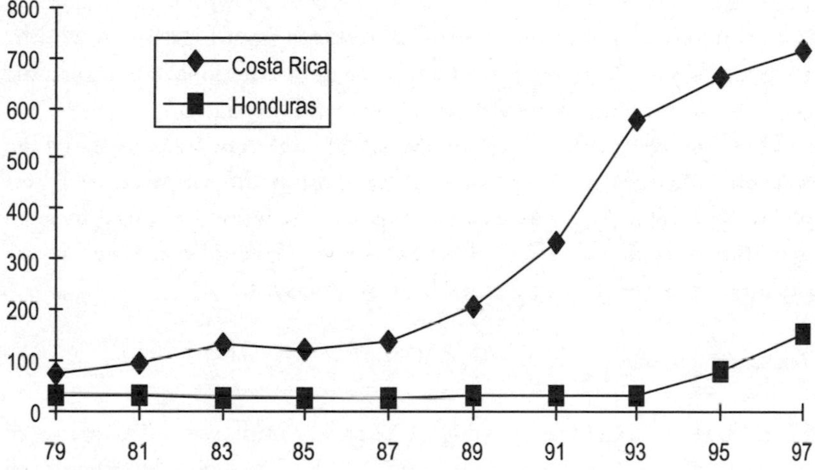

Fig. 7.2 Tourist revenues in $US millions, 1979–1997

44. One may assume that Costa Rica would have a much better infrastructure than Honduras. This is not necessarily true. My experience (at least before Hurricane Mitch) is that the Honduran highway system is in much better condition than that of Costa Rica, where dodging the potholes is a dangerous drawback to any travel. Honduras also has four international airports, compared to two in Costa Rica.

Costa Rica, from $71 million to $714 million. How important are tourism revenues for Costa Rica? In 1997, international tourism earned roughly double the revenues of coffee exports. Tourism was the number one generator of new employment in the past decade, creating 128,000 new jobs, or 44 percent of all new jobs. Twelve percent of the occupied labor force works in the tourism industry. Stated simply, Costa Rica's economy would be significantly weaker without the development of this industry. In addition, tourism has had an important impact outside of the Central Valley where most industry is located; 71.5 percent of tourism activity is found outside the Central Valley and has been an engine for growth in some of the poorest regions of the country. Finally, tourism has created thousands of micro-businesses owned by local residents: 73 percent of hotels have less than twenty rooms and one can travel throughout the country staying at locally owned hotels and eating in locally owned restaurants (*Unidad Social Cristiana* Platform: Tourism, www.nacion.co.cr/In_ee/elecciones/programa/turismo.html).

In contrast, international tourism revenues in Honduras were moribund—$29 million in 1979 and $32 million in 1993.[45] The situation is so pathetic in Honduras that in 1993, this poor country with significant tourism promise had a net loss in currency reserves from tourism, as wealthy Hondurans were spending $6 million more in international travel than the country was receiving from foreign visitors (IHT 1994, 79).

How can one possibly explain the starkly different trajectories of the tourism industries in these two countries? I put this question to a host of industry officials, media experts, political commentators, and tourism operators in both countries.[46] There was near universal consensus on the explanation, which can be divided into two sections.

Tourism Legislation

Costa Rican tourism was growing quite slowly until 1987. The principal reason for the sudden increase is found in 1985 Law 6990 (interview with

45. The situation for international tourism was far worse than these numbers indicate. Tourism revenues include money spent by missionaries, U.S. soldiers stationed in the country or participating in joint training maneuvers, and other similar visitors to the country who are not tourists.

46. In Costa Rica, interviews on tourism were held with Alfredo Oporta and Ireth Rodríguez of the Costa Rican Tourism Institute, tourism journalist for *La Nación* Emilia Mora, Catarina García of the public opinion firm UNIMER, U.S. embassy officials, former

Emilia Mora, 22 September 1997; ICT documents). In its 1998 party platform, the Unity Party (PUSC)—the PUSC was the opposition party in 1985 and not responsible for the law—admits that "The promulgation of the 1985 Law of Tourism Incentives No. 6990 opened the path for tourism to become a generating source of income and of employment" (PUSC Platform: Tourism). Tourism will not develop without a minimal level of services and hotels. Not only are hotels important for lodging, but they also promote the country through international advertising. In the early 1980s, Costa Rica did not possess the facilities for tourism and realized that an incentive was necessary. Law 6990 provided an incentive to invest in tourism by (1) allowing the duty-free importation of equipment, supplies, vehicles, boats, and other accouterments for tourism enterprises; and (2) tax benefits through an acceleration of depreciation (ICT 1997, 83–97). In addition, the Costa Rican Tourism Institute was given autonomy and a dedicated source of income for promotion that was derived from a 3 percent surcharge on hotel rooms and a fee for every airline ticket. The ICT has been able to spend large sums of money on international promotion and local capacity; in 1997 the ICT spent some $10 million on advertising in the United States, pushing the theme "Costa Rica: No Artificial Ingredients."

Investment incentives were quite successful; the number of hotel rooms in the country tripled from 1985 to 1993. Costa Rica first marketed itself as a destination for backpackers and ecotourists. The country is presently diversifying into high-end tourism with higher value-added products. In 1997, five mega projects with a total investment of $450 million were under construction, featuring five-star resorts and golf courses (*La Nación*, 5 October 1997).

One of the great frustrations for Honduran tourism officials is that legislation for ZOLT (*Zonas Libres Turísticas*, Tourism Free Zones) did not go into effect until 7 July 1992. The legislation was relatively simple and had goals similar to the 1985 Costa Rican tourism incentive legislation, permitting duty-free importation of tourism related materials and equipment as well as tax benefits (*La Gaceta*, 7 July 1992). The legislation was

presidents Oscar Arias and Luis Alberto Monge, and dozens of tourism entrepreneurs. In Honduras, interviews on tourism were held with Digna de Domínguez, Tatiana Cirque, Claudia Chávez, and Cristobal Silva of the Honduran Tourism Institute, political commentators Marvin Barahona and Rafael del Cid, U.S. embassy officials, and dozens of tourism entrepreneurs.

not controversial and did not create winners and losers among local elites in the same fashion that a shift from protected ISI industrialization to open ELG does.[47] Tourism officials had been lobbying for years for incentive legislation; they knew that they could capture a portion of the growing hemispheric tourist trade and that the legislation was critical. The legislation not only had no domestic opposition that I could identify, but did not require a large expenditure from the national treasury. Similar legislation was demonstrated to be effective in Costa Rica.

Why did tourism legislation come so late in Honduras? The answer hearkens back to the GAO statement that reforms will be slower when military objectives are primary. In the 1980–93 period, military security issues still dominated the agenda. Priorities were skewed away from the type of long-term policies represented by ZOLT. Elected officials were consumed during the "lost decade"of the 1980s with either short-term survival or putting out fires. Economic policy during these years existed, but instead of proactive planning of sustainable developmental policy it was reduced to crisis management and short-term reaction. This is largely the result of the military power and battle to control and/or reduce the power that characterized Honduras.

One may ask, how do we know that incentive legislation would actually spur tourism in Honduras? Perhaps the Hondurans are incapable of luring tourists? Passage of the ZOLT legislation in 1992 provides a test. After a lag period of two years, tourism revenues grew dramatically, from $32 million in 1992 to $80 million in 1995 and an estimated $150 million in 1997. That is a fivefold increase in five years after passage of the legislation. As of July 1997, nineteen hotels were under construction, bringing an estimated $100 million in new investment. IHT executive director Martínez provides the answer for the sudden success of the industry: "Martínez said that the growth of the tourism sector is the result of the Incentives Law that the government has been promoting, which includes the duty-free importation of goods and equipment, as well as the exoneration of taxes" (*El Heraldo*, 26 July 1997).[48]

IHT was also granted autonomy and I found the seventy-five employ-

47. Discussions of the tensions between domestic beneficiaries of import substitution and export-led-growth proponents, and possible solutions within a democratic polity, are found in Haggard and Kaufman (1995), Pastor and Wise (1994), and Przeworski (1991).

48. In an attempt to boost state capacity, President Callejas (1990–94) also sponsored the most extensive modernization of the state since Soto (1876–83) and Gálvez (1948–54).

ees to be both highly qualified and motivated. They are still no match for the Costa Rican Tourism Institute, which has 170 employees and twenty times the annual budget. IHT had no dedicated funding source, which limits long-term promotional planning and effectiveness. In May 1998, newly elected Honduran President Flores announced a 4 percent tax on hotel rooms, vehicle rentals, and tour agencies; the money would go to the Ministry of Tourism to promote Honduran tourism (*Honduras This Week*, 4 May 1998). Collecting the tourism tax has been problematic.

Image and Tourism

One other important linkage between the level of militarization and tourism is international image. Costa Rica has been nominated twelve times for the Nobel Peace Prize for the absence of a military; the country (and Oscar Arias) won the prize in 1989. The image of a peaceful and demilitarized country dovetailed nicely with the preferences and concerns of their targeted tourist market—ecotourists. According to a Menlo Consulting Group survey of 45,000 U.S. households, the U.S. tourists who would be most interested in visiting Costa Rica are well aware of Costa Rica's political climate. One of the reasons they would visit is "political stability in a part of the world known for military rule and instability" (1996, 6). "The research also shows a fairly high level of interest in understanding local conditions of the places they visit. For example, four in ten (41.1 percent) of Costa Rica's best prospects would want to understand the country's political and social structure" (1996, 14). Costa Rica has used the "no military" status extensively to lure these socially aware and progressive tourists. The three key points used in promotion are biodiversity, peace with no military, and the friendliness of Ticos (interview with ICT official Ireth Rodríguez, 16 September 1997, San José, Costa Rica). The "no military" status is emblazoned on popular T-shirts worn proudly by tourists: one T-shirt features beautiful native birds and the caption "The Costa Rican Air Force"; another features the massive leatherback turtles lumbering up a beach with the caption "The Costa Rican Navy."

In contrast, the international image of Honduras has been very negative. From the *Voice of America* references to the country as an "army with a country" to the U.S. press references to Honduras in the 1980s as the U.S.S. Honduras, the image of Honduras in the United States is of death squads, a mafia-like armed forces hiding behind sun glasses and tanks, and instability. This type of negative image can be overcome, but requires promotion and success stories in the international press.

Conclusion

Successful economic development requires a rational use of resources and opportunity maximization. Beginning in 1979, Costa Rica and Honduras entered a serious economic crisis. While the crisis in Costa Rica was deeper, the country was able to maximize opportunities created by the Contra war to obtain a great deal of economic assistance from the United States and reorient its economy from ISI to ELG. Hondurans and U.S. officials in the country had a different priority in the 1980s: a dramatic increase in military power and the subsequent challenge of reducing that power. This not only reduced the availability of U.S. economic assistance, but also limited the organizational capacity of the state and the commitment to economic response on the part of all actors.

Tourism is one segment of the economy that illustrates how militarization slowed the state response to economic opportunity. International factors created a great opportunity for Costa Rica and Honduras to reap tourism revenues. Costa Rica responded rationally and effectively. The Hondurans were fixated on crises and challenges resulting from a militarized response to the Cold War. They were slow to enact even a minimal proactive policy.

summation

PART

Conclusion

"Underdevelopment refers to the blockage which forestalls a rational transformation of the social structure in Third World countries. . . . Development is the increasing capacity to make rational use of natural and human resources for social ends" (Mittelman 1988, 22). In the final analysis, development is all about maximizing opportunities and minimizing losses. This book examines the relationship between militarization and development in Latin America during the Cold War. Has militarization encouraged or forestalled the rational use of natural and human resources for social ends? I theorized that where the armed forces are focused on internal threats, militarization has serious opportunity costs and undercuts two pillars of state capacity: economic resources and organizational resources/priorities. In addition, militarization more often than not tips power away from the popular classes and towards the oligarchy. The evidence is compelling and the verdict unambiguous—militarization has a substantial negative effect on political and material development in Latin America.

To reach this conclusion, my research design first partitioned the dependent variable—development—into three separate dependent variables: democracy, equity, and economic growth. The three resulting relationships were then assessed by triangulating diverse methods and sources of data on each relationship.[1] Cross-national quantitative data sources and inferential statistics were used to evaluate the relationship between militarization and democracy, equity, and economic growth in eighteen Latin American countries and often in larger samples of LDCs. I then employed militarization as a dichotomous variable and used comparative historical data to examine the relationship between militarization and democracy and material development in Costa Rica and Honduras.

I never proposed and the evidence never demonstrated that militarization is the single explanation for different levels of development in Latin America. Militarization is not the magic bullet. Indeed, in the quantitative chapters, many other control variables are employed that are highly significant and substantial parts of the explanation. And the explanation is

1. The equity variable was examined in the quantitative section but not in a comparative historical chapter. This is because the causal mechanism linking militarization with equity is regularly treated as the same causal mechanism as that linking militarization with economic growth. I chose to use economic growth in the comparative historical chapter, as the trade-off between military spending and social welfare is more obvious.

never complete, as a portion of the variance remains unexplained by the models. What is proposed and supported is that militarization is an important component of any explanation of democracy, equity, and economic growth during the Cold War.

Chapter 3 presents the quantitative analysis of the relationship between militarization and democracy. Militarization has a significant negative effect on democracy. No evidence exists to support reversed causality—high militarization causes low levels of democracy, low levels of democracy do not cause militarization. Finally, it is shown that the negative impact of militarization on democracy began to diminish in the late 1970s, such that the negative effect is much stronger in 1973–74 than in 1985–86.

Chapters 4 and 5 are comparative historical analyses of the militarization/democracy relationship in Costa Rica and Honduras. The oligarchy and the political opposition were strongly in favor of ousting Figueres in the 1950s through violence. Figueres was branded a communist both in Costa Rica and abroad, and many thought that he would be deposed soon after the overthrow of Jacobo Arbenz in Guatemala. Figueres's enemies had the will, but without an autonomous military did not have the means. It is highly probable that had a strong, autonomous military existed in Costa Rica in the 1950s, the country would have witnessed a democratic breakdown. Honduras was not so lucky. This country had no centralized autonomous military before 1954. The United States played a key role in militarizing the country despite an impressive public debate on the virtues of following Costa Rica's example and proscribing the armed forces. By 1957, the constitution granted absolute autonomy and tremendous power to the newly created armed forces. Villeda gained the presidency within this context. The similarities between Villeda and Figueres are extensive, as are their lists of enemies. On the eve of the 1963 elections (and the probability of electing an opponent of the armed forces and a continuation of progressive reforms), the military overthrew Villeda, ushering in two decades of military rule. The Honduran case is especially useful as it demonstrates how a near nonexistent military could grow with U.S. support into the arbiter of national politics in a short period of time. The same could have occurred in Costa Rica.

The results of the comparative historical chapter supplement the quantitative results. Militarization may not strongly impact the incidence of transition to democracy, but rather alters the quality of that democracy by restricting the autonomy of the elected government. Militarization does impact the incidence of democratic collapse. Even in the most highly educated countries that have the longest histories of consolidated democracy—Chile and Uruguay—very powerful military institutions accompanied democratic breakdown, military rule, and massive human rights violations.

Chapter 6 presents an empirical analysis of the relationship between militarization and material development (equity and economic growth). For eighteen Latin American countries, the size of the military has a strong and negative effect on increases in calorie consumption and economic growth. The militarization variable even outperforms the growth of the economy as a predictor of change in calorie consumption over a twenty-five-year period. The relationship with a large sample of LDCs is also examined, and demonstrates the very different effect of militarization on food consumption and economic growth by region. Context matters.

Chapter 7 examines the relationship between militarization and economic development in a comparative historical analysis of Costa Rica and Honduras in the 1980s and 1990s. The principal issue is how militarization affected the different responses to the 1980s economic crisis. I demonstrate that, due to the military's focus on internal security and its ability to plunder the state in the absence of serious external threats, military power in Honduras reduced the state's capacity as it shifted priorities away from economic development and towards issues of national security and the military. The newly installed democratic governments from 1982 to 1996 became a crisis manager that spent far too much effort putting out military fires. The U.S. embassy and the USAID office in Tegucigalpa also became far more interested in managing the Contras than in easing the economic depression.

I then explore U.S. economic and military assistance to Costa Rica and Honduras. Both countries received huge sums of U.S. largesse merely for sharing large borders with Nicaragua. Costa Rica received much more per capita economic assistance, and as a result was able to reorient its economy from ISI to ELG with minimal dislocation. Honduras received significant levels of economic aid, but also a great deal of military assistance that had no positive impact on the long-term restructuring of the economy. As a result of U.S. fixation on battling the Sandinistas, Costa Rica got a $500 million investment from INTEL and Honduras got a $500 million airport too far from any city for any rational use. Finally, the chapter details how the militarization variable helps to explain the successful development of the tourism industry in Costa Rica and the underdevelopment of the Honduran tourism industry.

In 1948–49, Costa Rica constitutionally proscribed a permanent military institution. In the 1950s, the emergence of the Cold War and a fear of communism forced governments to make a choice about how they were going to guard against leftist advances in Latin America. One option was to build citizen-centric security based on democracy, improved living standards, and co-optation. A second option was to base security on the ability to repress progressive change. This second option was strongly pushed by the United States and to one degree or another was followed by the countries of Latin America. Cold War militarization began in the early 1950s with bilateral military agreements and was enhanced after 1959 in response to the Cuban revolution. President Eisenhower announced a new comprehensive military policy for Latin America, one by which the United States might "strive to be the sole supplier of military hardware to Latin America" as "a means of maintaining U.S. influence over Latin American military forces and through such forces on the political orientation of Latin American Governments" (Rabe 1988, 108).

The bulking up and in some cases the creation of military institutions had serious long-term consequences for democracy, equity, and economic growth in Latin America. It led to a vicious cycle of higher military expenditures, greater economic deprivation, and greater political repression. Costa Rica was the exception that proves the rule. Instead of a spiral towards greater military expenditures, more autonomy for the generals, inadequate spending on social programs, and increased misery, Costa Rica was able to enter a virtuous circle. Defense expenditures as a percentage of GDP fell steadily. Larger portions of the national budget were dedicated to health care. Living standards and health standards increased dramatically. Democracy was legitimized and strengthened. And, in its weakened military condition, Costa Rica became more and not less secure than Honduras, which militarized its state under the aegis of the United States in 1954. The United States chose poorly, as did many Latin Americans, and the result was less democracy, increased human misery, thousands of "disappeared," wars, and slower economic growth.[2]

2. This is not to say that Costa Rica is a paradise or the ideal. Costa Rican democracy has serious shortcomings (see Seligson 2000). The economy is not growing as fast as it should. Inequalities are substantial. I consider Costa Rica, with limited natural resources, to be no more than the bare minimum of what every Latin American country should be able to achieve in regard to democracy, economic growth, and social development.

Contributions to Theory and Policy

This study provides a number of empirical, theoretical, and policy contributions. A large body of quantitative literature has concluded that militarization is universally beneficial for economic growth and equity in developing countries. I have exposed a serious flaw in this research. There are many different types of militarization that have different effects on development. When militaries face few or no credible external threats and when a military's enemies are largely comprised of fellow citizens, militarization has tremendous economic and social costs. This is especially true when a regional hegemon and a long historical trajectory enhance the internal missions of the armed forces. These conditions are presented in a simple typology in Chapter 2 and correspond with the Latin American experience.

The area-specific context of militarization makes an important and constructive contribution to the current debate over the value of nomothetic versus area-specific research agendas. Beginning with Geddes's critique of big-tent social science (1991) and reaching a peak with Bates's criticism of area scholars (1996), there has been an active campaign in some political science circles in favor of nomothetic deductive research over contextualized area studies research. This book shows that region-specific fields of inquiry are needed to understand development, and indeed may be more useful than nomological theory. At the same time, however, this research also shows that proponents of area-specific context must go much further than merely asserting that their country or region is "special" or "unique." Area scholars should clearly identify the area-specific characteristics that matter for context and demonstrate that those characteristics make a difference. I did not focus on Latin America without first identifying various area-specific characteristics and carefully confirming a regional effect of militarization on development.

Many excellent recent books have examined democratization in Costa Rica and Central America (including Booth 1998; Mahoney 2001; Molina and Lehoucq 1999; Paige 1997; Peeler 1998; Williams 1994; Wilson 1998; and Yashar 1997). This study challenges and advances the extant research. The timing of Costa Rican democratic consolidation is pushed back a full decade, from soon after the 1948 Civil War until after the 1958 elections. Bringing the 1950s into the analysis enhances our understanding of Costa Rican democratization and makes that consolidation much more conditioned by events and decisions of that decade and far less predestined by earlier structural, cultural, or institutional characteristics. This research lends support to Euraque's 1996 reinterpretation of Honduras. This country was closer than the conventional wisdom holds to consolidating democracy in the 1950–63 period.

Prospects for the Future

But now the Cold War is over. Communism is no longer a threat. The Left has largely abandoned the armed struggle (Castañeda 1993). Most countries of Latin America are formal democracies and formal democracies are not supposed to engage in wars with each other. Militaries have no credible national security rationale for large budgets. After the "lost decade" of the 1980s, all Latin American countries could use an influx of spending for improved education, health care, nutrition, debt service, or for roads and other economic infrastructure. Various authors have noted that the militaries of the region have retreated to the barracks and that militaries are being reduced. The end of the military as an arbiter of power has arrived! Or has it? Nunn (1995) has demonstrated that the thinking of the generals has not changed with the times. They still see enemies around every corner and see themselves as the guardian of the *Patria.* And in spite of the conventional wisdom that 1989 marked the demise of communism and the reduction of military budgets, the U.S. Arms Control and Defense Agency reveals a disturbing pattern in South American military budgets.

While Central American military budgets have fallen dramatically in the past decade (except for Guatemala), those of South America have risen substantially. In 1985, South America's share of the world's military expenditure was 1.4 percent and nearly doubled to 2.7 percent in 1995. In 1991–95, South America had a real annual growth rate of military spending of 5.2 percent, even while military spending in the world was dropping by an average of 7.1 percent per annum. In constant 1995 dollars, Brazilian defense expenditure rose from $5.3 billion in 1985 to $11.6 billion in 1995 and to $14.1 billion in 1997. In the summer of 2001, the *Folha de Sao Paulo* reported that the Brazilian military was using these resources to spy on and harass domestic human rights and peasant organizations. Their enemies are still fellow citizens. Chilean expenditures rose from $1.07 billion to $2.86 billion over the same period. Colombian military expenditures jumped from $1.51 billion to $3.46 billion (constant dollars) in the decade ending in 1997, and are now skyrocketing in the current war on drugs. Military spending in Ecuador, Mexico, and Uruguay has risen in real terms by large percentages in recent years (ACDA 1998).

The case of Uruguay is most enlightening. While the country faces no credible external threats, Uruguay continues to dedicate more money to the military than to health care or the police.[3] I interviewed a number of Uruguayans in July 2001, asking why they did not follow the Costa Rican model and demilitarize. Invariably, the answer was the same whether the person was from the political right (pro-military) or left (anti-military): the Uruguayan armed forces act as an insurance policy or praetorian guard in case the progressive former mayor of Montevideo (Tabaré Vásquez) wins the presidency and challenges the status quo. Recent decisions by the Peruvians, Chileans, and Ecuadorians to invest in advanced fighter jets only add to the recent trends. In Central America, despite the end of the Cold War and the region's civil wars, Guatemala continues to spend 15 percent—just as it did in the late 1980s during the war—of government expenditures on the military, even as the people suffer from grossly inadequate investment in education and health.

The decision by the Clinton administration to end the U.S. ban on advanced weapons sales to Latin America is ominous. Of course U.S. arms manufacturers argue that with a declining world market for advanced weapons, they must expand markets in order to achieve the economies of scale required to invest greater R&D for the next generation of attack helicopters or jet fighters. In addition, selling F-15s to Chile would feed families in Marietta, Georgia. Besides, they argue, if the United States does not sell to Latin America, someone else will. These arguments for ending the ban are less than satisfying. Latin America, with poor people to feed, educate, and employ, should not be subsidizing weapons development in the United States. Selling cocaine in Marietta feeds families in Bogota and rural Peru and that will not justify a change in U.S. drug policy. Finally, while Latin American countries can buy multimillion-dollar fighter jets from Belarus or Sweden or France, if the United States enters the market it legitimizes arms expenditures. The United States

3. Uruguay spends in excess of $350 million on the armed forces in addition to $294 million for police forces. Public health receives $318 million (2000 budget in *Búsqueda*, 26 July 2001).

gives the green light to a new arms race in the Southern Cone, which will lead to less security and more misery.

In addition to encouraging greater arms expenditures, the United States is currently hard at work bolstering the capacity of Latin American militaries to counter "potential internal threats." U.S. special operations forces were deployed some two hundred times in Latin America in 1998 to train counterinsurgency troops. "A big component of the program is what U.S. military officials call 'foreign internal defense' (FID) training, designed to help foreign nations defend against existing or potential internal threats" (*Washington Post*, 13 July 1998). According to some observers, military training "is undermining the Latin American trend toward demilitarization, democratization, and respect for human rights" (*Washington Post*, 13 July 1998). According to Robert Pastor, "The administration has not either formulated an overall strategy nor does it have the capacity on the ground or in Washington to do so. The result could very well be a short-sighted gain for anti-drug fighters in the U.S. government and special forces on the ground but lead to a long-term failure" (quoted in *Washington Post*, 13 July 1998).

U.S. policy in the 1950s and 1960s to enhance military powers led to shortsighted gains for the anticommunists but long-term failure. At a time when the United States has a golden opportunity to bolster the capabilities of civilian institutions vis-à-vis the militaries, once more it is placing short-term interests above the interests of the Latin American people by pushing weapons sales and counterinsurgency training.

If any country should know the benefits of severing the military from domestic security concerns, it is the United States. The Posse Comitatus Act of 1878 barred the participation of the armed forces in U.S. domestic affairs and police functions. Healthy civil-military relations require militaries to have a single function, external defense. This principle is so ingrained in U.S. military culture that some 90 percent of military personnel are opposed to military participation in the domestic war on drugs. One must wonder why, then, U.S. policy calls for training and massive aid packages to involve Latin American militaries in domestic security concerns and drug fighting. The drug war has become the new raison d'être for many of the region's armed forces, even as many are participants in the trafficking. And yet, even as the armed forces are being transformed and in many cases gaining larger budgets, most observers seem to believe that the post–Cold War military is benign. In the 1960s, observers as respected as Lieuwen (1961) announced that the military had been, by 1960, permanently extirpated from politics in Bolivia, Uruguay, and Chile. Of course, his prediction turned out to be incorrect and current prognostications may also turn out wrong unless Latin American militaries reorient their missions to external defense and recalibrate their size based on credible external threats. One wonders why the Central American countries need any armed forces at all.

Over forty years ago, as Honduras debated the pros and cons of establishing a military, a schoolteacher from Copán predicted that the establishment of a military would become a great headache for Honduras for many years. Another Honduran wrote to the newspaper, exclaiming that "now that the budget is in tatters, now when it would be wise to be economical with government expenditures, it would be a stupendous measure if the government would eliminate the defense minister, and with him all the commanders and soldiers in the country and establish in their place an efficient civil guard, and a mounted police to insure individual security in a civilized manner" (*El Cronista*, 9 May 1955). In 1963, Costa Rican officials visited Honduras at the height of the election campaign, urging the country to follow the Tico example of demilitarization. Things might have been very different in that country if this view had prevailed.

In 2001, Costa Rican President Miguel Angel Rodríguez visited the Southern Cone with the same demilitarization message. In Argentina, Rodríguez asserted that the elimination of the armed forces was a great "blessing, because it stopped the existence of a separate caste. We do not have this enormous and unproductive military expenditure. And we do not suffer from the temptation to use this power. We have seen how militaries use this power in Latin America" (*Clarín*, 16 August 2001). He told the Uruguayans to transfer military resources to education, infrastructure, job creation, and health. "The countries of Latin America should eliminate their armies because we are poor and we need these resources to develop human capital" (*La República*, 2 August 2001). The colonels bristled; many citizens cheered.

Of course this is foolishness. No civilized country could eliminate the defense minister, destroy the tanks, and close the barracks. This is a pipe dream. Some thirty-eight years after the proscription of the armed forces in his country, speaking to the U.S. Congress just weeks before receiving the Nobel Peace Prize, Costa Rican President Oscar Arias reported the results of his country's pipe dream:

I belong to a small country that was not afraid to abolish its army in order to increase its strength. In my homeland you will not find a single tank, a single artillery piece, a single warship, or a single military helicopter. In Costa Rica we are not afraid of freedom. We love democracy and respect the law. . . . We have made considerable progress in education, health, and nutrition. In all of these areas our levels are comparable to the best in Latin America. Although we are poor, we have so far been able to reach satisfactory social goals. This is largely because we have no arms expenditures and because the imbedded practice of democracy drives us to meet the needs of the people. Almost forty years ago we abolished our army. Today we threaten no one, neither our own people nor our neighbors. Such threats are absent not because we lack tanks, but because there are few of us who are hungry, illiterate, or unemployed. (22 September 1987)

References

Acuña, Miguel. 1977. *¡El 55: Te Mataron Hermano!* San José, Costa Rica: Libreria Lehmann.

Acuña, Víctor Hugo. 1993. "Clases Subalternas y Movimientos Sociales en Centroamérica (1870–1930)." In *Historia General de Centroamérica: Las Repúblicas Agroexportadoras*, ed. Víctor Hugo Acuña Ortega. Madrid: FLACSO.

ACDA (U.S. Arms Control and Disarmament Agency). Various years. *World Military Expenditures and Arms Transfers.* Washington, D.C.: U.S. Arms Control and Disarmament Agency.

Adelman, Irma, and Cynthia T. Morris. 1967. *Society, Politics, and Economic Development: A Quantitative Approach.* Baltimore: Johns Hopkins University Press.

Agüero, Felipe. 1995. *Soldiers, Civilians, and Democracy: Post-Franco Spain in Comparative Perspective.* Baltimore: Johns Hopkins University Press.

Aguilar Bulgarelli, Oscar. 1975. *La Constitución de 1949.* San José, Costa Rica: Editorial Costa Rica.

———. 1977. *Democracia y Partidos Políticos en Costa Rica.* San José, Costa Rica: Editorial Costa Rica.

———. 1978. *Costa Rica y sus Hechos Políticos de 1948.* San José, Costa Rica: Editorial Costa Rica.

———. 1983. *Costa Rica y sus Hechos Políticos de 1948: Problemática de una Década.* San José, Costa Rica: Editorial Costa Rica.

———. 1986. *La Constitución de 1949: antecedentes y proyecciones.* San José, Costa Rica: Editorial Costa Rica.

Aguilar Bulgarelli, Oscar, and Irene Alfaro Aguilar. 1997. *La Esclavitud Negra en Costa Rica: Origen de la Oligarchía Económica y Política Nacional.* San José, Costa Rica: Progreso Editorial.

Aguilera Peralta, Gabriel. 1994. *Seguridad, Función, Militar y Democracia.* Guatemala: FLACSO.

Alba, Victor. 1962. "The Stages of Militarism in Latin America." In *The Role of the Military in Underdeveloped Countries*, ed. John J. Johnson. Princeton: Princeton University Press.

Ali, Sonia M., and Richard H. Adams, Jr. 1996. "The Egyptian Food Subsidy System: Operation and Effects on Income Distribution." *World Development* 24 (11): 1777–91.

Allison, Paul D. 1990. "Change Scores as Dependent Variables in Regression Analysis." In *Sociological Methodology*, ed. Clifford C. Clogg. Oxford: Basil Blackwell.

Ameringer, Charles D. 1978. *Don Pepe: A Political Biography of José Figueres of Costa Rica.* Albuquerque: University of New Mexico Press.

———. 1989. "The Thirty Years War Between Figueres and the Somozas." In *The Costa Rican Reader*, ed. Marc Edelman and Joanne Kenen. New York: Grove Weidenfeld.

———. 1996. *The Caribbean Legion: Patriots, Politicians, Soldiers of Fortune: 1946–1950.* University Park: The Pennsylvania State University Press.

Ames, Barry. 1987. *Political Survival: Politicians and Public Policy in Latin America.* Berkeley and Los Angeles: University of California Press.

Amnesty International. 1988. *Honduras: Civilian Authority—Military Power, Human Rights Violations in the 1980s.* New York: Amnesty International.

Anderson, Lisa. 1986. *The State and Social Transformation in Tunisia and Libya, 1830–1980.* Princeton: Princeton University Press.

Anderson, Thomas P. 1981. *The War of the Dispossessed.* Lincoln: University of Nebraska Press.

———. 1988. "Politics and the Military in Honduras." *Current History* 87 (533 December): 425–31.

Andreski, Stanislav. 1954 (1968 Second Edition with Postscript). *Military Organization and Society.* Stanford: Stanford University Press.

Argueta, Mario. 1988. *Tiburcio Carías: Anatomía de una Epoca.* Tegucigalpa: Guaymuras.

———. 1990. *Diccionario Histórico-Biográfico Hondureño.* Tegucigalpa: Editorial Universitaria.

Argueta, Mario, and Edgardo Quiñónes. 1983. *Historia de Honduras.* Tegucigalpa: Escuela Superior de Profesorado Francisco Morazán.

Arias Sánchez, Oscar. 1989. "1987 Address to the United States Congress." In *The Costa Rica Reader*, ed. Marc Edelman and Joanne Kenan. New York: Grove Weidenfeld.

———. 1990. *La Semilla de la Paz.* San José, Costa Rica: Presidencia de la República.

———. 1991. "A New Opportunity for Panama." *Harvard International Review* 13 (3 March): 25–27, 62.

Ayoob, Mohammmed. 1991. "The Security Problematic of the Third World." *World Politics* 43 (January): 257–83.

Babin, Nehama. 1989. "Military Spending, Economic Growth, and the Time Factor." *Armed Forces and Society* 15: 249–62.

Backer, James. 1978. *La Iglesia y el Sindicalismo en Costa Rica.* San Jose, Costa Rica: Editorial Costa Rica.

Bahry, Donna. 1991. "Crossing Borders: The Practice of Comparative Research." In *Empirical Political Analysis*, ed. Jarol B. Mannheim and Richard C. Rich. New York: Longman.

Bakit, Oscar. 1990. *Cuentos Mariachis.* San José, Costa Rica: Editorial San José.

Ball, Nicole. 1988. *Security and Economy in the Third World.* Princeton: Princeton University Press.

———. 1992. *Pressing for Peace: Can Aid Induce Reform?* Washington, D.C.: The Overseas Development Council.

Barahona, Marvin. 1989. *La Hegemonía de los Estados Unidos en Honduras (1907–1932).* Tegucigalpa: CEDOH.

———. 1991. *Evolución Histórica de la Identidad Nacional.* Tegucigalpa: Editorial Guaymuras.

Barro, Robert J. 1991. "Economic Growth in a Cross Section of Countries." *Quarterly Journal of Economics* 106 (May): 407–43.

———. 1997. *Determinants of Economic Growth: A Cross-Country Empirical Study.* Cambridge, Mass.: MIT Press.

Barro, Robert J., and Xaviar Sala-i-Martin. 1995. *Economic Growth*. New York: McGraw-Hill.

Barry, Tom, and Deb Preusch. 1982. *Dollars and Dictators*. Albuquerque: The Resource Center.

———. 1986. *The Central America Fact Book*. New York: Grove Press.

———. 1988. *The Soft War: The Uses and Abuses of U.S. Aid in Central America*. New York: Grove Press.

Bates, Robert H. 1981. *Markets and States in Tropical Africa*. Berkeley and Los Angeles: University of California Press.

———. 1996. "Area Studies and the Discipline." *APSA-CP Newsletter* 7 (1): 1–2.

Becerra, Longino. 1983. *Evolución Histórica de Honduras*. Tegucigalpa: Editorial Baktún.

———. 1994. *El poder político*. Two volumes. Tegucigalpa: Editorial Baktún.

Bell, John Patrick. 1971. *Crisis in Costa Rica: The 1948 Revolution*. Austin: University of Texas Press.

Belsley, David A., Edwin Kuh, and Roy E. Walsh. 1980. *Regression Diagnostics: Identifying Influential Data and Sources of Collinearity*. New York: Wiley & Sons.

Bennett, Andrew, and Alexander George. 1998. "An Alliance of Statistical Methods: Research on the Interdemocratic Peace." *American Political Science Association Comparative Politics Newsletter* 9 (1): 6–9.

Benoit, Emile. 1973. *Defense and Economic Growth in Developing Countries*. Lexington, Mass.: Lexington Books.

Biesanz, Mavis H., Richard Biesanz, and Karen Z. Biesanz. 1998. *The Ticos: Culture and Social Change in Costa Rica*. Boulder, Colo.: Lynne Rienner Publishers.

Black, Jan Knippers. 1986. *Sentinals of Empire: The United States and Latin American Militarism*. New York: Glenwood Press.

Blasier, Cole. 1985. *The Hovering Giant: U.S. Responses to Revolutionary Change in Latin America 1910–1985*. Pittsburgh: University of Pittsburgh Press.

———. 1987. "The United States and Democracy in Latin America." In *Authoritarians and Democrats: Regime Transition in Latin America*, ed. James M. Malloy and Mitchell Seligson. Pittsburgh: University of Pittsburgh Press.

Bollen, Kenneth A. 1980. "Issues in the Comparative Measurement of Political Democracy." *American Sociological Review* 45 (3): 370–90.

———. 1983. "World System Position, Dependency, and Democracy: The Cross-National Evidence." *American Sociological Review* 48 (4 August): 468–79.

———. 1991. "Political Democracy: Conceptual and Measurement Traps." In *On Measuring Democracy*, ed. Alex Inkeles. New Brunswick, N.J.: Transaction.

Bollen, Kenneth A., and Robert W. Jackman. 1985. "Political Democracy and the Size Distribution of Income." *American Sociological Review* 50: 438–57.

———. 1989. "Democracy, Stability and Dichotomies." *American Sociological Review* 54 (4): 612–21.

———. 1995. "Income Inequality and Democratization Revisisted: Comment on Muller." *American Sociological Review* 60 (December): 983–89.

Bonilla, Harold H. 1975. *Figueres and Costa Rica: An Unautherized Political Biography.* San José, Costa Rica: Editorial Texto Limitada.

Booth, John A. "War and the Nicaraguan Revolution." *Current History* 85 (December 1986): 405–8, 432–34.

———. 1989. "Costa Rica: The Roots of Democratic Stability." In *Democracy in Developing Countries: Latin America,* ed. Larry Diamond and Juan V. Linz. Boulder, Colo.: Lynne Rienner Publishers.

———. 1998. *Costa Rica: Quest for Democracy.* Boulder, Colo.: Westview Press.

Booth, John A., and Thomas W. Walker. 1993. *Understanding Central America: Second Edition.* Boulder, Colo.: Westview Press.

Boudreaux, Richard. 2 September 1990. "Trying to Tame the Latin 'Tiger'." *The Los Angeles Times.*

Bowman, Kirk S. 1996. "Taming the Tiger: Militarization and Democracy in Latin America." *Journal of Peace Research* 33 (3): 289–308.

———. 1997. "Should the Kuznets Effect be Relied on to Induce Equalizing Growth?: Evidence from Post-1950 Development." *World Development* 25 (1): 127–43.

———. 1999. "Taming the Tiger in Honduras." *Latin American Studies Forum* 30 (1): 9–12.

———. 2000. "¿Fue el Compromiso y Consenso de las Elites lo que Llevó a la Consolidación Democrática en Costa Rica?: Evidencias de la Década 1950." *Revista de Historia* 41: 91–127.

———. 2001. "The Public Battles over Militarisation and Democracy in Honduras, 1954–1963." *Journal of Latin American Studies* 33 (3): 539–60.

Bowman Kirk, and Sean Eudaily. 1999. "The Democratic Peace through a Comparativist Lens." Delivered to the Annual Meeting of the Southern Political Science Association, Savannah, Ga.

Brenes, Lidiette. 1990. *La Nacionalización Bancaria en Costa Rica: Un Juicio Histórico.* San José, Costa Rica: FLACSO.

Brockett, Charles. 1987. "Public Policy, Peasants, and Rural Development in Honduras." *Journal of Latin American Studies* 19 (1): 69–86.

———. 1991. *Land, Power, and Poverty.* Boulder, Colo.: Westview Press.

———. 1992. "Measuring Political Violence and Land Inequality in Central America." *American Political Science Review* 86 (1): 169–76.

Brunk, Gregory G., Gregory Caldeira, and Michael S. Lewis-Beck. 1987. "Capitalism, Socialism, and Democracy: An Empirical Inquiry." *European Journal of Political Research* 15 (4): 459–70.

Brzoska, Michael. 1981. "The Reporting of Military Expenditures." *Journal of Peace Research* 18 (3): 261–75.

Bullock, Brad, and Glen Firebaugh. 1990. "Guns and Butter? The Effect of Militarization on Economic and Social Development in the Third World." *Journal of Political and Military Sociology* 18 (2): 231–66.

Bulmer-Thomas, Victor. 1987. *The Political Economy of Central America since 1920.* Cambridge: Cambridge University Press.

———. 1993. "La Crisis de la Economía de Agroexportación: 1930–1945." In *Historia General de Centroamérica: Las Repúblicas Agroexportadoras,* ed. Víctor Hugo Acuña Ortega. Madrid, FLACSO.

Burkhart, Ross E., and Michael S. Lewis-Beck. 1994. "Comparative Democracy: The Economic Development Thesis." *American Political Science Review* 88 (4 December): 903–10.

Burton, Michael, Richard Gunther, and John Higley. 1992. "Elite Transformations and Democratic Regimes." In *Elites and Democratic Consolidation in Latin America and Southern Europe*, ed. John Higley and Richard Gunther. Cambridge: Cambridge University Press.

Bury, Douglas P. 1968. "Political Instability in Latin America: The Cross-Cultural Test of a Causal Model." *Latin America Research Review* 3: 17–66.

Busey, James L. 1958. "Foundations of Political Contrasts: Costa Rica and Nicaragua." *Western Political Quarterly* 11 (September): 627–59.

Cañas, Alberto F. 1982. *Los Ocho Años.* San José, Costa Rica: EUNED.

Cardona Quirós, Edgar. 1992. *Mi Verdad.* San José, Costa Rica: García Hermanos.

Casas, Kevin. 1995. "Military Expenditure in Central America: Which Way Now?" *Central American Dialogue* no. 2: 2–3.

Castañeda, Jorge G. 1993. *Utopia Unarmed: The Latin American Left after the Cold War.* New York: Alfred A. Knopf.

CENPRO. 1996. *Exporters: Costa Rican Export Directory.* San José, Costa Rica: CENPRO.

Cerdas Albertazzi, Ana Luisa, and Gerardo A. Vargas Cambronero. 1988. *La Abolición del Ejército en Costa Rica.* San José, Costa Rica: Comisión Nacional de Conmemeraciones Históricas.

Céspedes, Víctor Hugo, and Ronulfo Jiménez. 1995. *La Pobreza en Costa Rica.* San José, Costa Rica: Academia de Centroamérica.

Chalker, Cynthia H. 1995. "Elections and Democracy in Costa Rica." In *Elections and Democracy in Central America, Revisited*, ed. Mitchell Seligson and John Booth. Chapel Hill: University of North Carolina Press.

Chan, Steve. 1989. "Income Inequality among LDCs: A Comparative Analysis of Alternative Perspectives." *International Studies Quarterly* 33: 45–65.

———. 1992. "Defense, Welfare, and Growth: Introduction." In *Defense, Welfare, and Growth*, ed. Steve Chan and Alex Mintz. London: Routledge.

Clark, Mary A. 1995. "Non-Traditional Export Promotion in Costa Rica: Sustaining Export-Led Growth." *Journal of Interamerican Studies and World Affairs* 37 (2): 181–223.

———. 1997. "Transnational Alliances and Development Policy in Latin America: Nontraditional Export Promotion in Costa Rica." *Latin American Research Review* 32 (2): 71–97.

Coleman, James S., and Belmont Brice, Jr. 1962. "The Role of the Military in Sub-Saharan Africa." In *The Role of the Military in Underdeveloped Countries*, ed. John J. Johnson. Princeton: Princeton University Press.

Collier, David. 1993. "The Comparative Method." In *Political Science: The State of the Discipline*, ed. Ada W. Finifter. Washington, D.C.: American Political Science Association.

Collier, David, and Robert Adcock. 1999. "Democracy and Dichotomies: A Pragmatic Approach to Choices about Concepts." *Annual Review of Political Science* 2: 537–65.

Collier, Ruth Berins, and David Collier. 1991. *Shaping the Political Arena: Critical Junctures, the Labor Movement, and the Regime Dynamics in Latin America.* Princeton: Princeton University Press.

Columbus, Georgia, and Roy Bourgeois. 1 September 1994. "USA: 'School for Dictators' under Fire." *Latinamerica Press.*

Comité de Abogados por los Derechos Humanos. 1994. *Análisis del Informe del Departamento de Estado Reporte de Países Acerca de los Derechos Humanos para 1993.* New York: Comité de Abogados por los Derechos Humanos.

Cook, Thomas, and Donald Campbell. 1979. *Quasi-Experimentation: Design and Analysis Issues for Field Settings.* Chicago: Rand McNally.

Creedman, Theodore. 1977. *Historical Dictionary of Costa Rica.* Metuchen, N.J.: Scarecrow Press.

———. 1991. *Historical Dictionary of Costa Rica.* Metuchen, N.J.: Scarecrow Press.

Cruz, Ramón Ernesto. 1982. *La Lucha Política de 1954 y la Raptura del Orden Constitucional.* Tegucigalpa: Editorial Universitaria.

Cuadernos Centromericanos de Ciencias Sociales. 1981. "Crisis en Costa Rica: Un Debate." Issue 8.

Cutright, Phillips. 1963. "National Political Development: Measurement and Analysis." *American Sociological Review* 28 (2): 253–64.

Cutright, Phillips, and James A. Wiley. 1969. "Modernization and Political Representation: 1927–1966." *Studies in Comparative International Development* 5 (1): 23–44.

Dahl, Robert A. 1971. *Polyarchy.* New Haven: Yale University Press.

Davis, Byron L., Edward L. Kick, and David Kiefer. 1989. "The World-System, Militarization, and National Development." In *War in the World System,* ed. Robert K. Schaeffer. New York: Greenwood Press.

Deger, Saadet, and Ron Smith. 1983. "Military Expenditure and Growth in Less Developed Countries." *Journal of Conflict Resolution* 13: 67–83.

del Cid, Rafael. 1991. *Honduras: Crisis Económica y Proceso de Democratización Política.* Tegucigalpa: Lithopress Industrial.

Deninger, Klaus, and Lyn Squire. 1996. "A New Data Set Measuring Income Inequality." *World Bank Economic Review* 10 (September): 565–91.

Desaparecidos. 1993 (Junio). Tegucigalpa: COFADEH.

Desch, Michael C. 1999. *Civilian Control of the Military: The Changing Security Environment.* Baltimore: Johns Hopkins University Press.

Di Palma, Giusseppe. 1990. *To Craft Democracies.* Berkeley and Los Angeles: University of California Press.

Díaz Sánchez, Miguel. 1996. *Soldados Empresarios en Centroamérica: Los Negocios de los Militares.* San José, Costa Rica: Arias Foundation for Peace and Human Progress.

Dickey, Christopher. 1987. *With the Contras: A Reporter in the Wilds of Nicaragua.* New York: Simon and Schuster.

Dixon, William J., and Bruce E. Moon. 1986. "The Military Burden and Basic Human Needs." *Journal of Conflict Resolution* 30 (4): 660–84.

Durham, William. 1979. *Scarcity and Survival in Central America: Ecological Origins of the Soccer War.* Stanford: Stanford University Press.

Dyer, Gwynne. 1979. "Costa Rica." In *World Armies*, pp. 150–153. London: Macmillan.

Eckstein, Susan, 1989. "Power and Popular Protest in Latin America.'" In *Power and Popular Protest*, ed. Susan Eckstein, pp. 1–60. Berkeley and Los Angeles: University of California Press.

ECLAC, various years. *Statistical Yearbook for Latin America and the Caribbean.* Santiago, Chile: United Nations.

Edelman, Marc. 1983a. "Recent Literature on Costa Rica's Economic Crisis." *Latin American Research Review* 28 (2): 166–80.

———. 21 May 1983. "Costa Rica Next?" *The Nation*, p. 626.

———. 1999. *Peasants against Globalization: Rural Social Movements in Costa Rica.* Stanford: Stanford University Press.

Edelman, Marc, and Joanne Kenen. 1989. *The Costa Rica Reader.* New York: Grove Weidenfeld.

Eder, George Jackson. 1968. *Inflation and Development in Latin America: A Case History of Inflation and Stabilization in Bolivia.* Ann Arbor: University of Michigan Press.

Ellis, Frank. 1983. *Las Trasnacionales del Banano en Centroamérica.* San José, Costa Rica: EDUCA.

Escudé, Carlos. 1993. "International Relations Theory: A Peripheral Perspective." Working Paper. Buenos Aires: Universidad Torcuato di Tella.

Etchison, Don L. 1975. *The United States and Militarism in Central America.* New York: Praeger.

Euraque, Darío A. 1986. "Social Structure and the Emergence of the Bourgeois Press in Honduras: A Historical Perspective." Master's thesis, University of Wisconsin.

———. 1996. *Reinterpreting the Banana Republic: Region and State in Honduras, 1870–1972.* Chapel Hill: University of North Carolina Press.

Evans, Peter B. 1979. *Dependent Development: The Alliance of Multinational State and Local Capital in Brazil.* Princeton: Princeton University Press.

———. 1994. "Predatory, Developmental and Other Apparatuses: A Comparative Political Economy Perspective of the Third World State." In *Comparative National Development*, ed. A. Douglas Kincaid and Alejandro Portes. Chapel Hill: University of North Carolina Press.

Evans, Peter B., Dietrich Rueschemeyer, and Theda Skocpol. 1985. *Bringing the State Back In.* New York: Cambridge University Press.

Evans, Peter B., and John D. Stephens. 1988. "Studying Development Since the 1960s: The Emergence of a New Comparative Political Economy." *Theory and Society* 17: 713–45.

Fallas Barrantes, Roger. 1984. "Processo Histórico de la Abolición del Ejército en Costa Rica." Licenciatura Thesis, University of Costa Rica.

Farah, Douglas. 24 April 1993. "Honduras Assesses Military Role." *Washington Post.*

FBIS (Foreign Broadcast Information Service), various issues. Washington, D.C.

Figueres Ferrer, José. 1956. *Cartas a un Ciudadano.* San José, Costa Rica: Imprenta Nacional.

Finer, Samuel E. 1988 (1962). *The Man on Horseback: The Role of the Military in Politics.* Boulder, Colo.: Westview Press. Second, Enlarged Edition, Revised and Updated.

Físchel, Astrid. 1990. *Consenso y represión: Una interpretación socio-política de la educación costarricence.* San José, Costa Rica: Editorial Costa Rica.

———. 1992. *El Uso Ingeniouso de la Ideología en Costa Rica.* San José, Costa Rica: EUNED.

Fitch, J. Samuel. 1986. "Armies and Politics in Latin America: 1975–1985." In *Armies and Politics in Latin America,* ed. Abraham F. Lowenthal and J. Samuel Fitch. New York: Holmes and Meier.

———. 1998. *The Armed Forces and Democracy in Latin America.* Baltimore: Johns Hopkins University Press.

Foster, Phillips, and Howard D. Leathers. 1999. *The World Food Problem,* second edition. Boulder, Colo.: Lynne Rienner Publishers.

Franco, Nora. 21 July 1994. "Argentine Military Had Role in 'Dirty War.'" *Latinamerica Press.*

Franko, Patrice. 1994. "De Facto Demilitarization: Budget-Driven Downsizing in Latin America." *Journal of Interamerican Studies and World Affairs* 36 (1): 37–74.

Frederiksen, Peter C., and Robert E. Looney. 1983. "Defense Expenditures and Economic Growth in Developing Countries." *Armed Forces and Society* 9: 633–45.

Funes, Matías H. 1995. *Los Deliberantes: El Poder Militar en Honduras.* Tegucigalpa: Editorial Guaymuras.

Gardner, John W. 1971. "The Costa Rican Junta of 1948–1949." Ph.D. dissertation, St. John's University.

Gardner, Mary A. 1963. "The Press in Honduras: A Portrait of Five Dailies." *The Journalism Quarterly* 40: 75–82.

Geddes, Barbara. 1991. "Paradigms and Sand Castles in the Comparative Politics of Developing Areas." In *Political Science: Looking to the Future,* vol. 2, ed. William Crotty. Evanston: Northwestern University Press.

General Accounting Office. 1996. "School of the Americas: U.S. Military Training for Latin American Countries." GOA/NSIAD-96-178. USGAO: Washington, D.C.

Gerschenkron, Alexander. 1962. *Economic Backwardness in Historical Perspective: A Book of Essays.* Cambridge, Mass.: Belknap Press of Harvard University Press.

Gibbs, David. 1994. "Taking the State Back Out: Reflections on a Tautology." *Contention* 3 (3): 115–38.

Gills, Barry, Joel Racamora, and Richard Wilson, eds. 1993. *Low Intensity Democracy.* London: Pluto.

Gleijeses, Piero. 1991. *Shattered Hope: The Guatemalan Revolution and the United States, 1944–1954.* Princeton: Princeton University Press.

Goldstone, Jack. 1997. "Methodological Issues in Comparative Macrosociology." *Comparative Social Research* 16 (1997): 107–20.

González Vargas, Alvaro. 1990. "Entre la Diplomacia del Buen Vecino de la Doctrina Monroe: Supuestos Históricos de la Presunción Hegemónica de los Estados Unidos (1914–1955)." Master's thesis, Universidad de Costa Rica.

Gonzáles-Vegas, Claudio, and Víctor Hugo Céspedes. 1993. "Costa Rica." In *The Political Economy of Poverty, Equity, and Growth: Costa Rica and Uruguay*, ed. Simon Rottenberg. Oxford: Oxford University Press.

Goodman, Louis W., Johanna S. R. Mendelson, and Juan Rial, eds. 1990. *The Military and Democracy: The Future of Civil-Military Relations in Latin America.* Lexington, Mass.: Lexington Books.

Granato, Jim, Ronald Inglehart, and David Leblang. 1996. "The Effect of Cultural Values on Economic Development: Theory, Hypothesis, and Some Empirical Tests." *American Journal of Political Science* 40 (3): 607–32.

Gudmundson, Lowell. 1986. *Costa Rica before Coffee.* Baton Rouge: Louisiana State University Press.

Gujarati, Domodar N. 1988. *Basic Econometrics*, second edition. New York: McGraw-Hill.

Gurr, Ted Robert, Keith Jaggers, and Will Moore. 1991. "The Transformation of the Western State: The Growth of Democracy, Autocracy, and State Power since 1800." In *On Measuring Democracy*, ed. Alex Inkeles. New Brunswick, N.J.: Transaction Publishers.

Gyamah-Brempong, Kwabena. 1989. "Defense Spending and Economic Growth in Sub-Saharan Africa." *Journal of Peace Research* 26 (1): 79–90.

Hadenius, Axel. 1992. *Democracy and Development.* Cambridge: Cambridge University Press.

Haggard, Stephan, and Robert Kaufman. 1995. *The Political Economy of Democratic Transitions.* Princeton: Princeton University Press.

Hall, Carolyn. 1982. *El Café y el Desarrollo Histórico-Geográfico de Costa Rica.* San José, Costa Rica: Editorial Costa Rica.

Hamilton, Nora. 1982. *The Limits of State Autonomy: Post-Revolutionary Mexico.* Princeton: Princeton University Press.

Harrison, Lawrence E. 1985. *Underdevelopment Is a State of Mind.* Boston: Harvard Center for International Affairs.

Hartlyn, Jonathan. 1994. "Crisis-Ridden Elections (Again) in the Dominican Republic: Neopatrimonialism, Presidentialism, and Weak Electoral Oversight." *Journal of Interamerican Studies and World Affairs* 36 (4): 91–144.

Heller, Claude. 1981. "Military Relations between the United States and Latin America: An Attempt at Evaluation." In *The Military as an Agent of Social Change*, ed. Claude Heller, pp. 145–70. Mexico City: El Colegio de México.

Hellinger, Stephen. 1988. *Aid for Just Development: Report on the Future of Foreign Assistance.* Boulder, Colo.: Lynne Rienner Publishers.

Higley, John, and Richard Gunther, eds. 1992. *Elites and Democratic Consolidation in Latin America and Southern Europe.* New York: Cambridge University Press.

Hirschman, Albert O. 1958. *The Strategy of Economic Development.* New Haven: Yale University Press.

———. 1963. *Journeys Towards Progress: Studies of Economic Policy-Making in Latin America.* New York: Twentieth Century Fund.

———. 1984. "A Dissenter's Confession: 'The Strategy of Economic Development' Revisited." In *Pioneers in Development*, ed. G. M. Meier and D. Seers. Oxford: Oxford University Press.

Holden, Robert H. 1993. "The Real Diplomacy of Violence: United States Military Power in Central America, 1950–1990." *The International History Review* 20 (2 May): 283–322.

———. 1996. "Constructing the Limits of State Violence in Central America: Towards a New Research Agenda." *Journal of Latin American Studies* 28: 435–59.

Honduras Human Rights Commission. 1994. *The Facts Speak for Themselves*. Tegucigalpa: Human Rights Commission.

Honey, Martha. 1994. *Hostile Acts: U.S. Policy in Costa Rica in the 1980s*. Gainesville: University Press of Florida.

Horowitz, Irving Louis. 1975. "Militarization, Modernization and Mobilization: Third World Development Patterns Reexamined." In *Militarism in Developing Countries*, ed. Kenneth Fidel. New Brunswick, N.J.: Transaction Books.

Høivik, Tord, and Solveig Aas. 1981. "Demilitarization in Costa Rica: A Farewell to Arms?" *Journal of Peace Research* 18 (4): 333–51.

Huber, Evelyne. 1995. "Assessments of State Strength." In *Latin America in Comparative Perspective: New Approaches to Methods and Analysis*, ed. Peter Smith. Boulder, Colo.: Westview Press.

Hunter, Wendy. 1997. *Eroding Military Influence in Brazil: Politicians against Soldiers*. Chapel Hill: University of North Carolina Press.

Huntington, Samuel P. 1957. *The Soldier and the State*. Cambridge, Mass.: The Belknap Press of Harvard University Press.

———. 1962. *Changing Patterns of Military Politics*. New York: The Free Press of Glencoe.

———. 1968. *Political Order in Changing Societies*. New Haven: Yale University Press.

———. 1984. "Will More Countries Become Democratic?" *Political Science Quarterly* 99 (1): 193–218.

———. 1987. "The Goals of Development." In *Understanding Political Development*, ed. Myron Weiner and Samuel P. Huntington. New York: Harper Collins.

———. 1991. *The Third Wave: Democratization in the Late Twentieth Century*. Norman: University of Oklahoma Press.

IMF. 14 December 1992. "Seminar Panelists Discuss Ways and Means to Reform Military Spending." *IMF Survey*.

IMF. Various years. *International Financial Statistics*. Washington, D.C.

Inglehart, Ronald, and María Carballo. 1997. "Does Latin America Exist (And Is There a Confucian Culture?): A Global Analysis of Cross-Cultural Differences." *PS: Political Science and Politics* 30 (1): 34–46.

Inkeles, Alex. 1966. "The Modernization of Man." In *Modernization: The Dynamics of Growth*, ed. Myron Wiener, pp. 138–50.

Instituto Costarricense de Turismo. 1997. *Normas que Regulan las Empresas y Actividades Turísticas*. San José, Costa Rica: ICT.

Instituto Hondureño de Turismo. 1994. *Boletín Estadístico de Turismo*, no. 5. Tegucigalpa: IHT.

IPM (Instituto de Previsión Militar de Honduras). 1993. Program for Sixth Congress of Central American Pension Funds. Tela, Honduras.

Isacson, Adam. 1997. *Altered States: Security and Demilitarization in Central America.* Washington, D.C.: Center for International Policy and the Arias Foundation for Peace and Human Progress.

Itzigsohn, José. 2000. *Developing Democracy: The State, Labor Market Deregulation, and the Informal Economy in Costa Rica and the Dominican Republic.* University Park: The Pennsylvania State University Press.

Jackman, Robert W. 1976. "Politicians in Uniform: Governments and Social Change in the Third World." *American Political Science Review* 70 (4): 1078–97.

———. 1985. "Cross-National Statistical Research and the Study of Comparative Politics." *American Journal of Political Science* 29 (1): 161–82.

Janowitz, Morris. 1960. *The Professional Soldier: A Social and Political Portrait.* New York: Free Press.

———. 1964. *The Military in the Political Development of New Nations.* Chicago: University of Chicago Press.

———. 1977. *Military Institutions and Coercion in the Developing Nations.* Chicago: University of Chicago Press.

———. 1981. "Introduction." In *Civil Military Relations*, ed. Morris Janowitz. Beverly Hills: Sage Publications.

Johnson, John J. 1964. *The Military and Society in Latin America.* Stanford: Stanford University Press.

Johnson, Kenneth F. 1977. "Research Perspectives on the Revised Fitzgibbon-Johnson Index of the Image of Political Democracy in Latin America, 1945–1975." In *Quantitative Latin American Studies*, ed. James W. Wilkie and Kenneth Ruddle. Los Angeles: UCLA Latin American Center Publications.

Jonas, Susanne. 2000. *Of Centaurs and Doves: Guatemala's Peace Process.* Boulder, Colo.: Westview Press.

Kantor, Harry. 1958. *The Costa Rican Election of 1953: A Case Study.* Gainesville: University of Florida Press.

Karl, Terry Lynn. 1990. "Dilemmas of Democratization in Latin America." *Comparative Politics* 23 (1): 1–21.

Kasliwal, Pari. 1995. *Developmental Economics.* Cincinnati, Ohio: South-Western Publishing.

Katzenstein, Peter J. 1985. *Small States in World Markets.* Ithaca: Cornell University Press.

Kepner, Charles D., and Jay Soothill. 1949. *El Imperio del Banano.* Mexico: Ediciones del Caribe.

Kick, Edward L., and Bam Dev Sharda. 1986. "Third World Militarization and Development." *Journal of Developing Societies* 2: 49–67.

Kick, E. L., R. Nasser, B. L. Davis, and L. Bean. 1990. "Militarization and Infant Mortality in the Third World." *Journal of Political and Military Sociology* 18 (winter): 285–305.

Kincaid, Douglas. 1989. "Costa Rican Peasants and the Politics of Quiescence." In *The Costa Rica Reader*, ed. Marc Edelman and Joanne Kenen. New York: Grove Weidenfeld.

———. 1987. "Peasants into Rebels: Community and Class in Rural El Salvador." *Comparative Studies in Society and History* 29 (3): 466–94.

King, Gary, Robert O. Keohane, and Sidney Verba. 1994. *Designing Social Inquiry*. Princeton: Princeton University Press.

———. 1995. "The Importance of Research Design in Political Science." *American Political Science Review* 89 (2): 475–80.

Kmenta, Jan. 1986. *Elements of Econometrics*, second edition. New York: Macmillan.

Kohli, Atul. 1995. "The Role of Theory in Comparative Politics: A Symposium." *World Politics* 48 (October): 1–49.

Kornblugh, Peter. 1987. *Nicaragua: The Price of Intervention*. Washington, D.C.: Institute for Policy Studies.

Krasner, Stephen D. 1978. *Defending the National Interest*. Princeton: Princeton University Press.

Kruijt, Dirk, and Edelberto Torres-Rivas. 1991. "Presentación." In *America Latina: Militares y Sociedad-I*, ed. Dirk Kruijt and Edelberto Torres-Rivas. San José, Costa Rica: FLACSO.

Kuznets, Simon. 1955. "Economic Growth and Income Inequality." *American Economic Review* 45: 1–28.

LaFeber, Walter. 1984. *Inevitable Revolutions: The United States in Central America*. New York: Norton.

Laitin, David D. 1995. "Disciplining Political Science." *American Political Science Review* 89 (2): 454–56.

Lehoucq, Fabrice Edouard. 1992. "The Origins of Democracy in Costa Rica in Comparative Perspective." Ph.D. dissertation, Duke University.

———. 1996. "The Institutional Foundations of Democratic Cooperation in Costa Rica." *Journal of Latin American Studies* 28 (2 May) 329–55.

———. 1997. *Lucha Electoral y Sistema Político en Costa Rica: 1948–1998*. San José, Costa Rica: Editorial Porvenir.

———. 1997b. "Institutionalizing Democracy: Constraint and Ambition in the Politics of Electoral Reform." Paper presented to the American Political Science Association, Washington, D.C.

———. 2000. "Institutionalizing Democracy: Constraint and Ambition in the Politics of Electoral Reform." *Comparative Politics* 32 (4): 459–78.

Lehoucq, Fabrice Edouard, and Iván Molina. Forthcoming. *Fraud, Electoral Reform and Democracy: Costa Rica in Comparative Perspective*. New York: Cambridge University Press.

LeoGrande, William O. 1998. *Our Own Backyard: The United States in Central America, 1977–1992*. Chapel Hill: University of North Carolina Press.

Lerner, Daniel. 1958. *The Passing of Traditional Society: Modernizing the Middle East*. Glencoe, Ill.: Free Press.

Levine, Ross, and David Renelt. 1992. "A Sensitivity Analysis of Cross-Country Growth Regressions." *American Economic Review* 82 (4): 942–63.

Levitsky, Steve. 1992. "Taming the Honduran Military." *Hemisphere* 4 (3): 36–38.

Levy, Myron J., Jr. 1966 (1996). *Modernization and the Structure of Societies.* Princeton: Princeton University Press.

Lieuwin, Edwin. 1960. *Arms and Politics in Latin America.* New York: Praeger.

———. 1961. "The Changing Role of the Military in Latin America." *Journal of Inter-American Studies* 3 (4): 559–69.

———. 1965. *United States Policy in Latin America.* New York: Praeger.

Lijphart, Arend. 1975. "The Comparative-Cases Strategy in Comparative Research." *Comparative Political Studies* 8 (2 July): 158–77.

Lipset, Seymour Martin. 1959/1981. "Some Social Requisites of Democracy: Economic Development and Political Legitmacy." *American Political Science Review* 53. Reprinted in S. M. Lipset, *Political Man,* exp. ed. Baltimore: Johns Hopkins University Press.

———. 1960 (1981). *Political Man.* Baltimore: Johns Hopkins University Press.

Longley, Kyle. 1997. *The Sparrow and the Hawk: Costa Rica and the United States during the Rise of José Figueres.* Tuscaloosa: University of Alabama Press.

Loveman, Brian. 1993. *The Constitution of Tyranny: Regimes of Exception in Spanish America.* Pittsburgh: University of Pittsburgh Press.

———. 1994. "'Protected Democracies' and Military Guardianship: Political Transitions in Latin America, 1978–1993." *Journal of Interamerican Studies and World Affairs* 36 (2):105–90.

———. 1999. *For La Patria: Politics and the Armed Forces in Latin America.* Wilmington, Del.: Scholarly Resources.

Loveman, Brian, and Thomas M. Davies, Jr., eds. 1997. *The Politics of Antipolitics: The Military in Latin America.* Wilmington, Del.: Scholarly Resources.

Lowenthal, Abraham F., ed. 1975. *The Peruvian Experiment: Continuity and Change under Military Rule.* Princeton: Princeton University Press.

———. 1976. *Armies and Politics in Latin America.* New York: Holmes and Meier.

———. 1991. *Exporting Democracy: The United States and Latin America.* Baltimore: Johns Hopkins University Press.

———. 1992. "Changing U.S. Interests and Policies in a New World." In *The United States and Latin America in the 1990s,* ed. Jonathan Hartlyn, Lars Schoultz, and Augusto Varas. Chapel Hill: University of North Carolina Press.

Lowenthal, Abraham F., and J. Samuel Fitch. 1986. *Armies and Politics in Latin America,* revised edition. New York: Holmes and Meier.

Luxner, Larry. 30 September 1993. "Honduran Election Focuses on Two Candidates." *Latinamerica Press.*

MacCameron, Robert. 1983. *Bananas, Labor, and Politics in Honduras: 1954–1963.* Syracuse: Syracuse University Press.

MacIntyre, Alasdair C. 1971. "Is a Comparative Science of Politics Possible?" In *Against the Self-Image of the Age,* ed. Alasdair C. MacIntryre. New York: Shocken Books.

Maddala, G. S. 1971. "The Use of Variance Components Models in Pooling Cross Section and Time Series Data." *Econometrica* 39 (2): 341–58.

Mahoney, James. 1999. "Nominal, Ordinal, and Narrative Appraisal in Macrocausal Analysis." *American Journal of Sociology* 104 (4):1154–87.

———. 2001. *Path Dependence and Political Change: Liberal Origins of National Regimes in Central America.* Baltimore: Johns Hopkins University Press.

Mahoney, James, and Dietrich Rueschemeyer, eds. 2003. *Comparative Historical Analysis in the Social Sciences.* New York and Cambridge: Cambridge University Press.

Malloy, James M. 1970. *Bolivia: The Uncompleted Revolution.* Pittsburgh: University of Pittsburgh Press.

Mairena, José. 1995. "Indios y Negros Bajo la Piel." *Rumbo*, October.

Mares, David R. 1998a. "Civil Military Relations, Democracy, and the Regional Neighborhood." In *Civil Military Relations: Building Democracy and Regional Security in Latin America, Southern Asia, and Central Europe*, ed. David R. Mares. Boulder, Colo.: Westview Press.

———. 1998b. "Civil Military Relations in Comparative Perspective." In *Civil Military Relations: Building Democracy and Regional Security in Latin America, Southern Asia, and Central Europe*, ed. David R. Mares. Boulder, Colo.: Westview Press.

Mariñas Otero, Luis. 1987. *Honduras.* Tegucigalpa: Editorial Universitaria.

Martz, John D. 1959. *Central America, the Crisis and the Challenge.* Chapel Hill: University of North Carolina Press.

McKeown, Timothy. 1998. "Why Is a Single Case Important?" *APSA Comparative Politics Newsletter* 9 (1): 12–15.

McSherry, J. Patrice. 1997. *Incomplete Transition: Military Power and Democracy in Argentina.* New York: St. Martin's Press.

Menlo Consulting Group. 1996. *Americans as International Travelers: Focus on Costa Rica.* Palo Alto, Calif.: Menlo Consulting Group.

Merrill, Tim L., ed. 1995. *Honduras: A Country Study*. Washington, D.C.: Library of Congress.

Meza, Víctor. 1981. *Política y Sociedad en Honduras: Comentarios.* Tegucigalpa: Editorial Guaymuras.

———. 1988. "Los Militares Hondureños en la Hora de Washington." In *Honduras-Estados Unidos: Subordinación y Crisis*, ed. Víctor Meza. Tegucigalpa: CEDOH.

———. 1991. *Historia del Movimiento Obrero Hondureño.* Tegucigalpa: CEDOH.

MIDEPLAN. 1997a. *Costa Rica Panorama Nacional 1996: Balance Anual Social, Económico y Ambiental.* San José, Costa Rica: MIDEPLAN.

———. 1997b. *Principales Indicadores Sociales de Costa Rica.* San José, Costa Rica: MIDEPLAN.

Migdal, Joel. 1988. *Strong Societies and Weak States: State-Society Relations and State Capabilities in the Third World.* Princeton: Princeton University Press.

Minello, Nelson. 1981. "Militarism in Uruguay as a Response to the Hegemonic Crisis." In *The Military as an Agent of Social Change*, ed. Claude Heller, pp. 193–217. Mexico City: El Colegio de México.

Mittelman, James H. 1988. *Out from Underdevelopment: Prospects for the Third World.* New York: St. Martin's Press.

Molina Jiménez, Iván. 1991. "El Legado Colonial del Valle Central de Costa Rica: Jueces y Juicios." In *Historia Económica y Social de Costa Rica: 1750–*

1990, ed. Víctor Hugo Acuña and Iván Molina J. San José, Costa Rica: Porvenir.

Molina Jiménez, Iván, and Fabrice Lehoucq. 1999. *Urnas de lo inesperado: Fraude electoral y lucha política en Costa Rica: 1901–1948.* San José, Costa Rica: Universidad de Costa Rica.

Molina Jiménez, Iván, and Steven Palmer. 1997. *Costa Rica 1930–1996: Historia de una Sociedad.* San José, Costa Rica: Editorial Porvenir.

Monge Alfaro, Carlos. 1989 "The Development of the Central Valley." In *The Costa Rica Reader*, ed. Marc Edelmand and Joanne Kenan. New York: Grove Weidenfeld.

Mora Valverde, Eduardo. Forthcoming. Untitled manuscript.

Morley, Morris. 1994. *Washington, Somoza, and the Sandinistas: State and Regime in U.S. Policy Toward Nicaragua, 1969–1981.* New York: Cambridge University Press.

Morris, James A. 1984. *Honduras: Caudillo Politics, and Military Rulers.* Boulder, Colo.: Westview Press.

Muller, Edward N. 1985. "Dependent Economic Development, Aid Dependence on the United States, and Democratic Breakdown in the Third World." *International Studies Quarterly* 29 (4 December): 445–69.

———. 1988. "Democracy, Economic Development, and Income Inequality." *American Sociological Review* 53 (February): 50–68.

———. 1995a. "Economic Determinants of Democracy." *American Sociological Review* 60 (December): 966–82.

———. 1995b. "Income Inequality and Democratization: Reply to Bollen and Jackman." *American Sociological Review* 60 (December): 990–96.

Mundlak, Yair. 1978. "On the Pooling of Time Series and Cross Section Data." *Econometrica* 46 (1): 69–85.

Munro Dana. 1918. *The Five Republics of Central America.* New York: Oxford University Press.

Muñoz Guillén, Mercedes. 1990. *La Abolición del Ejército: 1914–1949.* San José, Costa Rica: Editorial Porvenir.

Murga Frasinetti, Antonio. 1985. *La Crisis Económica en Honduras: 1981–1984.* Tegucigalpa: Centro de Documentación de Honduras.

Murillo Jíménez, Hugo. 1978."Wilson and Tinoco: The United States and the Policy of Non-Recognition in Costa Rica, 1917–1919." Ph.D. dissertation, University of California at San Diego.

———. 1981. *Tinoco y los Estados Unidos: Génesis y Caída de una Régimen.* San José, Costa Rica: EUNAD.

Nagle, John M. 1992. "Honduras Bites the Economic Bullet." *Washington Report on the Hemisphere* 22 (12): 6.

Natalini de Castro, Stefanía, María de los Angeles Mendoza Saborro, and Joaquín Pagan Solorzano. 1985. *Significado Histórico del Gobierno del Dr. Ramón Villeda Morales.* Tegucigalpa: Editorial Universitaria.

Needler, Martin C. 1966. "Political Development and Military Intervention in Latin America." *American Political Science Review* 60 (3): 616–26.

———. 1974. "The Causality of the Latin American Coup D'État: Some Numbers, Some Speculations." In *Soldiers in Politics*, ed. Steffen Schmidt and Gerald A. Dorfman. Los Altos, Calif.: Geron-X.

Nelson, Harold D., ed. 1984. *Costa Rica: A Country Study*. Washington, D.C.: American University Press.

Norden, Deborah. 1996. *Military Rebellion in Argentina: Between Coups and Consolidation*. Lincoln: University of Nebraska Press.

Nordlinger, Eric A. 1970. "Soldiers in Mufti: The Impact of Military Rule upon Economic and Social Change in the Non-Western States." *American Political Science Review* 64 (December): 1131–48.

———. 1977. *Soldiers in Politics: Military Coups and Governments*. Englewood Cliffs, N.J.: Prentice-Hall.

Norsworthy, Kent. 1993. *Inside Honduras: The Essential Guide to Its Politics, Economy, Society and Environment*. Albuquerque: Inter-Hemispheric Education Resource Center.

Nunn, Frederick M. 1983. *Yesterday's Soldiers: European Military Professionalism in South America*. Lincoln: University of Nebraska Press.

———. 1992. *The Time of the Generals: Latin American Professional Militarism in World Politics*. Lincoln: University of Nebraska Press.

———. 1995. "The South American Military and (Re)Democratization: Professional Thought and Self Perception." *Journal of Interamerican Studies and World Affairs* 37 (2): 1–56.

Obregón L., Rafael. 1951. *Conflictos Militares y Políticos en Costa Rica*. San José, Costa Rica: La Nación.

O'Donnell, Guillermo, 1973. *Modernization and Bureaucratic-Authoritarianism*. Berkeley: Institute of International Studies.

O'Donnell, Guillermo, and Philippe C. Schmitter. 1986. *Transitions from Authoritarian Rule: Tentative Conclusions about Uncertain Democracies*. Baltimore: Johns Hopkins University Press.

Olander, Marcia. 1996. "Costa Rica in 1948: Cold War or Local War." *Americas* 52 (4): 465–94.

Olson, Mancur. 1965. *The Logic of Collective Action*. Cambridge: Harvard University Press.

———. 1982. *The Rise and Decline of Nations*. New Haven: Yale University Press.

Oquelí, Ramón. 1981. "Cronología de la Soberanía Militar." *Revista Tegucigalpa* 59 (October): 3–6.

———. 1982. *Cronología de la Soberanía Militar*. Tegucigalpa: Centro de Estudios y Promoción del Desarrollo.

———. 1983. *La Viscera Entrañable*. Tegucigalpa: CEDOH.

———. 1995. *Gente y Situaciones: Tomo III*. Tegucigalpa: Editorial Universidad Autónoma de Honduras.

Organski, A. F. K., 1965. *The Stages of Political Development*. New York: Alfred A. Knopf.

Paige, Jeffery M. 1978. *Agrarian Revolution: Social Movements and Export Agriculture in the Underdeveloped World*. New York: Free Press.

———. 1987. "Coffee and Politics in Central America." In *Crisis in the Caribbean*, ed. Richard Tardanico. Newbury Park: Sage Publications.

———. 1997. *Coffee and Power: Revolution and the Rise of Democracy in Central America*. Cambridge: Harvard University Press.

Palmer, Steven. 1995. "Hacia la 'Auto-Inmigración': El Nacionalismo Oficial en Costa Rica 1870–1930." In *Identidades Nacionales y Estado Moderno en Centroamérica*, ed. Arturo Taracena and Jean Piel. San José, Costa Rica: Editorial de la Universidad de Costa Rica.

———. Forthcoming. *From Popular Medicine to Medical Populism: Doctors, Healers and Public Power in Costa Rica, 1800–1940*. Durham: Duke University Press.

Pastor, Manuel, and Carol Wise. 1995. "The Origins and Sustainability of Mexico's Free-Trade Policy." *International Organization* 48 (3): 459–89.

Pastor, Robert A. 1987. *Condemned to Repetition: The United States and Nicaragua*. Princeton: Princeton University Press.

———. 1992. *Whirlpool: U.S. Foreign Policy Toward Latin America and the Caribbean*. Princeton: Princeton University Press.

Pateman, Carole. 1970. *Participation and Democratic Theory*. Cambridge: Cambridge University Press.

Payne, James L. 1989. *Why Nations Arm*. Oxford: Blackwell.

Peeler, John A. 1985. *Latin American Democracies: Colombia, Costa Rica, Venezuela*. Chapel Hill: University of North Carolina Press.

———. 1992. "Elite Settlements and Democratic Consolidation: Colombia, Costa Rica, and Venezuela." In *Elites and Democratic Consolidation in Latin America and Southern Europe*, ed. John Higley and Richard Gunther. New York: Cambridge University Press.

———. 1995. "Elites and Democracy in Central America." In *Elections and Democracy in Central America Revisited*, ed. John A. Booth and Mitchell A. Seligson. Chapel Hill: University of North Carolina Press.

———. 1998. *Building Democracy in Latin America*. Boulder, Colo.: Lynne Rienner Publishers.

Pérez Brignoli, Héctor. 1988. *Breve Historia de Centroamérica*. Madrid: Alianza Editorial.

Pion-Berlin, David. 1995. "The Armed Forces and Politics: Gains and Snares in Recent Scholarship." *Latin American Research Review* 30 (1): 147–62.

———. 1997. *Through the Corridors of Power: Institutions and Civil-Military Relations in Argentina*. University Park: The Pennsylvania State University Press.

Posas, Mario. 1993. "La Plantación Bananera en Centroamérica: 1870–1929." In *Historia General de Centroamérica: Las Repúblicas Agroexportadoras*, ed. Víctor Hugo Acuña Ortega. Madrid: FLACSO.

Posas, Mario, and Rafael del Cid. 1983. *Construcción del Sector Pública y del Estado Nacional en Honduras: 1876–1979*. Tegucigalpa: Editorial Universitaria Centroamericana.

Proyecto Estado de la Nación. 1995. *Estado de la Nación: El Desarrollo Humano Sostenible*. San José, Costa Rica: Proyecto Estado de la Nación.

Przeworski, Adam, and Fernando Limongi. 1997. "Modernization: Theories and Facts." *World Politics* 49 (2): 155–83.

Psacharopoulos, George, Samuel Morley, Ariel Fiszbein, Haeduch Lee, and Bill Wood. 1994. *Poverty and Income Distribution in Latin America: The Story of the 1980s*. Latin America and Caribbean Technical Department Report no. 27. New York: World Bank.

Putnam, Robert D. 1967. "Toward Explaining Military Intervention in Latin America." *World Politics* 20 (October): 83–110.

———. 1993. *Making Democracy Work: Civic Traditions in Modern Italy.* Princeton: Princeton University Press.

Pye, Lucien W. 1964. "Armies in the Process of Political Modernization." In *The Military and Society in Latin America,* ed. J. Johnson. Stanford: Stanford University Press.

Quinn, Dennis. 1997. "The Correlates of Change in International Financial Regulation." *American Political Science Review* 9 (3): 531–52.

Quirós V., Claudia. 1989. *Los Tribunales de Probidad y de Sanciones Inmediatas.* San José, Costa Rica: Editorial Costa Rica.

Rabe, Stephen G. 1988. *Eisenhower and Latin America: The Foreign Policy of Anti-communism.* Chapel Hill: University of North Carolina Press.

Ragin, Charles C. 1987. *The Comparative Method.* Berkeley and Los Angeles: University of California Press.

Ram, Rati. 1993. "Conceptual Linkages between Defense Spending and Economic Growth and Development: A Selective Review." In *Defense Spending and Economic Growth,* ed. James E. Payne and Anandi P. Sahu. Boulder, Colo.: Westview Press.

Ramsey, Russell W. 1997. *Guardians of the Other Americas.* Lanham, Md.: University Press of America.

Remmer, Karen. 1989. *Military Rule in Latin America.* Boston: Unwin Hyman.

———. 1990. "Democracy and Economic Crisis: The Latin American Experience." *World Politics* 42 (3): 315–26.

Reutlinger, Shlomo, and Marcelo Selowsky. 1976. *Malnutrition and Poverty: Magnitude and Policy Options.* Washington D.C.: World Bank, Staff Occasional Paper No. 23.

Rial, Juan. 1990. "The Armed Forces and the Question of Democracy in Latin America." In *The Military and Democracy,* ed. Louis W. Goodman, Johanna S. R. Mendelson, and Juan Rial. Lexington, Mass.: Lexington Books.

Robinson, William L., and Kent Norsworthy. 1987. *David and Goliath: The U.S. War Against Nicaragua.* New York: Monthly Review Press.

Rodríguez, Linda Alexander, ed. 1994. *Rank and Privilege: The Military and Society in Latin America.* Wilmington, Del.: Scholarly Resources.

Rodríguez, Miguel Angel. "Echandi y la Unidad Nacional." *La Nación,* 5 October 1997.

Rodríguez V., Adrián. 1986. "El Gasto Público en Salud y su Impacto en la Distribución del Ingreso Familiar." Instituto de Investigaciones en Ciencias Económicas number 100. San José, Costa Rica: Universidad de Costa Rica.

Rodríguez Vega, Eugenio. 1954. "Deber y Haber del Hombre Costarricence." *Revista de la Universidad* (10): 9–32.

Rojas Bolaños, Manuel. 1986. *Lucha Social y Guerra Civil en Costa Rica, 1940–1948.* San José, Costa Rica: Alma Mater.

———. 1993. "La Política." In *Hístoria General de Centroamérica: De la Posguerra a la Crisis,* ed. Héctor Pérez Brignoli. Madrid: FLACSO.

Román Trigo, Ana Cecilia. 1995. *Las Finanzas Publicas de Costa Rica: Metodología y Fuentes (1870–1948).* San José, Costa Rica: CIHAC.

Ropp, Steve C. 1974. "The Honduran Army in the Sociopolitical Evolution of the Honduran State." *The Americas* 30 (4 April): 504–28.

Rosenberg, Mark B. 1990. "El Indicador Hondureño: Militares y Demócratas en la América Central." In *Honduras: Pieza Clave de la Política de Estados Unidos en Centro América*, ed. Victor Meza. Tegucigalpa: CEDOH.

———. 1995. "Democracy in Honduras: The Electoral and the Political Reality." In *Elections and Democracy in Central America, Revisited*, ed. Mitchell Seligson and John Booth. Chapel Hill: University of North Carolina Press.

Rosenberg, Tina. 1991. *Children of Cain: Violence and the Violent in Latin America.* New York: Penguin.

Rostow, Walt W. 1960. *The Stages of Economic Growth: A Non-Communist Manifesto.* Cambridge: Cambridge University Press.

Rouquié, Alain. 1984. *El Estado Militar en América Latina.* Mexico City: Siglo 21.

———. 1986. "Demilitarization and the Institutionalization of Military-Dominated Polities in Latin America." In *Transitions from Authoritarian Rule: Comparative Perspectives*, ed. Guillermo O'Donnell, Philippe C. Schmitter, and Laurence Whitehead. Baltimore: Johns Hopkins University Press.

Rovira Mas, Jorge. 1988. *Estado y Política Económica en Costa Rica: 1948–1970.* San José, Costa Rica: Editorial Porvenir.

———. 1989. *Costa Rica en los Años Ochenta.* San José, Costa Rica: Editorial Porvenir.

———. 1990. "Costa Rica: Partidos Políticos y Régimen Democrático." *Polémica* 11 (May): 44–60.

Rueschemeyer, Dietrich, Evelyne Huber Stephens, and John D. Stephens. 1992. *Capitalist Development and Democracy.* Chicago: University of Chicago Press.

Rueschemeyer, Dietrich, and John D. Stephen. 1997. "Comparing Historical Sequences—A Powerful Tool for Causal Analysis." *Comparative Social Research* 16: 55–72.

Ruhl, J. Mark, 1997. "Doubting Democracy in Honduras." *Current History* (February): 81–86.

Russet, Bruce M. 1964. "Inequality and Instability: The Relation of Land and Tenure to Politics." *World Politics* 16 (3): 442–54.

Ruttan, Vernon W. 1996. *United States Development Assistance Policy: The Domestic Politics of Foreign Economic Aid.* Baltimore: Johns Hopkins University Press.

SALA. Various years. *Statistical Abstract of Latin America.* Los Angeles: UCLA Latin American Center Publications.

Salazar, Jorge Mario. 1995. *Crisis Liberal y Estado Reormista: Análisis Político-Electoral (1914–1949).* San José, Costa Rica: Editorial de la Universidad de Costa Rica.

Salazar Mora, Orlando. 1990. *El Apogeo de la República Liberal en Costa Rica: 1870–1914.* San José, Costa Rica: Editorial de la Universidad de Costa Rica.

Salomón, Leticia, 1991. "*Honduras: La Transición de la Seguridad a la Democracia.*" In *América Latina: Militares y Sociedad-I*, ed. Dirk Kruijt and Edelberto Torres Rivas. San José, Costa Rica: FLACSO.

———. 1992. *Política y Militares en Honduras.* Tegucigalpa: CEDOH.

———. 1995. "Challenges to Demilitarizing Public Order: Honduras and Guatemala." *Demilitarizing Public Order.* Washington Office on Latin America.

Samper K., Mario. 1988. "Fuerzas Sociopolíticas y Procesos Electorales en Costa Rica, 1921–1936." *Revista de Historia*, special issue: 157–222.

———. 1993. "Café, Trabajo y Sociedad en Centroamérica (1870–1930): Una Historia Común y Divergente." In *Historia General de Centroamérica: Las Repúblicas Agroexportadoras*, ed. Víctor Hugo Acuña Ortega. Madrid: FLACSO.

———. 1994. "El Significado Social de la Caficultura Costarricense y Salvadoreña: Análisis Histórico Comparado a partir de los Censos Cafetaleros." In *Tierra, Café, y Sociedad*, ed. Héctor Pérez Brignoli and Mario Samper. San José, Costa Rica: FLACSO.

Sarkesian, Sam C. 1978. "A Political Perspective on Military Power in Developing Areas." In *The Military and Security in the Third World: Domestic and International Impacts*, ed. Sheldon W. Simon. Boulder, Colo.: Westview Press.

———. 1984. "Two Conceptions of Military Professionalism." In *The Military, Militarism, and the Polity*, ed. Michel Louis Martin and Ellen Stern McCrate. New York: Free Press.

Sartori, Giovani. 1987. *The Theory of Democracy Revisited.* Chatham, N.J.: Chatham House.

Scheetz, Thomas. 1992. "The Evolution of Public Sector Expenditures: Changing Political Priorities in Argentina, Chile, Paraguay and Peru." *Journal of Peace Research* 29 (2): 175–90.

Scheetz, Thomas, Edgar Pape, and Carlos Kulikowski. 1997. "Gastos Militares en Guatemala: Su Impacto Fiscal y Microeconómico." *Fuerzas Armadas y Sociedad* 12 (3): 29–37.

Schifter, Jacobo. 1986. *Las Alianzas Conflictivas.* San José, Costa Rica: Libro Libre.

Schirmer, Jennifer. 1991. "Guatemala: Los Militares y la Tesis de Estabilidad Nacional." In *América Latina: Militares y Sociedad-I*, ed. Dirk Kruijt and Edelberto Torres Rivas. San José, Costa Rica: FLACSO.

———. 1999. *The Guatemalan Military Project: A Violence Called Democracy*. Philadelphia: University of Pennsylvania Press.

Schlesinger, Stephen, and Stephen Kinzer. 1982. *Bitter Fruit: The Untold Story of the American Coup in Guatemala.* Garden City, N.Y.: Doubleday.

Schmitter, Philippe C., ed. 1973. *Military Rule in Latin America: Function, Consequences and Perspectives.* Beverly Hills: Sage.

Schmitz, David F. 1999. *Thank God They're on Our Side: The United States and Right-Wing Dictatorships, 1921–1965.* Chapel Hill: University of North Carolina Press.

Schoultz, Lars. 1981. *Human Rights and United States Policy toward Latin America.* Princeton: Princeton University Press.

———. 1987. *National Security and United States Policy toward Latin America.* Princeton: Princeton University Press.

———. 1998. *Beneath the United States: A History of U.S. Policy toward Latin America.* Cambridge: Harvard University Press.

Schulz, Donald E. 1993. *Como Honduras Evitó la Violencia Revolucionaria.* Tegucigalpa: CEDOH.

Schulz, Donald, and Deborah Sundloff Schulz. 1994. *The United States, Honduras, and the Crisis in Central America.* Boulder, Colo.: Westview Press.

Seckinger, Ron. 1981. "The Central American Militaries: A Survey of the Literature." *Latin American Research Review* 16 (2): 246–58.

Seligson, Mitchell A. 1980. *Peasants of Costa Rica and the Development of Agrarian Capitalism.* Madison: University of Wisconsin Press.

———. 1987. "Development, Democratization, and Decay: Central America at the Crossroads." In *Authoritarians and Democrats: Regime Transition in Latin America,* ed. James M. Malloy and Mitchell A. Seligson. Pittsburgh: University of Pittsburgh Press.

———. 2000. "Trouble in Paradise? The Erosion of System Support and the Centralamericanization of Costa Rica: 1978–1999." Paper presented to conference on La Democracia de Costa Rica ante el Nuevo Siglo (1986–2000). San José, Costa Rica, May 2000.

Sieder, Rachel. 1995. "Honduras: The Politics of Exception and Military Reformism, 1972–1978." *Journal of Latin American Studies* 27: 99–127.

———. 1998. *Elecciones y Democratización en Honduras desde 1980.* Tegucigalpa: Editorial Universitaria.

Simpson, Miles. 1990. "Political Rights and Income Inequality." *American Sociological Review* 55 (6 December): 682–93.

Singer, J. David, and Melvin Small. 1993. *Correlates of war project: International and civil war data,* 1816–1992 Computer file\ Ann Arbor, Mich.: J. David Singer and Melvin Small, producers\ Ann Arbor, Mich.: Inter-University Consortium for Political and Social Research.

Sirowy, Larry, and Alex Inkeles. 1991. "The Effects of Democracy on Economic Growth and Inequality: A Review." In *On Measuring Democracy,* ed. Alex Inkeles. New Brunswick, N.J.: Transaction Publishers.

Sivard. Ruth. Various years. *World Military and Social Expenditures.* Leesburg, Va.: World Priorities.

Skidmore, Thomas E., and Peter H. Smith. 1997. *Modern Latin America,* fourth edition. New York: Oxford University Press.

Sklar, Holly. 1988. *Washington's War on Nicaragua.* Boston: South End Press.

Skocpol, Theda, and Margaret Somers. 1980. "The Uses of Comparative History in Macrosocial Inquiry." *Comparative Studies in Society and History* 22: 174–97.

Smith, Peter H. 1996. *Talons of the Eagle: Dynamics of U.S.-Latin American Relations.* New York: Oxford University Press.

Smith, Tony. 1994. *America's Mission: The United States and the Worldwide Struggle for Democracy in the Twentieth Century.* Princeton: Princeton University Press.

Solís Salazar, Edwin, and Carlos González Pacheco. 1991. *El Ejército en Costa Rica: Poder Político, Poder Militar, 1821–1890.* San José, Costa Rica: Editorial Alma Mater.

Stepan, Alfred. 1971. *The Military in Politics: Changing Patterns in Brazil.* Princeton: Princeton University Press.

———, ed. 1973. *Authoritative Brazil.* New Haven: Yale University Press.

———. 1978. *The State and Society: Peru in Comparative Perspective*. Princeton: Princeton University Press.

———. 1986. "The New Professionalism of Internal Warfare and Military Role Expansion." In *Armies and Politics in Latin America*, ed. Abraham F. Lowenthal and J. Samuel Fitch. New York: Holmes and Meier.

———. 1988. *Rethinking Military Politics: Brazil and the Southern Cone*. Princeton: Princeton University Press.

Stephens, Evelyne Huber. 1980. *The Politics of Workers' Participation: The Peruvian Approach in Comparative Perspective*. New York: Academic Press.

Stephens, John D. 1998. "Historical Analysis and Causal Assessment in Comparative Research." *American Political Science Association Comparative Politics Newsletter* 9 (1): 22–25.

Stimson, James A. 1985. "Regression in Space and Time: A Statistical Essay." *American Journal of Political Science* 29 (4): 915–47.

Stokes, William S. 1950. *Honduras: An Area Study in Government*. Madison: University of Wisconsin Press.

Stone, Samuel. 1975. *La Dinastía de los Conquistadores*. San José, Costa Rica: EDUCA.

Streeten, Paul. 1981. *First Things First: Meeting Basic Needs in Developing Countries*. New York: Oxford University Press.

Summers, Robert, and Allen Heston. 1984. "Improved International Comparisons of Real Product and Its Composition." *Review of Income and Wealth* 30: 207–62.

———. 1991. "The Penn World Table (Mark 5): An Expanded Set of International Comparisons, 1950–1988." *Quarterly Journal of Economics* 106 (2): 327–68.

Tábora, Rocío. 1995. *Masculinidad y Violencia en la Cultura Política Hondureña*. Tegucigalpa: CEDOH.

Tarrow, Sidney. 1995. "Bridging the Quantitative-Qualitative Divide in Political Science." *American Political Science Review* 89 (2): 471–74.

Tetlock, Philip E., and Aaron Belkin. 1996. "Counterfactual Thought Experiments in World Politics: Logical, Methodological, and Psychological Perspectives." In *Counterfactual Thought Experiments in World Politics*, ed. Philip E. Tetlock and Aaron Belkin. Princeton: Princeton University Press.

Tilly, Charles. 1990. *Coercion, Capital, and European States, A.D. 990–1990*. Cambridge: Cambridge University Press.

Torres-Rivas, Edelberto. 1975. *Interpretación del Desarrollo Social Centroamericano*. San José, Costa Rica: EDUCA.

———, ed. 1993. *Historia General de Centroamérica*, 6 volumes. Madrid: FLACSO.

Tourism 2000: Honduran Tourism Magazine. 1997. No. 56.

Umaña Aglietti, Miguel A. 1978. "Militares y Civiles en Costa Rica." Licenciatura thesis, University of Costa Rica.

United Nations Development Programme. Various years. *Human Development Report*. New York: Oxford University Press.

United Nations. Various years. *FAO Production Yearbook*. United Nations.

United States Arms Control and Disarmament Agency. various years. *World Military Expenditures and Arms Transfers.* Washington, D.C.: ACDA.

United States General Accounting Office (GAO). 1989. *Central America: Impact of U.S. Assistance in the 1980s.* Report to the Chairman, Committee on Foreign Relations, U.S. Senate.

Urcuyo, Constantino. 1990. "Civil-Military Relations in Costa Rica: Militarization or Adaptation to New Circumstances." In *The Military and Democracy*, ed. Louis W. Goodman, Johanna S. R. Mendelson, and Juan Rial. Lexington, Mass.: Lexington Books.

U.S. Bureau of the Census. 1997. *Statistical Abstract of the United States*, 117th ed. Washington, D.C.

USAID. Various years. *U.S. Overseas Loans and Grants.* Washington, D.C.: USAID.

USAID. 1992. *Country Development Strategy Statements, Costa Rica FY92–96.* Washington, D.C.: USAID.

USAID. 1992. *Country Development Strategy Statements, Honduras FY92–96.* Washington, D.C.: USAID.

Valladares, Olban Francisco. 1993. "El PINU Comparte la Idea de la Necesidad de Modernizar el Estado." In *La Modernización del Estado.* Tegucigalpa: Gobierno de Honduras.

Varas, Augusto. 1985. *Militarization and the International Arms Race in Latin America.* Boulder, Colo.: Westview Press.

———, ed. 1989. *Democracy Under Siege: New Military Power in Latin America.* New York: Greenwood Press.

Vargas Araya, Armando. 1993. *El Siglo de Figueres.* San José, Costa Rica: Editorial Juricentro.

Velásquez Cerrato, Armando. 1954. *Las Fuerzas Armadas en una Democracia.* Tegucigalpa: Talleres Typográficos Nacionales.

Villeda Bermudez, Ramón. 1993. "Un Ejército con un Pais." *Puntos de Vista* 7: 46–47.

Villegas Hoffmeister, Guillermo. 1986. *El Cardonazo.* San José, Costa Rica: Casa Gráfica.

Walker, Thomas W., ed. 1987. *Reagan Versus the Sandinistas: The Undeclared War on Nicaragua.* Boulder, Colo.: Westview Press.

Washington Office on Latin America. 1995. *Demilitarizing Public Order: The International Community, Police Reform and Human Rights in Central America and Haiti.* Washington, D.C.: WOLA.

Washington Report on the Hemisphere. Various issues. Washington, D.C.: Council on Hemispheric Affairs.

Weaver, Federick Stirton. 1994. *Inside the Volcano: The History and Political Economy of Central America.* Boulder, Colo.: Westview Press.

Weber, Christof Anders. 1993. "United States Foreign Assistance to Central America, 1946–89: A Tool of Foreign Policy." In *Statistical Abstract of Latin America*, ed. James W. Wilkie et al. Los Angeles: UCLA Latin American Center Publications.

Weber, Diane Cecilia. 1999. "Warrior Cops: The Ominous Growth of Paramilitarism in American Police Departments." Washington, D.C.: Cato Institute Briefing Paper no. 50.

Weede, Erich, 1983. "Military Participation Ratios, Human Capital Formation, and Economic Growth." *Journal of Political and Military Sociology* 11 (1): 11–19.

———. 1986. "Rent-Seeking, Military Participation, and Economic Performance in LDCs." *Journal of Conflict Resolution* 30 (2): 291–314.

———. 1992. "Military Participation, Economic Growth, and Income Inequality: A Cross-National Study." In *Defense, Welfare, and Growth*, ed. Steven Chan and Alex Mintz. London: Routledge.

———. 1993. "The Impact of Military Participation on Economic Growth and Income Inequality: Some New Evidence." *Journal of Political and Military Sociology* 21 (winter): 241–58.

Weede, Erich, and Horst Tiefenbach. 1981a. "Some Recent Explanations of Income Inequality." *International Studies Quarterly* 25: 255–82.

———. 1981b. "Correlates of the Size Distribution of Income." *Journal of Politics* 43: 1029–41.

Whelan, James, and Franklin A. Jaeckle. 1988. *The Soviet Assault on America's Southern Flank*. Washington, D.C.: Regnery Gateway.

Whynes, David. 1979. *The Economics of Third World Military Expenditure*. London: Macmillan.

Wiarda, Howard J., and Harvey F. Kline, eds. 1996. *Latin American Politics and Development*, fourth edition. Boulder, Colo.: Westview Press.

Wilkie, James W., and Carlos A. Contreras, eds. Various years. *Statistical Abstract of Latin America*. Los Angeles: UCLA Latin American Center Publications.

Williams, Phillip J, and Knut Walter. 1997. *Militarization and Demilitarization in El Salvador's Transition to Democracy*. Pittsburgh: University of Pittsburgh Press.

Williams, Robert G. 1986. *Export Agriculture and the Crisis in Central America*. Chapel Hill: University of North Carolina Press.

———. 1994. *States and Social Evolution: Coffee and the Rise of National Governments in Central America*. Chapel Hill: University of North Carolina Press.

Wilson, Bruce. 1998. *Costa Rica: Politics, Economics, and Democracy*. Boulder, Colo.: Lynne Rienner Publishers.

Winson, Anthony. 1989. *Coffee and Democracy in Modern Costa Rica*. New York: St. Martin's Press.

Wolpin, Miles D. 1975. "External Political Socialization as a Source of Conservative Military Behavior in the Third World." In *Militarism in Developing Countries*, ed. Kenneth Fidel. New Brunswick, N.J.: Transaction Books.

Woodward, Ralph Lee, Jr. 1985. *Central America: A Nation Divided*. New York: Oxford University Press.

World Tourism Organization. 1997. *Yearbook of Tourism Statistics*. Madrid: WTO.

Wright, Thomas C. 1991. *Latin America in the Era of the Cuban Revolution*. New York: Praeger.

Yashar, Deborah J. 1995. "Civil War and Social Welfare: The Origins of Costa Rica's Competitive Party System." In *Building Democratic Institutions: Parties and Party Systems in Latin America*, ed. Scott Mainwaring and Timothy R. Scully. Stanford: Stanford University Press.

———. 1997. *Demanding Democracy: Reform and Reaction in Costa Rica and Guatemala, 1970s–1950s*. Stanford: Stanford University Press.

Zoninsein, Jonas. 1994. "Military Expenditures, Investment Funds, and Economic Growth." In *Seeking Security and Development: The Impact of Military Spending and Arms Transfers*, ed. Norman A. Graham. Boulder, Colo.: Lynne Rienner Publishers.

Index